THEORIES OF INTERNATIONAL RELATIONS

THEORIES OF INTERNATIONAL RELATIONS

Second Edition

Scott Burchill, Richard Devetak,
Andrew Linklater, Matthew Paterson,
Christian Reus-Smit and Jacqui True

palgrave

First published 2001 by
PALGRAVE
Houndmills, Basingstoke, Hampshire RG21 6XS and
175 Fifth Avenue, New York, N.Y. 10010
Companies and representatives throughout the world

PALGRAVE is the new global academic imprint of
St. Martin's Press LLC Scholarly and Reference Division and
Palgrave Publishers Ltd (formerly Macmillan Press Ltd).

ISBN 0–333–91417–1 hardback
ISBN 0–333–91418–X paperback

This book is printed on paper suitable for recycling and made from fully managed and sustained forest sources.

A catalogue record for this book is available from the British Library.

Library of Congress Cataloging-in-Publication Data

Theories of international relations / Scott Burchill ... [et al.].–2nd ed.
    p. cm.
  Rev. ed. of: Theories of international relations / Scott Burchill. c1996.
  Includes bibliographical references and index.
    ISBN 0–333–91417–1 (cloth) – ISBN 0–333–91418–X (pbk.)
    1. International relations–Philosophy. I. Burchill, Scott, 1961- II. Burchill, Scott, 1961- Theories of international relations.

JZ1242 .T48 2001
327.1'01–dc21   2001040150

10   9   8   7   6   5   4   3   2
10   09 08 07 06 05 04 03 02

Copy-edited and typeset by Povey–Edmondson
Tavistock and Rochdale, England

Printed and bound in Great Britain by Creative Print & Design (Wales) Ebbw Vale

Contents

Preface to the Second Edition

For the second edition, each chapter has been updated and fully revised. A new chapter on constructivism by Christian Reus-Smit has also been added to reflect the evolving nature of theory in the study of International Relations.

Andrew Linklater was again the driving intellectual force behind the new edition. The depth of his knowledge and the wisdom of his counsel have enhanced the quality of every chapter. The comments of an anonymous reviewer, the editing skills of Dan Flitton and the support of our publisher Steven Kennedy have all improved the final version.

SCOTT BURCHILL

Preface to the First Edition

The origins of this book lie in the decision of the school of Australian and International Studies at Deakin University to introduce a Master of Arts (International Relations) programme in 1995 for students learning via distance education. The provision of high-quality materials for every off-campus student enabling them to study for their degree anywhere in Australia or overseas was considered essential to the success of the programme.

As preparation of the programme proceeded it was decided that each student should receive a solid grounding in international theory before choosing a range of specialist options. However, it was felt that no one existing text adequately covered all the approaches the course designers believed should be included: the books were either too narrow in their theoretical focus or did not take sufficient account of contemporary developments in the field. It was therefore decided to write an entirely new book which would meet the requirements of both staff and students. Early drafts of Chapters 1 to 7 were piloted in the initial year of the programme, after which they were redrafted for publication. At this point Chapters 8 and 9 were added to broaden the coverage of more recent theoretical influences in International Relations.

I am very grateful to Andrew Linklater of Keele University for his excellent contributions to this volume, his invaluable comments on the other chapters, and for suggesting the other contributors. I am similarly grateful to Richard Devetak, Matthew Paterson and Jacqui True, whose work has been a pleasure to edit. I would also like to acknowledge the encouragement and support given by Gary Smith of Deakin University. The comments of an anonymous reviewer and our publisher, Steven Kennedy, have also significantly improved the quality of the manuscript.

Scott Burchill

CHAPTER 1

Introduction

Scott Burchill

Although in the modern era we have grown accustomed to the idea of theories within the 'natural sciences', the suggestion that the political and social worlds also lend themselves to theoretical enquiry remains problematic for many. As one sceptic has noted, in the analysis of international relations for example, 'historical conditions are too varied and complex for anything that might plausibly be called "a theory" to apply uniformly'.[1] If by theory our sceptic is referring to the levels of certainty and exactness, standards of proof and 'scientific rigour' normally associated with the 'physical' sciences, then he has a point when he claims that 'if there is a body of theory, well tested and verified, that applies to the conduct of foreign affairs or the resolution of domestic or international conflict, its existence has been kept a well guarded secret'.[2] There is a world of difference between the 'physical' and the 'social' sciences, and it is difficult to argue that the methodology of the former, with its emphasis on testable propositions and the production of falsifiable hypotheses, can be automatically applied to theoretical endeavours in the latter without serious problems arising.[3] Is it therefore misleading to speak of 'theories of international relations'?

One of the purposes of this book will be to argue that the term 'theory' is not limited to its 'scientific' or positivist formulation and that explanatory theories, of the kind which flow from the adoption of a positivist methodology, are only one type of international theory. There is now an increasingly large group of theorists who recognise a second category of theory which reflects upon the very process of theorising. These theorists are concerned with the social and political purposes of knowledge, the cognitive interests and assumptions of the observer and the way in which the principal actors construct their images of the political world. They believe we should be just as concerned with how we approach the study of world politics as we are with explaining events, issues and the behaviour of actors in the global system. One commentator has argued that these two categories of theory represent a fundamental division within the discipline 'between theories which seek to offer *explanatory* accounts of international relations, and those that see theory as *constitutive* of that reality'.[4] Recognising and understanding these two 'types' of theory will be the entry point for this introduction to international theory. The contributors to this book believe that both types of theory represent important paths of intellectual inquiry and that no contemporary survey of international theory could legitimately ignore either category.

It would be a mistake to regard constitutive theories as merely a prevailing or transitory intellectual fashion, after which the discipline will return to its normal explanatory concerns. As early as 1972 Hedley Bull argued that

> the reason we must be concerned with the theory as well as the history of the subject is that all discussions of international politics ... proceed upon theoretical assumptions which we should acknowledge and investigate rather than ignore of leave unchallenged. The enterprise of theoretical investigation is at its minimum one directed towards criticism: towards identifying, formulating, refining, and questioning the general assumptions on which the everyday discussion of international politics proceeds. At its maximum, the enterprise is concerned with theoretical construction: with establishing that certain assumptions are true while others are false, certain arguments valid while others are invalid, and so proceeding to erect a firm structure of knowledge.[5]

Bull believes that not only is there room for explanatory and constitutive theory, but that theoretical enterprise itself would be incomplete without both processes. Although he wrote this in the early 1970s, it wasn't until later in the decade that constitutive theory began to leave its mark on the discipline, thanks largely to the influence of the cognate fields of political and social theory. Since then, the growth of interest in international theory and the recent production of texts which address theoretical concerns in International Relations, indicates a widening acceptance that constitutive theory has a important place in the study of global politics. As Steve Smith argues, 'theories do not simply explain or predict, they tell us what possibilities exist for human action and intervention; they define not merely our explanatory possibilities, but also our ethical and practical horizons'.[6] This view is shared by the contributors to this volume.

At the outset our sceptic suggests a positivist bias by implying that 'theory' should be defined as the opposite of 'reality'. The authors of this book reject the suggestion that 'theory' and 'reality' are antonyms on the grounds that, as theoreticians, they are active agents in research which is conditioned by their own historical experiences. These experiences cannot be artificially separated from their work because they are embedded in the theoretical worlds they construct. As Cox explains, theorists cannot stand outside of the political and social worlds that they are examining because theory follows reality. It also precedes and shapes reality. That is to say, there is a real historical world in which things happen; and theory is made through reflection upon what has happened. The separation of theory from historical happenings is ... only a way of thinking, because theory feeds back into the making of history by virtue of the way those who make history ... think about what they are doing. Their understanding of what the historical context allows them to do, prohibits them from doing, or requires them to do, and the way they formulate their purposes in acting, is the product of theory.[7]

As we shall discover, although it is extremely difficult to reach an agreed definition of theory within the study of international relations, the contributors to this volume share a sense of the importance of theory because they regard the *theory versus reality* divide as a false dichotomy. Whether they like it or not, even those in the field of international relations who reject the value and purpose of international theory cannot avoid the fact that their work is theoretically informed and has theoretical and political implications.[8] The burgeoning literature on ethics and international politics, as well as the growing body of feminist studies in the field, reminds us of just how central to our daily lives theoretical questions and issues are.

International Relations can be cast as a discipline of theoretical disagreements. Though it is a comparatively new subject in the Western academy, almost every aspect of its nature is contested. What should be studied in the discipline? How should it be studied? Is the discipline politically biased, or conceived in such a way as to limit the possibilities for discussion and analysis? The discipline of International Relations (IR) is internally divided on the notions of the *subject matter* to be analysed, the appropriate *methodology* to be used when studying international politics, and the *epistemological structure* of the theories. These internal divisions have sometimes taken the form of 'great debates' which have served as watersheds in the short history of the discipline. More recently, they have been re-considered as a consequence of the application of contemporary developments in social theory to the study of global politics. International Relations has belatedly joined the ranks of the introspective academic disciplines.

In this introductory chapter we will examine these and other issues under the following headings:

1. The foundation of the discipline of International Relations
2. Theories and disciplines
3. Explanatory and constitutive theory
4. What do theories of international relations differ about?
5. What criteria exist for evaluating, comparing and contrasting theories?

Initially we will discuss the notion of 'theory' in the context of studying international relations and briefly examine how the term is variously understood. This has become a more complex task since questions of methodology, epistemology and ontology joined the discipline's theoretical agenda, first in the 1960s with the 'behaviourist revolution' and again in the 1980s with the application of critical, feminist and post-modern theory to IR. We will then examine the relationship between theories and academic disciplines, before distinguishing between two broad categories of international theory – explanatory and constitutive. It will also be necessary to examine a range of criteria for differentiating between the theories selected for explication in the book. This should help to explain the proliferation of theories over the last two decades and why a number of theoreticians appear to 'talk past' each other rather than engage in intellectual exchanges. We will also identify ways in which meaningful comparisons between the various perspectives of international relations can be made. It will be important to bear these points in mind as we sweep through a selection of some of the most influential theoretical traditions in the field. Before then, however, a brief introduction to the foundation of the discipline will help to set the scene for the more specific analysis to follow.

The Foundation of International Relations

Though scholars and thinkers have long devoted their thoughts to international politics, the formal recognition of international relations as a separate discipline within the Western academy dates from the end of the First World War with the establishment of a Chair of International Relations at the University of Wales at Aberystwyth in 1919. Until this time, the province of international politics was shared by a number of older disciplines, including law, philosophy, economics, politics and diplomatic history.

It is difficult to separate the foundation of the discipline of International Relations from the intellectual reaction to the horrors of the First World War. As far as the historians were concerned there was relatively little interest in the war itself. The great subject which eclipsed all others and monopolised their interest was how and why the war began. Historians established their reputations as authorities on the origins of the First World War – Gooch in England, Fay and Schmitt in the United States, Renouvin and Camille Bloch in France, Thimme, Brandenburg, and von Wegerer in Germany, Pribram in Austria, Pokrovsky in Russia, to name just a few.[9] Their task was one guided by a genuinely moral purpose: to discover the causes of the war so the world might avoid a similar catastrophe in the future.

At least initially, the experiences of 1914–18 brought into intellectual and diplomatic prominence those who considered the old assumptions and prescriptions of power politics to be totally discredited (for example, Zimmern, Noel-Baker, Wilson). Peace, they believed, could only be preserved by a system of collective security; this involved transferring the concepts and practices of domestic society to the international sphere. Together with a nineteenth century belief in the inevitable progress of mankind, these 'idealists' or 'utopians' as they came to be pejoratively called, invested their hopes for a new, peaceful world order in the idea of a 'Concert', and specifically in international organisations such as the League of Nations. At the basis of their proposals was a critique of the doctrine of the balance of power as the main guarantor of state sovereignty, and an emphasis on the need to extend the concept of citizenship to include membership of the global community of nation-states.

However, it was widely felt amongst students of the causes of the First World War that, to a certain extent, the war had highlighted the inadequacy of history as a guide to the future. In its aftermath, therefore, a discipline devoted specifically to the comprehensive and systematic study of international conflict emerged within universities in the victorious nations, specifically the United Kingdom and the United States. The discipline of International Relations was founded in reaction to the unprecedented horrors of the conflict. The war had shaken the confidence of those who thought diplomacy operated effectively and was properly understood. As an instrument of statecraft war had proven to be immoral, costly and dysfunctional. Early scholars in the field, almost exclusively from the 'satisfied' or 'status quo' nations, therefore agreed that three questions would dominate their studies:

1. What had war achieved, other than death and misery for millions?
2. Were there lessons from the war that could be learnt to prevent a recurrence of conflict on this scale?
3. Was the war caused by mistake, misunderstanding or evil intent?

In response to these questions, the first 'school' or 'theory' of international relations emerged to dominate the discipline's early history. The idealists (also known as liberals and utopians) argued that war was not a product of human nature, but the result of misunderstandings by politicians who had lost control of events leading up to hostilities in 1914. If 'secret diplomacy' could be replaced by collective security, and autocratic rule by democracy, war would be seen as a senseless and destructive tool of international statecraft. Thus a more peaceful and just world order could be established if the lessons of the First World War were understood and acted upon.[10] According to Bull,

> the distinctive characteristic of these writers was their belief in progress: the belief, in particular, that the system of international relations that had given rise to the First World War was capable of being transformed into a fundamentally more peaceful and just world order; that under the impact of the awakening of democracy, the growth of the 'international mind', the development of the

League of Nations, the good works of men of peace or the enlightenment spread
by their own teachings, it was in fact being transformed; and that their responsibility as students of international relations was to assist this march of progress
to overcome the ignorance, the prejudices, the ill-will, and the sinister interests
that stood in its way.[11]

The important point to note here is the normative character of the early
discipline. Founded in a climate of reaction against the barbarity of the First
World War, the discipline was established with the conviction that war
must never happen again: the Great War, as it was initially called, was to be
the 'war to end all wars'. Only the rigorous study of the phenomenon of
war could reveal its underlying causes so that its recurrence could be
prevented. The initial preoccupation of the discipline with this question
coloured the questions that practitioners in the field asked about the world,
the methods they employed to conduct their studies and the conclusions
they eventually reached. With each generation of scholars, these questions
were re-asked and re-answered. What is significant is not so much the
answers the first generation of thinkers emerged with, but the direction
they initially gave to the discipline's trajectory. The reaction of scholars to
the liberal-utopians dominates the discipline's early life. The realist critique
of the liberal-utopian school launched by E. H. Carr immediately before the
Second World War, sometimes referred to as the discipline's first 'great
debate', gave the discipline of International Relations its early definition:
the dualism between idealism and realism. As we shall see in subsequent
chapters, as each theoretical approach rises to dominance in the discipline it
exercises its hegemony over the field of study, in part, by restructuring the
focus and content of the entire discipline.

It should be obvious from this that in the discipline's formative stages
there was an explicit connection between theory and practice and between
means and ends. The very purpose of intellectual endeavour was to change
the world for the better by eradicating the scourge of war. This was really
the only function international theory had. It was not a remote and disconnected vocation. Idealism was 'a way of thinking in which some higher
or better state is projected as a way of judging conduct or of indicating
action'.[12] Liberals were intellectuals who believed 'the world to be profoundly other than it should be, and who have faith in the power of human
reason and human action so to change it that the inner potential of all
human beings can be more fully realised'.[13]

As the discipline grew this foundational normative concern of International Relations became supplemented by other theoretical issues. Whilst
the preoccupation with conflict and war remained, the discipline became
more generally concerned with a wider range of other international actors
and phenomena as well as a series of introspective philosophical questions.
By the 1990s, the discipline had undergone a 'rapid transition from an

essentially problem-solving approach to strategic interaction between existing bounded communities to a normatively-engaged analysis of the history of bounded communities and the possibility of improved forms of political community'.[14] This represents nothing short of a revolutionary transformation of the discipline's principal focus. The early consensus about the nature of the discipline has collapsed and been replaced by a spectrum of contending theoretical approaches. The traditional intellectual boundaries of International Relations have been widened to the point where it would be barely recognisable to its early practitioners. Interdisciplinary research and influences from cognate fields have so deeply affected the subject it is now possible to ask whether International Relations still has a clearly bounded intellectual domain or even a distinctive subject matter.[15] One of the tasks of this book will be to map many of these changes and offer a range of answers to this question.

Theories and Disciplines

Although earlier it was claimed that 'idealism' or 'liberal internationalism' constituted the first school or theory of International Relations, this is in many ways a retrospective judgement. As late as 1966 Martin Wight posed the question, 'why is there no international theory?', by which he meant an equivalent body of knowledge to that which comprised political theory. Wight argued that there was no body of international theory ('speculation about the society of states, or the family of nations, or the international community') to match the achievements of political theory ('speculation about the state') because the character of international politics was 'incompatible with progressivist theory'. Political theory was philosophically rich because it was concerned with the 'theory of the good life', whereas 'international theory is the theory of survival' in a world where 'international politics is the realm of recurrence and repetition'. Because theorising 'has to be done in the language of political theory and law', a language 'appropriate to man's control of his social life', Wight believed it was inappropriate for thinking about the international domain where state survival was the principal concern.[16]

Three decades later the poverty of international theory which Wight identified has been substantially alleviated. We hope to demonstrate in this book that there is now a rich and diverse field of international theory which is not constrained by a preoccupation with state survival or the absence of an appropriate vocabulary with which to theorise about global politics. We hope to refute the claim that the character of international politics is either consensually recognised or determined, and challenge the view that the discipline needed to create an autonomous theory of international relations.

By arguing that international theory is not analytically distinct from the cognate fields of social and political theory, it is possible to open up new areas of theoretical endeavour which Wight could not have anticipated in the 1960s.

Thanks to an explosion of theoretical activity in field since the 1970s, it is now possible to regard International Relations as a discipline comprising a range of alternative, overlapping and competing theories of world politics. As we proceed through this book we will be examining a number of the most influential theories, including liberal internationalism, neo-realism, and rationalism, as well as less influential approaches such as Marxism and newer perspectives such as constructivism, feminism and green political theory. We are unable to trace the intellectual history of the entire discipline, but it is possible to examine a broad range of theories, both explanatory and constitutive, which currently influence the discipline's agenda.

We will call these approaches theories, but in the literature we will also see them referred to as perspectives, paradigms, discourses, schools of thought, images and philosophical traditions: there isn't any agreement within the discipline about what these divisions of knowledge should be called. For convenience we will call them theories or theoretical traditions, but what are they? What do they seek to do? And how do they differ from each other? The following definitions of theory show how varied the notion of theory can be for scholars in the field:

-    theories explain laws which identify invariant or probable associations (Waltz)
-    to abstract, generalise and to connect (Hollis and Smith)
-    a tradition of speculation about relations between states (Wight)
-    using observation to test hypotheses about the world (empirical theory)
-    a representation of the way the world ought to be (normative theory)
-    ideological critique of the present which opens up alternative future paths to change, freedom and human autonomy (critical theory)
-    reflections upon the process of theorising, including questions of epistemology and ontology (constitutive theory)

Putting aside for a moment the difficulty of formulating coherent ideas about an area of such complexity and diversity as world politics, it is clear from the above list that practitioners in the field do not agree about what they are actually doing when they theorise about international relations. This makes comparisons between their work all the more difficult, for we might in effect be comparing and contrasting unlike things. Post-modernists, for example, would deny the worthiness of 'grand theories' and reject the suggestion that their own contribution to the study of world politics constitutes a 'school' or even a unified theoretical approach. If further evidence of diversity is needed, the plurality of names used to describe essentially the same theoretical approach is another indication of this confusion (for example utopianism, idealism, liberal internationalism and interdependency theory are alternative descriptions of essentially the same theoretical tradition). We may have to live with fact that there are categories of theory, such as the division made earlier between explanatory and constitutive theory, which are incommensurable and perhaps incompatible.

Even the term 'international relations' is misleading because it no longer defines the field. It implies that all we are concerned with is relations between the nations of the world, which in effect means relationships between nation-states – a concession to state-centric realism. And yet in the contemporary world, this is only one of the discipline's principal concerns. It is now a broader and more eclectic field of study, which in part accounts for the diversity of definitions of theory, and explains why some argue that 'global politics' is a more appropriate description of the subject. Though by no means an exhaustive list, below are some of the discipline's recent preoccupations:

- *relationships* – economic interdependence, relations of dominance and dependence that led to Third World and increasing global inequalities, international trade, new forms of political identity and citizenship, regimes, international society of states, the nature of anarchy, regional economic associations, balances of power, democratisation, post-Cold War security
- *actors* – nation-states, transnational corporations, finance markets, non-government organisations, supra and sub-national political communities, UN peacekeepers, new social movements, G8, IMF-World Bank
- *empirical issues* – globalisation and fragmentation, human rights, intervention and sovereignty, aid, refugees, ethnic nationalism, women's issues, environmental conservation, aids, drugs, organised crime, identity politics
- *ethical and philosophical issues* – questions of epistemology, ontology and methodology, gender perspectives, inter-paradigm debates, ethics and foreign policy, new forms of political community, moral issues between the West and non-Western societies, questions of inclusion, exclusion and difference

According to Halliday, who argues that International Relations retains its distinctive subject matter, it is possible to identify three 'constituent elements' which have produced an enormous variety of specialist sub-fields, inter-disciplinary studies and theoretical approaches. They are: (1) the inter-state; (2) the transnational; and (3) the systemic.[17] Halliday is suggesting that international relations occur on more than one level, and possibly three. When it was founded over eighty years ago, the subject was primarily, though not exclusively concerned with (1) the inter-state. However, within the framework of a contemporary International Relations syllabus you might find scholars working on US–Russia diplomatic relations side by side with a finance market or Third World debt analyst who could be sitting across the table from a neo-Marxist theoretician. The field is now more open and it is almost as difficult to see where the discipline's distinctive subject matter ends as it is to pinpoint where it actually begins.

In contrast to Halliday, critical theorists and post-modern approaches refuse to treat the discipline of International Relations as a discrete discourse with its own rigid intellectual boundaries, distinctive concepts, language and subject matter. For post-modernists this would involve an intolerable process of exclusion – an arbitrary and unjustifiable choice of what goes in and what is left out of academic consideration. Instead, they regard disciplinary boundaries, such as the division between sociology and history, for example, as artificially imposed demarcation lines which distort our capacity to understand the world. For them, knowledge has no boundaries – the borders between neatly packaged fields of study merely reflect the conservative nature of the academy, a process which, in turn, obstructs our intellectual endeavours. Marxists would want to make a similar point by rejecting 'the epistemological and methodological foundations of "bourgeois" social science with its fragmentation into arbitrarily delimited disciplines'.[18] Clearly the domain of International Relations is a matter of some dispute.

Another question which effects our study of the discipline's theoretical terrain, is the changing fortunes of each theory in policy making circles. In his study of US foreign policy at the beginning of the Cold War, Daniel Yergin traces the alternating influence which realism (the 'Yalta axioms') and totalitarian theory (the 'Riga axioms') had over the Roosevelt and Truman administrations in the 1940s.[19] His purpose was to demonstrate how intellectuals and arguments compete for influence over government policy, and why any one particular perspective can move from being in the ascendancy (hegemonic) to the margins (dissenting) in influencing government policy, depending on the turn of world events and changing political personalities. What needs to be stressed here is that there are two domains in which theories compete for hegemony, and they can often be unrelated to each other: there is (1) the (foreign policy) behaviour of the state and (2) debate and discussion within the academy (the universities and the general intellectual domain). Realism's clear dominance over US foreign policy during the Nixon and Kissinger years occurred at a time when its influence within the academy was under one of its first important challenges. In the 1980s when neo-liberalism dominated the economic agendas of many Western governments, it was under substantial attack from neo-mercantilists and economic nationalists within the discipline of political economy. Dominance in one domain does not necessarily mean control in the other: the reasons can be quite different.[20]

In response to this uncertainty, a number of scholars have sought to explain the relationship between *theories* and *disciplines*. In an attempt to understand how academic disciplines in the natural sciences evolved, Kuhn suggested that the growth of knowledge proceeds via a series of distinct stages, each dominated by a particular frame of assumptions (paradigms) which render knowledge in one particular period of time incommensurate with knowledge in another. These successive periods of knowledge are separated by confrontations between opposing sets of ideas which in turn change the actual shape of the discipline. As human knowledge expands, paradigms become intellectually exhausted and impoverished, and are continually superseded as scholars find within them anomalies which cannot be explained.

Instead of viewing research as a procession of random and momentary fads without apparent logic or justification, Kuhn's model claims that what passes for knowledge at any given time in the history of a discipline is not objective but 'paradigm dependent'. A dominant paradigm is primarily a frame of assumptions dialectically conceived and consensually recognised as the cumulative wisdom of the discipline at any specific time in its evolution. These dominant paradigms give direction to the field of study within the discipline, shape the fundamental assumptions that can be made about the world, and determine the kind of questions that can be meaningfully posed and answered.[21]

There is much debate over the relevance and applicability of Kuhn's epistemological model to the social sciences, with suggestions that realism, for example, has been the dominant paradigm within the discipline of International Relations. It then becomes possible for scholars to cast theoretical disagreements and rivalries within the discipline as representing 'inter-paradigm debates', the implication being that a dominant theory becomes hegemonic within a discipline because of its intellectual merit.[22] This explanation may err in discounting the role played by politics, and specifically ideology, in the structure of the Western academy. Kuhn's approach may also militate against theoretical diversity by arguing that the emergence of *one* dominant paradigm within a discipline is both normal and desirable.[23]

Bull poses and interesting challenge for Kuhn's approach by arguing that intellectual progress in International Relations is quite different to intellectual progress in the natural or 'hard' sciences. Research in the 'hard' sciences proceeds on the assumption that logical argument and empirical verification will render certain hypotheses proven beyond reasonable doubt. Once a consensus of views within the scientific community is formed, theoretical inquiry can be built upon the acceptance of certain views as established fact: progress occurs as old ideas are superseded by superior accounts. According to Bull, this type of intellectual progress is not possible within the study of international relations because the matter under investigation cannot be subject to proof or strict confirmation. New ideas will certainly add to knowledge about an issue or event but their superiority to previous accounts can never be conclusively demonstrated. In International Relations, there is rarely a consensus about when theoretical progress is made and the central questions of the discipline are never finally settled: they will always be open to new interpretations and further refinement. Applying Kuhn's model to a subject such as International Relations, therefore, may in fact impede theoretical progress. 'The rhetoric of scientific progress itself, misapplied to a field in which progress of a strictly scientific sort does not take place, has the effect of constricting and obscuring the sort of advance that is possible'.[24]

However appropriate Kuhn's model may be, without further elaboration it is clear that the factors which determine whether a theory within a discipline is the dominant paradigm at any point may be quite different from the reasons why a government appears to be following a particular policy path. The world of international diplomacy is affected by a range of factors which may have nothing to do with the intellectual merits of the protagonists in a theoretical dispute, including most importantly, economic and political interests. It is therefore important to keep the domains separate in our minds as we survey the field of international theory.

It is necessary to stress the politicised nature of the discipline because the politics of International Relations can determine how broad the spectrum of 'legitimate theoretical opinion' can actually be. A brief review of the early history of the discipline can serve to illustrate the point more clearly. A number of Marxist scholars have highlighted the limits of expressible dissent in the discipline's attempt to uncover the cause of the First World War. They point to the conceptual and ideological parameters beyond which the investigators into war causes could not, or would not proceed. For opinion to be considered legitimate it had to fall between the poles of 'idealism' at one end of the spectrum and 'realism' at the other. According to these Marxists, certain facts were axiomatically excluded as not belonging to the inquiry at all. Tensions within society, such as class struggles, and economic competition between colonial powers – during this period a popular Marxist explanation of the origins of war – were not considered seriously within the discipline at this time. One commentator has suggested that the theory of imperialism was deliberately excluded because, since it located the causes of war within the nature of the capitalist system, it posed a direct threat to the social order of capitalist states: 'this false doctrine had to be refuted in the interest of stabilising bourgeois society ... the [historians] acted and reflected within the social context the bourgeois university, which structurally obstructed such revolutionary insights'.[25] Feminists have made a similar claim about the exclusion of their identity and perspectives from the concerns of International Relations, arguing that the organisation of the academy is designed in a way which prevents inquiry into masculine power. We need to be aware that because of its very subject matter, International Relations is a politicised discipline and this can affect the way we read texts and theorise about the world. We cannot take it for granted that any question can be posed or that the discipline values each theoretical approach equally, or on the same terms.

Explanatory and Constitutive Theory

Rather than proclaiming an 'official' definition of international relations theory, it might be better to state the purpose to which these theories are being put. This will enable us to distinguish between *explanatory* and *constitutive* international theory.

One aim of studying a wide variety of IR theories is to make international politics more intelligible and better understood - to make better sense of the institutions, events and processes which exist in the contemporary world. At times the theories will involve testing hypothesis, proposing causal explanations, describing events and explaining general trends and phenomena, with the aim of constructing a plausible image of the world. We will call these *explanatory* theories of international relations. To the extent that these theories broaden and deepen our understanding of contemporary world politics, they will be performing an important function.

But why study international relations in this way, that is via explanatory theories? Do we need theories at all? Surely facts are sufficient? Halliday's three answers to this question are instructive.

> First, there needs to be some preconception of which facts are significant and which are not. The facts are myriad and do not speak for themselves. For anyone, academic or not, there need to be criteria of significance. Secondly, any one set of facts, even if accepted as true and as significant, can yield different interpretations: the debate on the 'lessons of the 1930s' is not about what happened in the 1930s, but about how these events are to be interpreted. The same applies to the end of the Cold War in the 1980s. Thirdly, no human agent, again whether academic or not, can rest content with facts alone: all social activity involves moral questions, of right and wrong, and these can, by definition, not be decided by facts. In the international domain such ethical issues are pervasive: the question of legitimacy and loyalty – should one obey the nation, a broader community (even the world, the cosmopolis), or some smaller sub-national group; the issues of intervention – whether sovereignty is a supreme value or whether states or agents can intervene in the internal affairs of states; the question of human rights and their definition and universality.[26]

Theories provide intellectual order to the subject matter of international relations. They enable us to conceptualise and contextualise both past and contemporary events. They also provide us with a range of ways of interpreting complex issues. Theories help us to orientate and discipline our minds in response to the bewildering phenomena around us. They help us to think critically, logically and coherently. A solid grounding in explanatory theories of International Relations will make empirical studies of world politics that much more intelligible. As Banks argues, theory consists of both analysis and synthesis. To analyse is to unravel, to separate the strands, or to take to pieces. To synthesise is to reassemble, to piece together the parts in such a way as to compose a whole that makes sense. General theory in IR, then, consists of dividing the human race into sections, noting the significant properties of each, examining the relationships between them, and describing the patterns formed by the relationships. Interesting problems arise at every stage. Some of these are methodological. How should we set about observing things, defining them, measuring them and comparing them? Others are theoretical, because theory consists of forming ideas or concepts to describe aspects of the world, classifying them, and considering the various ways in which they interact. ... In short, what are the appropriate units of analysis, what are the significant links between them, and what are the right levels on which to conduct the analysis? And there are further theoretical questions even beyond these, because all theories of society are, at root, ideological. Theories simultaneously express the political values of the theorist, and also help to shape the world which is being analysed.[27]

To the scholar of the 'international', theories are unavoidable. After all, the interpretation of 'reality' is always contingent on theoretical assumptions of one kind or another. To reiterate the point, the events and issues which comprise international relations can only be interpreted and understood by reference to a conceptual framework. The theory of International Relations provides us with a choice of conceptual frameworks.

The functions we perform when theorising are also in dispute and, as Bull insisted, they require critical and reflective examination. Gellner asks whether is it possible or meaningful to distinguish 'between a world of fact "out there" and a cognitive realm of theory that *retrospectively* orders and gives meaning to factual data'?[28] In separating 'theory and practice', 'object and subject' in this way, might we place ourselves in debt to positivist-based empirical science when this methodology may be ideologically biased or inappropriate to our task? Are we fooling ourselves in pretending to be detached from the task of theorizing – the process by which we give meaning to an allegedly objectified world 'out there' – if, as some post-modernists tell us, there is no Archimedean point of ultimate reference from which we can make judgements about the world?

These questions lead us to a second category of theory, *constitutive* international theory. Everyone comes to the study of international relations with preconceptions, experiences and beliefs which affect the way they understand the subject. Language, culture, religion, ethnicity, class and ideology are just a few of the factors which shape our world view. Indeed it is only possible to understand and interpret the world within particular cultural and linguistic frameworks: these are the *lenses* through which we see the world. One of the primary purposes for studying theory is to enable us to examine our own lenses to discover just how controlled or distorted our world view is. Why do we focus on some images (for example states) and why are we unable to see others (such as class)? Why do we gaze in one direction (for example the international system) and seemingly turn a blind eye to others (such as the domestic environment)? And in which interpretation of *social reality* are our intellectual endeavours grounded?

We need to examine our own background assumptions to reveal and explain our selections, priorities and prejudices because 'all forms of social analysis ... raise important questions about the moral and cultural constitution of the observer'.[29] In the theory of international relations we are as concerned with how we *approach* the study of world politics as we are with the events, issues and actors in the global system. We need to understand how individuals think about their world by promoting a wider self-awareness of our belief systems. As Linklater argues, 'all social analysts [should] reflect upon the cognitive interests and normative assumptions which underpin their research'.[30] It should be remembered that the 'international' is refracted through the mind of the observer. Constitutive international theory is directly concerned with the importance of human reflection on the nature and character of world politics.

Often our views may not be particularly coherent, rigorous or well founded in knowledge. This is accepted as inevitable, given that no-one's mind is absolutely blank or completely neutral on questions concerning the study of international relations, however poorly informed they may be. All that can be asked is that as human beings we need to be acutely aware of our own assumptions, prejudices and biases. We should not attempt anything as futile or unrealistic as dispensing with our intellectual and emotional baggage, but we are duty bound to subject these assumptions to critical analysis and review. We cannot hope to understand the complex field of international politics until we understand ourselves, in particular the inherent assumptions we bring to the task. International relations theory is fundamentally concerned with asking questions about these prior assumptions.

What do Theories of International Relations Differ About?

We should not assume that even within the same theoretical tradition, scholars share a consensus of views. Although they may share many basic assumptions, there can be as much diversity within the one school of thought as there is between the various theoretical perspectives. Marxism and Feminism are examples of very broad 'churches' with almost as many variations, strains and factions as there are scholars in each field. They could not be described as monolithic or homogenous theoretical traditions. The same is increasingly true for Constructivism. This should not come as a surprise to students in the field of international relations. It is perfectly normal for there to be scope for differences of views within the same theoretical school. Indeed some of the most interesting debates within IR theory are between intellectuals from the same theoretical tradition. Heterogeneity can be a strength. There are few benefits to be gained from theoretical purity.

Comparing unlike things would be a fruitless activity. However, theories of international relations have enough in common to make contrasts and comparisons an insightful activity. Perhaps an odd starting point for this task is the identification of things about which the theories *disagree*. According to Linklater there are four fundamental points on which the various theories of international relations differ.[31] These will be used as the basis for our discussion.

The first is the *object of analysis and the scope of the enquiry*. This is sometimes called the level of analysis debate. Here the differences centre on the very nature of the subject matter under analysis. Which actors or phenomena should be studied in International Relations – nation-states, war, international organisations, class, transnational corporations, bureaucracies, the environment or the makers of foreign policy? What characteristics of global political processes should theorists be concerned with – the pursuit of power, the successful management of the international system, the exclusion of women, the social construction of norms, the evolution of a diplomatic culture or the exploitation of classes and the dependent relationships between states? And what kinds of outcomes are favoured – preservation of the existing state-system, greater levels of interdependency between individuals across the world, new forms of political community or the revolutionary transformation of the international order?[32]

In his survey of approaches to the causes of wars, Kenneth Waltz argued that there were three levels of analysis: (a) the nature of individuals; (b) the nature of states and societies; and (c) the nature of the international system. According to which level of analysis is chosen, certain actors will be emphasised and de-emphasised in any study of the causes of war. So for a neo-realist like Waltz, the object of analysis in the study of international relations is the struggle for power and security by nation-states in an anarchical international system (level c). For a Marxist, however, who wishes to understand the prospects for global political and economic change, it is the internal class nature of capitalist societies which is significant (level b). A psychologist, who explains war by looking at the innate aggressiveness of humankind, will focus on the individual in her explanation of its causes (level a). Again, depending on the level at which the question is addressed, certain actors or agents will be privileged over others.

The scope of the inquiry can often extend to questions of ontology and epistemology which underpin the very nature of theorising. Here we are indebted to the work of critical theorists and post-modernists who correctly point out that debates over the nature of knowledge, meaning, interpretation, language and reality have until the last two decades, largely been ignored within the discipline of International Relations. And yet questions which focus on what is the 'knowable reality' of global politics, for example, are central to our task. For many theorists, the scope of their inquiries extends to subjecting the reality 'out there', and assumptions that this reality is palpable, perceptible, universally accepted and understood, to ideological critique. Post-modernists, for example, believe the interpretation of social reality which underwrites neo-realism is narrowly conceived and highly contestable: it is not widely agreed as Waltz and others assume. For them 'reality' is a discursive phenomenon and is 'never a complete, entirely coherent "thing", accessible to universalized, essentialist or totalized understandings of it ... [it] is always characterised by ambiguity, disunity, discrepancy, contradiction and difference'.[33] Feminists would similarly argue that women are too often excluded from the neo-realist 'reality' of international politics. Women should not be an invisible feature of the theoretical landscape, as the hegemonic perspectives would have them drawn. Constructivists are concerned with how national and state identities and interests change as social norms evolve. They are also interested in questions of political agency and identity, and ethical conduct by states.

For the theorist of international relations, questions of ontology are unavoidable. As Cox argues, 'ontology lies at the beginning of any enquiry. We cannot define a problem in global politics without presupposing a certain basic structure consisting of the significant kinds of entities involved and the form of significant relationships among them'.[34] All theories have ontological foundations of some kind because ontology is the study of 'how political actors construct the political world and imagine its purposes'.[35] Even the shape of the discipline itself and the content of its curriculum are an expression of ontological preference. Again Cox reminds us that 'ontological presuppositions [are] inherent in ... terms such as "international relations", which seems to equate nation with state and to define the field as limited to the interactions among states'. Perhaps the term 'global politics' is less restrictive and more appropriate?[36] At the very least these ontological questions cast doubt on whether a politically neutral or objective interpretation of an external 'reality' is possible, or even makes sense.

Over the last decade discussion of exactly what constitutes the 'knowable reality' of international relations (that is, ontological questions) has been matched by debates over how knowledge is generated in theories of international relations (that is, epistemological questions). The focus of an increasing number of theoreticians has been on the social and political purposes of knowledge, specifically the relationship between knowledge and power. The intellectual inquiries of critical theorists have centred on the construction of an epistemological taxonomy, the most frequently cited being Habermas's three categories of knowledge-constitutive interests (technical, practical and emancipatory), and their application across the theoretical breadth of the discipline. The purpose of this approach has been to evaluate the respective perspectives on international relations by revealing the theory of knowledge which underpins each of them. Linklater, for example, has suggested that in this way neo-realism can be seen to be based on positivist methodology, rationalism on hermeneutics and critical theory on an emancipatory cognitive interest. The epistemological basis of each theory is said to be an important factor in determining what it privileges and assumes in its account of world politics.

Cox has distinguished between theories such as neo-realism which produce knowledge 'which made it possible for a political order that favoured dominant interests to function more smoothly', and critical approaches which generate knowledge with an emancipatory interest and a transformative intent.[37] Similarly, feminists can demonstrate how knowledge about structures and beliefs functions to exclude, subordinate or marginalize a specific social group, while ecological theorists can show how positivism is biased towards producing knowledge which privileges anthropocentricism, industrialism and economic growth, thus giving legitimacy to humankind's mastery over nature.

Evaluating the theories of International Relations from an epistemological perspective can be difficult because it involves a high order of abstraction. Nevertheless, it can tell us much about the assumptions each theorist makes and the conclusions each perspective on world politics reaches. The only danger in pursuing the philosophy of social science as an avenue of research (constitutive theory) is that scholars may, in the process, neglect or be distracted from the important fields of empirical research which deserve to be explored.[38]

The second point of difference between theories is the *purpose of social and political enquiry*. What is the underlying reason behind the theoretical undertaking? For many who work in the field, the answer is obvious. The purpose of theoretical enquiry is to find ways of making international politics more pacific and just. This is a consistent normative thread which can be traced back to the discipline's origins. But it is not seen as the only purpose of theory.

For neo-realists like Waltz, it is to ensure, by understanding the international system better, that relations between states are managed as smoothly as possible in an effort to minimise the potential for conflict and war: its purpose is problem-solving. For neo-liberals the purpose of social and political enquiry is to produce optimal economic outcomes for the citizens of each country based on efficiencies produced by market applications. Specifically, this means exposing and removing the corrupting influence of the state from the lives of individual citizens. Critical theorists and feminists are normatively committed to promoting human understanding and emancipation by explaining and exposing the constraints upon human autonomy in the contemporary world. For them, the purpose of social enquiry is to be actively libertarian by opening the paths to changing the international system. They are seeking new arrangements which will improve the circumstances of subordinate and marginal groups.[39]

Different purposes for social and political enquiry is the basis of the distinction between *problem solving theory* and *critical* theory made by Robert Cox in his assessment of the impact of recent developments in social theory for the study of International Relations. Cox distinguishes between theoretical approaches on the basis of the purpose of theory: 'theory is always *for* someone and *for* some purpose. ... The world is seen from a standpoint definable in terms of nation or social class. ... There is ... no such thing as theory in itself, divorced from a standpoint in time and space. When any theory so represents itself, it is the more important to examine it as ideology, and to lay bare its concealed perspective'.[40] Theory never exists in a void. It can 'either be a guide [to] solving problems within the terms of a particular perspective [problem-solving theory], or it can reflect on the process of theorising itself, which raises the possibility of choosing a different perspective [critical theory]'.[41]

Cox claims that problem solving theory 'takes the world as it finds it, with the prevailing social and political relations and institutions into which they are organised, as the given framework for action.[42] The general aim of problem-solving theory is to make these relationships and institutions work smoothly by dealing effectively with particular sources of trouble'. Problem solving theory does not question the pattern of relationships and institutions in question and can 'fix limits or parameters to a problem area' which in turn limits 'the number of variables which are amenable to relatively close and precise examination'.[43] Problem-solving theory has the effect of legitimising the status-quo.

Critical theory, on the other hand, 'stands apart from the prevailing order of the world and asks how that order came about. Critical theory, unlike problem-solving theory, does not take institutions and social and power relations for granted but calls them into question by concerning itself with their origins and how and whether they might be in the process of changing. It is directed towards an appraisal of the very framework of action ... which problem-solving theory accepts as its parameters'. Whereas problem-solving theory is 'a guide to tactical actions which, intended or unintended, sustain the existing order', critical theory provides a 'a guide to strategic action for bringing about an alternative order'.[44]

This is just one scholar's method of distinguishing between theoretical approaches to the study of international relations. In this case Cox wants to expose the ideology of neo-realism by demonstrating that it is a 'problem solving' theory in contrast to 'critical theory' which is informed by the emancipatory commitment of the Marxist tradition. There are many different approaches to theoretical distinction and classification in International Relations. And there are obviously a variety of purposes which animate the work of international theorists. Some want to bring greater intellectual cohesion to the field while others want to abandon the search for a resolution of the discipline's major theoretical disputes. More recent practitioners want to subvert ruling orthodoxies and breakdown disciplinary boundaries. Others want to admit previously marginal and dissident concerns into the mainstream of the discipline.[45] The proliferation of purposes and motives reflects the discipline's recent receptiveness to new theoretical possibilities. International Relations is now more inclusive than at any time in its short history.

The third point of difference centres on the *appropriate methodology for the study of international relations*. Should it be an empirical vocation, one based on the rigorous application of the scientific method, or should there be a clear preference for either a systemic or reductionist approach? In the discipline's 'great debate' over methodology in the 1960s, 'traditionalists' emphasised the relative utility of history, law, philosophy and other classical methods of academic inquiry, whilst the 'behaviourists' argued in favour of scientific conceptualisation, including the quantification of variables, formal hypothesis testing and model building, to reveal the 'realities' of the international system.

This debate formed part of a much longer discussion about the extent to which like the natural world, the 'laws' of the social world could also be uncovered by applying the scientific method. At the end of the eighteenth century, when science had contributed so much to our understanding of the natural world and our own physical nature, it began to be asked whether science might also further our understanding of the social world. Could the method by which science studied the natural world be applied to the study of human affairs? The creation of 'social science' therefore sprung from the application of a specific set of methodological principles (scientific empiricism) which had proved so successful in other disciplines. Methodological debates in the 'social sciences' generally, and International Relations specifically, have therefore centred on the relevance and applicability of this approach. Does emulating the natural sciences make sense when the subject matter is human and social?

In the 1980s more critically orientated theorists reopened the debate by attacking the positivist methodology of neo-realism, believing that this explained both the dominance and conservative nature of the perspective. According to critical theorists influenced by the Frankfurt School and the work of Habermas, methodology should be grounded in an emancipatory interest in freeing human beings from unnecessary social constraints and not a technical interest in social control.[46] Debates over methodology are relatively common in the 'social sciences', with certain approaches being more widely favoured in one country over others (the impact of behaviourism on the US IR community was much greater than its impact elsewhere). In International Relations these arguments are a long way from being resolved. Perhaps they shouldn't or can't be resolved, only debated? After all, different modes of social inquiry will inevitably produce different outcomes.

By the 1980s the idea of a politically neutral, value free methodology came under challenge as the study of International Relations became influenced by intellectual developments in other fields, most notably European political and social theory. Borrowing ideas from critical theory, writers such as Cox and Ashley began to expose the links between theoretical methodology and the legitimation of political orders which favoured the interests of ruling elites. Having subverted the somewhat naive belief that positivism could provide the student of International Relations with an impartial or politically objective world view, these influences ensured that questions of methodology, and subsequently ontology and epistemology, would be brought in from the margins of the discipline to occupy a central place on its research agenda.

The fourth point of departure centres on *whether each theory sees International Relations as being distinct from, or related to, other areas of intellectual endeavour*. Is the study of international relations distinct from political science, sociology, diplomatic history, political philosophy, and so on, or are these demarcation lines contrived and artificial? Is it important to have a separate, specialised field dealing with the international context? These are epistemological questions as well as questions concerned with the history and structure of the Western academy. What do these disciplinary boundaries represent anyway? Do they facilitate or limit enquiry? What do they tell us about the way the university system packages knowledge? Can the disciplinary boundaries be explained by the careerist motives of academics?

Each theoretical approach has different answers to these questions and places greater or lesser emphasis on the importance of disciplinary boundaries. Though they might borrow their methodological approach from other disciplines, neo-realists see the international system as a 'domain apart' (Waltz) which deserves separate treatment in the academy. For them, the discipline is unique. Critical theorists, on the other hand, dispute the discrete nature of the discipline and are concerned with the relevance of recent developments in social theory and historical sociology for the study of international politics. Many post-modernists are highly suspicious of what they call the 'metanarratives' of liberation and progress. Unlike anarchists who believe the libertarian promise of the Enlightenment is still to be consummated, and critical theorists who wish to recast the Enlightenment project, many post-modernists want to abandon it altogether, believing it to be a dehumanising and ultimately oppressive tradition. They regard disciplinary boundaries as exclusionary and part of a structure of intellectual repression.

Feminists and ecologists have recently joined the debates within International Relations because of the increasingly porous state of the discipline's boundaries. Their perspectives could no longer be ignored or marginalised, and their influence is a direct product of inter-disciplinary research. Questions of identity, patriarchy and exclusion are central to the concerns of feminists, although most discussion of these topics has taken place outside the IR pantheon. Similarly, it is research into ecological sustainability and environmental degradation conducted in other disciplines, such as environmental studies, which is finally impacting on international theory.

Just as the shape of contemporary political boundaries was being altered by the forces of globalisation and fragmentation, so too the intellectual boundaries of International Relations were being eroded by the influences of cognate disciplines such as jurisprudence and international law, sociology and political economy. In a sense, the fate of the nation-state became a metaphor for the discipline which has claimed exclusive jurisdiction over the study of its external behaviour. The power of finance markets, transnational corporations and regional trade associations, together with developments in information technology, have undermined the immutability of political boundaries and the sovereign integrity of the modern nation-state. Similarly, the ideas of theorists such as Habermas, Foucault, Derrida, and the political force of social and intellectual movements centred on feminism and environmentalism, have undermined the safe and traditional certainties of international thought: as a result, the intellectual boundaries of International Relations have been contested and are being redrawn. Given the collapse of the consensus about its actual nature, whether International Relations should continue to stand alone as a separate discipline within the academy is now a central question for those who work in the field.

It is possible to find other points of difference between the theories of International Relations. In fact in the 1980s debates about this issue often filled the discipline's journals and pre-occupied the intellectual lives of teachers and students. The four points of difference just outlined can be seen as a template for conceptualising the seemingly endless and complex disputes within the field.

Evaluating Theories for Contrasts and Comparisons

We should not ask too much of these theories. For scholars who locate themselves in the post-modern tradition, grand theories are by definition problematic and should be either treated with suspicion or dispensed with. A single theory cannot, by itself, completely identify and explain all the key structures and dynamics in the international system. Some will be more convincing in explaining certain specific features of international politics.

Others will be more persuasive in their understanding of the process of theorising. Most are deficient in some way. This may be initially frustrating for students seeking a single comprehensive meta-theory of international relations. It will soon be apparent, however, that each approach has something important and insightful to say, though this may depend on each theory's relevance for a specific topic or period of history. The end of the Cold War and the process of globalisation forced scholars to reconsider the relevance of their theoretical outlooks in the 1990s. The failure of IR theory adequately to detect and predict patterns of behaviour at the global level has been particularly noticeable in recent years. Neither the collapse of the Soviet Union, the Gulf War nor the ethnic conflicts in the Balkans were anticipated or adequately explained by any of the major traditions of speculation about international politics.

As has been suggested earlier, the selection of theories for this book has been based on what the authors regard as the most influential and informative in contemporary theoretical discussion – a theoretical stocktake. Our approach has therefore been pluralist and, at times, inter-disciplinary – or to put it in religious terms, we have tried to be ecumenical and non-denominational. We do not claim that this is a definitive survey covering all theoretical traditions. Nor do we deny the claims of other IR theories for representation here. We have selected nine theoretical traditions with at least one eye on where we believe theoretical research in the discipline is currently heading. By definition the process of selection demands a degree of arbitrary decision making.

The biases of the authors should be apparent because there has been no conscious attempt to conceal them. And it is quite normal for scholars to identify, or be identified, with one perspective in preference to others, however misleading or inaccurate the label may be. This is often no more than a form of intellectual shorthand which purports to make the process of classifying intellectuals easier. Readers, however, are encouraged to reach their own conclusions about the strengths and weaknesses of each perspective, regardless of the preferences of the authors. The important point to remember is one made by Wight, that no one theory can ever be proven correct, but it is the debate between them that is important: truth is not an attribute of any one tradition, but of the dialogue between them.[47]

Establishing criteria for evaluating theories of international relations is not an easy task. Kegley's argues that 'a theory of international relations needs to perform four principal tasks. It should describe, explain, predict and prescribe'.[48] As criteria for evaluating the performance of explanatory theories, this list may be sufficient. However, it would exclude from consideration constitutive theory which, by definition, could not meet these criteria. It is only possible, then, to suggest that theories of international relations can be evaluated against one or more of the following criteria:

1. A theory's *understanding* of an issue or process
2. The *explanatory* power of the theory
3. The theory's success in *predicting* events
4. The theory's intellectual *consistency* and *coherence*
5. The *scope* of the theory
6. The theory's capacity for critical *self-reflection* and intellectual *engagement* with contending theories

This list of six points is not a definitive one but it should help the reader to conceptualise the complex field of alternative conceptions of international relations. The processes of appraisal and discrimination are higher order cognitive skills which make considerable demands upon the student of international theory. In this book we hope to make these tasks both stimulating and rewarding.

In Chapters 2 and 3 Scott Burchill discusses the traditions of liberalism and realism. These theories represent the oldest and arguably the most influential perspectives in the field, dominating speculation for at least the first fifty years of the discipline's life. Although no longer unchallenged for theoretical dominance, they remain highly influential within the field. As far as economic relationships are concerned, global politics in the new century resonates with many of the ideas originally promoted by nineteenth century liberals. Conversely, the writings of early realists such as Carr and Morgenthau still influence discussion within the discipline over half a century after they were published. Neo-realism emerged in the 1970s to occupy a position of intellectual hegemony in the discipline, particularly in the United States, though its influence would appear to be currently in decline. A measure of neo-realism's dominance, however, has been the extent to which dissenting approaches have felt obliged to address many of the central concerns of theorists such as Waltz, most notably the nature and importance of anarchy in the international system.

In Chapters 4 and 5 Andrew Linklater analyses rationalism and Marxism, two perspectives which have had less historical influence on the discipline than the first three, but have nevertheless had a significant impact upon contemporary thought. Rationalism came to prominence in the 1970s in Australia and the United Kingdom as a substantial theoretical qualification to the pessimism of realism and the idealism of liberal-internationalism. The work of Wight, Vincent and Bull remain central to any discussion of an 'international society of states' and the prospects for universal human rights. Marxism, which was widely thought to have neglected the central foci of International Relations, re-emerged in the 1980s to stake its claim as a progressivist account of international politics based on its emancipatory credentials. Although it is still widely seen as a theory of domestic society, Marxism nevertheless mounts an important critique of neo-realism's exogenous approach to world politics.

Marxism also provides the intellectual inheritance for critical theory, which is discussed by Richard Devetak in Chapter 6. The relevance of critical theory for the study of international relations reflects the influence of European social theory across disciplinary boundaries. The importance of the work of Habermas, Ashley, Cox and Linklater can be measured by both their reclamation of the emancipatory spirit of Marxism, and their exploration of the epistemological bases of the most influential traditions of thought within International Relations. In Chapter 7 Richard Devetak evaluates the theoretical contribution of Derrida, Foucault and Lyotard, and the likely effects of their writings on the trajectory of the discipline. Challenging the premises of the Enlightenment 'project', including the assumption that modernity is linear and progressive, is at the core of much post-modernist theory. Together with a focus on issues such as *exclusion*, *difference* and *ontology*, these central themes pose a fundamental challenge to the way scholars have thought about international politics. Depending on the reader's own position, the influence of post-modernism on International Relations can be viewed as either an exciting development which opens up new avenues of research or a disturbing trend which threatens to tear the discipline apart.

Constructivism, discussed by Christian Reus-Smit in Chapter 8, has recently impacted across the discipline and now represents a broad spectrum of theoretical thought, from liberal to post-modern variations. Explaining state policy and national behaviour by focusing on how the norms which guide policy makers are socially constructed – and therefore change over time – has re-opened debates about the sources of political identity and national interests. Unlike the other new theories under consideration, constructivism has largely grown from discussion and research within the discipline rather from external influences.

In Chapter 9 Jacqui True sheds light on a subject which, until recently, has been largely neglected: feminist perspectives on international relations. Ostensibly invisible to a male-dominated discipline, the contributions of feminist scholarship are some of the most innovative and original challenges to orthodoxy within the field and should not be seen as marginal. Feminist approaches to international relations have developed their own distinctive foci and agendas, in particular highlighting the extent to which masculinity has distorted conceptions of power and epistemology within the discipline. As arguments for theory which is sensitive to the concerns of gender, they have significantly enriched the study of world politics.

Developments within ecological theory, discussed by Matthew Paterson in Chapter 10, also have important implications for the study of global politics. Environmental degradation and threats to the continuing diversity of species caused by assumptions of infinite economic growth and unbridled capitalism pose problems which can only be seriously addressed at the global level. Ecological theory and green politics are responses which will continue to reorientate the discipline of International Relations towards ways of thinking which consider humanity's common fate and the shared destiny of life on earth as the moral starting point for intellectual research.

The authors of this book believe that theoretical developments within the discipline of International Relations have reached an exciting stage marked by rapid intellectual challenges, most notably the influences of cognate fields of research and need to grasp the extraordinary changes currently taking place in global politics. Consideration of issues such as ethics, identity, agency, and globalisation – to name only four – have given con-temporary theorists much food for thought. The authors do not share the pessimism of our early sceptic, believing that a knowledge of a range of theories of international relations, both explanatory and constitutive, is not only possible but is actually an essential prerequisite to understanding the modern world. This volume is their contribution to an ongoing dialogue.

Notes

1. N. Chomsky, *World Orders, Old and New* (London, 1994), p. 120.
2. N. Chomsky, *American Power and the New Mandarins* (Harmondsworth, 1969), p. 271.
3. Hence the debate over the impact of positivism in the area. See S. Smith, K. Booth and M. Zalewski (eds), *International Theory: Positivism and Beyond* (Cambridge, 1996). For an excellent review of theoretical development in the discipline, see A. Linklater (ed.), *Theories of International Relations* (London, 2000), Introduction.
4. S. Smith, 'The Self-Image of a Discipline: A Genealogy of International Relations Theory', in K. Booth and S. Smith (eds), *International Relations Theory Today* (Cambridge, 1995), pp. 26–7.
5. H. Bull, 'The Theory of International Politics, 1919–1969' (1972), reproduced in J. Der Derian (ed.), *International Theory: Critical Investigations* (Basingstoke, 1995), pp. 183–4.
6. S. Smith, 'Positivisim and Beyond', in Smith, Booth and Zalewski (1996), p. 13.
7. R. W. Cox, 'Towards a post-hegemonic conceptualization of world order: reflections on the relevancy of Ibn Khaldun', in J. N. Rosenau and E.-O. Czempiel (eds), *Governance Without Government: Order and Change in World Politics* (Cambridge, 1992), p. 133.
8. For an excellent introductory discussion of these issues, see C. Brown, *Understanding International Relations* (Basingstoke, 1997).
9. A. J. P. Taylor, *The Origins of the Second World War* (Harmondsworth, 1961), p. 30.
10. For a fuller discussion see Chapter 2 of this volume.

11. Bull quoted in M. Hollis and S. Smith *Explaining and Understanding International Relations* (Oxford, 1990), p. 20.
12. R. Williams *Keywords* (London, 1983), p. 152.
13. M. Howard, *War and the Liberal Conscience* (Oxford, 1978), p. 11.
14. J. Macmillan and A. Linklater (eds), *Boundaries in Question: New Directions in International Relations* (London, 1995), p. 15.
15. Macmillan and Linklater (1995), p. 4.
16. M. Wight, 'Why is there No International Theory?' (1966), reprinted in Der Derian (1995), pp. 15, 25-6 and 32.
17. F. Halliday, 'The Pertinence of International Relations', *Political Studies*, 38 (1990), p. 503.
18. V. Kubalkova and A. Cruickshank, 'The "new cold war" in critical international relations studies', *Review of International Studies*, 12 (1986), p. 164.
19. D. Yergin, *Shattered Peace*, revised edn (London, 1990).
20. Think of the influence of prevailing intellectual fashions and careerism on the academy.
21. T. Kuhn, *The Structure of Scientific Revolutions* (Chicago, 1970).
22. See M. Banks, 'The inter-paradigm debate', in M. Light and A. J. R. Groom (eds), *International Relations: A Handbook of Current Theory* (London, 1985) and M. Hoffman, 'Critical theory and the inter-paradigm debate', *Millennium*, vol. 16, no. 2 (1987).
23. For a celebration of theoretical diversity from an anarchist perspective, see P. Feyerabend, *Against Method* (London, 1975).
24. Bull (1972) in Der Derian (1995), p. 204. See also pp. 202-6.
25. E. Krippendorff, *International Relations as a Social Science* (Brighton, 1982), p. 27.
26. F. Halliday, *Rethinking International Relations* (London, 1994), p. 25.
27. Banks (1985), pp. 8-9.
28. E. Gellner, *Legitimation of Belief* (Cambridge, 1974), p. 175.
29. Macmillan and Linklater (1995), p. 9.
30. A. Linklater, 'The question of the next stage in international relations theory: a critical-theoretical point of view', *Millennium*, vol. 21, no. 1 (1992).
31. See Linklater (1992).
32. See R. Little and M. Smith (eds), *Perspectives on World Politics* (London, 1991), pp. 4-12.
33. J. George, *Discourses of Global Politics: A Critical (Re)Introduction* (Boulder, 1994), p. 11.
34. Cox (1992), p. 132.
35. Macmillan and Linklater (1995), p. 10.
36. Cox (1992), p. 132.
37. Cox (1992), p. 132-3.
38. R. Keohane, 'International Institutions: Two Approaches', *International Studies Quarterly*, vol. 32, no. 4, (1988), pp. 379-91.
39. Macmillan and Linklater (1995), p. 9.

40. R. W. Cox, 'Social forces, states and world orders: beyond international relations theory', *Millennium*, 10 (1981), p. 128.
41. Hoffman (1987), p. 237.
42. For a discussion of both Horkheimer's and Habermas' theoretical constructions, see R. Bernstein, *The Restructuring of Social and Political Theory* (London, 1976), pp. 191–200 and Hoffman (1987), pp. 231–8.
43. Cox (1981), pp. 128–9.
44. Cox (1981), pp. 128–30.
45. Linklater (1992).
46. Linklater (1992).
47. Cited by Smith in Booth and Smith (1995), p. 13.
48. C. W. Kegley Jr (ed.), *Controversies in International Relations Theory: Realism and the Neo-Liberal Challenge* (New York, 1995), p. 8.

CHAPTER 2

Liberalism

Scott Burchill

Liberalism has had a profound impact on the shape of all modern industrial societies. It has championed limited government and scientific rationality, believing individuals should be free from arbitrary state power, persecution and superstition. It has advocated political freedom, democracy and con-stitutionally guaranteed rights, and privileged the liberty of the individual and equality before the law. Liberalism has also argued for individual competition in civil society and claimed that market capitalism best pro-motes the general welfare by most efficiently allocating scarce resources within society. To the extent that its ideas have been realised in recent democratic transitions in both hemispheres and manifested in the globali-sation of the world economy, liberalism clearly remains a powerful and influential doctrine.

However, according to C. B. Macpherson there is a tension within liberal thought between two conceptions of the human condition.

> The first of these is the liberal, individualist concept of man as essentially a consumer of utilities, an infinite desirer and infinite appropriator. This concept was fitting, even necessary, for the development of the capitalist market society, from the seventeenth century on: it antedates the introduction of democratic principles and institutions, which did not amount to anything before the nine-teenth century. The other is the concept of man as an enjoyer and exerter of his uniquely human attributes or capacities, a view which began to challenge the market view in the mid nineteenth century and soon became an integral part of the justifying theory of liberal democracy.[1]

These two strands within the liberal tradition – between the market view of human beings as consumers maximising their utilities and the ethical view of humans striving to realise their potential – are defining characteristics of the species. But as views of the human essence they also remain largely irreconciled. They form two quite distinct and at times contradictory sub-traditions within a broad philosophical outlook. Consequently their under-lying principles and the tension between them must form the organising themes of any assessment of liberalism's contribution to international thought.

The chapter will begin with an analysis of the revival of liberal thought after the Cold War. It will then examine the origins of ethical liberalism, including traditional liberal attitudes to war and the importance of democracy and human rights in liberal internationalism. The influence of market or economic liberalism will then be assessed before the role of liberal thought in the debate about globalisation is measured. The conclusion will judge the contribution of liberalism to the theory of International Relations.

After the Cold War

The demise of Soviet Communism at the beginning of the 1990s enhanced the influence of liberal theories of international relations within the academy, a theoretical tradition long thought to have been discredited by perspectives which emphasise the recurrent features of international relations. In a confident reassertion of the teleology of liberalism, Fukuyama claimed that the collapse of the Soviet Union proved that liberal democracy had no serious ideological competitor: it was 'the end point of mankind's ideological evolution' and the 'final form of human government'. It is an argument that has been strengthened by recent transitions to democracy in Africa, East Asia and Latin America.

For Fukuyama the end of the Cold War represented the triumph of the 'ideal state' and a particular form of political economy, 'liberal capitalism', which 'cannot be improved upon': there can be 'no further progress in the development of underlying principles and institutions'. According to Fukuyama, the end of the East–West conflict confirmed that liberal capitalism was unchallenged as a model of, and endpoint for, humankind's political and economic development. Like many liberals he sees history as progressive, linear and 'directional', and is convinced that 'there is a fundamental process at work that dictates a common evolutionary pattern for *all* human societies – in short, something like a Universal History of mankind in the direction of liberal democracy'.[2]

Fukuyama's belief that Western forms of government and political economy are the ultimate destination which the entire human race will eventually reach poses a number of challenges for orthodoxy within International Relations. First, his claim that political and economic development always terminates at liberal-capitalist democracy assumes that the non-Western world is striving to imitate the Western route to modernisation: to put in another way, that the Western path to modernity no longer faces a universal challenge of the kind posed by communism, and will eventually command global consent.

Secondly, Fukuyama's argument assumes that the West is the progenitor of moral and political truths which progress will oblige all societies to observe, regardless of national and cultural distinction.

Thirdly, Fukuyama's observation that the spread of capitalism now faces little or no resistance raises vital questions about governance and political community. What are the implications of globalisation for nation-states and their sovereign powers?

Fourthly, Fukuyama believes that progress in human history can be measured by the elimination of global conflict and the adoption of principles of legitimacy which have evolved over time in domestic political orders. This constitutes an 'inside-out' approach to international relations, where the exogenous behaviour of states can be explained by examining their endogenous political and economic arrangements. It also leads to Doyle's claim that 'liberal democracies are uniquely willing to eschew the use of force in their relations with one another', a view which refutes the realist contention that the anarchical nature of the international system means states are trapped in a struggle for power and security.[3]

Liberal Internationalism: Inside Looking Out

Fukuyama revives a long held view amongst liberal internationalists that the spread of legitimate domestic political orders will eventually bring an end to international conflict. This neo-Kantian position assumes that particular states, with liberal-democratic credentials, constitute an ideal which the rest of the world will emulate. Fukuyama is struck by the extent to which liberal democracies have transcended their violent instincts and institutionalised norms which pacify relations between each other. He is particularly impressed with the emergence of shared principles of legitimacy amongst the great powers, a trend which can be expected to continue now that the ideological contest of the Cold War has passed into history. The projection of liberal-democratic principles to the international realm is said to provide the best prospect for a peaceful world order because 'a world made up of liberal democracies ... should have much less incentive for war, since all nations would reciprocally recognise one another's legitimacy'.[4]

This approach is rejected by neo-realists who claim that the moral aspirations of states are thwarted by the absence of an overarching authority which regulates their behaviour towards each other. The anarchical nature of the international system homogenises foreign policy behaviour by socialising states into the system of power politics. The requirements of strategic power and security are paramount in an insecure world, and they soon override the ethical pursuits of states, regardless of their domestic political complexions. Waltz, for example, highlights the similarity of foreign policy behaviour amongst states with diverse political orders, and argues that if any state was to become a model for the rest of the world, one would have to conclude that 'most of the impetus behind foreign policy is internally generated'. The similarity of United States and Soviet foreign policy during the Cold War would suggest that this is unlikely, and that their common location in the international system is a superior explanation.[5]

By stressing the importance of legitimate domestic orders in explaining foreign policy behaviour, Waltz believes that liberals such as Fukuyama and Doyle are guilty of 'reductionism' when they should be highlighting the 'systemic' features of international relations. This conflict between 'inside-out' and 'outside-in' approaches to international relations has become an important line of demarcation in modern international theory. The extent to which the neo-realist critique of liberal internationalism can be sustained in the post-Cold War era will be a major feature of this analysis.[6]

Fukuyama's argument is not simply a celebration of the fact that liberal capitalism has survived the threat posed by Marxism. It also implies that neo-realism has overlooked 'the foremost macropolitical trend in contemporary world politics: the expansion of the liberal zone of peace'.[7] Challenging the view that the nature of anarchy conditions international behaviour is Doyle's argument that there is a growing core of pacific states which have learnt to resolve their differences without resorting to violence. The likely expansion of this pacific realm is said to be the most significant feature of the post-Communist landscape. If this claim can be upheld it will constitute a significant comeback for an international theory widely thought to have been seriously challenged by Carr in his critique of liberal utopianism over 50 years ago. It will also pose a serious challenge to a discipline which until recently has been dominated by assumptions that war is a recurrent and endemic feature of international life.

I War, Democracy and Free Trade

The foundations of contemporary liberal internationalism were laid in the eighteenth and nineteenth centuries by liberals proposing preconditions for a peaceful world order. In broad summary they concluded that the prospects for the elimination of war lay with a preference for democracy over aristocracy, free trade over autarky, and collective security over the balance of power system. In this section we will examine each of these arguments in turn and the extent to which they have informed contemporary liberal thought.

Prospects for peace

For liberals, peace is the normal state of affairs: in Kant's words, peace can be perpetual. The laws of nature dictated harmony and co-operation between peoples. War is therefore both unnatural and irrational, an artificial contrivance and not a product of some peculiarity of human nature. Liberals have a belief in progress and the perfectibility of the human condition. Through their faith in the power of human reason and the capacity of human beings to realise their inner potential, they remain confident that the stain of war can be removed from human experience.[8]

A common thread running through liberal thought, from Rousseau, Kant and Cobden, to Schumpeter and Doyle, is that wars were created by militaristic and undemocratic governments for their own vested interests. Wars were engineered by a 'warrior class' bent on extending their power and wealth through territorial conquest. According to Paine in *The Rights of Man*, the 'war system' was contrived to preserve the power and the employment of princes, statesmen, soldiers, diplomats and armaments manufacturers, and to bind their tyranny ever more firmly upon the necks of the people'.[9] Wars provide governments with excuses to raise taxes, expand their bureaucratic apparatus and thus increase their control over their citizens. The people, on the other hand, were peace-loving by nature, and only plunged into conflict by the whims of their unrepresentative rulers.

War was a cancer on the body politic. But it was an ailment that human beings, themselves, had the capacity to cure. The treatment which liberals began prescribing in the eighteenth century hasn't changed: the 'disease' of war could be successfully treated with the twin medicines of *democracy and free trade*. Democratic processes and institutions would break the power of the ruling elites and curb their propensity for violence. Free trade and commerce would overcome the artificial barriers between individuals and unite them everywhere into one community.

For liberals like Schumpeter, war was the product of the aggressive instincts of unrepresentative elites. The warlike disposition of these rulers drove the reluctant masses into violent conflicts which, while profitable for the arms industries and the military aristocrats, were disastrous for those who did the fighting. For Kant, the establishment of republican forms of government in which rulers were accountable and individual rights were respected would lead to peaceful international relations because the ultimate consent for war would rest with the citizens of the state.[10] For both Kant and Schumpeter, war was the outcome of minority rule, though Kant was no champion of democratic government. Liberal states, founded on individual rights such as equality before the law, free speech and civil liberty, respect for private property and representative government, would not have the same appetite for conflict and war. Peace was fundamentally a question of establishing legitimate domestic orders throughout the world.

'When the citizens who bear the burdens of war elect their governments, wars become impossible'.[11]

The dual themes of domestic legitimacy and the extent to which liberal-democratic states exercise restraint and peaceful intentions in their foreign policy have been taken up more recently by Doyle and Russett. In a restatement of Kant's argument that a 'pacific federation' (*foedus pacificum*) can be built by expanding the number of states with democratic constitutions, Doyle claims that liberal democracies are unique in their ability and willingness to establish peaceful relations between themselves. This pacification of foreign relations among liberal states is said to be a direct product of their shared legitimate political orders based on democratic principles and institutions. The reciprocal recognition of these common principles – a commitment to the rule of law, individual rights and equality before the law, representative government based on popular consent – means that liberal democracies evince little interest in conflict with each other and have no grounds on which to contest each other's legitimacy: they have constructed a 'separate peace'.[12] This does not mean that they are less inclined to make war with non-democratic states, and Doyle is correct to point out that democracies maintain a healthy appetite for conflicts with authoritarian states. But it does suggest that the best prospect for bringing an end to war between states lies with the spread of liberal-democratic governments across the globe. The expansion of the zone of peace from the core to the periphery is the basis of Fukuyama's optimism about the post-Communist era.[13]

This is an argument extended by Rawls, who claims that liberal societies are also 'less likely to engage in war with nonliberal outlaw states, except on grounds of legitimate self-defence (or in the defence of their legitimate allies), or intervention in severe cases to protect human rights'.[14]

A related argument by Mueller claims that we are already witnessing the obsolescence of war between the major powers. Reviving the liberal faith in the capacity of people to improve the moral and material conditions of their lives, Mueller attempts to demonstrate that, just as duelling and slavery were eventually seen as morally unacceptable, war is increasingly viewed in the developed world as repulsive, immoral and uncivilised. That violence is more widely seen as an anachronistic form of social intercourse is not due to any change in human nature or the structure of the international system. According to Mueller, the obsolescence of major war in the late twentieth century was the product of moral learning, a shift in ethical consciousness away from coercive forms of social behaviour. Because war brings more costs than gains and is no longer seen as a romantic or noble pursuit, it has become 'rationally unthinkable'.[15]

The long peace between states of the industrialised world is a cause of profound optimism for liberals such as Mueller and Fukuyama, who are confident that we have already entered a period in which war as an instrument of international diplomacy is becoming obsolete. But if war has been an important factor in nation-building, as Giddens, Mann and Tilly have argued, the fact that states are learning to curb their propensity for violence will also have important consequences for forms of political community which are likely to emerge in the industrial centres of the world. The end of war between the great powers may have the ironic effect of weakening the rigidity of their political boundaries and inspiring a wave of sub-national revolts. If war has been a binding as well as destructive force in international relations, the problem of maintaining cohesive communities will be a major challenge for metropolitan centres.

Far from sharing the optimism of the liberals, neo-realists such as Waltz and Mearsheimer are profoundly disturbed by the collapse of Soviet strategic power. If mutual nuclear deterrence between the United States and the Soviet Union accounted for the high level of international stability in the post-war period, the end of bipolarity casts an ominous shadow over the future world order. Because there is no obvious replacement for the Soviet Union, which can restore the balance of strategic power, the world has entered an uncertain and dangerous phase. As Waltz concedes, 'in international politics, unbalanced power constitutes a danger even when it is American power that is out of balance'.[16]

Waltz and Mearsheimer continue to stress the importance of strategic interaction in shaping the contours of international relations. For them, the distribution and character of military power remain the root causes of war and peace.[17] Instead of highlighting the spread of liberal democracy and a concomitant zone of peace, they regard the rapid demise of bipolarity as the single most dramatic change in contemporary world politics. The pacification of the core, while desirable and perhaps even encouraging, is merely a transient stage which needs to be superseded by a restoration of the strategic balance amongst the great powers. Echoing Carr's critique of liberal utopianism on the eve of the Second World War, Waltz believes that the 'peace and justice' which liberals claim is spreading beyond the central core 'will be defined to the liking of the powerful'.[18]

According to Waltz and Mearsheimer, the recurrent features of international relations, most notably the struggle for power and security, will eventually reassert themselves: 'in international politics, overwhelming power repels and leads others to try to balance against it'.[19] However, the absence of a countervailing power to the United States means there are few clues about the current period. According to Mearsheimer, the long peace of the Cold War was a result of three factors: the bipolar distribution of military power in continental Europe, the rough equality of military power between the United States and the Soviet Union, and the pacifying effect of the presence of nuclear weapons.[20] The collapse of the Soviet Union removed the central pillar upon which the bipolar stability was built. Multipolar systems, on the other hand, are notoriously less stable than bipolar systems because the number of potential bilateral conflicts is greater, deterrence is more difficult to achieve, and the potential for misunderstandings and miscalculations of power and motive is increased.[21] Based on the experience of previous multipolar systems, in particular both pre-world war periods, the post-Cold War era is more a cause for concern than celebration.

Recent conflicts in the Persian Gulf, the Balkans and the former Soviet Union – all involving major industrial powers – are a reminder that the post-Cold War period remains volatile and suggest that war may not yet have lost its efficacy in international diplomacy. None of these constitute conflicts between democratic states but they are no less important to the maintenance of world order. These and other conflicts in so called 'failed states' such as Somalia, and possibly Indonesia and Papua New Guinea, highlight the fact that the fragmentation of nation-states and civil wars arising from secessionist movements have not been given the same attention by liberals as more conventional inter-state wars.

Neo-realists have regarded nuclear weapons, and the rough parity between East and West, as a source of stability and pacification during the Cold War. They provided security to both blocs, generated caution amongst decision makers, imposed a rough equality, and created a clarity of relative power between both camps.[22] The absence of a first strike capability and the destructive potential of a direct conflict forced the United States and the Soviet Union to learn to manage their differences without recourse to violence. In addition, the binding force of having a common enemy imposed a discipline upon and within each bloc. According to Mearsheimer, if this level of stability is to be reached in the multipolar environment, the 'carefully managed proliferation' of nuclear weapons in Europe may be required to preserve the peace, or at least keep a check on the strategic primacy of the United States.[23]

Maintaining strategic stability in Europe in a multipolar environment is just one of many major challenges for liberals. On the question of how liberal states should conduct themselves with non-liberal states, Fukuyama and Doyle are equally and surprisingly silent. Rawls, on the other hand, is concerned with the extent to which liberal and non-liberal peoples can be equal participants in a 'Society of Peoples'. He argues that principles and norms of international law and practice – the 'Law of Peoples' – can be developed and shared by both liberal and non-liberal or decent hierarchical societies, without an expectation that liberal democracy is the terminus for all. The guidelines and principle basis for establishing harmonious relations between liberal and non-liberal peoples under a common Law of Peoples, takes liberal international theory in a more sophisticated direction because it explicitly acknowledges the need for utopian thought to be realistic.[24]

As the number of East Asian and Islamic societies which reject the normative superiority of liberal democracy grows, considerable doubt is cast on the belief that the non-European world is seeking to imitate the Western route to political modernisation. Perhaps the answer here, as Linklater suggests, is not so much the spread of liberal democracy *per se*, 'but the idea of limited power which is present within, but not entirely synonymous with, liberal democracy'.[25] The notion of limited power and respect for the rule of law contained within the idea of 'constitutionalism' may be one means of solving the exclusionary character of the liberal zone of peace. It is a less ambitious project and potentially more sensitive to the cultural and political differences among states in the current international system. It may avoid the danger of the system bifurcating into a privileged inner circle and a disadvantaged and disaffected outer circle.[26] The greatest barrier to the expansion of the zone of peace from the core is the perception within the periphery that this constitutes little more than the domination of one culture by another. These suspicions are well founded given that peripheral states have consistently been the victims of Western intervention.

The spirit of commerce

Eighteenth and nineteenth century liberals felt that the spirits of war and commerce were mutually incompatible. Many wars were fought by states to achieve their mercantilist goals. According to Carr, 'the aim of mercantilism ... was not to promote the welfare of the community and its members, but to augment the power of the state, of which the sovereign was the embodiment ... wealth was the source of power, or more specifically of fitness for war'. Until the Napoleonic wars, 'wealth, conceived in its simplest form as bullion, was brought in by exports; and since, in the static conception of society prevailing at this period, export markets were a fixed quantity not susceptible of increase as a whole, the only way for a nation to expand its markets and therefore its wealth was to capture them from some other nation, if necessary by waging a trade war'.[27]

Free trade, however, was a more peaceful means of achieving national wealth because, according to the theory of comparative advantage, each economy would be materially better off than if it had been pursuing nationalism and self-sufficiency (autarky). Free trade would also breakdown the divisions between states and unite individuals everywhere in one community. Artificial barriers to commerce distort perceptions and relations between individuals, thereby causing international tension. Free trade would expand the range of contacts and levels of understanding between the peoples of the world and encourage international friendship and understanding. According to Kant, unhindered commerce between the peoples of the world would unite them in a common, peaceful enterprise. 'Trade ... would increase the wealth and power of the peace-loving, productive sections of the population at the expense of the war-orientated aristocracy, and ... would bring men of different nations into constant contact with one another; contact which would make clear to all of them their fundamental community of interests'.[28] Similarly Ricardo believed that free trade 'binds together, by one common tie of interest and intercourse, the universal society of nations throughout the civilised world'.[29]

Conflicts were often caused by states erecting barriers which distorted and concealed the natural harmony of interests commonly shared by individuals across the world. The solution to the problem, argued Adam Smith and Tom Paine, was the free movement of commodities, capital and labour. 'If commerce were permitted to act to the universal extent it is capable, it would extirpate the system of war and produce a revolution in the uncivilised state of governments'.[30] Writing in 1848, John Stuart Mill also claimed free trade was the means to bring about the end of war: 'it is commerce which is rapidly rendering war obsolete, by strengthening and multiplying the personal interests which act in natural opposition to it'.[31] The spread of markets would place societies on an entirely new foundation. Instead of conflicts over limited resources such as land, the industrial revolution raised the prospect of unlimited and unprecedented prosperity for all: material production, so long as it was freely exchanged, would bring human progress. Trade would create relations of mutual dependence which would foster understanding between peoples and reduce conflict. Economic self-interest would then be a powerful disincentive for war.

Free trade, according to Cobden, was 'eternal in its truth and universal in its application'. It was the key to global harmony and peace: 'the triumph of free trade was a triumph of pacific principles between all nations of the earth'.[32] As it was understood by Bright, free trade was the means for 'undermining the nationalist ambitions of nation-states by encouraging cosmopolitanism (meaning free from national limitations), and making nations so interdependent that wars and military budgets became unthinkable. Imperialism and autarky were regarded by liberals as the work of illiberal and reactionary forces and as a direct cause of wars'.[33] Free trade meant

> breaking down the barriers that separate nations; those barriers behind which nestle feelings of pride, revenge, hatred and jealousy which every now and then break their bonds and deluge whole countries with blood; those feelings which nourish the poison of war and conquest, which assert that without conquest we can have no trade, which foster that lust for conquest and dominion which sends forth your warrior chiefs to sanction devastation through other lands.[34]

It was felt that unfettered free commercial exchange would encourage links across frontiers and shift loyalties away from the nation-state. Leaders would eventually come to recognise that the benefits of free trade outweighed the costs of territorial conquest and colonial expansion. The attraction of going to war to promote mercantilist interests would be weakened as societies learn that war can only disrupt trade and therefore the prospects for economic prosperity. Interdependence would replace national competition and defuse unilateral acts of aggression and reciprocal retaliation.

Interdependence and liberal institutionalism

Free trade and the removal of barriers to commerce is at the heart of modern interdependency theory. The rise of regional economic integration in Europe, for example, was inspired by the belief that the likelihood of conflict between states would be reduced by creating a common interest in trade and economic collaboration amongst members of the same geographical region. This would encourage states which traditionally resolved their differences militarily, such as France and Germany, to co-operate within a commonly agreed economic and political framework for their mutual benefit. States would then have a joint stake in each other's peace and prosperity. The European Union is the best example of economic integration engendering closer economic and political co-operation in a region historically bedevilled by national conflicts.

As Mitrany argued, initially co-operation between states would be achieved in technical areas where it was mutually convenient, but once successful it could 'spill over' into other functional areas where states found that mutual advantages could be gained.[35] In a development of this argument, Keohane and Nye have explained how, via membership of international institutions, states can significantly broaden their conceptions of self-interest in order to widen the scope for co-operation. Compliance with the rules of these organisations not only discourages the narrow pursuit of national interests, it also weakens the meaning and appeal of state sovereignty.[36] This suggests that the international system is more normatively regulated than realists would have us believe, a position further developed by the English School of rationalists such as Wight and Bull.

A development of this argument can be found in liberal institutionalism which shares with neo-realism an acceptance of the importance of the state and the anarchical condition of the international system, though liberal institutionalists argue that the prospects for co-operation, even in an anarchical world, are greater than neo-realists would have us believe.[37] Accepting the broad structures of neo-realism, but employing rational choice and game theory to anticipate the behaviour of states, liberal institutionalists seek to demonstrate that co-operation between states can be enhanced even without the presence of a hegemonic player which can enforce compliance with agreements. For them, anarchy is mitigated by regimes and institutional co-operation which brings higher levels of regularity and predictability to international relations. Regimes constrain state behaviour by formalising the expectations of each party to an agreement where there is a shared interest. Institutions then assume the role of encouraging co-operative habits, monitoring compliance and sanctioning defectors.

Neo-realists and neo-liberals disagree about how states conceive of their own interests. Whereas neo-realists, such as Waltz, argue that states are concerned with 'relative gains' – meaning gains are assessed in comparative terms (who will gain more?), neoliberals such as Keohane claim that states are concerned with maximising their 'absolute gains' – an assessment of their own welfare rather than their rivals (what will gain me the most?). Accordingly, neorealists argue that states will baulk at co-operation if they expect to gain less than their rivals. Liberal-institutionalists, on the other hand, believe international relations does not need to be a zero-sum game, as many states feel secure enough to maximise their own gains regardless of what accrues to others. Mutual benefits arising out of co-operation are possible because states are not always preoccupied with relative gains.

Liberal-institutionalists acknowledge that co-operation between states is likely to be fragile, particularly where enforcement procedures are weak. However, in an environment of growing regional and global integration, states can often discover – with or without the encouragement of a hegemon – a coincidence of strategic and economic interests which can be turned into a formalised agreement determining the rules of conduct.

According to Rosecrance, the growth of economic interdependency has been matched by a corresponding decline in the value and importance of territorial conquest for states. In the contemporary world the benefits of trade and co-operation among states greatly exceed that of military competition and territorial control. Nation-states have traditionally regarded the acquisition of territory as the principal means of increasing national wealth. In recent years, however, it has become apparent that additional territory does not necessarily help states to compete in an international system where the 'trading state' rather than the 'military state' is becoming dominant. In the 1970s state elites began to realise that wealth is determined by their share of the world market in value-added goods and services. This understanding has had two significant effects. First, the age of the independent, self-sufficient state is over. Complex layers of economic interdependency ensure that states cannot act aggressively without risking economic penalties imposed by other members of the international community. It also makes little sense for a state to threaten its commercial partners, whose markets and capital investment are essential for its own economic growth. Secondly, territorial conquest in the nuclear age is both dangerous and costly for rogue states. The alternative, economic development through trade and foreign investment, is a much more attractive and potentially beneficial strategy. In an environment of free and open trade, the conquest of territory would not only be burdensome, it would also undermine the system upon which economic success in the global economy rests.[38]

Neo-realists have two responses to the liberal claim that economic interdependency is pacifying international relations. First, they argue that in any struggle between competing disciplines, the anarchic environment and the insecurity it engenders will always take priority over the quest for economic prosperity. Economic interdependency will never take precedence over strategic security because states must be primarily concerned with their survival. Their capacity to explore avenues of economic co-operation will therefore be limited by how secure they feel, and the extent to which they are required to engage in military competition with others. Secondly, the idea of economic interdependence implies a misleading degree of equality and shared vulnerability to economic forces in the global economy. Interdependence does not eliminate hegemony and dependency in interstate relations because power is very unevenly distributed throughout the world's trade and financial markets. Dominant players such as the United States have usually framed the rules under which interdependency has flourished. Conflict and co-operation is therefore unlikely to disappear, though it may be channelled into more peaceful forms.

Human rights

The advocacy of democracy and free trade foreshadows another idea which liberal internationalism introduced to international theory. Liberals have always believed that the legitimacy of domestic political orders was largely contingent upon upholding the rule of law and the state's respect for the human rights of its citizens. If it is wrong for an individual to engage in socially unacceptable or criminal behaviour, it is also wrong for states.

References to essential human needs are implicit in some of the earliest written legal codes from ancient Babylon, as well as early Hindu, Buddhist and Confucian texts, though the first explicit mention of universal principles governing common standards of human behaviour can be found in the West.

The idea of universal human rights has its origins in the Natural Law tradition, debates in the West during the Enlightenment over the 'rights of man' and in the experience of individuals struggling against the arbitrary rule of the state. The Magna Carta in 1215, the development of English Common Law and the Bill of Rights in 1689 were significant, if evolutionary steps along the path to enshrining basic human rights in law, as were intellectual contributions from Grotius (the law of nations), Rousseau (the social contract) and Locke (popular consent, limits of sovereignty). An early legal articulation of human rights can be found in the American Declaration of Independence in 1776 ('we take these truths to be self-evident, that all men are created equal, and that they are endowed by their Creator with certain unalienable Rights, that amongst these are Life, Liberty and the pursuit of Happiness') and in France's Declaration of the Rights of Man and the Citizen in 1789 ('all men are born free and equal in their rights').

Human beings are said to be endowed – purely by reason of their humanity – with certain fundamental rights, benefits and protections. These rights are regarded as inherent in the sense they are the birthright of all, inalienable because they cannot be given up or taken away, and universal since they apply to all regardless of nationality, status, gender or race.

The extension of these rights to all peoples has a particularly important place in liberal thinking about foreign policy and international relations for two reasons. First, these rights give a legal foundation to emancipation, justice and human freedom. Their denial by state authorities is an affront to the dignity of all and a stain on the human condition. Secondly, states which treat their own citizens ethically and allow them meaningful participation in the political process are thought to be less likely to behave aggressively internationally. The task for liberals has been to develop and promote moral standards which would command universal consent, knowing that in doing so states may be required to jeopardise the pursuit of their own national interests.

This has proven to be a difficult task, despite evident progress on labour rights, the abolition of slavery, the political emancipation of women in the West, the treatment of indigenous peoples and the end of white supremacism in South Africa.

The creation of important legal codes, instruments and institutions in the post-Second World War period is a measure of achievement in the area. The most important instruments are the Universal Declaration of Human Rights (1948), the International Covenant on Civil and Political Rights (1966) and the International Covenant on Economic, Social and Cultural Rights (1966), while the International Labour Organisation and the International Court of Justice play a significant institutional and symbolic role in the protection of human rights.

In his seminal account, Vincent identified the right of the individual to be free from starvation as the only human right which is likely to receive the support of a global consensus. The world community, regardless of religious or ideological differences, agrees that a right to subsistence was essential to the dignity of humankind.[39] Beyond this right, nation-states struggle to find agreement, not least because the developing world is suspicious that human rights advocacy from metropolitan centres is little more than a pretext for unwarranted interference in their domestic affairs. Most states are reluctant to give outsiders the power to compel them to improve their ethical performance, although there is a growing belief that interference in domestic affairs should no longer be used by governments as a credible excuse for avoiding legitimate international scrutiny.

Marxists have dismissed human rights as mere bourgeois freedoms which fail to address the class-based nature of exploitation contained within capitalist relations of production. Realists would add that 'conditions of profound insecurity for states do not permit ethical and humane considerations to override their primary national considerations'.[40] After all it is interests which determine political action and in the global arena, politics is the amoral struggle for power to advance these interests.

Liberals battle to avoid the charge that their conceptions of democracy and human rights are culturally specific, ethnocentric and therefore irrelevant to societies which are not Western in cultural orientation. To many societies, the claim to universality may merely conceal the means by which one dominant society imposes its culture upon another, while infringing on its sovereign independence. The promotion of human rights from the core to the periphery assumes a degree of moral superiority – that the West not only possesses moral truths which others are bound to observe, but that it can sit in judgement on other societies.

The issue is further complicated by the argument that economic, social and cultural rights should precede civil and political rights – one made earlier by Communist states and more recently by a number of East Asian governments, and which is a direct challenge to the idea that human rights are indivisible and universal – a revolt against the West. It implies that the alleviation of poverty and economic development in these societies depends on the initial denial of political freedoms and human rights to the citizen. However, the claim that rights can be prioritised in this way or that procedural and substantive freedoms are incompatible is problematic and widely seen, with some justification, as a rationalisation by governments for authoritarian rule.

An increasing number of conservative political leaders in the region have also argued that there is a superior Asian model of political and social organisation comprising the principles of harmony, hierarchy and consensus (Confucianism) in contrast to what they regard as the confrontation, individualism and moral decay which characterises Western liberalism. Regardless of how self-serving this argument is – and it is rarely offered by democratically elected rulers – it poses a fundamental challenge to Fukuyama's suggestion that in the post-Cold War period liberal democracy faces no serious universal challenge. It is clear that these states are not necessarily striving to imitate the Western route to political modernisation.

It is also ironic that the basic procedural freedoms and rights which citizens in liberal democracies take for granted, including freedom of association, the right to organise and collectively bargain, the right to work in a safe environment, the prevention of forced labour, and so on, are being denied in a number of developing East Asian societies by policies of market liberalisation which Western liberals are encouraging. In recent years, industrial accidents due to poor or non existent safety standards have been rising in China and Thailand. Trade unionists have been attacked, arrested and murdered in Indonesia. Workers' rights in Malaysia and Singapore are routinely denied in the interests of 'economic development'. Child labour is exploited in South Korea and China. Attempts by US governments to draw attention to these abuses have been condemned by other liberal democracies more enamoured with the ideology of free trade and concerned by any threats to the region's comparative advantage in cheap labour.

Even if universal rules and instruments could be agreed upon, how could compliance with these standards be enforced? Liberals are divided over this issue, between non-interventionists who defend state sovereignty, and those who feel that the promotion of ethical principles can justify intervention in the internal affairs of other states.[41] Recent examples of so called 'humanitarian intervention' in Somalia, Cambodia, Rwanda, Serbia and East Timor pose a growing challenge to the protection from outside interference traditionally afforded by sovereignty claims. As does the prosecution of those suspected of committing war crimes and crimes against humanity by international tribunals such as the International Court of Justice.[42]

Modern forms of humanitarian intervention follow a pattern established in the middle of the eighteenth century when the British and Dutch successfully interceded on behalf of Prague's Jewish community, which was threatened with deportation by authorities in Bohemia. The protection of Christian minorities at risk in Europe and in the Orient in the eighteenth and nineteenth centuries by the Treaty of Kucuk-Kainardji (1774) and the Treaty of Berlin (1878) are also part of the same legal precedent, as is the advocacy of British Prime Minister Gladstone in the second half on the nineteenth century and US President Wilson early in the twentieth century. Vietnam's invasion of Cambodia in 1978, when refracted through the ideological prism of the Cold War, highlighted both the underdeveloped and politically contingent nature of humanitarian intervention in the modern period. Liberals who support both the sovereign rights of independent states and the right of external intervention in cases where there is an acute humanitarian crisis, find it difficult to reconcile both international norms.[43]

Secret diplomacy, the balance of power and collective security

As much as any other factor, liberals argue for democracy because they are profoundly suspicious of concentrated forms of power, especially state power. When they looked at the international system, liberals of the nineteenth and early twentieth centuries saw power being exercised in the interests of governing elites and against the wishes of the masses. 'Secret diplomacy' was the name they gave to the way unrepresentative elites practiced international relations in the pre-democratic era. Liberals disputed the view that foreign policy was a specialised art which was best made by professional diplomats behind closed doors and away from the influences of national politics. If the democratisation of domestic politics could produce important economic and social reforms there would be a commensurate improvement in the conduct of foreign policy as a result of popular participation.[44] And if popular consent was to be fully realised in the liberal state, there would need to be an adequate machinery for ensuring the democratic control of foreign policy.

From the time of Bright and Cobden, liberals have regarded the balance of power as the most pernicious aspect of 'secret diplomacy'. It was, in Bright's words, 'a foul thing' which gave no credence to the common interests of humankind and the just claims of small nations seeking self-determination. The balance of power was the product of elite collusion which resulted in international relations being 'arranged' to suit the interests of those who ruled Great Powers. For Cobden the 'balance of power' was both the veil behind which the armaments industries enriched themselves through state expenditure on weapons of war and a smokescreen which concealed British imperial interests.[45]

Consistent with their preference for the minimalist state was liberal belief that governments get in the way of peaceful relations between individuals, hence Cobden's call for 'as little intercourse as possible between Governments, as much connection as possible between nations of the world'. To realise their world view, liberals wanted to replace autocratic regimes with ones based on democratic accountability and values. However, a major obstacle to the transformation of international relations was the balance of power system, which helped to sustain tyrannical regimes by denying nationalities the opportunity to overthrow the structures of state power. Empires and authoritarian governments were propped up by those with vested interests in maintaining the integrity of European states-system, regardless of the political aspirations of the peoples of Europe.[46]

The balance of power is technically defined as the absence of a preponderant military power in the international system. As it operated in Europe, the balance of power system described the process whereby smaller powers would form temporary alliances of convenience which would act as a countervailing power to the dominant military state in the region. Membership of these alliances would change over time as new hegemons emerged, and from time to time war would be necessary to cut down the dominant state and distribute strategic power in the region more evenly. To defenders of the balance power, conflict was a regrettable but necessary and sometimes desirable feature of the international system.

Liberal critics of the balance of power claim the concept is vague and unintelligible and the method by which great powers pursue their commercial and strategic interests at the expense of small powers, often in violation of international law. Realist defenders of the concept, on the other hand, argue that liberals have missed the point of the system. The principle function of the balance of power is not to preserve peace, but to preserve the system of states. On certain occasions war may in fact be necessary to recalibrate the differentials of power in the international system. Smaller powers may be absorbed or partitioned in the process, and international law may be sporadically breached, but this is the necessary cost of keeping order in the system.[47]

Until 1914 most scholars and statesmen assumed that the 'balance of power' was a self-regulating system, the political equivalent of the law of economics. The First World War discredited the laws of both economics and politics. The self-operating laws had failed to prevent one of the most destructive conflicts in human history. The balance of power had failed to prevent the war because, instead of allowing for the flexibility of realigning each other against the aggressor, the great powers had locked themselves into two antagonistic blocs. The liberal alternative idea of collective security was designed to prevent this situation recurring by ensuring that in the future, the aggressor would be confronted by all other states. In other words, a balance of power would be institutionalised. According to its proponents, collective security would have two beneficial results. First, it would make the balance of power more effective because there would be less chance of a preponderant power emerging. Secondly, it would ensure that violence, if necessary, would always be used in a legitimate manner. Since power is vested in the international community, it would not be abused in the way it was by individual nation-states.[48] Henceforth, all members of the international community would take collective responsibility for keeping the peace. This responsibility would be formally enshrined in the institutional form of the League of Nations.

Consistent with the view that peace depended on the spread of democracy, collective security was an attempt to reproduce the concepts and processes of domestic law at the international level. Liberals believed that the destructive forces of international anarchy could only be brought to an end if the international system was regulated in the same way as domestic society. Then there would no longer be any need for covert alliances between governments because secret diplomacy would be replaced by open discussion within the Assembly of the League. The commitment of member states to the principle of collective security would override any other alliance or strategic obligations. States would formally renounce the use of force as a means of settling international disputes.

Regrettably, it was all a forlorn hope. The idea of collective security failed in the 1930s because it depended on the general acceptance by states of a particular configuration of international power: a distribution of influence, territory and military potential that clearly favoured the victors of the First World War at the expense of the defeated powers. Why should Germany, for example, accept forever the injustice of a discriminatory peace settlement imposed on them in 1918? To those states which lost the First World War, and who wished to revise the frontiers and conditions imposed by the

Versailles settlement, the League of Nations seemed dedicated to the preservation of the status quo rather than the preservation of peace. As Carr
was soon to point out, the insecurity states feel in the international system
does not afford them the luxury of forswearing the use of violence to
uphold a principle. States are extremely reluctant to reduce their freedom
of manoeuvre in an anarchical international environment.

And what could be done about states which didn't accept these new
diplomatic norms, such as the rule of law, controls on the use of force in
international disputes, and the authority of the collective security organisation (that is, states which didn't accept the idea of constitutionalism[49])?
When Japan moved into Manchuria in 1931 and Italy invaded Abyssinia in
1935-6, the League of Nations lacked both the collective will and the
enforcement power to reverse these acts of aggression. Collective security
was seen as inherently contradictory, if not hypocritical. If its principal
motivation was outlawing the recourse to war, should the enforcement of
its provisions in the final instance be dependent on the threat of the use
of force?

Ironically, although the League of Nations was properly seen as one of
the principal instruments of collective security, its creation had the effect of
consolidating conceptions of national sovereignty as the 'natural' political
condition of humankind. Far from representing a stage beyond the nation-
state as a representation of political community, the League operated on the
principle that 'statehood' was universally applicable: it should be extended
to all ethnic and national groups. As a critique of the balance of power as
the principal guarantor of sovereignty, the League of Nations was an
alternative means of legitimating national sovereignty, not an alternative
to national sovereignty. The restructured territorial divisions which arose as
a result of the new entitlement to statehood merely ensured that, after 1918,
hostilities between ethnic or national minorities would become conflicts
between states.[50]

Liberals internationalists had been wrong to assume that there was a self-
evident value system, committed to international harmony and co-operation, which had universal validity. As Carr commented, 'these supposedly
absolute and universal principles were not principles at all, but the unconscious reflections of national policy based on a particular interpretation of
national interest at a particular time'.[51] Collective security, as it was practised in the early phase of the inter-war years, was little more than the
preservation of the status quo congenial to the interests of the victorious
powers.

At the very least, a collective security system requires 'a degree of mutual
confidence, a homogeneity of values and a coincidence of perceived interests'.[52] This level of cultural homogeneity is never easy to find in the
international system. Later in the century collective defence would prove
to be more successful when attempted at the regional level, especially in
limited strategic alliances against a common enemy.

II   The Economic Dimension

Fukuyama's post-Cold War optimism is on firmer ground if we consider the extent to which economic liberalism has become the dominant ideology of the contemporary period. The move towards a global political economy organised along neo-liberal lines is a trend as significant as the likely expansion of the zone of peace. As the new century dawns, the world economy more closely resembles the prescriptions of Smith and Ricardo than at any previous time. And as Macpherson forecast, this development is also a measure of 'how deeply the market assumptions about the nature of man and society have penetrated liberal-democratic theory'.[53]

In this section we will assess the significance of this trend for both the internal nature of modern capitalist societies and the relationships between nation-states in the modern period. We will begin by examining a previous liberal attempt to construct a 'market society' in nineteenth century Britain, followed by an exploration of the ideology of free trade.

Society and the 'free market' (Polanyi's critique)

In his seminal account of the abandonment of *laissez-faire* capitalism, Karl Polanyi argues that contrary to economic orthodoxy, the arrival of *laissez-faire* in the early nineteenth century was neither inevitable nor the result of an evolutionary process. According to Polanyi, it was the product of deliberate state policy and 'nothing less than a self-regulating market on a world scale' could ensure its proper functioning. The crucial step towards the *laissez-faire* economy was the commodification of land and labour in the eighteenth century, while the expansion of the market system in the nineteenth century was dependent on the spread of international free trade, the creation of a competitive (national) labour market, and the linking of the currency to the gold standard.[54]

Polanyi seeks to explode a number myths which underwrite economic liberalism and the claims it makes for market capitalism as the superior form of economic organisation. The first of these is the suggestion that the pursuit of material self-gain is the natural condition of humankind. This has been an article of faith for economic liberals who, since the time of Adam Smith, have argued that society is comprised of individuals with an innate propensity to 'truck, barter and trade'. Polanyi argues that the pursuit of material self-gain has become an institutionally enforced incentive. 'Only in the nineteenth-century self-regulating market did economic self-interest become the dominant principle of social life, and both liberalism and Marxism made the ahistorical error of assuming that what was dominant in that society had been dominant throughout human history'.[55] According to Polanyi, 'the pursuit of material gain compelled by *laissez-faire* market rules is still not seen as behaviour forced on people as the only way to earn a living in a market system, but as an expression of their inner being; individualism is regarded as the norm, and society remains invisible as a cluster of individual persons who happen to live together without responsibility for anyone other than kin'.[56]

Secondly, according to Polanyi *laissez-faire* capitalism was a 'unique and transitory event', given birth in England between 1750 and 1850, but dying in Europe and America during the 1930s and 1940s.[57] Polanyi claims that the great achievement of economic liberals has been to present a transitory, historical state of economic and social relations as if they were permanent, neutral and eternal. 'The market mechanism ... created the delusion of economic determinism as a general law for all human society', he says.[58]

Thirdly, according to Polanyi the discipline of economics was invented on the assumption of an artificial and misleading separation of the polity and the economy. As Block points out, 'the neo-classical insistence that the economy is analytically distinct from the rest of society makes it logical to see government regulation of business or government provision of welfare as an external interference with a market economy. While economists may disagree as to whether particular types of interference are benign or malignant, they share the view that they are *external*'.[59] This is both wrong and a distortion of reality.

Paradoxically, the expansion of the market system after the Industrial Revolution could only be maintained by state intervention. According to Polanyi, 'the road to the free market was opened and kept open by an enormous increase in continuous, centrally organised and controlled intervention'. Despite the claims of liberals that *laissez-faire* was a natural, organic development, 'there was nothing natural about *laissez-faire*; free markets could never have come into being merely by allowing things to take their course'.[60] The liberal doctrine of non-intervention disguised the extent to which governments were expected to maintain conditions for markets to function.

Markets are often the products of states, not their alternatives or rivals. 'Economic history reveals that the emergence of national markets was in no way the result of the gradual and spontaneous emancipation of the economic sphere from governmental control. On the contrary, the market has been the outcome of a conscious and often violent intervention on the part of government which imposed the market organisation on a society for non-economic needs'.[61] Gramsci endorses this view, claiming that 'it must be made clear that *laissez-faire* too is a form of State 'regulation', introduced and maintained by legislative and coercive means. It is a deliberate policy, conscious of its own ends, and not the spontaneous, automatic expression of economic facts'.[62] Another observer agrees, adding that 'in the last analysis, markets come out of the barrel of a gun, and to establish an integrated world economy on capitalist lines requires the international mobilisation of political power'.[63]

Importantly, as Chomsky has noted, economic historians such as Alexander Gerschenkron have long been arguing that a sharp departure from neo-liberal doctrines was a pre-requisite for economic development in our own century. In fact in the post-war period, the experience of Japan and the other dynamic economies of East Asia has demonstrated that 'late development' would appear to be critically dependent on state intervention in the economy.[64] There are few, if any examples of *laissez-faire* transitions to economic development. This view of economic development runs directly counter to neo-liberal orthodoxy.

According to Polanyi, the abandonment of market principles and the protective intervention of the state in late nineteenth-century Britain arose out the need to safeguard the public from the more odious conditions of modern industrial life: 'the market economy was a threat to the human and natural components of the social fabric', and 'to allow the market mechanism to be the sole director of the fate of human beings and their natural environment, indeed, even of the amount and use of purchasing power, would result in the demolition of society'.[65]

Far from being 'strangled by shortsighted trade unionists, Marxist intellectuals, greedy manufacturers and reactionary landlords', the abandonment of *laissez-faire* principles was demanded by a public which required protection from the perils inherent within the market system.[66] Social legislation covering working hours, public health, factory conditions and trades unions were acts of community self-defence. They were a response of both the organised working class and the middle class protecting their own respective interests. 'Paradoxically enough, not human beings and natural resources only but also the organisation of capitalistic production itself had to be sheltered from the devastating effects of a self-regulating market'.[67]

Adam Smith had understood this. 'The invisible hand, he wrote, will destroy the possibility of a decent human existence 'unless government takes pains to prevent' this outcome, as must be assured in 'every improved and civilised society'.[68] *Laissez-faire* capitalism in the nineteenth century collapsed because of the free operation of the self-regulating market, which in turn prompted calls for state protection – an authentic expression of community fear that without state intervention, society would be annihilated by the market.[69]

Whilst it is possible for liberals to support the market on grounds of economic efficiency, as Macpherson suggests, it is more difficult to defend market society on moral grounds. The devastating effects of unrestricted economic competition were only overcome in the industrialised North by protecting society from market forces. In the post-Cold War period, however, 'protection' is now widely demonised: in the discourse of the ruling elites in many industrialised societies it is a pejorative term, associated with intrusive and inefficient government. Attempts to create a 'market society' on a global scale may not be as desirable as some liberals would have us believe. Fukuyama's triumphalism may be somewhat premature, for as Derrida remarks 'never in history has the horizon of the whole thing whose survival is being celebrated (namely, all the old models of the capitalist and liberal worlds) been seen as dark, threatening and threatened'.[70]

From Polanyi's critique of both the theory and practice of economic liberalism, we now turn to the second category of concerns about liberal internationalism: the politics of 'free trade'.

Free trade imperialism

Two of the difficulties we face with the term 'free trade' is its benign symbolism and the gap which often exists between the rhetoric of it progenitors and the reality of their behaviour. As we will see later, in contemporary world politics free trade agreements, for example, are rarely 'free' nor are they specifically about 'trade'. Moreover, the most prominent advocates of free trade often behave as if the idea was non-reciprocal: it's a policy honoured more in the breach than in the observance.

To those societies which have had the 'beneficence' of free trade thrust upon them by metropolitan powers, the policy can appear anything but benign. After all, free trade and market forces tend to overwhelm and even dissolve traditional social relations and institutions: they are a powerful source of social and political change. The introduction of free trade and market relations produces a competition for efficiency which drives out the inefficient and forces all members of society to adapt to new ways. Free trade also affects the distribution of wealth and power within and between societies, establishing new hierarchies, dependencies and power relationships. Within states, community life is transformed into market life, in accordance with the requirements of efficient production, export earnings and the international division of labour. Outside, in the international system, not all states are able to take advantage of the opportunities presented by free trade or capable of influencing market forces to their own advantage. Only wealthy societies seem capable of harnessing the power of the market, and sometimes they struggle to do so.

Recipients may view free trade as a rationale for the exploitation of subordinate sectors by rich and powerful states determined to secure domestic economic advantages for themselves. 'Free trade undermines national autonomy and state control by exposing the economy to the vicissitudes and instabilities of the world market and exploitation by other, more powerful economies'.[71] This argument was first articulated during the middle of the nineteenth century, the so called 'golden age' of liberalism when British colonialism and industrial expansion was at its peak.[72]

The case of those who felt the malign effects of 'free trade' has been argued by political economists such as Friedrich List who regarded free trade in the mid-nineteenth century as merely the 'veil behind which the British state ruthlessly pursued its own national interests and exploited its particular advantages – the great productivity of its industries and their consequent dominance of world trade'.[73] It was not until 1846 that British manufacturers were sufficiently powerful to allow the Corn Laws to be repealed, confident in the knowledge that free trade policies would now serve their particular interests. According to List, the British used the power of the state to protect their infant industries against foreign competition while weakening their opponents by military force, and only became champions of free trade after having achieved technological and industrial supremacy over their rivals. They had pursued protectionist policies until British industry was strong enough to out compete all rivals. Having reached this point, they then sought to advance their own 'national' economic interests by gaining unimpeded access to foreign markets through free trade.[74] 'In contemporary terms, once they had established the "level playing field" to their incontestable advantage, nothing seemed more high-minded than an "open world" with no irrational and arbitrary interference with the honest entrepreneur, seeking the welfare of all'.[75] Free trade, as List argued, was the correct policy for an industrially-dominant nation like Great Britain in the nineteenth century, but only policies of protection could enable weaker power to challenge the hegemon's supremacy.

From the very beginning free trade was a middle class movement. Though it was only to last until 1931, when free trade was introduced in Britain in 1846 it was rightly seen by Cobden as a victory for the interests of manufacturers over aristocratic and landed interests. Having discovered that free trade policies promoted their own prosperity, British manufacturers were convinced that free trade also promoted British prosperity as a whole: their interests were said to be indivisible and 'in harmony' with the interests of the whole society. According to Marx, 'the assertion that free competition is the final form of development of productive forces, and thus of human freedom, means only that the domination of the middle class is the end of world history'.[76] Thus when workers struck for higher pay and better working conditions they damaged the manufacturers and merchants, and therefore by definition, they hurt Britain. Logically, industrial action became unpatriotic, if not treacherous behaviour.

The class-based nature of free trade advocacy continues to be reflected in the second half of the twentieth century.[77] Only a few economic historians would contest the view that the rise of Britain to industrial and commercial superiority at this time had little to do with methods guided by free trade principles: hence the suffix 'imperialism' was attached by critics of 'free trade' to the original description of international market relations. As one American commentator declared in 1866, 'free trade was a system devised by England to enable her to plunder the world'.[78]

Little needs to be added to the truism that all the modern advanced societies in this century also industrialised behind protective walls (the US in 1816 and most advanced states by the 1880s): 'it seems altogether rash to suppose that economic nationalism is necessarily detrimental to states which practice it'.[79] On this subject, economic history remains almost uniform. However, what is not generally acknowledged in the scholarly literature is the dual standards of economic development which hegemonic states apply on the one hand to themselves, and on the other to economically subordinate societies. Nowhere is this more graphically illustrated than in the post-war period where the means by which the burgeoning US had climbed to economic maturity were to be denied to later entrants in the race. As Chomsky argues, 'it should be stressed that the economic doctrines preached by the powerful are intended for others, so they can be more efficiently robbed and exploited. No wealthy developed society accepts these conditions for itself, unless they happen to confer temporary advantage; and their history reveals that sharp departure from these doctrines was a pre-requisite for development'.[80]

The creation of a liberal free-trading regime by the United States in the post-war period was a conscious act of state policy. The United States emerged from the Second World War with 'preponderant power' and in an unprecedented position to re-construct the world economy 'so American business could trade, operate and profit without restrictions everywhere'.[81] This meant creating an open world economy conducive to the free movement of goods, capital and technology. US planners wanted to break down Britain's sterling bloc, create convertible currencies, and establish conditions for free trade. Crucially, raw materials had to be made available to all nations, though particularly to the advanced industrialised states, without discrimination. It was clear from official statements that the US was ready to assume Britain's former role as the world's financial hegemon, and realised this could only be achieved by exercising considerable state power.[82]

The regions of the world would have to be 'opened' – to investment, the repatriation of profits, access to resources, and so on – and dominated by the United States.[83] It flows from this analysis that the Soviet Union was considered by US planners to be the major threat to the liberal international order because of its very existence as a great power controlling an imperial system that could not be incorporated within the US sphere.[84] A country or bloc which succeeded in exempting itself from the US dominated system might expect hostility from the US because this would constitute a reduction in the potential resource base and market opportunities available to the hegemonic economy. 'We believe passionately', Acheson stated, 'that the dissemination of free enterprise abroad was essential to its preservation at home'.[85] If necessary the doors barring access to US capital may need to be opened by force.

The historical record suggests two fundamental exceptions to the free trade model of economic development. The doors which barred free and non-discriminatory access to raw materials, and which blocked the path to currency convertibility, could only be pushed open by the state, in the post-war period the United States. Left alone they would have remained shut. As Calleo and Rowland have argued, 'it is, in fact, difficult to sustain any free trade system without a concomitant political hegemony'.[86] Beyond that, the markets so necessary to absorb America's vast industrial production at the end of the war had to be created by the state. Foreign trade had to be subsidised. The reconstruction of the economies of Western Europe was therefore only partially altruistic. At one level it was designed to deal decisively with the Franco-German problem. But it was also the only way US capitalism could expand at the necessary rate.

Secondly, the distinction between the state and the private economy is more blurred than the liberals would argue. Not only does the state periodically intervene on behalf of private companies, transnational corporations frequently return the compliment. As Leffler argues, 'in a world free of barriers to the movement of goods and capital ... the private sector could serve as an instrument, albeit not a docile one, of state power'. Thus US based multinational oil companies could help ensure American control over the world's most important raw material.[87]

The critique of 'free trade imperialism' exposes both the double standards of states which espouse free trade and the extent to which the economic world order advocated by liberals paradoxically requires state intervention for its realisation. Free trade has never been embraced as enthusiastically in developing societies as it has by the elites in wealthy industrial states. They tend to see free trade as a weapon used by dominant players to open up their societies to resource exploitation, foreign investment, access to raw materials and the repatriation of profits. Invariably this means that free trade can lead to a diminution in their economic sovereignty, at the same time blocking paths to alternative forms of economic development.

III   Liberalism and Globalisation

To a significant extent, the globalisation of the world economy coincided with a renaissance of neo-liberal thinking in the western world. The political triumph of the 'New Right' in Britain and the United States in particular during the late 1970s and 1980s, was achieved at the expense of Keynesianism, the first coherent philosophy of state intervention in economic life. According to the Keynesian formula, the state intervened in the economy to smooth out the business cycle, provide a degree of social equity and security, and maintain full employment. Neo-liberals, who had always favoured the free play of 'market forces' and a minimal role for the state in economic life, wanted to 'roll back' the welfare state, in the process challenging the social-democratic consensus established in most Western states during the post-war period.

Just as the ideological predilection of Western governments became more concerned with efficiency and productivity and less concerned with welfare and social justice, the power of the state to regulate the market was eroded by the forces of globalisation, in particular the de-regulation of finance and currency markets. The means by which domestic societies could be managed to reduce inequalities produced by inherited social structures and accentuated by the natural workings of the market, declined significantly. In addition, the disappearance of many traditional industries in Western economies, the effects of technological change, increased competition for investment and production, and the mobility of capital, undermined the bargaining power of labour. The sovereignty of capital began to reign over both the interventionary behaviour of the state and the collective power of organised working people.

There is nevertheless a considerable debate over globalisation, between liberals who believe it constitutes a fundamentally new phase of capitalism and statists who are sceptical of such claims.[88] Liberals point to the increasing irrelevance of national borders to the conduct and organisation of economic activity. They focus on the growth of free trade, the capacity of transnational corporations to escape political regulation and national legal jurisdictions, and the liberation of capital from national and territorial constraints.[89] Sceptics, on the other hand, claim that the world is less open and globalised at the end of the twentieth century than it was in the nineteenth. They suggest that the volume of world trade relative to the size of the world economy is much the same as it was in 1914, though they concede that the enormous explosion of short-term speculative capital transfers since the collapse of the Bretton Woods system in the early 1970s has restricted the planning options for national governments. Significantly, sceptics want to distinguish between the idea of an international economy with growing links between separate national economies which they concede, and a single global political economy without meaningful national borders or divisions – which they deny.[90]

This section will examine the claims made by liberals and the extent to which their ideas have shaped the current economic order. It will focus on the contemporary nature of world trade and the question of sovereignty and foreign investment.

The nature of 'free trade'

For neo-liberals, the principles of free trade first enunciated by Smith and Ricardo, continue to have contemporary relevance. Commercial traders should be allowed to exchange money and goods without concern for national barriers. There should be few legal constraints on international commerce, and no artificial protection or subsidies constraining the freedom to exchange. An open global market, where goods and services can pass freely across national boundaries, should be the objective of policy makers in all nation-states. Only free trade will maximize economic growth and generate the competition that will promote the most efficient use of resources, people and capital.

Conversely, 'protectionism' is seen as a pernicious influence on the body politic. Policies which protect uncompetitive industries from market principles corrupt international trade, distort market demand, artificially lower prices and encourage inefficiency, while penalising fair traders. Protection is the cry of 'special' or 'vested' interests in society and should be resisted by government in 'the national interest'. It penalises developing nations by excluding them from entry into the global marketplace where they can exploit their domestic advantage in cheap labour.

The cornerstone of the free trade argument is the theory of 'comparative advantage', which discourages national self-sufficiency by advising states to specialise in goods and services they can produce most cheaply – their 'factor endowments'. They can then exchange their goods for what is produced more cheaply elsewhere. As everything is then produced most efficiently according to the price mechanism, the production of wealth is maximised and everyone is better off. For Smith, the 'invisible hand' of market forces directs every member of society in every state to the most advantageous position in the global economy. The self-interest of one becomes the general interest of all.

The relevance of the theory of comparative advantage in the era of globalisation has recently come under question.[91] The first difficulty is that it was devised at time when there were national controls on capital movements. Ricardo and Smith assumed capital was immobile and only available for national investment. They also assumed that the capitalist was first and foremost a member of a national political community, which was the context in which he established his commercial identity: Smith's 'invisible hand' presupposed the internal relations and bondings of community, so that the capitalist feels a 'natural disinclination' to invest abroad. Smith and Ricardo could not have foreseen 'a world of cosmopolitan money managers and transnational corporations which, in addition to having limited liability and immorality conferred on them by national governments, have now transcended those very governments and no longer see the national community as their context'. The emergence of capitalists who had freed themselves from community obligations and loyalties, and who had no 'natural disinclination' to invest abroad, would have appeared absurd.[92] Highly mobile and volatile capital markets are a major challenge for the theory of comparative advantage.

The second problem arises from the fact that the forms of international trade have dramatically changed over recent decades. The idea of national, sovereign states trading with each other as discrete economic units is becoming an anachronism. Intra-industry or intra-firm trade dominates the manufacturing sector of the world economy. Over 40 per cent of all trade now comprises of intrafirm transactions, which are centrally managed interchanges within transnational corporations (that cross international borders) guided by a highly 'visible hand', to quote Alfred Chandler: these are what Robert Reich has called a 'global web' of linkages and exchanges. Intra-firm trade runs counter to the theory of comparative advantage which advises nations to specialise in products where factor endowments provide a comparative cost advantage. The mobility of capital and technology, and the extent to which firms trade with each other, means that 'governments in virtually all industrial societies now take an active interest in trying to facilitate links between their own domestic firms – including offshoots of multinationals – and the global networks' in the strategic industries. They can no longer remain at arms length from business as neo-liberal economic theory demands.[93]

Similarly, the globalisation of the world economy has seen the spread of manufacturing industries to many developing countries and the relocation of transnational manufacturing centres to what are often low wage, high repression areas – regions with low health and safety standards where organised labour is frequently suppressed or illegal. Transnational corporations are becoming increasingly adept at finding ways of circumventing national borders in their search for cheap labour and access to raw materials, and few states can refuse to play host to them. The creation of new centres of production occurs wherever profit opportunities can be maximised because investment decisions are governed by absolute profitability and no longer by comparative advantage. For liberals, this is nevertheless the best way of encouraging much needed foreign investment in the developing world and establishing a trade profile for countries which might otherwise be excluded from world trade altogether.

Modern trading conditions have diverged significantly from the assumptions which underpin the neo-liberal analysis of how markets and trade actually work. The internationalisation of production, the mobility of capital and the dominance of transnational corporations (20 per cent of world production, 70 per cent of world trade) are just three developments which render theories of comparative advantage somewhat anachronistic. The idea of national sovereign states trading with each other as discrete economic units is steadily becoming the exception rather than the rule.

Neo-mercantilist theory, which stresses the maximisation of national wealth, also fails to explain contemporary trade realities. A more accurate description is 'corporate mercantilism', with 'managed commercial interactions within and among huge corporate groupings, and regular state intervention in the three major Northern blocs to subsidise and protect domestically-based international corporations and financial institutions'.[94] If there is such a thing as a nation's comparative advantage it is clearly a human achievement and certainly not a gift of nature, though this view remains unorthodox within powerful economic circles.

The third challenge to the relevance of the theory of comparative advantage is the steady erosion of the rules which have underpinned multilateral trade in the post-war era. Whilst there has been a reduction in barriers to trade *within* blocs such as the EU and NAFTA, they have been raised *between* blocs. Tariffs have come down but they have been replaced by a wide assortment of non-tariff barriers, including import quotas and voluntary restraint agreements. This is a concern to small, 'fair' traders which are incapable of matching the subsidies provided by Europeans and North Americans. States which unilaterally adopt free market doctrines while leading industrial societies head in the opposite direction, place themselves in a very vulnerable position in the world economy. But regardless of whether tariff and non-tariff barriers were dismantled, the world market would not be 'free' in any meaningful sense, because of the power of the transnational corporations to control and distort markets through transfer pricing and other devices.

The proliferation of free trade agreements and organisations such as NAFTA, APEC and the WTO and the growing importance of international organisations such as the G8, IMF and World Bank is indicative of the influence of neo-liberalism in post-Cold War period. These are powerful transnational bodies which embody free trade as their governing ideology. To their supporters they provide developing societies with the only opportunity overcome financial hardship and modernise their economies. To their critics, however, they impose free market strictures on developing societies. They are primarily organisations which formalise and institutionalise market relationships between states. By locking the developing world into agreements which force them to lower their protective barriers, NAFTA and the WTO for example, prevent the South from developing trade profiles which diverge from the model dictated by their supposed 'comparative advantage'. The IMF and the World Bank, on the other hand, make the provision of finance (or more accurately 'debt') to developing societies conditional on their unilateral acceptance of free market rules for their economies – the 'conditionality' of so called 'structural adjustment programs'.

The new institutions of governance, such as the World Bank and NAFTA, are dominated by the wealthy industrialised societies of the North. They enshrine the liberal principle that unfettered competition between privately owned enterprises is the only efficient form of economic organisation. And they believe that economic growth is the one and only road to development for all societies. They regard recent East Asian and Latin American success stories as vindicating their approach. Critics, on the other hand, highlight the effects of free trade policies which are imposed on subordinate societies, including environmental degradation, growing disparities of wealth and income, and the creation of economic dependencies. They are also concerned by the lack of democratic accountability in these institutions.

Most importantly, critics attack these institutions for legitimising only one kind of global order, based on unequal market relations. Specifically, the institutions are criticised for imposing identical prescriptions for economic development on all countries, regardless of what conditions prevail locally. Developing societies are expected to adopt the free market blueprint (sometimes called the 'Washington consensus') – opening their economies up to foreign investment, financial de-regulation, reductions in government expenditure and budgetary deficits, the privatisation of government-owned enterprises, the abolition of protection and subsidies, developing export-orientated economies – or risk the withholding of much needed aid and finance. And because they are required to remove national controls on capital movements – which make it possible for states to reach their own conclusions about investment and spending priorities – the direction of their economic development is increasingly set by amorphous financial markets which act on profit opportunities rather than out of any consideration of national or community interest. The price of financial assistance to and investment in these states is the loss of their economic sovereignty. This fulfils the traditional requirements of liberal internationalism: the distorting power of the state to interfere in commercial relations between individuals is curtailed. The sovereignty of the state is replaced by the sovereignty of capital.

Arguments for free trade are still powerfully made on the grounds of economic efficiency and as the only way of integrating the developing world into the wider global economy. Protectionism within the North is said to primarily hurt the South by pricing their economies out of markets in the industrialised world, thus denying them the opportunity to modernise their economies.

For leading players, however, free trade is often non-reciprocal and an ideological weapon used to regulate the economic development of subordinate societies. Their rhetoric supporting the sanctity of market principles is rarely matched by their own economic behaviour. This tendency, together with fundamental changes to the structure of the world economy and the forms of international trade, casts some doubt on the extent to which liberals can explain the globalisation of the world economy solely on their own terms.

Sovereignty and foreign investment

The enormous volumes of unregulated capital liberated by the collapse of the Bretton Woods system in the early 1970s, have transformed the relationships between states and markets. Credit (bonds and loans), investment (FDI) and money (foreign exchange) now flow more freely across the world than commodities. The resulting increase in the power of transnational capital and the diminution of national economic sovereignty is perhaps the most dramatic realisation of liberal economic ideas.[95]

The relationship between a nation's economic prosperity and the world's money markets is decisive. Because most states are incapable of generating sufficient endogenous wealth to finance their economic development, governments need to provide domestic economic conditions which will attract foreign investment into their countries. In a world where capital markets are globally linked and money can be electronically transferred around the world in microseconds, states are judges in terms of their comparative 'hospitality' to foreign capital: that is, they must offer the most attractive investment climates to relatively scarce supplies of money. This gives the foreign investment community significant leverage over policy settings and the course of a nation's economic development generally, and constitutes a diminution in the country's economic sovereignty.

The power of transnational finance capital in the modern period can scarcely be overestimated. The volume of foreign exchange trading in the major financial centres of the world, estimated at over $US 1.5 trillion per day, has come to dwarf international trade by at least 60 times. Recent UN statistics suggest that the world's 100 largest transnational corporations, with assets of over $A4.6 trillion, account for a third of the total foreign direct investment of their home states, giving them increasing influence over the economies of host countries.

The brokers on Wall Street and in Tokyo, the clients of the 'screen jockeys' in the foreign exchange rooms, and the auditors from credit ratings agencies such as Moody's and Standard & Poors, can now pass daily judgements on the management of individual economies, and signal to the world's financial community the comparative profit opportunities to be found in a particular country. Inappropriate interventionary policies by government can be quickly deterred or penalised with a (threatened) reduction in the nation's credit rating, a 'run' (sell off) on it's currency or an investment 'strike'. The requirements of the international markets can only be ignored at a nation's economic peril. Not only have nation-states lost direct control over the value of their currencies and the movements of capital around the world, they can no longer determine the institutional settings in which capital markets operate. Many neo-liberal financial commentators regard this development as a positive change, believing that markets rather than the governments know what is in peoples' best interests.

Finance markets, dominated by large banks and financial institutions, insurance companies, brokers and speculators, exist only to maximise their own wealth. There is no compelling reason for them to act in the interests of the poor, the homeless, the infirm or those who are deprived of their basic human rights by their own governments. These are irrelevant considerations, unless they impinge in some way on the 'stability' of the host economy. States which cede economic sovereignty to these global players in the name of free trade and commerce therefore run the risk of elevating private commercial gain to the primary foreign policy objective of the state. As Marx wrote in 1848,

> What is free trade under the present conditions of society? It is freedom of capital. When you have overthrown the few national barriers which still restrict the progress of capital, you will merely have given it complete freedom of action. ... All the destructive phenomena which unlimited competition gives rise to within one country, are reproduced in more gigantic proportions on the world market. It breaks up old nationalities and pushes the antagonism of the proletariat and the bourgeoisie to the extreme point.[96]

When the foreign investment community is freed from state barriers and controls, and able to choose the most profitable location for its capital, it has the effect of homogenising the economic development of nation-states across the globe. In what is effectively a bidding war for much needed infusions of capital, states are driven by the lowest common denominator effect to reduce their regulations, standards, wages and conditions, in order to appear attractive to the investor community: in contemporary parlance, this is what is meant by 'international competitiveness'. Priority is given to the drive for efficiency and profits. The threat of disinvestment becomes the stick for markets to wield over the heads of government. For liberals this is a pleasing reversal of modern history which they see as a struggle for liberation from the clutches of arbitrary state power. Ironically, in many instances the key to attracting overseas investment is for the host government to provide the transnational investor with subsidies and protection from market forces. In some cases this is the only way states can win and maintain the confidence of global markets.

The demand for the liberalisation of finance and services by the investment community allows transnational banks to displace domestic rivals so that it is difficult for developing economies to carry out the kind of national economic planning that enabled the rich countries to develop – usually behind high protectionist walls with extensive state intervention to protect domestic elites from the destructive effects of the market. This again illustrates the changing differentials of power between states and markets over the last two decades.

There are many other examples which highlight the shift of economic power in the contemporary period. To take just one, interest rate settings, which are nominally set by central banks, are now ultimately determined by the pressures of highly integrated global financial markets, over which even the most powerful economies have limited control or influence.

The ill-fated Multilateral Agreement on Investments (MAI) was a vivid illustration of just how far governments in the developed world are pre-pared to go in surrendering their discretionary economic power to the markets. In this case OECD members were offering voluntarily to restrict their own ability to discriminate against foreign capital. The MAI is a reminder that, as with the establishment of national markets in the nine-teenth century, globalisation is not the result of the gradual and sponta-neous emancipation of the economic sphere from government control. On the contrary, it has been the outcome of conscious and sometimes violent state intervention by advanced capitalist states. Just as domestically the labour market can only be 'freed' by legislative restrictions placed on trades unions, the creation of the post-war liberal trading regime and the de-regulation of the world's capital markets in the 1970s required deliberate acts by interventionary states.

During the current phase of globalisation national economic sovereignty has not so much been lost, but either enthusiastically given away or begrudgingly surrendered. The state's capacity to direct the national econ-omy has been deliberately and significantly undercut by the globalisation of relations of production and exchange. Sovereign power has been ceded to bond holders, funds managers, currency traders, speculators, transnational banks and insurance companies – groups that by definition are democra-tically unaccountable in any national jurisdiction. In effect, the world economy has come to resemble the global strategic environment. It has become anarchic in character and, as a consequence, the competition for economic security is as intense as the search for strategic security.

In the nineteenth century citizens were able to look to the state to protect them from market forces which, according to Polanyi, if left unregulated would demolish industrial society. The transition from *laissez-faire* capital-ism to state capitalism acknowledged the need for interventionary beha-viour by the state. Earlier this century Keynes provided the intellectual justification for abandoning free market principles. By the year 2000, how-ever, globalisation had liberated the power of financial markets from the authority of the overarching state. The state appears to be in retreat and is either no longer willing or capable of providing its citizens with protection from the vicissitudes of global markets. In many ways international relations at the dawn of a new century fulfils the dream of eighteenth and nineteenth century liberals. The state is in decline, democracy is spreading and international commerce is almost unfettered. Only the recurrence of war outside the central core defies the liberal prescription for a better world order.

Conclusion

At the beginning of this chapter it was argued that liberalism was an 'inside-out' approach to international relations, because liberals favour a world in which the endogenous determines the exogenous. The challenge is to extend the legitimacy of domestic political arrangements found within democratic states to the relationships between all nation-states. To put it another way, liberals believe democratic society, in which civil liberties are protected and market relations prevail, can have an international analogue in the form of a peaceful global order. The domestic free market has its counterpart in the open, globalised world economy. Parliamentary debate and accountability is reproduced in international fora such as the United Nations. And the legal protection of civil rights within liberal democracies is extended to the promotion of human rights across the world. With the collapse of Communism as an alternative political and economic order, the potential for continuity between the domestic and the international is greater that in any previous period.

Fukuyama has reason to be optimistic. The spread of liberal democracies and the zone of peace is an encouraging development, as is the realisation by states that trade and commerce is more closely correlated with economic success than territorial conquest. The number of governments enjoying civilian rather than military rule is increasing, and there are signs that ethical considerations and ideas of human justice have a permanent place on the diplomatic agenda. The collapse of Marxism as a legitimate alternative political order removes a substantial barrier to the spread of liberal democracies, and there can be little doubt that the great powers are now much less inclined to use force to resolve their political differences.

The globalisation of the world economy means there are few obstacles to international trade. Liberals have long sort to remove the influence of the state in commercial relations between businesses and individuals, and the decline of national economic sovereignty is an indication that the corrupting influence of the state is rapidly diminishing. Transnational corporations and capital markets wield unprecedented influence over the shape of the world economy, in the process homogenising the political economies of every member state of the international community. The objective of creating a market society on a global scale is within sight.

Globalisation has undermined the nation-state in other ways that have pleased liberals. The capacity of each state to control the political loyalties of its citizens has been weakened by an increasing popular awareness of the problems faced by the entire human species. The state cannot prevent its citizens turning to a range of sub-national and transnational agents to secure their political identities and promote their political objectives. Sovereignty is no longer an automatic protection against external interference called 'humanitarian intervention'. And decision making on a range of environmental, economic and security questions has become internationalised, rendering national administration often much less important than transnational political co-operation.

Despite these important changes, realists would nevertheless argue that liberals such as Ohmae are premature in announcing the demise of the nation-state. They would remind the enthusiasts for globalisation that as a preferred form of political community, the nation-state still has no serious rival. There are currently over 200 nation-states in the world asserting their political independence.

Realists can cite a number of important powers retained by the state despite globalisation, including monopoly control of the weapons of war and their legitimate use, and the sole right to tax its citizens. They would argue that only the nation-state can still command the political allegiances of its citizens or adjudicate in disputes between them. And it is still only the nation-state which has the exclusive authority to bind the whole community to international law.

As liberals always intended, globalisation has certainly weakened the authority of nation-states. Its inefficient and corrupting influence in commercial relations is being removed. National economic planning is no longer possible. However, those who celebrate these developments are wise to be wary of consigning the nation-state to history just yet.

There is a growing number of states which reject the argument that Western modernity is universally valid or that political development always terminates at liberal-capitalist democracy. They claim that the West's political and human rights agenda is a form of cultural imperialism and have demonstrated impressive economic success without the procedural freedoms championed by liberal internationalists. They would agree with Carr that liberalism is the ideology of the comfortable which is being imposed by the West on others.

Liberal states have yet to learn how to conduct themselves peacefully with these societies, though Rawls has at least begun to explore the basis of toleration between liberal and non-liberal peoples. Liberal internationalists have not shown how liberal states can overcome their insecurity engendered by the anarchic international system, a condition further aggravated by the collapse of the balance of power and mutual nuclear deterrence with the end of the Cold War. The uncertainties of a multipolar world and the inherent weaknesses of collective security arrangements are a cause of considerable disquiet amongst neo-realists.

Furthermore, the triumph of free trade appears somewhat misleading given that the leading economic powers have achieved economic success by explicitly violating the market principles they often seek to impose on the developing world. Left unregulated, free trade policies exacerbate disparities of wealth internally and between the rich and poor worlds. They overwhelm and often destroy community life in traditional societies by prescribing only one path to economic development. Meanwhile the globalisation of the world economy leaves the power of transnational corporations and financial markets unchallenged and largely unaccountable.

As suggested by Macpherson, liberalism is bifurcated between its ethical and market strands. Both have made impressive gains in the post-Cold War period, even though they remain largely irreconciled and their impact is resisted in some quarters. The end of the Cold War has increased the influence of liberal theories of international relations in the academy. No matter how flawed, their claims about the future of the international order deserve serious investigation and intellectual engagement with contending approaches. To continue to believe that liberalism was fatally discredited in the 1930s would be grossly to underestimate its intellectual resilience and the extent to which the contours of contemporary international relations have come to resemble its programme.

Notes

1. C. B. Macpherson, *Democratic Theory* (Oxford, 1973), p. 24. See also J. L. Richardson, 'Contending Liberalisms – Past and Present', *European Journal of International Relations*, vol. 3, no. 1 (March 1997).
2. F. Fukuyama, *The End of History and the Last Man* (London, 1992), pp. xi–xii and 48.
3. A. Linklater, 'Liberal Democracy, Constitutionalism and the New World Order', in R. Leaver and J. Richardson (eds), *The Post-Cold War Order: Diagnoses and Prognoses* (St Leonards, 1993), p. 29.
4. Fukuyama (1992), p. xx.
5. K. Waltz, 'America as a Model for the World?', *PS: Political Science and Politics*, vol. 24, no. 4 (1991), p. 667. See also Linklater (1993), pp. 29–31.
6. See M. Doyle, 'Liberalism and World politics', *American Political Science Review*, vol. 80, no. 4 (1986), pp. 1151–69.
7. Linklater (1993), p. 29.
8. For a survey of liberal internationalism, see Richardson (1997) and M. W. Zacher and R. A. Matthew, 'Liberal International Theory: Common Threads,

Divergent Strands', in C. W. Kegley Jr (ed.), *Controversies in International Relations Theory* (New York, 1995), pp. 107–50. See also R. N. Gardner, 'The Comeback of Liberal Internationalism', *The Washington Quarterly*, vol. 13, no. 3 (Summer 1990), pp. 23–39 and S. Hoffmann, 'The Crisis of Liberal Internationalism', *Foreign Policy*, 98 (1995), pp. 159–77.

9.   M. Howard, *War and the Liberal Conscience* (Oxford, 1978), p. 31.
10. I. Kant, *Kant's Political Writings*, edited by H. Reiss and translated H. Nisbet (Cambridge, 1970), p. 100.
11. Doyle (1986), p. 1151.
12. Doyle (1986), p. 1161. See also Fukuyama (1992), p. xx.
13. See Doyle (1986) and M. W. Doyle, 'Liberalism and World Politics Revisited', in Kegley Jr (1995), pp. 83–106. See also B. Russett, *Grasping the Democratic Peace* (Princeton, 1993) and M. W. Doyle, *Ways of War and Peace* (New York, 1997).
14. J. Rawls, *The Law of Peoples* (Harvard, 1999), p. 49.
15. J. Mueller, *Retreat From Doomsday* (New York, 1989).
16. Waltz (1991), p. 670.
17. J. L. Mearsheimer, ' "Back to the Future": Instability in Europe After the Cold War', *International Security*, vol. 15, no. 1 (Summer 1990), p. 6.
18. Waltz (1991), p. 669.
19. Waltz (1991), p. 669.
20. Mearsheimer (1990), pp. 6–7.
21. Mearsheimer (1990), pp. 14–19.
22. Mearsheimer (1990), p. 32.
23. Mearsheimer (1990), pp. 7–8.
24. Rawls (1999), pp. 11–23.
25. Linklater (1993), p. 33–6. See also Rawls (1999).
26. Linklater (1993), p. 33.
27. E. H. Carr, *Nationalism and After* (New York, 1945), pp. 5–6.
28. Howard (1978), p. 20. See also A. Walter, 'Adam Smith and the Liberal Tradition in International Relations', in I. Clark and I. B. Neumann (eds), *Classical Theories of International Relations* (Oxford, 1996).
29. D. Ricardo, *The Principles of Political Economy and Taxation* (London, 1911), p. 114.
30. Paine quoted in Howard (1978), p. 29.
31. Quoted in Howard (1978), p. 37.
32. Quoted in A. Arblaster, *The Rise and Decline of Western Liberalism*, (Oxford, 1984), p. 261.
33. A. Gamble, *An Introduction to Modern Social and Political Thought* (London, 1981), pp. 81–2.
34. Cobden in 1843 quoted in Howard (1978), p. 43.
35. D. Mitrany, 'The Functional Approach to World Organisation', *International Affairs*, 24 (1948), pp. 350–63.
36. R. O. Keohane and J. S. Nye, *Power and Interdependence: World Politics in Transition* (Boston, 1977).

37. See J. S. Nye, 'Neorealism and Neoliberalism', *World Politics*, vol. 40 (1988) and R. Powell, 'Anarchy in international relations theory: the neorealist–neoliberal debate', *International Organisation*, 48 (1994).

38. R. Rosecrance, *The Rise of the Trading State* (New York, 1986). See also S. Strange, 'New World Order: Conflict and Co-operation', *Marxism Today*, January (1991), pp. 30–1.

39. J. Vincent, *Human Rights and International Relations* (Cambridge, 1986). See also S. Hoffmann, *Duties Beyond Borders* (Syracuse, 1981) and T. Dunne and N. J. Wheeler (eds), *Human Rights in Global Politics* (Cambridge, 1999).

40. A. Linklater, 'What is a Good International Citizen?', in P. Keal, *Ethics and Foreign Policy* (Canberra, 1992), p. 27.

41. See H. Bull (ed.), *Intervention in World Politics* (Oxford, 1984).

42. See I. Forbes and M. Hoffman (eds), *Political Theory, International Relations and the Ethics of Intervention* (Basingstoke, 1993) and G. Robertson, *Crimes Against Humanity* (London, 1999).

43. For a critical discussion, see N. Chomsky, *The New Military Humanism* (Monroe, 1999).

44. See I. Clark, *The Hierarchy of States* (Cambridge, 1989), pp. 147–8.

45. Cobden quoted in M. V. Kauppi and P. R. Viotti (eds), *The Global Philosophers* (New York, 1992), pp. 208–9.

46. For a lively survey of British Liberal thinking on war, see A. J. P. Taylor, *The Troublemakers* (London, 1957).

47. Bull (1977), pp. 106–12.

48. Clark (1989), p. 23.

49. For a discussion of constitutionalism and its relationship to liberal internationalism, see Linklater (1993), pp. 33–8.

50. A. Giddens, *The Nation-State and Violence* (Cambridge, 1985), pp. 258–61.

51. E. H. Carr, *The Twenty Years' Crisis 1919–1939* (London, 1939), p. 87.

52. Howard (1978), p. 132.

53. C. B. Macpherson, *The Life and Times of Liberal Democracy* (Oxford, 1977), p. 21.

54. K. Polanyi, *The Great Transformation* (Boston, 1944), pp. 137–9.

55. F. Block and M. Somers, 'Beyond the Economistic Fallacy: The Holistic Social Science of Karl Polanyi', in T. Skocpol (ed.), *Vision and Method in Historical Sociology* (Cambridge, 1984), p. 63.

56. K. Polanyi, 'Our Obsolete Market Mentality', in G. Dalton (ed.), *Primitive, Archaic and Modern Economies* (New York, 1968), p. xxvii.

57. Dalton (1968), pp. i and xxx.

58. Polanyi (1968), p. 70.

59. F. Block, *Postindustrial Possibilities* (Berkeley, 1990), p. 39.

60. Polanyi (1944), pp. 139–40.

61. Chomsky (1993), p. 250.

62. A. Gramsci, *Selections From Prison Notebooks* (New York, 1971), p. 160.

63. Stephen Hymer quoted in G. Hodgson, *The Democratic Economy* (Harmondsworth, 1984), p. 79.

64. See, for example, F. Pollock, 'State Capitalism', in S. E. Bronner and D. M. Kellner (eds), *Critical Theory and Society* (New York, 1989), Polanyi (1944) and A. Gershenkron, *Economic Backwardness in Historical Perspective* (Harvard, 1962).
65. Polanyi (1944), p. 73.
66. Polanyi (1944), p. 150. See also D. P. Calleo and B. M. Rowland, *America and the World Political Economy* (Bloomington, 1973), pp. 23–4.
67. Polanyi (1944), p. 132.
68. N. Chomsky, 'Notes on Nafta', Massachusetts Institute of Technology, (Cambridge, MA, 1993a). See also T. Fitzgerald, *Between Life and Economics* (Crows Nest, 1990), pp. 12–15.
69. See Polanyi (1944), p. 73.
70. J. Derrida, *Specters of Marx* (New York, 1994), p. 52.
71. R. Gilpin, *The Political Economy of International Relations* (Princeton, 1987), p. 183.
72. It is generally agreed that the term free trade imperialism was coined by J. Gallagher and R. Robinson, 'The Imperialism of Free Trade', *Economic History Review*, vol. 6, no. 1 (1953), pp. 1–15.
73. Gamble (1981), p. 145.
74. Gilpin (1987), p. 181.
75. Chomsky (1993), p. 10. According to Robinson, free trade was 'believed in only by those who will gain an advantage from it' (J. Robinson, *The New Mercantilism* (Cambridge, 1966), p. 108.
76. K. Marx, *Grundrisse* (St Albans, 1970), p. 153.
77. P. Deane, *The First Industrial Revolution* (Cambridge, 1979), pp. 212–3 and Hobsbawm (1969), pp. 106–7 and 137–40.
78. Arblaster (1984), p. 262.
79. Carr (1939), p. 72.
80. N. Chomsky, 'Correspondence with Author' (1992a), p. 2.
81. For a definition of preponderant power see M. Leffler, *A Preponderance of Power* (Stanford, 1992), pp. 12 and 19. The quotation is from Kolko and Kolko (1972), p. 2.
82. Leffler (1992), p. 16.
83. Leffler (1992), p. 16.
84. N. Chomsky, *Necessary Illusions* (Boston, 1989), p. 25.
85. Leffler (1992), p. 63.
86. Calleo and Rowland (1973), p. 12.
87. Leffler (1992), p. 16.
88. For a summary of the debate see D. Held, A. McGrew, D. Goldblatt and J. Perraton, *Global Transformations* (Cambridge, 1999), Introduction and D. Held and A. McGrew (eds), *The Global Transformations Reader* (Cambridge, 2000), Introduction.
89. See K. Ohmae, *The End of the Nation State* (New York, 1995); T. Friedman, *The Lexus and the Olive Tree* (London, 2000); J. Micklewait and A. Wooldridge, *A Future Perfect: The Challenge and Hidden Promise of Globalisation* (New York, 2000).

90. See L. Weiss, *The Myth of the Powerless State: Governing the Economy in a Global Era* (Cambridge, 1998); N. Chomsky, *Profit Over People: Neoliberalism and the Global Order* (New York, 1999); P. Hirst and G. Thompson, *Globalisation in Question* (Cambridge, 1999); E. Hobsbawm, *The New Century* (London, 2000).

91. See S. Strange, 'Protectionism and World Politics', *International Organisation*, vol. 39, no. 2 (Spring 1985). See also H. E. Daly and J. B. Cobb Jr, *For the Common Good* (Boston, 1st edn, 1989; 2nd edn, 1994) and P. Bairoch, *Economic and World History* (Chicago, 1993). See also F. F. Clairmont, *The Rise and Fall of Economic Liberalism* (Penang, 1996) and N. Chomsky, *Profit Over People: Neoliberalism and Global Order* (New York, 1999).

92. Daly and Cobb (1989), p. 215. See more generally, pp. 209–35.

93. H. V. Emy, *Remaking Australia* (Melbourne, 1993), p. 173.

94. Chomsky (1993), p. 95.

95. See S. Strange, *The Retreat of the State* (Cambridge, 1996) and S. Strange, *Mad Money* (Michigan, 1998). See also Held *et al.* (1999), ch. 4.

96. K. Marx, 'Address to the Democratic Association of Brussels' (1848), quoted by E. Wheelwright, 'Free Trade?', *Arena* (February/March 1993).

CHAPTER 3

Realism and Neo-realism

Scott Burchill

Realism is widely regarded as the most influential theoretical tradition in International Relations, even by its harshest critics. Its ancient philosophical heritage, its powerful critique of liberal internationalism and its influence on the practice of international diplomacy have secured it an important, if not dominant position in the discipline. No other theory has given as much form and structure to the study of international politics, especially to the sub-fields of Security Studies and International Political Economy (IPE).[1]

As its name implies, realism seeks to describe and explain the world of international politics *as it is*, rather than how we might like it to be. Accordingly, the world is revealed to realists as a dangerous and insecure place, where violence is regrettable but endemic. In their account of the conflictual nature of international politics, realists give high priority to the centrality of the nation-state in their considerations, acknowledging it as the supreme political authority in the world. Explaining the violent behaviour of nation-states can only be done, however, by focussing on the role of power and the importance of the most powerful – the Great Powers. The relevance of an approach which accords priority to military power, perceptions of vulnerability, superpowers, wars and the perpetuation of a system which seems chronically troubled, was obvious to all in the most violent of all centuries – the twentieth.

Realists are unified in their pessimism about the extent to which the international political system can be made more peaceful and just. The international realm is characterised by conflict, suspicion and competition between nation-states, a logic which thwarts the realisation of alternative world orders. Realism is a pessimistic theoretical tradition. Fundamental changes to the structure of the international system are unlikely, even if they are needed. The apparent immutability of the international system means that it will not come to resemble domestic liberal orders, however desirable the analogue may be. For realists, international politics is a world of recurrence and repetition, not reform or radical change.

In this chapter we will examine the work of E. H. Carr and Hans Morgenthau, widely regarded as the founding fathers of modern or 'traditional' realism. We will also analyse the neo-realism of Kenneth Waltz which emerged in the 1980s as arguably the dominant theory of international relations, as well as the contribution of other structural realists such as Barry Buzan. The responses of neo-realists such as Waltz, Stephen Krasner and Robert Gilpin to recent liberal arguments for globalisation will round off the chapter.

The Early Realists

The first coherent expressions of a realist approach to the study of international politics evolved out of the apparent failure of liberal principles to sustain peace in Europe after the First World War. Realists believed that no amount of wishful thinking or the application of domestic political principles to the international sphere would change the nature of global politics, in particular its endemic violence. However desirable progress towards the pacification of international politics might be, unless the 'realities of power' were given priority in understanding international relations, few advances could be made and normative expectations would not be met.

Unlike their successors, the early realists recognised the need for international political reform and were not blind to alternative forms of political organisation. For them, the nation-state was not necessarily the ultimate expression of political community. And though their accounts now seem unscientific and lacking in intellectual precision, many early realists believed that they could uncover the patterns and laws of international politics through a more sophisticated understanding of human nature. The most important of these early realists are E. H. Carr and Hans Morgenthau.

Carr

E. H. Carr's *The Twenty Years' Crisis* (1939) is not a textbook of international theory, but a critique of the prevailing wisdom of its day. Published on the eve of the Second World War, it was a devastating attack on liberal 'utopianism' which had inspired the post-Great War political arrangements in Europe, most particularly the idea of collective security as it was enshrined in the institution of the League of Nations. It was a book which set much of the discipline's initial agenda, and continues to inform contemporary debates in the field.[2]

In response to the horrors of the First World War, liberal internationalists, or 'utopians' as Carr called them, sought to abolish war as an instrument of statecraft. Liberals were convinced that the forms of international diplomacy could be restructured to make them more peaceful. Self-determination and statehood ‾would be available to all national groups. Secret diplomacy would be abolished and replaced by public consent in the conduct of foreign policy. The balance of power principle would give way to a system of collective security, where individual acts of aggression would. be met by the collective force of world opinion and military power. Finally, international fora such as the League of Nations would be established to mediate the peaceful resolution of conflicts.

Carr's initial concern with the liberal-utopian position was its underlying normative character. It was dangerous, he believed, to base the study of international politics on an imaginary desire of how we would *like* the world to be. According to Carr, 'the teleological aspect of the science of international politics has been conspicuous from the outset ... the passionate desire to prevent war determined the whole initial course and direction of the study' which, consequently, made it 'markedly and frankly utopian'. As a result of its preoccupation with the 'end to be achieved' (international peace), International Relations in its initial stage was a discipline 'in which wishing prevails over thinking, generalisation over observation, and in which little attempt is made at a critical analysis of existing facts or available means'. Until the 1930s, International Relations was, according to Carr, a discipline in which teleology preceded analysis.[3]

For Carr, although we might *wish* the world was more peaceful and harmonious, this was not a useful basis on which to erect a scientific study of world politics. 'Events which have occurred since 1931', writes Carr in 1939, 'clearly revealed the inadequacy of pure aspiration as the basis for a science of international politics, and made it possible for the first time to embark on serious critical and analytical thought about international problems'.[4] The failure of the League of Nations to prevent Japan's invasion of Manchuria and Italy's occupation of Abyssinia had dashed the hopes of many liberals who believed the world could be made peaceful simply by wishing it to be so. What was needed, according to Carr, was a more rigorous approach which emphasised the realities of power in international politics rather than one which took as its starting point, an image of how the world could be: in other words, what *is* rather what *ought* to be.

> The impact of thinking upon wishing which, in the development of a science, follows the breakdown of its first visionary projects, and marks the end of its specifically utopian period, is commonly called realism. Representing a reaction against the wish-dreams of the initial (utopian) stage, realism is liable to assume a critical and somewhat cynical aspect. In the field of thought, it places its emphasis

on the acceptance of facts and on the analysis of their causes and consequences. It tends to depreciate the role of purpose and to maintain, explicitly or implicitly, that the function of thinking is to study a sequence of events which it is powerless to influence or alter. In the field of action, realism tends to emphasise the irresistible strength of existing forces and the inevitable character of existing tendencies, and to insist that the highest wisdom lies in accepting, and adapting oneself to these forces and these tendencies.[5]

Carr believed that realism was 'a necessary corrective to the exuberance of utopianism' which had ignored the central element of power in its consideration of international politics.[6] Until the unequal distribution of power in the international system became the central focus of a dispassionate analysis, the root causes of conflict and war would not be properly understood. Carr believed the liberal utopians were so concerned with eradicating the scourge of war they had completely neglected its underlying rationale.

Liberals had also imputed common interests to states, interests which were clearly not as widely shared as they thought. They believed, for example, that every nation had an identical interest in peace and that any state which behaved aggressively or failed to respect the peace was acting irrationally and immorally.[7] According to Carr, this was in fact nothing more than an expression of the 'satisfied powers' with a vested interest in the preservation of the 'status quo'. The post-war system had been created by the victors of the war, and it was an arrangement from which they stood to gain the most at the expense of 'revisionist' powers. 'The post-war utopia became the tool of vested interests and was perverted into a bulwark of the status quo ... a cloak for the vested interests of the privileged'. The rhetoric of liberal internationalism, if it were to be taken seriously, was based on 'the illusion of a world society possessing interests and sympathies in common'.[8] In reality the post-war order reflected the specific interests of 'satisfied powers', and was therefore unlikely to receive the support of those states, such as Germany, which clearly felt aggrieved by the 1919 Versailles settlement.

Carr refutes the liberals' belief that international concord could be achieved by the widest possible application of their views. This is because 'these supposedly absolute and universal principles (peace, harmony of interests, collective security, free trade) were not principles at all, but the unconscious reflexions of national policy based on a particular interpretation of national interest at a particular time'.[9] Britain's own particular experience, for example, was seen as the foundation upon which international peace could be built for all states. These allegedly universal principles form part of the doctrine of the *harmony of interests*, a central pillar of liberal internationalism, which is revealed as little more than the selfish and particular interests of the elites within the 'satisfied powers':

the doctrine of the harmony of interests ... is the natural assumption of a prosperous and privileged class, whose members have a dominant voice in the community and are therefore naturally prone to identify its interest with their own. In virtue of this identification, any assailant of the interests of the dominant group is made to incur the odium of assailing the alleged common interest of the whole community, and is told that in making this assault he is attacking his own higher interests. The doctrine of the harmony of interests thus serves as an ingenious moral device invoked, in perfect sincerity, by privileged groups in order to justify and maintain their dominant position.[10]

Assuming particular interests are commonly shared is not a new practice in politics and government. 'Once industrial capitalism and the class system had become the recognised structure of society, the doctrine of the harmony of interests ... became ... the ideology of a dominant group concerned to maintain its predominance by asserting the identity of its interests with those of the community as a whole'.[11] Its adoption in the international arena by the liberal utopians, however, resulted in the collapse of the inter-war peace. According to Carr, 'just as the ruling class in a community prays for domestic peace, which guarantees its own security and predominance, and denounces class war, which might threaten them, so international peace becomes a vested interest of predominant powers'.[12] For a state which wishes to revise its territorial boundaries or its economic and strategic power, 'international peace' is an oppressive tyranny masquerading as universal harmony. It is the slogan of those players powerful enough to impose their will on subordinate societies. For realists, the liberal idea that every international conflict is unnecessary, if not immoral, is nothing more than an attempt to enshrine an existing economic and political order which is favourable to ruling classes within dominant states. There is no natural harmony of interests between states in the international system, only a temporary and transient reflection of a particular configuration of global power. War may in fact be the only way in which power can be recalibrated in the international system.

Carr cites the example of *laissez-faire* economics to refute the notion of a *harmony of interests* between states. *Laissez-faire* is the ideology of the ruling elites within dominant economic states which claims that what is good for them is, by definition, of benefit to all. In the nineteenth century, the British manufacturer and merchant, 'having discovered that *laissez-faire* promoted his own prosperity, was sincerely convinced that it also promoted British prosperity as a whole'. In turn, British statesmen in the same period, 'having discovered that free trade promoted British prosperity, were sincerely convinced that, in doing so, it also promoted the prosperity of the world as a whole'.[13] Carr, invoking List, points out that while free trade was the correct policy for a nation like Great Britain, which was industrially dominant at the time, only policies of protection would enable weaker nations to break the British stranglehold. There was no evidence that the economic nationalism practised by the United States and Germany had achieved anything less than enabling those states to challenge Britain's economic power.[14] 'Laissez-faire, in international relations as in those between capital and labour, is the paradise of the economically strong. State control, whether in the form of protective legislation or of protective tariffs, is the weapon of self defence invoked by the economically weak'.[15] Accordingly, there is no underlying and natural harmony of interests between nations, only asymmetrical power. Common interests between states, if they are to emerge, must be artificially harmonised by state action.[16]

The liberal utopians had wanted to eliminate power as a consideration for states in the international system. Realists on the other hand, believed the pursuit of national power was a natural drive which states neglected at their peril. Nation-states which eschewed the pursuit of power on principle simply endangered their own security. For Carr, the pursuit of power by individual states took the form of promoting 'national interests', a term later to be more broadly defined as the foreign policy goals of the nation but understood by realists specifically to mean strategic power. Clashes of national interests were inevitable: it was futile and dangerous to suggest otherwise. The only way to minimise such clashes, and therefore the incidence of war, was to ensure that a rough balance of power existed between the states in the international system. To put it another way, the best safeguard against international conflict was the prevention of one state emerging with predominant power. Far from being a cause of international conflict as the liberals had argued, the balance of power system resembled the laws of nature: it was the normal expression of international power and the best guarantee of peace. Collective security, the liberal alternative, was little more than a method of placing predominant power in the hands of the victorious states, thus institutionalising the status quo. The League of Nations proved to be incapable of rising above the national interests of its principal members, failing to take account of the shifting differentials of power between the status quo and revisionist states.

It is a mistake to believe that Carr was dismissive of the notion of change in the international system, or that he discounted the role of utopian thought entirely. For realists, peaceful change comes with adjustments to new relations of power: that is, shifting strategic alliances between states. Peace comes through diplomacy, negotiation and compromise, recognising the different interests of status quo and revisionist powers. This is what is meant by 'the irresistible strength of existing forces and the inevitable character of existing tendencies'. Shrewd diplomacy involves accommodation and adaptation to these forces, rather than the naive neglect of them. Power has a rational flow of its own and it is pointless to attempt to swim against the tide.[17] However, although realism is an important corrective to the naivety of liberal thought, 'utopianism must (also) be invoked to counteract the barrenness of realism'. Both, therefore, have their place in 'sound political thought' – realism to expose the fact that utopianism serves the interests of the privileged and powerful, and utopianism to deny that 'altruism is an illusion' and demonstrate that 'pure realism can offer nothing but a naked struggle for power which makes any kind of international society impossible'.[18] The 'science of international politics' requires a blend of both forms of thinking. Its reputation for sterility, pessimism and resistance to change are not entirely well deserved.

Critics of Carr's position point to the irreconcilable antinomies between realism and idealism. Carr's response was to defend 'national policy which aimed at the extension of moral obligation and the enlargement of political community'.[19] Unlike his successors, Carr was not wedded to the belief that the state was the final evolutionary form of political community: there was no need to assume that the nation was the 'ultimate group unit of human society'. He envisaged other political units which were not necessarily territorially based, such as religion, class and ethnicity. Few things in international politics had permanent form, including the size and shape of political communities. Carr predicted that the nation-states of the world would pass through a tumultuous period of integration and disintegration in their search for 'optimal size'. In the process, the concept of sovereignty would become 'even more blurred and indistinct than it is at the present'.[20]

Whatever its final form, Carr was convinced that a new international order would be shaped by the realities of global power rather than morality. He was not arguing that morality was an irrelevant consideration, in fact he believed that international peace was most likely when the dominant power is 'generally accepted as tolerant and unoppressive or, at any rate, as preferable to any practical alternative'.[21] But this was the closest he came to conceding that there might be a moral basis for international order. He preferred to stress that 'power is a necessary ingredient of every political order'.[22] This conviction exposed Carr to critics who claimed he was privileging power and its pursuit by states, above all other factors. How could he explain, for example, that states often forgo their national interests (as narrowly defined by realists) in the interests of international humanitarianism? And why is it so 'wise' for smaller states to 'adapt' to 'irresistible forces and tendencies' which they are 'powerless to alter' but which perpetuate injustice and inequalities?

For Carr, as for all realists, conflict between states was inevitable in an international system without an overarching authority regulating relations between them. The absence of a compulsory jurisdiction for states – an 'anarchical' international system – confirmed the principal distinction between domestic and international politics. In civil society, an individual must submit to the rule of law or pay the consequences: voluntary compliance is not an option. In the international system on the other hand, there is no equivalent regulatory system which can enforce compliance on states.

There is no binding international law or legal system which can bring states to account for their behaviour. States can 'get away' with whatever their power allows them to achieve. Carr expresses the same domestic-international distinction in another way. 'Nationalism was one of the forces by which the seemingly irreconcilable clash of interest between classes within the nation was reconciled. There is no corresponding force which can be invoked to reconcile the seemingly irreconcilable clash of interest between nations'. Moreover, appeals to the common interests of states were an 'illusion', the voice of preponderant power, and often at the expense of the weak and disadvantaged.[23]

Carr's work should be understood as primarily a critique of liberal internationalism, or what he called utopian thinking. It was not put forward as a meta-theory of international relations. It is not a comprehensive theoretical account. It is the kind of explanation one could expect from an historian who believed that history was a sequence of cause and effect which could only be properly appreciated by intellectual effort. Carr believed that the theory of international relations would emerge from the ways in which those relations were practised, and not the other way around. For him, ethics was a function of politics and morality was the product of power.[24] It is not surprising that he thought it was important to defend realism and highlight its relevance in explaining the drift towards another global conflagration. In neglecting the importance of power as a consideration in international relations, Carr was convinced that the architects of the Versailles peace had set the world on an inevitable course to further conflict.

Morgenthau

Hans Morgenthau's *Politics Among Nations* (1948) comes closer to being a realist textbook. It was written in the aftermath of the Second World War as the United States was emerging as a major world economic and strategic power. It became not only an attempt to consolidate the principles of realism, which had seemingly been vindicated by the war, but it was also designed to provide intellectual support for the role the United States was to play in the post-war world. Morgenthau's most important work therefore straddled two worlds: it was an intellectual statement destined to influence generations of students in the academy and a series of guidelines for US foreign policy makers confronted by the uncertainties of the Cold War.

From the tone and style of the book it is possible to sense the extent to which the US academic community was influenced, if not enthralled by developments in the natural sciences during this period. Morgenthau took up Carr's challenge to create a 'science of international politics' by applying the positivist methodology of the 'hard' or natural sciences to the study of international relations. The intellectual rigour of this approach would reveal the underlying 'reality' of world politics, from which certainties and predictions could be deduced. Not surprisingly, Morgenthau's writings are scattered with references to laws and principles, objectivity and science.

His definition of theory, for example, is explicitly borrowed from the natural sciences. Theories, according to Morgenthau, should be judged 'not by some pre-conceived abstract principle or concept unrelated to reality', but by their purpose which is 'to bring order and meaning to a mass of phenomena which without it would remain disconnected and unintelligible'. They must be 'consistent with the facts and within itself'. In other words, theories must be factual, independent and retrospective. Theories must also satisfy strict empirical and logical criteria: 'do the facts as they actually are lend themselves to the interpretation the theory has put on them, and do the conclusions at which the theory arrives follow with logical necessity from its premises?'[25] Morgenthau clearly believes there is a 'knowable reality' or 'rational essence' of foreign policy which theories can reveal.[26] This is the methodological approach of positivism and its application to the study to international politics was designed to provide the field with greater coherence, rigour and intellectual respect. It later inspired the discipline's epistemological debates which erupted in the 1980s.

Morgenthau's account of world politics is underpinned by the contrast he draws between two schools of modern political thought and their conceptions of the nature of humanity, society and politics. The first, which closely resembles liberal utopianism, 'believes that a rational and moral political order, derived from universally valid abstract principles' can be achieved by conscious political action. It 'assumes the essential goodness and infinite malleability of human nature, and blames the failure of the social order to measure up to the rational standards on [a] lack of knowledge and understanding, obsolescent social institutions, or the depravity of certain isolated individuals or groups. It trusts in education, reform, and the sporadic use of force to remedy these defects'. This school believes in the perfectibility of the human condition.

By contrast the second school, with which Morgenthau identifies and that he calls realism, believes the world's imperfections are 'the result of forces inherent in human nature'. According to this approach, 'to improve the world one must work with those forces, not against them'. In a world where conflicts of interest are endemic, moral principles can never be fully realised, only approximated through a temporary balancing of interests. Absolute good cannot be achieved, but a system of checks and balances can help to produce acceptable outcomes. Principles of universal relevance can be deduced from historical experience rather than abstract moral or ethical codes.[27] Like Carr, Morgenthau begins his approach by defining his position in opposition to what he sees as the influence, if not the dominance, of the liberal-utopian perspective.

From this contrast between utopian and realist conceptions of the nature of politics, Morgenthau lists 'six principles of political realism' which, taken together, summarise his theoretical approach to the study of international relations. Below is a brief precis of each point.

(1) Politics is governed by *objective laws* which have their root in human nature. These laws do not change over time and are impervious to human preference. A rational theory of politics and international relations can be based on these laws, in fact any such theory should reflect these objective laws. Following this approach it is possible to distinguish between truth or facts on the one hand, and opinion on the other. These laws provide us with certainty and confidence in predicting rational political behaviour.

(2) The key to understanding international politics is the concept of interest defined in terms of *power*. Reference to this concept enables us to see politics as an autonomous sphere of action. It 'imposes intellectual discipline upon the observer, infuses rational order into the subject matter of politics, and thus makes the theoretical understanding of politics possible'.[28] The idea of interest defined in terms of power reveals the true behaviour of politicians and guards us against two popular misconceptions about the determination of a state's foreign policy – the motives of statesmen and ideological preferences. Whilst political leaders will cast their policies in ideological terms (defence of democracy and so on) they are inevitably confronted by the distinction between what is desirable and what is actually possible. There is no room for moral or ethical concerns, prejudice, political philosophy or individual preference in the determination of foreign policy because actions are constrained by the relative power of the state. The 'national interest', which ought to be the sole pursuit of statesmen, is always defined in terms of strategic and economic capability'.

(3) The forms and nature of state power will vary in time, place and context but the concept of interest remains consistent. The political, cultural and strategic environment will largely determine the forms of power a state chooses to exercise, just as the types of power which feature in human relationships change over time. In addition, realists ought not to be wedded to a perennial connection between interest and the nation-state which is 'a product of history, and therefore bound to disappear'. There is no reason why 'the present division of the political world into nation states will [not] be replaced by larger units of a quite different character, more in keeping with the technical potentialities and moral requirements of the contemporary world'. Change in the international system, however, will only occur 'through the workmanlike manipulation of the perennial forces that have shaped the past as they will the future'.[29]

(4) Universal *moral principles* do not guide state behaviour, though state behaviour will certainly have moral and ethical implications. Individuals are influenced by moral codes, but states are not moral agents. Any attempt

to explain the international behaviour of states should not, therefore, concentrate on the stated moral principles which are said to underpin the conduct of foreign policy. Whereas ethical behaviour is judged according to whether it conforms with a set of moral principles, political behaviour is evaluated according to the political consequences which ensue: there is a tension between moral action and the expedient requirements of political action. Prudential behaviour based on a judicious assessment of the consequences arising out of alternative political choices is the guiding law for realists.

(5) There is no *universally* agreed set of moral principles. Though states from time to time will endeavour to clothe their behaviour in ethical terms (human rights advocacy), the use of moral language to justify external behaviour is designed to confer advantage, legitimacy and further the national interests of the state. It ought not to be mistaken for political motives which in reality are restricted to the pursuit of interest defined in terms of power. Universal moral principles are not a reliable guide to state behaviour. When states proclaim these universal principles they are merely projecting their *particular* national or cultural codes onto the world as a whole. 'Interest is the perennial standard by which political action must be judged and directed'.[30]

(6) Intellectually, the political sphere is *autonomous* from every other sphere of human concern, whether they be legal, moral or economic. This enables us to see the international domain as analytically distinct from other fields of intellectual inquiry, with its own standards of thought and criteria for the analysis and evaluation of state behaviour (interest defined in terms of power). Key questions such as 'how does this policy affect the power of the nation?' are central to the concerns of this autonomous sphere of intellectual analysis.

Like Carr's account, Morgenthau's principles of political realism reflected the intellectual mood of the age. They were designed as an antidote to liberal utopianism which was widely held to be responsible for shaping the intellectual climate as Europe drifted towards the Second World War. For Morgenthau, international politics was a struggle for power between states: the pursuit of national interests was a normal, unavoidable and desirable activity. Above everything else, Morgenthau wanted to attack the idea that any state could attempt to universalise its own particular moral and ethical principles. This was reckless utopianism which breached the laws of politics. Although there were certain moral goals which mankind should aspire to, the exigencies of world politics render it difficult, if not futile, to attempt to realise them.[31] Human nature, however imperfect, is fixed and ought to be accepted for what it is rather than what it might be. To the extent that it can be maintained for long periods of time, peace can only be realised when the rational pursuit of power by statesmen acting according to the laws of politics is more widely understood. Radical changes to the international system will be doomed to failure and might possibly be counter-productive, if they challenge the 'laws of politics'.

Realists such as Morgenthau spoke with an air of certainty about politics because they believed it to be governed by immutable laws, 'deriving either from human nature itself, or from the dynamics of inter-state competition'.[32] After all, the concept of interest defined as power 'imposes discipline upon the observer' and 'infuses rational order into the subject matter of politics'.[33] It provides us with unshakeable knowledge about how states will behave. For Morgenthau, national interests are permanent conditions which provide policy makers with a rational guide to action: they are fixed, politically bipartisan and always transcend changes in government. They are 'a fact to be discovered rather than a matter of contingent and constructed preferences'.[34]

The 'national interest ... is not defined by the whim of a man or the partisanship of party but imposes itself as an objective datum upon all men applying their rational faculties to the conduct of foreign policy'.[35] Peace, on the other hand, is never a permanent feature of the international system. It is merely a temporary truce based on a rough equilibrium of state power, between inevitable periods of tension and conflict. The balance of power system is an essential stabilising factor in international relations, and the best way of managing the tendency for states to accumulate strategic power.

It is usually taken for granted that realists regard the nation-state as the primary actor in international politics, however neither Carr nor Morgenthau regarded it as the final expression of political community. Writing in 1970, Morgenthau anticipated that the forces of globalisation would render the nation-state 'no longer valid' and soon 'obsolete'. The impact of 'nuclear power, together with modern technologies of transportation and communications, which transcends the ability of any nation-state to control and harness it and render it both innocuous and beneficial, requires a principle of political organisation transcending the nation-state'.[36] It was time to think of 'novel structures and types of organization' such as a 'supranational community and a world government, a political organization and structure that transcend the nation-state'.[37] The openness of this argument stands in stark contrast to the stereotypical image of realism as simply the conservative realm of recurrence and repetition. Clearly neither Carr nor Morgenthau was wedded to the idea of the nation-state as an indefinite fixture on the international landscape, a position which distinguishes them from their neo-realist successors.

Morgenthau's approach to international relations has been attacked from a number of directions. His infatuation with positivism and empirical science is not surprising, given that at the time of writing *Politics Among Nations* (1948), the natural sciences (particularly in the areas of physics, biology and chemistry) appeared to be providing humankind with a degree of mastery over nature. If science could subdue the natural world, perhaps

its methodology could do the same for international relations? As behaviourists, critical theorists and post-modernists would later demonstrate,
many questions have been raised over the application of scientific methodology to the social domain. Does the social aspect of the international
world really lend itself to being understood in terms of enduring, objective
laws and certainties? Just how authoritative is the scientific method and is it
relevant to the complexities of international relations?

Morgenthau's realism was based on *a priori* assumptions about human
nature (the rational pursuit of self-interest, utility maximisation, and so on)
which by definition cannot be tested or verified to any meaningful extent.
He makes a number of claims about the biological basis of the human drive
for power and domination, without explaining other aspects of the human
condition which are not as egoistic. What if these assumptions are flawed or
do not conform in any actual sense to a shared reality? How can altruism be
explained?[38]

What are the implications for Morgenthau's thesis if there are no laws of
politics at all, only subjective impressions? What happens to Morgenthau's
thesis if, as post-modernists claim, there is no 'objective truth' or if there is
no simple division between 'truth and rationality' on one hand and 'prejudice and subjective preference' on the other? Morgenthau's world is a
very limited one. He sees strengths in a dispassionate and amoral approach
to international relations when this may be little more than a cover for and
rationalisation of immoral and unethical behaviour.

Morgenthau's treatment of Marxism is paltry and ungenerous. His critique of theories of imperialism is simplistic and hostile. He largely ignores
economic considerations in the formulation of foreign policy and says very
little about the nature of capitalism and its effects on the international order.
He assumes the nation-state is a unitary actor but is uninterested in its
internal social or ideological nature, including the composition of its commercial and state elites. Other international actors, such as non-governmental authorities and international markets, are almost entirely neglected.
And though he rejects the prescriptive elements of liberal idealism
(utopianism), his message about the immutability of the 'laws of politics'
appears equally prescriptive, if not dogmatic. He also stands accused of a
masculine bias.[39]

Kenneth Waltz parts company with what he calls the 'traditional realism'
of Morgenthau by arguing that international politics can be thought of as a
system with a precisely defined structure. Realism, in his view, is unable to
conceptualise the international system in this way because it is limited by its
behavioural methodology which 'explains political outcomes through examining the constituent parts of political systems'. According to this approach, 'the characteristics and the interactions of behavioural units are
taken to be the direct cause of political events'.[40] Morgenthau explains
international outcomes by focussing on the actions and interactions of the

units – the principles of human nature, the idea of interest defined in terms of power, the behaviour of statesmen – rather than highlighting the systemic constraints of international politics. He infers political outcomes from 'the salient attributes of the actors producing them' and ignores the effects of structure on state behaviour. According to Waltz traditional realists could not explain behaviour at a level above the nation-state – theirs is an endogenous account.[41] Whereas Morgenthau argued that power is rooted in the nature of humankind, Waltz points to the anarchical condition of the international realm which he claims imposes the accumulation of power as a systemic requirement on states. The former explanation relies on a particular understanding of human nature to explain conflict in international politics. The latter abandons such a reliance, preferring to treat the international system as a separate domain which conditions the behaviour of all states within it.

Morgenthau sought to create a guidebook for students and statesmen at a time when existing conventions and understandings about the international order were under challenge. He wanted to instil certainty into the field of international politics by providing an interpretative guide which would help us to 'look over the shoulder' of a statesman, enabling us to 'read and anticipate his very thoughts'.[42] The extent of his success can be measured by the fact that *Politics Among Nations* is regularly re-printed and still widely used by students of statecraft.

Problems with Traditional Realism

The realist school, as its name suggests, formulated their views in reaction to the liberal utopians of the 1920s and 1930s. Whereas liberals had called for the repudiation of power politics as a feature of international behaviour, realists saw power politics as a necessary and endemic feature of all relationships between sovereign states. Realists drew attention to the reality of conflict in international relations, and the lessons to be learnt from its cyclical and recurrent patterns. Unlike the idealists, realists stressed the positive functions of those features of international diplomacy normally associated with 'power politics' – state sovereignty, the balance of power and limited war.

Although realists were not the first to think and write about international relations, they were the first to offer a comprehensive account of the international system in practice. In the sense that it 'codifies practice', realism can therefore be considered the other foundational theory of the discipline. In the two decades following the first World War, when serious debates about the appropriate forms of the discipline took place, there was a growing awareness that the purpose of the study should be to develop generalisations about patterns of behaviour in international relations, and to emphasise recurring phenomena rather than unique events. The early realists brought to the fledgling discipline a variety of experiences and intellectual antecedents which contributed significantly to the theoretical longevity of the discourse. In the United States, Hans Morgenthau, Arnold Wolfers, Klaus Knorr and Henry Kissinger were European émigrés who 'suffered at first hand the operations of unchecked power operating in support of an alien value system'.[43] E. H. Carr was alternately an historian and diplomat, whose twenty years in the British foreign service included membership of that country's 1919 peace delegation to what he later called the 'fiasco' of the Versailles negotiations. George Kennan was also an academic, but who as a senior US diplomat in Moscow during the 1950s was credited with responsibility for the authorship of the Truman Administration's policy of 'containment'.

Realists defined their own position in opposition to what Carr called 'utopian liberal internationalism' and the 'moralism' of creating a model of the international system which, however desirable, took little account of the realities of power. A number of incontrovertible assumptions formed the basis of their approach. The first concerned the primacy of the state. The modern nation-state was seen as the most viable existing form of political organisation: conceptions of national sovereignty were regarded as the 'natural' political condition of humankind. Consequently, the international system was considered 'anarchical' – that is, without an overarching authority to regulate the behaviour of nation-states.[44] International law was regarded sceptically, particularly if states believed that it infringed on their capacity to pursue their national interests. For realists, a state's assertion of its sovereignty, and its concomitant claim for protection under the doctrine of non-intervention, came before any right the international community might assert for intervention in 'the internal affairs' of that state. Furthermore, realists argued that states are the primary actors in international relations because they retain a monopoly on the legitimate use of violence.

As a result of a growing commonality of views and methodological approaches to the subject matter in its early years, International Relations was constituted as a discrete field of study concerned with the strategic and diplomatic behaviour of states. Contemporaneously, realism, which concerned itself with concepts such as sovereignty, the state, diplomacy, the balance of power and the causes of war, established itself as the discipline's leading discourse. In the first two decades after the Second World War the discipline and realism were widely regarded as one and the same thing.

Foundational texts such as those by Carr and Morgenthau ensured that realism would be concerned with a number of specific empirical and normative preoccupations, including: (a) sovereign states are both the primary actors and basic units of analysis; (b) inter-state behaviour takes place in an environment of ungoverned anarchy; and (c) the behaviour of states can be understood 'rationally' as the pursuit of power defined as interest. Taken collectively, these central concerns indicated an acceptance (however reluctant) of the present structure and operation of international relations: there was no point in denying its underlying 'reality'. Realism was an argument from necessity, based on the pursuit of national interest revealed by 'the evidence of history as our minds reflect it'.[45] It offered an account of the reproduction of the states-system, and in the sense that it contributed to the perpetuation of the international system by providing it with an intellectual rationale, realism obstructed paths to alternative historical developments. It persuasively explained why international politics was never likely to resemble liberal democratic orders.

Marxists have argued from this that realism is primarily concerned with the reinforcement and reproduction of capitalist relations of production, at both the domestic and international levels, and that the system of states structurally supports this mode of production. It is sometimes argued that there is a link between realism and ruling class interests in leading industrial societies.

The difficulty with this line of argument is establishing why capitalism specifically requires a states-system and could not operate globally with some alternative form of international organisation, and why a self-proclaimed 'revolutionary state' such as the Soviet Union became an leading agent for the reproduction of the states-system. It is perhaps helpful, then, to distinguish between realism as an intended expression of dominant class interests (a Marxist contention) and realism as an ideology which has the unintended consequence of preserving structures which favour such interests. Realism may well play a significant role in reproducing a world order which favours dominant classes. Cox's point that realism may be criticised for its failure to recognise how its contribution to international stability preserves social and economic inequalities within and between societies, is therefore more relevant than an axiomatic alignment between realism as a discourse for ruling class ideology.

Linked with this argument is the additional criticism that, in its concern with continuity and a logic of reproduction, realism has neglected the existence of a logic of change, though as we have noted neither Carr nor Morgenthau discount the eventual possibility of alternative structures in the international system. However, in suggesting that we 'must work *with* rather than against immutable forces inherent in human nature' (Morgenthau), that the laws of politics are 'impervious to our preferences' (Morgenthau), that the function of thinking is to study a sequence of events which we are 'powerless to influence or alter' (Carr), and that wisdom lies in 'accepting and adapting oneself' to the 'irresistible strength of existing forces and tendencies' (Carr), realism is nevertheless militating against structural change in the international system. It is effectively stifling the possibility of transforming, or at least renovating international relations by encouraging us to resign ourselves to the present.

Realism maintains that the search for power and security is the dominant logic in global politics, and that states as the primary actors in the arena have no choice but to accumulate the means of violence in the pursuit of self preservation: the 'international' is a self-help system. In a more recent study, Waltz draws the distinction between 'reductionist' and 'systemic' theories of international relations to emphasise the possibility of abstracting the states system or strategic interaction as 'a domain apart' from analyses that link foreign policy exclusively with the internal social and economic characteristics of states. Thus for neo-realists, the specific internal structure of states is largely irrelevant to their international behaviour. What is crucial in this 'systemic' approach is the state's location in the global power configuration. This is not to imply, however, that the pursuit of physical security through violence is completely unregulated. Through the skilful use of the balance of power, states can regulate their propensity for violence by maintaining strategic equilibrium between the major powers. According to realists, this can reduce, though not eliminate the incidence of war.

Clearly, if there is an identifiable ideology associated with realism it is the more general idea of conservatism.[46] Or, as Buzan puts it, realism is 'the natural home of those disposed towards conservative ideology'.[47] Ostensibly, realism purports to aim at an accurate representation of the 'reality' of global politics as opposed to a way of thinking in which some higher state is imagined or recommended as a course of action (idealism). In actual fact, realism can be both a conduit for and an expression of conservative ideology. As has been pointed out, realism seeks to resist change and foreclose alternative political practices.[48] How it encourages this process is more obvious when we look closely at its value system, ideas, and nomenclature.

The language of realism is said to be ideologically encoded. And yet one of the most powerful factors sustaining the dominance of realism has been the capacity of its authors to project the realist nomenclature (system of states, balance of power, strategy, stability, deterrence, national interest) as politically neutral and non-ideological: the language of realism has largely become the language of International Relations.[49] To some this may not be surprising, after all realism seeks to describe 'reality'. However, it is significant that the discipline's reference points come from one theoretical approach because ideology and values are transmitted through language. Through the selection of 'appropriate words', realists ask us to consider their theory as commonsense, normal and neutral.[50] Decoding the language of realism, however, reveals what some theorists regard as a value-laden dialogue which uses a vast array of lexical and grammatical devices to conceal an ideologically conservative predisposition. Its critics argue that even a rudimentary textual analysis exposes the manner in which realism fixes the domain of debate in International Relations. As Rothstein has argued,

> [realism] has fostered a set of attitudes that predisposed its followers to think about international politics in a particularly narrow and ethnocentric fashion, and to set very clear bounds around the kind of policies which it seemed reasonable to contemplate.[51]

Realism is concerned with the reproduction of the international system of states. It uses notions of order, stability, deterrence and especially the balance of power, to convey its message of constraint and to reify the structure of the international system.[52] At the same time it marginalises those theories offering alternative or contradictory accounts of the 'reality' of world politics.

Neo-realism

According to Stephen Krasner,

> Realism is a theory about international politics. It is an effort to explain both the behaviour of individual states and the characteristics of the system as a whole. The ontological given for realism is that sovereign states are the constitutive components of the international system. Sovereignty is a political order based on territorial control. The international system is anarchical. It is a self-help system. There is no higher authority that can constrain or channel the behaviour of states. Sovereign states are rational self-seeking actors resolutely if not exclusively concerned with relative gains because they must function in an anarchical environment in which their security and well-being ultimately rest on their ability to mobilise their own resources against external threats.[53]

Krasner's summary is an accurate if brief description of neo-realism, a modern variant of the broader realist tradition which emerged on the eve of the Second Cold War, partly as a response to the challenges posed by interdependency theory and partly as a restatement of the importance bipolarity and systemic factors in international politics. In the sub-discipline of international political economy, Robert Gilpin and Stephen Krasner sought to reclaim a role for the state in a world where transnational economic players threatened to undermine its primacy. Ideas such as 'regimes' and 'hegemonic stability theory' were invented to demonstrate the continuing importance of the nation-state in the world economy.[54] As we shall see these ideas also formed the basis of a challenge to neo-liberalism's advocacy of economic globalisation.

Waltz

In the more traditional provinces of International Relations, Kenneth Waltz has attempted to bring what he sees as the scientific and methodological rigour of disciplines such a anthropology and economics to the study of international politics. Waltz's 'neo-realism' or 'structural realism' is both a critique of traditional realism and a substantial intellectual extension of a theoretical tradition which was in danger of being outflanked by rapid changes to the contours of global politics. Waltz presents a more sophisticated theory than his predecessors in the realist tradition, to the extent that his account has often been referred to as occupying a position of intellectual hegemony in the discipline.

The nature of theory

A number of criticisms of Waltz's neo-realism centre on the charge that he has not produced an all encompassing account of international politics: there are said to be too many holes or omissions in his theory. However, according to Waltz his critics 'fail to understand that a theory is not a statement about everything that is important in international political life, but rather a necessarily slender explanatory construct'.[55] A number of his critics appear to have failed to understand Waltz's conception of theory, in particular his belief that theory is necessarily abstract and deliberately artificial.

Waltz cites the gains made in the understanding of political economy by the physiocrats of the seventeenth and eighteenth centuries. They were able to make important advances in their understanding of economic growth and prosperity because they invented the concept of *the economy* as distinct from the society and polity. The artificial demarcation of the economy meant that specific economic forces could be isolated and properly understood. For Waltz, this is the great value of the theoretical process. Theory is a tool which makes the task of intellectual explanation possible. Without theory all we are left with are disconnected and randomly selected facts which tell us very little about the subject of our inquiry. According to Waltz, a theory is an intellectual construction in which we select facts and interpret them. The challenge is to bring theory to bear on facts in ways that permit explanation and prediction. That can only be achieved by distinguishing between theory and fact.[56]

The process of theorising is therefore deliberately contrived, or as Waltz puts it, 'theory is artifice'. It becomes possible only 'if various objects and processes, movements and events, acts and interactions, are viewed as forming a domain that can be studied in its own right'.[57] The physiocrats were not claiming that an economy actually exists in isolation from society and polity, but that by treating it that way for the purpose of intellectual inquiry, it was possible to make 'radical advances' that might not otherwise have been made. By adopting this approach the rationality of human motives and the laws of supply and demand were discovered and then used as assumptions upon which broader theoretical constructions were built.

A theory selects and organises facts, processes and relationships into a separate domain so that importance and significance can be identified. The isolation of one domain from another in order to study it is artificial, but this is an intellectual strength rather than a weakness. Although the effect of such as process is to simplify complex forces and relationships, this is the only way meaningful explanations can be reached. Accordingly, Waltz applied the same approach to the study of international relations. His 'structural realism' argues that 'by depicting an international political system as a whole, with structural and unit levels at once distinct and connected, neo-realism establishes the autonomy of international politics and thus makes a theory about it possible'.[58] If the state-system is considered as a 'domain apart' from domestic considerations such as dominant ideology, religion, mode of production and social organisation, it becomes possible to make advances in our understanding of the nature of international relations. The idea that international politics can understood as a system with a precisely defined and separate structure is both the starting point for international theory and Waltz's point of departure from traditional realism.[59] As with the approach of the physiocrats to political economy, the abstraction of the international system as a 'domain apart' by neo-realists is an equivalent distortion of reality, but it is similarly necessary to delineate the central forces and principles of international politics.

For Waltz, a theory applies – or can be useful for prediction – 'when the conditions the theory contemplates are in effect'. Regardless of time and place, whenever a system is characterised by the same conditions – the reality of a self-help world in an anarchical environment – we should expect similar behavioural responses from the actors in that environment, the nation-states.[60]

Realism and neo-realism

The key question which Waltz poses and then proceeds to answer is: why do states exhibit similar foreign policy behaviour despite their different political systems and contrasting ideologies? Waltz cites the example of superpower behaviour during the Cold War to refute the argument that it is possible to infer the condition of international politics from the internal composition of states. The Soviet Union and the United States comprised quite different, if not antithetical political and social orders. And yet as

Waltz points out, their behaviour during the period of East–West tension is remarkably similar. Their pursuit of military power and influence, their competition for strategic advantage and the exploitation of their respective spheres of influence were strikingly parallel. The explanation, says Waltz, may be found in the systemic constraints on each state rather than their internal composition. These systemic forces homogenise foreign policy behaviour by interposing themselves between states and their diplomatic conduct. The identification of these systemic forces is perhaps neo-realism's single greatest contribution to international theory.

Waltz advances beyond what he calls 'traditional realism' by arguing that international politics may be thought of as a system with a precisely defined structure.[61] Realism was unable to conceptualise the international system in this way because it was limited by its behaviourist methodology which 'explains political outcomes through examining the constituent parts of political systems'. By this logic, 'the characteristics and the interactions of behavioural units are taken to be the direct cause of political events'.[62] Morgenthau attempted to understand and explain international outcomes by examining the actions and interactions of the units – the principles of human nature, the idea of interest defined in terms of power, the behaviour of statesmen – rather than focusing on the systemic constraints of international politics. He inferred political outcomes from 'the salient attributes of the actors producing them' and ignored the important effects of structure.

As Waltz argues, 'realists cannot handle causation at a level above states because they fail to conceive of structure as a force that shapes and shoves the units'.[63] Whereas realists such as Morgenthau argued that power is rooted in the nature of humankind, neo-realists such as Waltz point to the anarchical condition of the international realm which imposes the accumulation of power as a systemic requirement on states. The former account relies on a particular understanding of human nature to explain conflict in international politics, always a difficult approach to substantiate. The latter abandons such a reliance on reductionism, preferring to treat the international system as a separate domain which conditions the behaviour of all states within it.

Units and structure

Before examining exactly what Waltz understands by 'structure' and the nature of the international 'system', it is important to consider what he is rejecting. Waltz's concern with traditional realism is the same as his reservations with liberal and Marxist accounts of international relations, which he labels 'second image' or 'second level' explanations in his earlier work and 'reductionist' in his most detailed analysis.[64] Waltz rejects 'unit-level' theories because they attempt to explain the whole (the global system) by examining the interactions of its parts (domestic orders). These 'reductionist' approaches assume there is a direct link between the intentions of individual actors such as nation-states, and the results of their actions. What they fail to recognise are the structural conditions which belong to the international system, which impose themselves on all the units, and which therefore ultimately determine the outcomes of the interactions between states. Other theories err by explaining the behaviour of states at the unit level rather than at the system level. Realists emphasise human nature and the intentions of statesmen, liberals stress the importance of democracy and free trade, and Marxists highlight the class struggle between capital and labour. All ignore the overriding importance of the international system which comes between the intentions of states and the results of their interactions.

For the purpose of explaining its determining properties and distinguishing it from domestic political systems, Waltz believes the international system has a precisely defined structure with three important characteristics. These are (1) the ordering principle of the system, (2) the character of the units in the system, and (3) the distribution of the capabilities of the units in the system.[65]

In domestic political systems the ordering principle is hierarchic, with power and authority exerted through the compulsory jurisdiction of political and legal processes. The ordering principle of the international system is anarchic, with an absence of any overarching authority regulating the behaviour of nation-states towards each other. Nation-states, unlike individuals in domestic society, exist in a self-help environment where the quest for survival requires them to seek security through the accretion of military power. This security dilemma is common to all states, regardless of their domestic cultural or political complexions. In other words, the ordering principle of the international system forces states to perform exactly the same primary function regardless of their capacity to do so. In the process they become 'socialised' into behaviour which centres on mutual distrust, self reliance and the pursuit of security through the accumulation of the means to wage war against each other. This socialisation to the system of power politics occurs even to non-conformist states with revolutionary regimes, because a refusal to play the political game may risk their own destruction.[66] According to Waltz, the anarchical nature of the international system has been its ordering principle for several centuries, a pattern in international relations which has withstood the extraordinary changes to the internal composition of nation-states in recent years.[67]

According to Waltz, the character of the units in the system are identical or, to put in another way, all states in the international system are made functionally similar by the constraints of structure. The anarchic realm imposes a discipline on states: they are all required to pursue security before they can perform any other functions. In fact their concern about their own survival conditions much of their behaviour. However, although they are functionally similar, states differ vastly in their capabilities. There is an unequal and constantly shifting distribution of power across the international system. States 'are alike in the tasks that they face, though not in their abilities to perform them. The differences are of capability, not of function'.[68] The capacity of each state to pursue and achieve these common objectives varies according to their placement in the international system, and specifically their relative power. As a key to understanding the behaviour of states, the distribution of power in the international system overrides consideration of ideology or any other internal factor. Hence the important distinction neo-realists make between great and small powers.

Criticisms

As Linklater has pointed out, a major problem with Waltz's unit-structure relationship is that it leaves little or no room for systemic change induced by the units themselves.[69] Waltz is convinced that states are virtually powerless to alter the system in which they find themselves trapped, though he concedes that under certain conditions 'virtuosos' can resist the constraints of structure.[70] While this argument allows him to explain the persistence and longevity of the international system, it is by definition hostile to the idea that the system can be fundamentally altered by the states which comprise it. There is a contradiction and a weakness here. On the one hand Waltz argues that the values, ethics and moral aspirations of states are thwarted by the systemic constraint of anarchy. On the other he concedes to the arguments of liberal internationalists such as Doyle that 'on external as well as on internal grounds, I hope that more countries will become demo-cratic', which suggests that states can limit the influence of structure by changing their internal dispositions.[71] He appears too willing to discount the character of the units in the system. It may be that structure is simply not as important in conditioning state behaviour as Waltz would have us believe and that the system-level properties are not as historically immu-table as he suggests. This criticism would be in line with constructivist claims that anarchy itself is the creation of states, and not a given which states are powerless to alter.[72]

Waltz also denies that greater levels of economic interdependency amongst states pose a threat to the condition of anarchy, despite Rosecran-ce's claim that the 'trading state' is displacing the 'military state' in the contemporary world because competition for global market shares has become more important than territorial conquest.[73] Nevertheless it is clear that the use of force has become counter-productive in the post-Second World War period because it threatens the stability of the global trading and finance system, despite neo-realist incantations about strategic primacy. Doyle's argument that liberal democracies have transcended their violent instincts – and the insecurities engendered by anarchy – and have learnt to resolve their differences peacefully, is relevant here. The pacification of a core of liberal democracies and the increasing number of states choosing liberal-democratic orders poses a challenge for neo-realism's contention that the units can do little to alter the structure of the system.[74] Similarly, the apparent pacification of great power relations in the post-Cold War period is a significant trend in world politics that neo-realists could not acknowledge.

Waltz also discounts the rationalist view that though it is anarchic in structure, the international system is also normatively regulated. The idea of international society with common interests and values, rules and institutions, where conflict is mollified by mutually recognised requirements for co-existence undermines the neo-realist view that states are incapable of altruistic behaviour. Waltz appears to be suggesting that states cannot widen their conception of self-interest beyond the egoism of strategic interaction, despite the gains that can be made through co-operation, submission to the rules of a diplomatic culture, and membership of international organisations. For him, states will not subordinate the pursuit of their national interests for the sake of international order. Even the growing recognition of universal values such as humanitarianism, which occasionally overrides the sanctity of national sovereignty, has no apparent transformative potential for the system.

The epistemological critiques of neo-realism by Ashley and Cox expose the conservative ideology which underwrites Waltz's theoretical approach.[75] Both adopt a critical approach to neo-realism, highlighting the extent to which it naturalises or reifies the international system by treating structures which have a specific and transitory history as if they were 'permanent', 'normal' or 'given' political fixtures. This not only has the effect of legitimising the status quo, it also occludes arguments for alternative forms of political community which are more sensitive to changing social and ethnic identities and the exclusionary character of political boundaries. As Linklater argues, by emphasising recurrence and repetition in the international system, 'neo-realism cannot envisage a form of statecraft which transcends the calculus of power and control'.[76] Cox places neo-realism in the category of 'problem-solving theory' which 'takes the world as it finds it, with the prevailing social and political relations and institutions into which they are organised, as the given framework for action. The general aim of problem-solving theory is to make these relationships and institutions work smoothly by dealing effectively with particular sources of trouble'.[77] Problem-solving theory fails to question the pattern of relationships and institutions in question and can 'fix limits or parameters to a problem area' which in turn limits 'the number of variables which are amenable to relatively close and precise examination'.[78] For Cox, neo-realism reduces international relations to great power management by legitimating the very political order it is describing – one which favours the powerful and is hostile to change.

Critical theory, on the other hand, 'stands apart from the prevailing order of the world and asks how that order came about. Critical theory, unlike problem-solving theory, does not take institutions and social and power relations for granted but calls them into question by concerning itself with their origins and how and whether they might be in the process of changing. It is directed towards an appraisal of the very framework of action ... which problem-solving theory accepts as its parameters'. Whereas problem-solving theory is 'a guide to tactical actions which, intended or unintended, sustain the existing order', critical theory provides a 'a guide to strategic action for bringing about an alternative order'.[79] This is an approach which would directly undermine neo-realism's confidence in recurrence, repetition, and the cyclical pattern of international politics.

Structural realism

In parallel with Waltz's approach, Barry Buzan, Richard Little and Charles Jones have developed a structural realist approach which has already passed through three phases, from an early articulation of structural principles,[80] to an engagement between realism and the idea of international society as proposed by English rationalists such as Hedley Bull,[81] and most recently a marriage of IR theory and world history.[82]

Structural realism has made a significant contribution as both a sympathetic critique of Waltz's neorealism (a rejection of Waltz's narrow understanding of structure) and as a reminder of the need to synthesise orthodox international theory with world history, a long overdue and badly neglected task. However, it is the movement of the structural realist position towards the approach adopted by the English school of rationalists such as Hedley Bull and Martin Wight, which is arguably its most significant and theoretically interesting achievement.

According to Buzan, structural realism and its IPE 'sister' regime theory, contain assumptions about anarchy, the centrality of the state and the interactions of states, which are not inconsistent with the idea of an emerging international society. In what he describes as a 'functional account', Buzan maps the relationship between international systems and international society, and concludes that the need states have to develop rules, conventions, forms of mutual recognition and communication – in other words the need for order – is consistent with the moulding effects of systemic pressures. 'International societies [are] ... a natural product of the shoving and shaping forces of anarchy', a conclusion that Waltz could only half agree with.[83] This is an important concession for realists to make because it raises the possibility of levels of co-operation between states which have previously been dismissed as impractical.

By opening up a dialogue of this kind, structural realism not only rescues English rationalists from charges that it is 'history-bound' and doesn't have enough to say about contemporary international politics, it also helps modern realism shed some of the sterility and inflexibility associated with its emphasis on the anarchical condition of the global system. The complementarities of structural realism and English rationalism blur the lines between previously antagonistic approaches, expanding the possibilities for future research agendas.

Responses to Globalisation and Unipolarity

Contemporary economic and technological developments – grouped under the rubric 'globalisation' – are transforming the nature of international politics, and pose a number of challenges to realist thought. Cross border capital flows, trade liberalisation, the privatisation of government-owned enterprises, deregulation and the need to maintain economies open to foreign investment, are seen as both evidence of the dominance of neo-liberalism since the 1970s and the decline of state power.

Furthermore, the rising importance of non-state actors such as transnational corporations and the foreign investment community are said to not only endanger national economic sovereignty but, according to liberals, are also evidence of the growing interdependence of the world's economies and the commensurate pacification of international relations. To many liberals, globalisation and the promise of a 'borderless world' represents not only a change in the nature of diplomacy but also to the very structure of the international system.

Unsurprisingly, these developments, and the ideas which underpin them, represent a major challenge to realist thinking. However, only very recently have neo-realists such as Waltz, Krasner and Gilpin responded to the neo-liberal challenge. Their rebuttal has a number of separate components to it, but can be summarised in Krasner's claim that 'there is no evidence that globalisation has systematically undermined state control or led to the homogenisation of policies and structures. In fact, globalisation and state activity have moved in tandem'.[84]

First, neo-realists are sceptical of the extent to which economic globalisation is a truly global phenomenon. They point to Africa, Latin America, Russia and the Middle East as significant regions of the world which have been relatively untouched by the forces of globalisation. Globalisation remains predominantly a Western experience.[85]

Secondly, if trade or capital flows are measured as a percentage of Gross National Product, the level of economic interdependence in the world in 1999 approximately equals that of 1910. The figure is even lower if interdependence is measured by the mobility of labour, and lower still if measured by the mutual military dependence of states. Neo-realists are therefore unimpressed by claims made about the unprecedented levels of contemporary economic interdependence in the world.[86] They are willing to concede that money markets specifically, have been truly globalised as a result to the Nixon shocks of the 1970s and advances in information technology. As a consequence there has been a loss of state autonomy and control in this area. However, they also point out that financial markets in 1900 were at least as integrated as they are now.[87] And capital flows in the nineteenth century as a percentage of global economic product were far greater than current levels.[88]

Thirdly, in response to the liberal claim that only the market model will produce sustained levels of prosperity, Waltz reminds liberals that in the 1930s and 1950s, growth rates in the USSR were among the world's highest, as was Japan's in the 1970s and 1980s when a model of corporate mercantilism was practised. Historically a 'one size fits all' model of political economy, now called the 'Washington consensus', has not been the only route to economic modernisation or successful growth.

The anti-statism of neo-liberalism is also difficult to justify. Liberals forget or ignore the fact that 'states perform essential political, social and economic functions, and no other organisation rivals them in these respects. … States turn possession into property and thus make saving, production and prosperity possible. The sovereign state with fixed borders has proved to be the best organisation for keeping peace internally and fostering the conditions for economic well-being'.[89] It is important to remember the political underpinnings of globalisation and its management in any discussion of the virtues of a market economy.[90]

Neo-realists remind liberals that as a preferred form of political community, the nation-state has no serious rival. They can cite a number of important powers retained by the state despite globalisation, including monopoly control of the weapons of war and their legitimate use, and the sole right to tax its citizens. Only the nation-state can still command the political allegiances of its citizens or adjudicate in disputes between them. And it is the nation-state which has the exclusive authority to bind the whole community to international law. As Krasner argues, not all the constituent parts of a nation-state's sovereignty are equally vulnerable to globalisation.[91]

Fourthly, economic activity is not as global as some liberals would have us believe. The largest economies continue to conduct most of their business in their home markets – 90 per cent of the US economy, for example, produces goods and services for Americans rather than the export market.

The figure is similar in leading European economies. And if judged in terms of where assets, management, ownership, headquarters and R & D funding is principally located, transnational corporations are not as global as first thought. Despite their popular image, they remain largely anchored at home.[92]

Finally, as one would expect, neo-realists regard the military power of states as being far more important in conditioning international politics than economic globalisation. 'The most important events in international politics are explained by differences in the capabilities of states, not by economic forces operating across states or transcending them'. High levels of economic interdependence early last century failed to prevent the First World War, nor did economic integration forestall the break-up of Yugoslavia at the end of the century. When it comes to inhibiting conflict, neo-realists are in no doubt that nuclear weapons are more effective than shared economic interests. 'The uneven distribution of capabilities continues to be the key to understanding international politics'.[93]

The danger of unipolarity

Neo-realists such as Waltz and Mearsheimer are profoundly disturbed by the collapse of Soviet strategic power in the 1990s. If mutual nuclear deterrence between the United States and the Soviet Union accounted for the high level of international stability in the post-war period, the end of bipolarity casts an ominous shadow over the present world order. 'In a system of balanced states, the domination by one or some of them has in the past been prevented by the reactions of others acting as a counterweight'. For one state to remain predominant is 'a position without precedent in modern history'.[94] As Waltz concedes, 'in international politics, unbalanced power constitutes a danger even when it is American power that is out of balance'.[95] Unlike liberals, neo-realists are pessimistic about the prospects for peace in the new, unipolar world.

Waltz and Mearsheimer stress the importance of strategic capabilities in shaping the contours of international relations. For them, the distribution and character of military power remain the root causes of war and peace.[96] Instead of highlighting the spread of liberal democracy and a concomitant zone of peace, they regard the rapid demise of bipolarity as the single most dramatic change in contemporary world politics. 'The main difference between international politics now and earlier is not found in the increased interdependence of states but in their growing inequality. With the end of bipolarity, the distribution of capabilities among states has become extremely lopsided. Rather than elevating economic forces and depressing political ones, the inequalities of international politics enhance the political role of one country. Politics as usual prevails over economics'.[97]

The pacification of the core, while desirable and perhaps even encouraging, is merely a transient stage which is likely to be superseded by a restoration of the strategic balance amongst the great powers. Echoing Carr's critique of liberal utopianism on the eve of the Second World War, Waltz believes that the 'peace and justice' which liberals claim is spreading beyond the central core 'will be defined to the liking of the powerful'.[98] Current circumstances cannot be sustained indefinitely. 'The present condition of international politics is unnatural. Both the predominance of America and, one may hope, the militarisation of international affairs will diminish with time'.[99]

According to Waltz and Mearsheimer, the recurrent features of international relations, most notably the struggle for power and security, will reassert themselves: 'in international politics, overwhelming power repels and leads others to try to balance against it'.[100] According to Mearsheimer, the long peace of the Cold War was a result of three factors: the bipolar distribution of military power in continental Europe, the rough equality of military power between the United States and the Soviet Union, and the pacifying effect of the presence of nuclear weapons.[101] The collapse of the Soviet Union removes the central pillar upon which the bipolar stability was built. Multipolar systems, on the other hand, are notoriously less stable than bipolar systems because the number of potential bilateral conflicts is greater, deterrence is more difficult to achieve, and the potential for misunderstandings and miscalculations of power and motive is increased.[102] Unipolar systems are even more precarious.

Conclusion

The strength of the realist tradition is its capacity to argue from necessity. It seeks to describe reality, solve problems and understand the continuities of world politics. To accomplish this task it invokes a philosophical tradition, with Hobbes, Rousseau, Machiavelli re-employed to provide the theory with the authority of classicism. By reclaiming its intellectual antecedents realism again emphasises its timelessness and the importance of continuity in theoretical research. A normative concern with the causes of war and the conditions of peace, security and order will continue to guide research and teaching in International Relations because they are centrally important issues. Realism speaks to these concerns directly by privileging strategic interaction and the distribution of global power above other considerations. It explains the inevitably of competition and conflict between states by highlighting the insecure and anarchical nature of the international environment.

Neo-realism provides a convincing account of why the foreign policies of nation-states are so familiar, despite their very diverse internal natures. It also provides a more sophisticated explanation for the persistence of the international system. However, it exaggerates the autonomy states enjoy from their domestic conditions, overstates the importance of structure and underestimates the potential for states to transform the international system. Neo-realism implies that, in its present form, the nation-state is a seemingly perennial fixture in the international system and that the prospects for alternative expressions of political community are limited.[103] This claim is now being undermined by more critically orientated accounts of international relations, and from the various challenges economic globalisation poses for orthodox thinking in the field.

Interestingly, we seems to be back amongst the earliest debates in the field, with liberals and realists arguing about what is dominant in world politics and what is possible and impossible in relations between states. This largely explains realism's continuing centrality in international theory.

Notes

1. For recent evaluations of the realist tradition, see S. Guzzini, *Realism in International Relations and International Political Economy* (London, 1998) and J. Donnelly, *Realism and International Relations* (Cambridge, 2000).
2. For a contemporary assessment of Carr's contribution to the field, see M. Cox (ed.), *E. H. Carr: A Critical Appraisal* (London, 2000).
3. E. H. Carr, *The Twenty Years' Crisis* (London, 1939), pp. 11–12.
4. Carr (1939), p. 13.
5. Carr (1939), p. 14.
6. Carr (1939), p. 14.
7. Carr (1939), p. 67.
8. Carr (1939), pp. 289 and 297.
9. Carr (1939), p. 111.
10. Carr (1939), p. 102.
11. Carr (1939), p. 58.
12. Carr (1939), p. 104.
13. Carr (1939), p. 103.
14. Carr (1939), pp. 61 and 72. See also E. H. Carr, *Nationalism and After* (London, 1945), p. 17.
15. Carr (1939), p. 77.
16. Carr (1939), p. 66.
17. Carr (1939), pp. 283 and 14.
18. Carr (1939), pp. 14, 93 and 97.
19. A. Linklater, *Beyond Realism and Marxism: Critical Theory and International Relations* (Basingstoke, 1990), p. 7. See also A. Linklater, 'The Transformation

of Political Community: E. H. Carr; Critical Theory and International Relations', *Review of International Studies*, 23 (1997), pp. 321–38.

20. Carr (1939), pp. 292–6.
21. Carr (1939), pp. 301–2.
22. Carr (1939), p. 297.
23. Carr (1939), p. 297.
24. M. Hollis and S. Smith, *Explaining and Understanding International Relations* (Oxford, 1990), pp. 63–4.
25. H. J. Morgenthau, *Politics Among Nations*, 6th edn (New York, 1985), p. 3.
26. Morgenthau (1985), p. 7.
27. Morgenthau (1985), pp. 3–4.
28. Morgenthau (1985), p. 5.
29. Morgenthau (1985), p. 12.
30. Morgenthau (1985), p. 12.
31. I. Clark, *The Hierarchy of States* (Cambridge, 1989), p. 84.
32. Clark (1989), p. 87.
33. Morgenthau (1985), p. 5.
34. Donnelly (2000), p. 45.
35. H. Morgenthau in *The New Republic*, 22 January 1977.
36. H. Morgenthau, 'The Intellectual and Political Functions of Theory (1970)', in J. Der Derian (ed.), *International Theory: Critical Investigations* (Basingstoke, 1995), p. 50.
37. Morgenthau in Der Derian (1970), p. 52.
38. Donnelly (2000), pp. 44–9.
39. J. Ann Tickner, 'Hans Morgenthau's Principles of Political Realism: A Feminist Reformulation', *Millennium: Journal of International Studies*, vol. 17, no. 3 (Winter 1988).
40. K. N. Waltz, 'Realist Thought and Neo-Realist Theory', *Journal of International Affairs*, vol. 44, no. 1 (1990), p. 33.
41. Waltz (1990), p. 34.
42. Morgenthau (1985), p. 5.
43. M. Howard, *The Causes of Wars* (London, 1983), p. 41.
44. There were exceptions like Morgenthau who believed in the long term need for some form of world government.
45. Morgenthau cited in N. Chomsky, *Towards a New Cold War* (New York, 1982), p. 74.
46. See J. Rosenberg, 'What's the matter with realism?', *Review of International Studies*, 16 (1990), pp. 296–9.
47. B. Buzan, 'The Timeless Wisdom of Realism?', in S. Smith, K. Booth and M. Zalewski (eds), *International Theory: Positivism and Beyond* (Cambridge, 1996), p. 55.
48. R. D. McKinlay and R. Little, *Global Problems and World Order* (London, 1986), p. 5.

49. Thompson calls this process 'dissimulation' (J. B. Thompson, *Ideology and Modern Culture* (Oxford, 1990), p. 61.

50. This is what Thompson calls the 'legitimation' mode of ideological operation.

51. R. L. Rothstein, 'On the costs of Realism', in M. Smith, R. Little and M. Shackleton (eds), *Perspectives on World Politics* (London, 1981), pp. 388–97.

52. Reification here meaning that 'relations of domination may be established and sustained by representing a transitory, historical state of affairs as if it were permanent, natural [and] outside of time' (Thompson, 1990, p. 65).

53. S. Krasner, 'Realism, imperialism, and democracy', *Political Theory*, 20 (1992), p. 39.

54. See for example, S. D. Krasner, *Defending the National Interest* (Princeton, 1978) and R. Gilpin, *The Political Economy of International Relations* (Princeton, 1987).

55. Waltz (1990), p. 32.

56. Waltz (1990), p. 22.

57. Waltz (1990), p. 23. For an expansion of Waltz's conception of theory, see K. Waltz, *Theory of International Politics* (New York, 1979), pp. 1–17 and 116–23.

58. Waltz (1990), p. 29.

59. Waltz (1990), pp. 29–30.

60. F. Halliday and J. Rosenberg, 'Interview with Ken Waltz', *Review of International Studies*, 24 (1998), p. 383.

61. For a summary of the differences, see K. N. Waltz, 'The Origins of War in Neorealist Theory', *Journal of Interdisciplinary History*, 18 (1988), pp. 615–28.

62. K. N. Waltz, 'Realist Thought and Neo-Realist Theory', *Journal of International Affairs*, vol. 44, no. 1 (1990), p. 33.

63. Waltz (1990), p. 34.

64. 'Theories of international politics that concentrate causes at the individual or national level are reductionist; theories that conceive of causes operating at the international level as well are systemic' (Waltz, 1979, p. 19).

65. Waltz (1979), pp. 88–97, 104.

66. Waltz (1979), p. 128.

67. Waltz (1979), p. 66; Waltz (1990), p. 34.

68. Waltz (1979), p. 96.

69. A. Linklater, 'Neo-realism in Theory and Practice', in K. Booth and S. Smith (eds), *International Relations Theory Today* (Cambridge, 1995), pp. 251–4.

70. K. Waltz, 'Reflections on Theory of International Politics: A Response to My Critics', in R. O. Keohane (ed.), *Neorealism and its Critics* (New York, 1986), p. 343. For an extension of neo-realism, see B. Buzan, C. Jones and R. Little, *The Logic of Anarchy* (Columbia, 1993).

71. K. Waltz, 'America as a Model for the World?', *PS: Political Science and Politics*, vol. 24, no. 4 (1991), p. 670.

72. A. Wendt, 'Anarchy is what states make it: the social construction of power politics', *International Organisation*, 462 (1992), pp. 391–425.

73. R. Rosecrance, *The Rise of the Trading State* (New York, 1986). See also S. Strange, 'New World Order: Conflict and Co-operation', *Marxism Today* (January 1991), pp. 30–1.
74. See M. Doyle, 'Liberalism and World Politics', *American Political Science Review*, vol. 80, no. 4 (1986), pp. 1151–69.
75. R. K. Ashley, 'The Poverty of Neorealism', *International Organisation*, 38 (1984), pp. 225–86; R. W. Cox, 'Social Forces, States and World Order: Beyond International Relations Theory', *Millennium: Journal of International Studies*, 10 (1989), pp. 126–55.
76. Linklater (1995), p. 256.
77. For a discussion of both Horkheimer's and Habermas' theoretical constructions, see R. Bernstein, *The Restructuring of Social and Political Theory* (London, 1976), pp. 191–200; and Hoffman (1987), pp. 231–8.
78. Cox (1981), pp. 128–9.
79. Cox (1981), pp. 128–30.
80. B. Buzan, C. Jones and R. Little, *The Logic of Anarchy* (Columbia, 1993).
81. B. Buzan, 'From international system to international society: structural realism and regime theory meet the English school', *International Organization*, vol. 47, no. 3 (Summer 1993).
82. B. Buzan and R. Little, *International Systems in World History* (Oxford, 2000).
83. Buzan (1993), p. 352.
84. S. D. Krasner, *Sovereignty: Organised Hypocrisy* (Princeton, 1999), p. 223.
85. For an excellent summary of the neo-realist rebuttal, see K. N. Waltz, 'Globalization and American Power', *The National Interest* (Spring 2000).
86. Ibid. See also P. Hirst and G. Thompson, *Globalization in Question*, 2nd edn (Cambridge, 1999).
87. Waltz (2000), p. 2.
88. R. Gilpin, 'No One Loves a Political Realist', *Security Studies*, 5 (1996), p. 17.
89. Waltz (2000), p. 4.
90. See R. Gilpin, *The Challenge of Global Capitalism* (Princeton, 2000).
91. See Krasner (1999).
92. Krasner (1999), p. 3; Gilpin (1996), p. 24.
93. Waltz (2000), p. 4. See also Waltz (1988).
94. Waltz (2000), p. 6.
95. Waltz (1991), p. 670.
96. J. L. Mearsheimer, ' "Back to the Future": Instability in Europe After the Cold War', *International Security*, vol. 15, no. 1 (Summer 1990), p. 6.
97. Waltz (2000), p. 7.
98. Waltz (1991), p. 669.
99. Waltz (2000), p. 7.
100. Waltz (1991), p. 669.
101. Mearsheimer (1990), pp. 6–7.
102. Mearsheimer (1990), pp. 14–19.
103. Linklater (1995), pp. 258–9.

CHAPTER 4

Rationalism[1]

Andrew Linklater

Realism was first developed systematically by twentieth-century thinkers such as Morgenthau and Waltz although it is often associated with a great tradition of political thinkers which includes Thucydides, Hobbes and Machiavelli. Long the dominant perspective in International Relations, realism emphasises the unending competition for power and security in the world of states. Sovereignty, anarchy and the security dilemma are crucial terms in its lexicon; in the main the idea of global progress is absent from its vocabulary. Moral principles and social progress are seen as relevant to domestic politics where trust prevails since security is provided by the state, but cosmopolitan projects are said to have little importance for international relations where states must provide for their own security and trust few of their neighbours. In the latter domain, moral principles serve to legitimate national interests and to stigmatise principal competitors: they are not the basis for a new form of world political organisation which will supersede the nation-state.

The existence of a more or less unbridgeable gulf between domestic and international politics is a central theme in realist and especially in neo-realist thought. By contrast, cosmopolitan thinkers envisage a world order – but not necessarily a world government – in which universal moral principles are taken seriously and the gulf between domestic and international politics is reduced or eliminated. Global political reform is not only possible but of vital importance to end the struggle for power and security. The tension between these two approaches has been crucial to the history of international thought and was clearly evident in the early twentieth century debate between realists and idealists.

The characteristics of that debate need not detain us. Suffice it to note that it was largely about whether the development of a strong sense of moral obligation to human beings everywhere was the key to building peaceful international relations. Liberal internationalists believed that realism was unjustifiably pessimistic about the feasibility of radical change and lacked political imagination. Realists thought that liberal internationalists were naively optimistic about the prospects for a new world order based on the rule of law, open diplomacy and collective security, and they thought their ideas were dangerous because they distracted attention from the main task of foreign policy which is to ensure security and survival. The violence of 'the inter-war years' and the tensions peculiar to the bipolar era secured the victory of realism.

The rationalist approach which is associated with classical writers such as Grotius and Vattel, and with modern thinkers such as Wight, Bull, Watson and Vincent argues there is another way of thinking about international relations, albeit one that overlaps with realism and idealism to some degree. The overlap with realism is evident in Wight's influential essay 'Why is there no International Theory?'. There, in a much-quoted claim, Wight maintained that domestic politics is the sphere of the good life whereas international politics is the realm of security and survival.[2] Similarly realist is his argument that international relations is 'incompatible with progressivist theory'. In a statement that seems to place him squarely in the realist camp, Wight maintained that Sir Thomas More would have recognised the basic features of international politics in the 1960s since nothing fundamental has changed over the last few centuries.[3] Like realism, then, rationalism begins with the condition of anarchy but it is more inclined than realism to emphasise the ways in which the sense of belonging to the community of humankind has had its civilizing effect on international relations. Rationalists take arguments for global reform seriously, recognising however that the world political order frustrates many of the demands for international social justice and for the protection of human rights. In general, they are deeply sceptical of all the proposals for large-scale global reform and doubt that any of them will ever command the consent of the majority of nation-states or the most powerful of them.

Rationalists are attracted by elements of realism and idealism, yet occupy the middle ground between them, never wholly reconciling themselves to either point of view. This is how Wight described rationalism in a famous series of lectures delivered at the London School of Economics in the 1950s. He argued in those lectures that it was the 'via media' between realism and revolutionism which was Wight's term for those perspectives which were hostile to the current order and committed to its transformation.[4] Rationalism recognises that states are forced to provide for their own security in the condition of anarchy, unlike individuals in civil society, and that competition and conflict often accompany their efforts to realise their objectives. Yet the international system is not a state of war, and there is a surprisingly high level of international order given that states have an internal monopoly of control over the instruments of violence and, as sovereigns, no obligation to submit to a higher power.

Hedley Bull neatly captured the apparently paradoxical feature of the sovereign states-system in the title of his most famous work, *The Anarchical*

Society (1977). One of the main aims of that book was to demonstrate that there is more to international relations than the realist admits but less than the cosmopolitan desires. Rationalism has its own particular object of analysis. It is not primarily concerned with the struggle for power and security in the *international system* of states but it does not regard the current order as a mere stepping stone on the way towards a universal political community which will ensure justice for the whole of humankind. Rationalists concentrate on what they regard as the fundamental reality of world politics which realists and revolutionists ignore, namely the existence of an *international society* of states.

Realists have argued that the belief that states are constrained by international society underestimates the importance of national egoism.[5] From this vantage-point, rationalists are committed to the idea that a limited degree of progress has occurred in international relations. Critics with a radical political orientation have argued that the rationalism offers an apology for a society of states which safeguards the privileges of the leading powers and dominant political interests. From this standpoint rationalism is no more than a British variant on realism which has been superseded by critical approaches to the field.[6] These arguments deny the possibility of the *via media* and raise important criticisms of the rationalist account of order and change in international relations. Two points need to be made about these matters at the present stage.

First, rationalists are convinced that the realist emphasis on how states outmanoeuvre, control and seek to overpower one another in periods of war captures only part of the substance of world politics. Because of a common interest in placing restraints on the use of force, states also develop the art of accommodation and compromise which makes an international society possible. At times, rationalists suggest that the evolution of order and civility might be inevitable. Adam Watson has argued that a 'strong case can be made out, on the evidence of past systems as well as the present one, that the regulatory rules and institutions of a system usually, and perhaps inexorably, develop to the point where the members become conscious of common values and the system becomes an international society.'[7] Having noted that there may a universal tendency which transforms international systems into international societies, Watson added that the important point is to identify and understand the specific reasons for their development.[8]

The second point is that rationalists insist that international order should not be taken for granted since it is a precarious achievement which can be destroyed by the policies of aggressive or revolutionary powers. There is no guarantee that any international society will survive indefinitely or succeed in keeping crude self-interest at bay. Such progress as there is may not last forever, but as long as an international society endures it is important to ask whether it can be improved. Demands for morality and justice have always formed an important part of the history of international relations – hence Wight's interest in 'revolutionist' perspectives. Wight himself argued that 'the fundamental political task at all times [is] to provide order, or security, from which law, justice and prosperity may afterwards develop'.[9] Critics maintain that rationalists are generally sceptical of sweeping visions of alternative forms of world political organisation which their exponents regard as the key to greater peace and justice, and there is a great deal of truth in this remark. Even so, it is arguable that in the 1980s and 1990s some rationalists began to take a more explicitly normative stance on issues such as poverty and human rights. Whereas the core of the rationalist tradition has emphasised the precarious achievement of order, what has been called the critical international society approach has advocated greater justice in what may be the more propitious post-bipolar age.[10]

We will return to these themes later in this chapter which has four parts. Part I focuses on the idea of order and society in the main rationalist texts. Part II considers the rationalist analysis of the relative importance of order and justice in the traditional European society of states. Part III analyses the 'revolt against the West' and the emergence of the universal society of states in which various demands for justice are frequently heard. Part IV returns to the question of whether rationalism remains committed to the notion that only limited progress is possible in international relations and whether its claim to be the *via media* between realism and revolutionism is convincing in the light of current debates and developments in the field.

I   From Power to Order: International Society

Explaining the surprisingly high level of order which exists between in-dependent political communities in an anarchic condition is the main aim of the rationalist project. Rationalists such as Wight were fascinated by the small number of international societies which have existed in human history and by their relatively short life-spans, all previous examples hav-ing been destroyed by empire after a few centuries.[11] Wight also noted the propensity for internal schism in the form of international revolutions which brought transnational political forces and ideologies rather than separate states into conflict.[12] He posed the interesting question of whether commerce first brought different societies into contact and provided the context within which a society of states would later develop.[13] In his remarks about the three international societies about which a great deal is known (the Ancient Chinese, the Graeco-Roman and the modern society of states) Wight maintained each had emerged in a region with a high level of linguistic and cultural unity. Crucially, independent political communities felt they belonged to the civilised world and were superior to their neighbours.[14] Their sense of their 'cultural differentiation' from allegedly semi-civilised and barbaric peoples facilitated communication between them and made it easier to agree on the rights and duties which bound them together as members of an exclusive society of states.

Writing on the evolution of the modern society of states Wight's protégé, Hedley Bull, observed that in 'the form of the doctrine of natural law, ideas of human justice historically preceded the development of ideas of inter-state or international justice and provided perhaps the principal intellectual foundations upon which these latter ideas at first rested'.[15] This seems to echo Wight's position that some sense of cultural unity is needed before an international society can develop but, in the end, this was not Bull's position. He believed that international societies can exist in the absence of linguistic, cultural or religious agreement. To clarify the point, Bull introduced a distinction between an international system and an international society which does not exist in Wight's own work. A 'system of states (or international system)', he argued, 'is formed when two or more states have sufficient contact between them, and have sufficient impact on one another's decisions to cause them to behave – at least in some measure – as parts of a whole'.[16] A 'society of states', on the other hand, comes into being 'when a group of states, conscious of certain common interests and common values, form a society in the sense that they conceive themselves to be bound by a common set of rules in their relations with one another, and share in the working of common institutions'.[17] This is an important distinction which highlights the need to give a precise account of how international societies have evolved.

As we have seen, Bull maintained that order can exist between states which do not feel they belong to a common civilisation. John Vincent made the same point when he argued that international society is 'functional' or utilitarian rather than 'cultural' or moral in character.[18] A pragmatic need to co-exist is enough to produce what Bull called a 'diplomatic culture' – that is, a system of conventions and institutions which preserve order between states with radically different cultures, ideologies and aspirations.[19] He added that the diplomatic culture will be stronger if it is anchored in an 'international political culture' – that is if states have a similar way of life. Illustrating the point, Bull and Watson argued that the modern global society of states which is global does not rest on an international political culture in the way that the European society of states did in the nineteenth century. However, the basic rules of the international society which originated in Europe have been accepted by a large majority of its former colonies, now equal sovereign members of the first global society of states. There is no international political culture lending support to the diplomatic culture, yet Bull asked if this might change now that many different elites across the world belong to what he called the evolving 'cosmopolitan culture' of modernity.[20]

Bull's *The Anarchical Society* provides the most detailed analysis of the foundations of international order. He argues there that all societies – domestic and international – have arrangements for protecting three 'primary goals' of placing constraints on violence, upholding property rights and ensuring agreements are kept.[21] The fact that these primary goals are common to domestic and international society explains Bull's rejection of 'the domestic analogy' which is the idea that order will only come into being when states surrender their sovereign powers to centralised institutions of the kind that provide order within nation-states.[22] As we have seen, rationalists break with realism because they believe that states can enjoy the benefits of society without submitting to a higher authority. Bull's version of rationalism argues that states are usually committed to limiting the use of force, ensuring respect for property and preserving trust not only in relations between citizens but in their dealings with one another as independent political communities. This shared ground rather than any common culture is the real foundation of international society.

Domestic societies and international society are both concerned with the satisfaction of primary goals but the society of states is distinctive because it is an 'anarchical society' – there is no sovereign power which can impose its will on the constituent parts. Citizens of the modern state are governed by the 'primary rules' of society which set out how they should behave, and also by 'secondary rules' which determine how these basic rules concerning conduct should be created, interpreted and enforced.[23] In the modern state, central institutions have the right to make primary and secondary rules whereas in international society states create primary rules as well as secondary rules pertaining to their creation, interpretation and enforcement. A related point is that international society has a set of primary goals which are uniquely its own.[24] The idea that entities must be sovereign to acquire membership is a distinctive feature of the society of states, as is the conviction that the latter is the only legitimate form of global political organisation and the belief that states have a duty to respect the sovereignty of all others. These goals may conflict with one another, as Bull observed in his writings on order and justice which will be considered later in this chapter.

Societies of states exist because most political communities want to place constraints on the use of force and bring civility to their relations. An interesting question is whether some national societies are more likely than others to attach special value to international society and to take care of its institutions which include diplomacy, international law and the practice of balancing the power of states that aspire to lay down the law to others. Rationalists argue that international society can be multi-denominational and include states with different cultures and philosophies of government. A central task of diplomacy in their view is to find some common ground between radically different and mutually suspicious states. They are unconvinced by those who believe that the members of the society of states should have identical political ideologies, a point Wight made against liberals such as Kant.[25] However, rationalists have also argued that societies with a strong commitment to constitutional politics and a history of resistance to political absolutism played a vital role in the formation of the European society of states and in the development of international law.[26] It is worth considering this theme in the light of recent neo-realist and liberal discussions of the relationship between the international states-system and its constituent parts.

The neo-realist argument of Kenneth Waltz maintains that the international system compels all states to take part in an unceasing struggle for power and security. According to this approach, states cannot escape the politics of 'self-help' which separates the international political system from national politics.[27] The liberal argument of Michael Doyle argues in opposition to neo-realism that liberal states have a strong predisposition towards peace with each other though not with non-liberal states.[28] Rationalists agree with the liberals that the inside of the state matters and that neo-realists are guilty of divorcing the international system from national political systems (without assuming that liberalism is the essential precondition of peace). Rationalists are as interested in how the 'inside' affects the 'outside', in how domestic society shapes international society, as they are in influences that flow the other way. They are therefore interested in the attention states pay to internal developments within other societies, a necessary concern if it is indeed the case that a commitment to constitutionalism or its equivalent is necessary for the survival of international society. They are especially interested in how states reconcile this interest in one another's internal affairs with the duty to respect the principle of sovereign equality.

Wight's essay on international legitimacy illustrates the point. One part of this essay deals with the move from the dynastic principle of government to the conviction that the state should represent the nation as a whole, and with how the rules governing membership of international society changed in the process. In this context Wight noted that 'these principles of legitimacy mark the region of approximation between international and domestic politics. They are principles that prevail (or are at least proclaimed) *within* a majority of the states that form international society, as well as in the relations *between* them'.[29] Exactly the same point may be made about contemporary claims that the legitimate members of international society should respect human rights and be committed to democracy. This is one of the respects in which rationalism differs from realism and from neo-realism in particular. From the latter standpoint the relations between states are rather like the relations between firms in a market place – all actors are caught up in a world of quasi-physical forces. The interplay between domestic and international legitimacy is missing from this account. Rationalists reject this systemic approach to international politics and stress instead the inter-subjective legal and moral understandings which bring a measure of civility to the anarchic condition. It is this focus on the 'normative' and 'institutional' factors which give international society its distinctive 'logic' that distinguishes rationalism from other approaches in the field.[30]

II   Order and Justice in International Relations

Rationalists are interested in the processes which transform systems of states into societies of states and in the norms and institutions which prevent the collapse of civility and the re-emergence of unbridled power. They are also concerned with the question of whether societies of states can develop means of promoting justice for individuals and their immediate associations. Bull in particular distinguished between international societies and international systems but he also identified different types of international society in order to cast light on the relationship between order and justice in international relations.

In an early essay Bull distinguished between the 'solidarist' or 'Grotian' and 'pluralist' conceptions of international society. He maintained that the 'central Grotian assumption is that of the solidarity, or potential solidarity, of the states comprising international society, with respect to the enforcement of the law'.[31] Solidarism is apparent in the Grotian conviction that there is a clear distinction between just and unjust wars, and in the assumption 'from which [the] right of humanitarian intervention is derived ... that individual human beings are subjects of international law and members of international society in their own right'.[32] Pluralism, as expounded by the eighteenth century international lawyer, Vattel, rejects this approach, arguing that 'states do not exhibit solidarity of this kind, but are capable of agreeing only for certain minimum purposes which fall short of that of the enforcement of the law'.[33] A related argument is that states rather than individuals are the basic members of international society.[34] Having made this distinction, Bull asked whether there was any evidence that the pluralist international society of the post-Second World War era was becoming more solidarist. His answer in *The Anarchical Society* was that expectations of greater solidarity were seriously 'premature'.[35]

To understand the reasons for this conclusion it is necessary to turn to his discussion of the conflict between the primary goals of international society.[36] Bull argued that in the past the goal of preserving the sovereignty of each state has clashed with the goal of preserving the balance of power and maintaining peace. Polish independence was sacrificed in the eighteenth century for the sake of international equilibrium. The League of Nations chose not to defend Abyssinia from Italian aggression because Britain and France needed Italy to balance the power of Nazi Germany. In such cases, international order was in conflict with basic notions of justice which require that all sovereign states should be treated equally. Contemporary international society contains other examples of the tension between order and justice. Order requires efforts to prevent further additions to the nuclear club but justice suggests all states have an equal right to acquire weapons of mass destruction.[37]

A related point was that states have different and often conflicting ideas about justice and there is a danger that they will undermine international society if they try to impose their views on others. Efforts to apply principles of justice to international relations are often highly selective in any event, as was the case with the war crimes tribunals at the end of the Second World War.[38] What some thought was the reasonable response of the civilised world was Victor's Justice to others. The different responses to NATO's action against Serbia in 1999 demonstrate that such differences of interpretation survive to this day. On a separate front, Bull was keen to stress that Western liberal conceptions of individual human rights do not strike much of a chord in many parts of the non-western world. Rather than assume that other peoples are insufficiently enlightened, the advocates of universal human rights had to grasp that tensions over the meaning of such rights are inescapable in a multicultural society of states.[39]

States may not agree on the meaning of justice but, Bull argued, they often concur about how to maintain order amongst themselves. Most agree that each state should respect the sovereignty of the others and observe the principle of non-intervention. Each society can then promote its notion of the good life within its own territory, recognised as an equal by all others. But although Bull drew attention to the tension between order and justice, he also argued that international order has moral value since 'it is instrumental to the goal of order in human society as a whole'. 'Order among all mankind', he argued, '[is] of primary value, not order within the society of states',[40] and 'a world society or community' is a goal which all 'intelligent and sensitive persons' should take seriously.[41] This apparent cosmopolitanism stands uneasily alongside his conviction that there is little evidence that different societies are about to agree on the nature of a world community. But the implication seems to be that states should try to improve international society whenever circumstances allow.

Wight's claim that rationalism is the *via media* between realism and revolutionism is worth recalling at this point. Read alongside Bull's writings on order and justice, this can be taken to mean that rationalists believe that a limited amount of progress has taken place in international relations. At the very least, the existence of a society of states demonstrates progress in agreeing on the basic principles of coexistence and on some rudimentary forms of cooperation. Rationalists believe that realists fail to appreciate the importance of such phenomena. The tension between order and justice is a reminder that progress may not have advanced very far even though it is desirable that it develops further. Revolutionists are thought to fail to recognise the difficulty that states have in progressing together in the same normative direction. It follows that rationalists must always be interested in how the limited progress that has taken place may be undone by a lack of prudent diplomacy or by naked power; and they must also be interested in whether there are any signs that states are making progress in creating a more just international society.

The development of rationalist thinking about human rights is interesting in this regard. Bull argued that pluralism has prevailed over solidarism in the recent history of international society. In this period, the solidarist belief in the primacy of individual human rights 'has survived but it has gone underground'.[42] For the most part it would appear that states have entered into 'a conspiracy of silence ... about the rights and duties of their respective citizens'.[43] Most states – and Europe's former colonies in particular – have feared that human rights considerations might be used as a pretext for unwarranted interference in their domestic affairs. Bull was concerned that Western arrogance and complacency about human rights might damage the delicate framework of international society. He also noted that the relative silence of the diplomatic culture on the importance of human rights had produced a strong counteraction, and that states had come under pressure to promote their international protection.[44]

This is the starting-point of John Vincent's book, *Human Rights and International Relations*, which argued that the right of the individual to be free from starvation is one human right on which all states can agree despite their ideological differences.[45] Vincent argued that global action to end starvation is essential since the absence of the basic means of subsistence should always shock the conscience of humankind. Consensus on this matter would be a significant advance in relations between the Western world which has traditionally been concerned with order rather than justice and the non-western world which has fought for greater justice. In one of his last essays Vincent returned to the theme of his first book which defended the principle of non-intervention. He observed that states are increasingly open to external scrutiny and under pressure to comply with the international law of human rights.[46] Some violations of human rights might be so shocking that states had to set aside the convention that states should not intervene in each other's internal affairs. Whether and how they should do so are questions that have become central to international relations with the collapse of the Soviet bloc and genocide in Rwanda.[47] International action to try persons suspected of war crimes and gross human rights violations has progressed but, as the debate over NATO's military action against Serbia demonstrates, there is no global consensus about when sovereignty can be overridden for the sake of human rights.

The 'revolt against the West' is a subject for the next section but one of its dimensions, namely the demand for racial equality, is pertinent to the present discussion. Bull and Vincent argued that the rejection of white supremacism has been a central theme in the transition from a narrowly European to the first universal society of states.[48] The demand for racial equality demonstrated that international order will not endure unless Third World peoples realise their basic aspirations for justice. Although order was also an issue – disorder in Southern Africa was possible while white supremacist regimes endured – the deeper matter was the immorality of apartheid. This dimension of the revolt against racial equality adds force to Wight's point that the modern society of states differs from its predecessors in making the legitimacy or illegitimacy of particular forms of government a matter of importance for the entire international community.[49] Disgust with apartheid was a matter on which the whole of international society was agreed. Mindful of the ideological competition between the United States and the Soviet Union, Bull added that agreement on apartheid was about as far as the global moral consensus extended in the 1970s and 1980s.[50]

The revolt against white supremacism reveals how progress towards greater solidarism can be made. As Bull put it, if 'there is overwhelming evidence of a consensus in international society as a whole in favour of change held to be just, especially if the consensus embraces all the great powers (then) change may take place without causing other than a local and temporary disorder, after which the international order as a whole may emerge unscathed or even appear in a stronger position than before'.[51] Whether Bull thought that a global moral consensus could emerge in other areas is unclear although Watson maintains that Bull and he 'inclined (towards the) optimistic view' that states in the contemporary system are 'consciously working out, for the first time, a set of transcultural values and ethical standards'.[52] Perhaps a growing consensus about the need for democratic government – or at the very least for constitutional safeguards for human rights – reveals that further progress has been made. It is worth adding however that Bull wrote in the 1980s that neither superpower seemed to have the requisite 'moral vision' for dealing with the central problems between 'North' and 'South'.[53] A rationalist interpretation of international society at the present time might insist that any growing acceptance of liberal-democratic principles owes much to American or Western dominance and reflects the core's moral preferences and economic and political interests.

It is hard to tell whether Bull and Watson believed that the expansion of international society to include the West's former colonies would lead to greater solidarism or demonstrate that aspirations in that direction were still 'premature' – and few contemporary rationalists have built on their insightful comments.[54] Bull did point to an emerging elite cosmopolitanism – and observers might now add that he was dealing in tentative fashion with the impact of globalisation on the society of states – but he was quick to add that this 'nascent cosmopolitan culture ... is weighted in favour of the dominant cultures of the West'.[55] Incorporating non-western ideas in international law would help to overcome this problem but, Bull argued, there was clear evidence that the West and the Third World were drifting further apart:

> we have to remember that when these demands for justice were first put forward, the leaders of Third World peoples spoke as supplicants in a world in which the Western powers were still in a dominant position. The demands that were put forward had necessarily to be justified in terms of ... conventions of which the Western powers were the principal authors; the moral appeal had to be cast in terms that would have most resonance in Western societies. But as ... non-western peoples have become stronger ... and as the Westernised leaders of the early years of independence have been replaced in many countries by new leaders more representative of local or indigenous forces, Third World spokes-men have become freer to adopt a rhetoric that sets Western values aside, or ... places different interpretations upon them. Today there is legitimate doubt as to how far the demands emanating from the Third World coalition are compatible with the moral ideas of the West.[56]

Intriguing questions about the future of solidarism are raised by these comments which foreshadow the concerns of more recent analyses of the coming 'clash of civilisations'.[57] Yet nothing in Bull's writings suggests the imminent breakdown of international order. As we shall see in the next section, Bull believed that the majority of new states accepted the basic principles of international society including the ideas of sovereignty and non-intervention. Despite cultural and other differences which seemed to be increasing, new states and old could agree on some universal principles of co-existence and on some moral universals such as the principle of racial equality. How different societies come to agree on the universal principles pertinent to either a pluralist or solidarist conception of international so-ciety is the central theme in rationalist analysis which steers clear of the fatalism of neo-realism and a naive belief in the inevitability of global progress which occasionally surfaces in triumphalist forms of liberalism. In the end, diplomatic practice decides how far states can agree on moral and political universals which transcend cultural and other differences. On such foundations does the rationalist claim to be the *via media* between realism and revolutionism finally rest.

III The Revolt against the West and the Expansion of International Society

The impact of the revolt against the West upon the modern society of states was central to rationalist writings in the 1980s. The key question was whether the diverse civilizations which had been brought together by the expansion of Europe have similar views about how to maintain order and belong to an international society rather than an international system. To answer this question it was necessary to recall the world of the late eighteenth century. In that era, the European, Chinese, Islamic and Indian worlds were the four main regional international systems and 'most of the governments in each group had a sense of being part of a common civilization superior to that of the others'.[58] European states were committed to the principle of sovereign equality within their own continent but they rejected the view that other societies had the same sovereign rights. Exactly how Europe should behave towards its colonies was always a matter of dispute. Some claimed the right to enslave and to annihilate conquered peoples while others argued that they were equally members of the universal society of humankind and entitled to be treated humanely. The dominant theories of empire in the twentieth century, as expressed in the League of Nations mandates system and the trusteeship system of the United Nations, maintained that colonial powers had a duty to prepare non-European peoples for their eventual admission into the society of states on equal terms with Western members.

The Europeans believed that this transition would take decades, even centuries, in part because other civilizations had to divest themselves of a hegemonial conception of international society in which they were believed to be at the centre of the world. China, for example, saw itself as the Middle Kingdom which deserved tribute from other societies which were at a lower stage of social development. Traditional Islamic views of international relations distinguished between the House of Islam (*Dar al Islam*) and the House of War (*Dar al Harb*) – between believers and infidels – though the possibility of a temporary truce (*Dar al Suhl*) with non-Islamic powers was allowed. Also committed to hegemonial conceptions of international relations, the European powers believed that membership of the society of states was impossible for those that failed to reach their 'standard of civilization'.[59]

What this meant was that different civilisations belonged to an international system in the eighteenth century. With the expansion of Europe, other peoples were forced to comply with its conception of the world and, gradually, most of those societies came to accept European principles of international society. But they only came to enjoy equal membership of the international society of states after a long struggle to dismantle Europe's sense of its own moral superiority and political invincibility.

Bull called this struggle 'the revolt against the West' and argued that it had five main components.[60] The first was 'the struggle for equal sovereignty' undertaken by societies such as China and Japan which had 'retained their formal independence' but were thought 'inferior' to the Western powers. These societies were governed by unequal treaties 'concluded under duress'; because of the principle of 'extra-territoriality', they were denied the right to settle disputes involving foreigners according to domestic law. As a consequence of the legal revolt against the West, Japan joined the society of states in 1900, Turkey in 1923, Egypt in 1936 and China in 1943. The political revolt against the West was a second and related part of this process. In this case, the former colonies which had lost their former independence demanded freedom from colonial domination. The racial revolt against the West which included the struggle to abolish slavery and the slave trade as well as all forms of white supremacism was the third part of the quest for freedom and dignity; a fourth dimension was the economic revolt against the forms of inequality and exploitation associated with a Western-dominated global commercial and financial system. The fifth revolt, the cultural revolt, was a protest against all forms of Western cultural imperialism including the West's assumption that it was entitled to decide how other peoples should live, not least by universalising liberal-individualistic conceptions of human rights.

The first four dimensions of the revolt of the Third World appealed to Western conceptions of freedom and equality and argued that the colonial powers should take their own principles seriously when dealing with other parts of the world. This seemed to signify a desire to follow the West's own trajectory of development. But as already noted the cultural revolt was different because it was often 'a revolt against Western values as such'.[61] The inevitable question was whether the expansion of international society which was the immediate outcome of the revolt against the West would lead to new forms of ideological conflict with harmful consequences for international order.

This question remains central to debates about the future of international relations and at least three different answers have appeared in recent years. The first is Samuel Huntington's view that increasingly the main fault-lines in international society are those that divide civilisations.[62] According to this perspective, there are no guarantees that a pluralist form of international society will survive. The second is Francis Fukuyama's belief that liberal democracy will prevail in most parts of the world so expanding the liberal zone of peace.[63] The implication here is that major advances in realising a solidarist conception of international society are taking place, certainly within the liberal-democratic regions of the world. The third approach is Chris Brown's argument that the cultural revolt against the West has destroyed 'the modern requirement' which is the belief that the West can require other societies to live according to its moral conventions.[64] On this argument, the former colonies of the West are keen to preserve their sovereign independence. An acceptance of pluralist principles of world political organisation is not in doubt but movement in a solidarist direction is unlikely.

Bull and Watson's own position which predates these writings noted the simultaneous appearance of growing cultural conflict and an emerging

cosmopolitan culture of modernity. This is to add a fourth approach to the
ones already mentioned and to suggest that a tension between pluralist and
solidarist views is likely to remain a distinguishing feature of the first
universal international society. We can observe this in continuing disputes
about the nature of universal human rights which bring sovereignty into
conflict with liberal-democratic ideas about how societies everywhere
should be organised. Be that as it may, Bull and Watson argued that an
international order which reflects the interests of non-western states was
already 'in some measure' constructed,[65] but international society would
not command the support of the great majority of non-western peoples
unless more radical changes took place. As previously noted, international
law would have to absorb non-western ideas 'to a much greater degree' but
there would also need to be a radical redistribution of power and wealth
from North to South.[66] A rather different conception of the relationship
between order and justice emerged against this background. In his earlier
reflections on this subject, Bull stressed the tension between order and
justice. His last remarks on the subject reiterated the claim that 'justice is
best realised in the context of order' but they also elaborated the point that
the 'measures that are necessary to achieve justice for peoples of the Third
World are the same measures that will maximise the prospects of international order or stability, at least in the long run'.[67]

Bull did not live to witness the further expansion of international society
though the fragmentation of the Soviet bloc and the disintegration of
several states in the Third World. New challenges for international society
have been posed by national-secessionist movements which argue that
sometimes justice can only be realised 'at the price of order'.[68] New problems have been created by the appearance of 'failed states',[69] by gross
violations of human rights in civil conflicts, and by regimes which are in a
state of war with sections of their own population. But as we shall see, such
developments reinforce Bull and Watson's claim that modern international
society is divided between pluralist and solidarist principles of world
political organisation.

Robert Jackson's *Quasi-States in International Relations* remains the best
introduction to the problem of the failed state within the rationalist tradition.[70] His argument is that Third World states were admitted into the
society of states as sovereign equals without an assurance that they could
govern themselves well. An earlier principle that a people had to demonstrate a capacity for good government before it could acquire the right of
self-government was overturned by the United Nations General Assembly
in 1960. Many new states acquired 'negative sovereignty' – the right to be
free from external interference – when they clearly lacked 'positive sovereignty' – the ability to satisfy the basic needs of their populations. The
acquisition of sovereignty meant that political elites were legally free to do
what they wanted within their respective national jurisdictions. Violators of

human rights could appeal to Article 2 paragraph 7 of the United Nations Charter which asserts that the international community does not have the right 'to intervene in matters which are essentially within the domestic jurisdiction of any state'.

Jackson raised the question of whether there ought to have been a more effective system of global trusteeship to prepare the colonies for full membership of the society of states, and some have argued that the international community should take responsibility for governing states which are no longer economically or politically viable.[71] A related question in this context was whether the consent of the government of the target state is absolutely necessary before the international community can take action of this kind.[72]

Acts of genocide in Rwanda and human rights atrocities in the Balkans have reopened the question of whether there is a right of humanitarian intervention to protect the lives of vulnerable or endangered populations. The debate over NATO's involvement in Kosovo has revealed that there is no universal consensus on the matter of whether the right of sovereignty can be overridden by an allegedly higher moral principle of protecting human rights. Some observers supported NATO's actions on the grounds that states have duties to the whole of humanity and not just to co-nationals.[73] Others criticised NATO for what they saw as a breach of the United Nations Charter, for its highly selective interest in checking human rights violations and for acts of violence which brought added misery to the local population.[74] In these different reactions one can hear echoes of an older tension between the pluralist and solidarist conceptions of international society. One way of striking the balance between these rival views is suggested by the argument that states should be willing to intervene in the very worst cases of human rights atrocities but should remain 'critical of any general undermining of non-intervention'.[75] It remains to be seen whether the modern society of states can reach an agreed definition of intolerable human rights violations and come to strike the balance between pluralism and solidarism in this way.

IV   A Progressivist Interpretation of International Relations?

Quite how far progress in international relations is possible is one of the most intriguing questions in the field. In one essay, Wight maintained that the international system is 'the realm of recurrence and repetition', a formulation which is repeated in Waltz's classic statement of neo-realism.[76] The argument of this chapter is that rationalism is principally about progress in the form of agreements about how to maintain order and, to a lesser degree, about how to promote elementary principles of justice. Bull's writings on this subject often suggested that order is prior to justice, the point being that international order is a fragile achievement and that states have not found it easy to agree on the meaning of global justice. At times, Bull seems to be aligned with what Wight described as the 'realist' wing of rationalism but, on other occasions, he is much closer to its 'idealist' wing.[77] Towards the end of his life, it has been argued, Bull moved significantly towards a more solidarist point of view.[78]

This shift is most pronounced in the Hagey Lectures delivered at the University of Waterloo in Canada in 1983. It is illustrated by the comment that 'the idea of sovereign rights existing apart from the rules laid down by international society itself and enjoyed without qualification has to be rejected in principle', not least because 'the idea of the rights and duties of the individual person has come to have a place, albeit an insecure one' within the society of states 'and it is our responsibility to seek to extend it'.[79] The 'moral concern with welfare on a world scale' was evidence of a 'growth of ... cosmopolitan moral awareness' which amounted to 'a major change in our sensibilities'.[80] The changing global agenda made it necessary for states to become the 'local agents of a world common good'.[81]

It would be a mistake to suggest that Bull had come to think that solutions to global problems would be any easier to find and that 'agonising choices' would no longer have to be made.[82] Scepticism invariably blunted the visionary impulse. This is clear from Bull's observation that new, post-sovereign political communities might yet develop in Western Europe. An intriguing passage in *The Anarchical Society* states that the time may be ripe for new principles of regional political organization which recognise the need for sub-national, national and supranational tiers of government but reject the notion that any of them should enjoy exclusive sovereignty.[83] A 'neo-medievalist' Western Europe could 'avoid the classic dangers of the system of sovereign states' by encouraging 'overlapping structures and criss-crossing loyalties'.[84] Yet such a world would not be free from dangers. Mediaeval international society with its complex structure of overlapping jurisdictions and multiple loyalties had been even more violent than the modern system of states.[85] Bull thought it important to set out a qualified defence of the society of states and to argue against the revolutionists that the state played a 'positive role in world affairs'.[86]

We have considered the rationalist critique of realism; it is now necessary to turn to its assessment of the revolutionist tradition and its many visions of alternatives to the world of sovereign states. The essence of revolution-ism, Bull argued, could be found in the Kantian belief in 'a horizontal conflict of ideology that cuts across the boundaries of states and divides human society into two camps – the trustees of the immanent community of mankind and those who stand in its way, those who are of the true faith and the heretics, the liberators and the oppressed'.[87] The Kantian interpretation of international society assumed that diplomatic conventions could be set aside in the quest for the unification of humankind. 'Good faith with heretics' had no intrinsic value. It had no more than 'tactical convenience' because 'between the elect and the damned, the liberators and the oppressed, the question of mutual acceptance of rights to sovereignty or independence does not arise'.[88] This characterisation of Kantianism was false and, as Stanley Hoffmann has argued, Kant 'was much less cosmopolitan and universalist in his writings on international affairs than Bull suggests'. In fact, Kant believed in a cosmopolitan ethic and in a society of states which upheld the rights of sovereign communities and the duty of non-intervention.[89]

This is not to suggest that Kant's thinking and modern rationalism are identical. Wight argued that Kant was committed to the idea of 'doctrinal uniformity' since he thought that peace will not come about until the whole world consists of republican regimes.[90] Recent studies of Kant's theory of international relations have cast doubt on this interpretation,[91] but that does not alter the fact that rationalists were deeply opposed to all approaches which argue that the members of international society can and should live by the same ideology. Perhaps this was a good reason for the decision to bracket together thinkers as diverse as Kant, Lenin and Gandhi as revolutionists. But the immediate problem was that parallels between Kant's thought and contemporary rationalism were obscured, notwithstanding Wight's claim that rationalism and revolutionism are overlapping rather than completely separate doctrines. Questions then arise about whether rationalism is really the *via media* at all, about how far its own qualified cosmopolitanism could have been strengthened by assimilating ideas from thinkers such as Kant, and about whether this is how it can best contribute to the current theoretical debate.

Wight commented in his lectures that the least dangerous form of revolutionism is to be found in Kantian thought, adding that Kant is like the rationalist who is first and foremost 'a reformist, the practitioner of piecemeal social engineering'.[92] Perhaps the deepest similarity is a fascination with the three basic forms of community or claims on human loyalty evident in world society. Wight argued they are the sovereign state, the international society of states and the still wider imaginary community of humankind.[93] For his part, Kant reflected on the existence of three spheres of civility and law: domestic society (governed by the *ius civitatis*), the society of states (governed by the *ius gentium*) and the world community (governed by the ius *cosmopoliticum*).[94] Kant and Wight are united by the belief that national egoism may destroy the forms of international civility, although Kant was unquestionably the more optimistic of the two regarding the possibility of perpetual peace. They both thought the civil order between states is a significant achievement and both believed the problem of world politics was not only how to create order but how to promote justice. However Wight did not share Kant's conviction that states were moving steadily towards a global moral consensus.

Kant and the rationalists were drawn towards the analysis of the nature of domestic and international political community. Interestingly, Bull wrote that Karl Deutsch's writings on security communities, though underdeveloped, were 'pregnant with implications for a general theory of international relations'.[95] Deutsch was one of the few thinkers to reflect on 'the distinguishing features of a community, the different sorts of community that obtain, the elements that make up the cohesion of a community, the determinants of mutual responsiveness between one people and another'.[96] Here was a distinctive approach to international relations which focused on the nature of the social bond which simultaneously holds the members of a community together and separates them from the rest of humankind yet need not rule out 'responsiveness' to the concerns of other peoples. Bull's interest in Deutsch's thinking about such matters is unsurprising since after all a society of states can only exist if independent political communities do not close themselves off but are tolerant of very different points of view and sensitive to one another's legitimate interests.[97] The very existence of a society of states, and any significant progress in satisfying aspirations for global justice, requires forms of political community which are moved by purposes beyond themselves.[98]

It is useful to consider these matters in connection with other strands of international relations theory. The first point to make here is that rationalists have long argued that cooperation exists even in the context of anarchy, an orientation which has been at the heart of neo-liberal institutionalist analyses of international cooperation which seek to explain how rational egotists come to cooperate.[99] A second point is that there are parallels with more recent constructivist arguments that anarchy, sovereignty and state interests are socially constructed and mutable rather than given in some external and unchangeable reality. Alexander Wendt's claim that 'anarchy is what states make of it' has long been a central theme in rationalist thought.[100] As Bull points out they make an international system or an international society out of it, and there are times when they may be able to make that society conform with some basic principles of human justice.[101] Nothing is pre-ordained here; everything depends on how states separately and together construct themselves as separate political communities and how they determine their rights against and duties to the rest of humankind. This is why rationalists have a particular interest in the moral, cultural and institutional dimensions of international relations, and why their writings warrant close consideration by scholars who believe that these features of international political life have not received the attention they deserve, especially in the United States. In that country, constructivists have opened up the discussion of the normative and cultural sphere in important ways although they have not dealt with the tension between order and justice which rationalists regard as central to the field.

There are also interesting parallels between rationalism and critical theories of international relations, and a growing literature is concerned with bridging these different areas.[102] Two areas of overlap are worth noting. First, rationalists have been particularly interested in questions regarding cultural difference or otherness which have been at the heart of critical international theory in recent years. This is evident in Wight's comments on 'cultural differentiation' in international societies and in Bull and Watson's work on the emergence of the first universal society of states. Bull's analysis of the essentially contested nature of human rights invited Western liberals to take non-western constructions of human rights seriously. His position on human rights resonates with postmodern claims that no one society and civilisation has uncovered absolute truths about society and politics.

Second, rationalists believe it is always possible that states will use force to resolve some of their differences however, in practice, most states have wanted to preserve civility between themselves and have relied on the 'diplomatic dialogue'.[103] Bull's investigation into the revolt against the West asserts that force is no solution to the moral debates in contemporary international society. Agreements and compromises which command the consent of the world's peoples require forms of dialogue which are sensitive to cultural and religious differences. Recent interpretations of rationalism have suggested parallels with the strands of critical theory which argue that there are no established foundations for moral beliefs, and that open dialogue is the best way in which societies can try to bridge their differences.[104]

It has been argued that Bull's claim that the modern society of states should be reformed so that it rests on the consent of the world's peoples is developed further in ethical perspectives which hold that all human beings have the right to participate in making decisions that affect vital interests.[105] Although rationalists have been keenly interested in the history of international thought they have not sought to contribute to international moral and political theory in its own right.[106] Indeed, in Bull's writings one can detect impatience with visions of alternative forms of world political organisation which stray too far from the main issues facing international society and which disregard the practicalities of foreign policy.

That being so, it is intriguing to ask what Wight, Bull and Vincent would have made of recent efforts to weaken the grip of the principle of sovereign immunity and to prosecute those accused of committing war crimes. Yet Bull's last writings seem less remote from the view that one of the functions of international theory is to understand those trends that work against the current system and to defend them in a sophisticated way.[107] Further advances on that front would have required far more attention to the structure of the world economy, to the patterns of inequality which are inherent in it, and to the state's relationship with the increasing power of

global capital. The rationalist analysis of the normative and cultural framework of international relations steered clear of such themes which are more
central to the Marxist tradition, which was dismissed because of its revolutionism, and to the larger domain of international political economy.[108] A
more complex account of the trends working against the system would
have gained a great deal from Kant's theory which was centrally concerned
with how the society of states might make progress in realising commitments to dialogue and consent. Here too the importance of his thinking was
obscured by unhelpful comments about his revolutionism. The significance
of Kant's thought for the rationalist project is even greater today given
pressures to open the diplomatic dialogue to international non-governmental organisations as well as minority nations and indigenous peoples which
have not been adequately represented in the history of international society.
One possible future for rationalism is to ask whether the society of states
can progress towards democratic forms of global governance which tackle
the problems of world poverty and increasing international inequalities
while securing the rights of the culturally different.

Conclusion

In *The Twenty Years' Crisis* E. H. Carr argued that international theory
should avoid the 'sterility' of realism and the 'naivety' of idealism.[109]
Rationalists can claim that they have passed this test of a good international
theory. They have analysed elements of civility and society in international
relations which have been of little interest to realists. Although they have
been principally concerned with understanding international order they
have argued that the theory of international relations is incomplete if it
ignores claims that international society is fundamentally unjust. Rationalists do not argue that order should come before justice but they are not
convinced by the idealist or revolutionist view that states will eventually
settle their differences about morality and justice. The suggestion that
rationalism is the *via media* between realism and revolutionism rests on
such considerations.

Rationalists believe that international society is a precarious achievement
but that it is the only context within which more radical developments can
take place. The argument is that advances in the international protection of
human rights will not occur in the absence of international order. It is to be
expected that there will always be two sides to rationalism: the side that is
quick to detect threats to international society and the side that identifies
ways in which that society might become more responsive to the needs of
individuals and their most immediate associations. The relationship

between these different orientations changes and will continue to change in response to historical circumstances. The Cold War years did little to encourage the search for alternative principles of world order, and the solidarist conception of international society was deemed to be premature; in many respects the passing of bipolarity is more conducive to the development of solidarism although the question of whether states should intervene to prevent human rights violations once again brings the solidarist concern with individual rights into conflict with the pluralist stress on the dangers involved in breaching national sovereignty. The tension between these positions is almost certain to endure. Analysing this tension is sure to remain one of the ways in which rationalism will continue to contribute to understanding the relationship between sovereignty, intervention and human rights in contemporary world politics.

Notes

1. Rationalism is used here as an alternative to the Grotian tradition and to what has been called 'the English School'. The term was used by Martin Wight in the 1950s and 1960s to describe the long tradition of thought which analyses the nature of international society. Rationalism is widely used in the United Kingdom to refer to this approach. In the United States, as Chris Reus-Smit demonstrates in his chapter on constructivism, rationalism is used to describe a specific approach to international institutions and international cooperation. Robert Keohane used the term in this way in an article published in the late 1980s. The different meanings of rationalism may be a source of confusion; however, this chapter keeps faith with Wight's original meaning.
2. M. Wight, 'Why is there no International Theory', in H. Butterfield and M. Wight (eds), *Diplomatic Investigations, Essays in the Theory of International Relations* (London, 1966), p. 33.
3. Ibid., p. 26.
4. M. Wight, 'Western Values in International Relations', in Butterfield and Wight (1966), p. 91.
5. J. D. B. Miller, 'The Third World', in J. D. B. Miller, and R. J. Vincent (eds), *Order and Violence: Hedley Bull and International Relations* (Oxford, 1990), pp. 77–80.
6. For a critique of this view, see N. J. Wheeler and T. Dunne, 'Hedley Bull's Pluralism of the Intellect and Solidarism of the Will', *International Affairs*, 72 (1996), pp. 91–108.
7. A. Watson, 'Hedley Bull, States Systems and International Societies', *Review of International Studies*, 13 (1987), p. 151.
8. Watson (1987), p. 151.
9. M. Wight, *Systems of States* (Leicester, 1977), p. 192.

10. See Wheeler and Dunne (1999); also T. Dunne, *Inventing International Society: A History of the English School* (London, 1998).

11. Wight (1977), p. 43.

12. Wight (1977), pp. 35–9.

13. Wight (1977), p. 33.

14. Wight (1977), pp. 33–5.

15. H. Bull, *The Anarchical Society: A Study of Order in World Politics* (London, 1977), p. 82.

16. Bull (1977), pp. 9–10.

17. Bull (1977), p. 13.

18. R. J. Vincent, 'Edmund Burke and the Theory of International Relations', *Review of International Studies*, 10 (1984), p. 213.

19. Bull (1977), p. 316.

20. Bull (1977), pp. 316–17.

21. Bull (1977), pp. 53–5.

22. H. Suganami, *The Domestic Analogy and World Order Proposals* (Cambridge, 1989).

23. Bull (1977), p. 133.

24. Bull (1977), pp. 16–20.

25. M. Wight, *International Theory: The Three Traditions* (Leicester, 1991), p. 41–2.

26. See A. Linklater, 'Liberal Democracy, Constitutionalism and the New World Order', in R. Leaver and J. L. Richardson (eds), *Charting the Post-Cold War Order* (Colorado, 1993).

27. K. N. Waltz, *Theory of International Politics* (New York, 1979).

28. M. Doyle, 'Liberalism and World Politics', *American Political Science Review*, 80 (1986), pp. 1151–69.

29. Wight (1977), p. 153; author's italics.

30. H. Bull and A. Watson (eds), *The Expansion of International Society* (Oxford, 1984), p. 9.

31. H. Bull, 'The Grotian Conception of International Society', in Butterfield and Wight (1966) p. 52.

32. Bull (1966), p. 64.

33. Bull (1966), p. 52.

34. Bull (1966), p. 68.

35. Bull (1977), p. 73.

36. Bull (1977), p. 16–18 and ch. 4.

37. Bull (1977), p. 227–8.

38. Bull (1977), p. 89.

39. Bull (1977), p. 126. See also Bull's essay on 'Human Rights and World Politics', in R. Pettman (ed.), *Moral Claims in World Affairs* (London, 1979).

40. Bull (1977), p. 22.

41. Bull (1977), p. 289.

42. Bull (1977), p. 83.

43. Bull (1977), p. 83.

44. H. Bull, 'Justice in International Relations', *The Hagey Lectures*, The University of Waterloo (Ontario, 1984).
45. R. J. Vincent, *Human Rights and International Relations* (Cambridge, 1986).
46. R. J. Vincent and P. Wilson, 'Beyond Non-Intervention', in I. Forbes and M. Hoffman (eds), *Political Theory, International Relations and the Ethics of Intervention* (London, 1994), p. 128–9.
47. See T. Dunne and N. J. Wheeler (eds), *Human Rights in Global Politics* (Cambridge, 1999).
48. R. J. Vincent, 'Racial Equality', and H. Bull, 'The Revolt Against the West', in Bull and Watson (1984).
49. Wight (1977), p. 41.
50. H. Bull, 'The West and South Africa', *Daedalus*, 11 (1982), p. 266.
51. Bull (1977), p. 95.
52. Watson (1987), p. 152.
53. H. Bull, 'The International Anarchy in the 1980s', *Australian Outlook*, 37 (1983), pp. 127–31.
54. But see J. Mayall (ed.), *The New Interventionism 1991–1994: United Nations Experience in Cambodia, former Yugoslavia and Somalia* (Cambridge, 1996); also N. J. Wheeler, *Saving Strangers: Humanitarian Intervention in International Society* (Oxford, 2000).
55. Bull (1977), p. 317.
56. Bull (1984), p. 6.
57. S. Huntington, 'The Clash of Civilisations', *Foreign Affairs*, 72 (1993), pp. 22–49.
58. Bull and Watson (1984), p. 87.
59. G. Gong, *The Standard of Civilisation in International Society* (Oxford, 1984).
60. Bull and Watson (1984), pp. 220–4.
61. Bull and Watson (1984), p. 223.
62. Huntington (1993).
63. F. Fukuyama, *The End of History and the Last Man* (London, 1992).
64. C. Brown, 'The Modem Requirement: Reflections on Normative International Theory in a Post-European World', *Millennium*, 17 (1988), pp. 339–48.
65. Bull and Watson (1984), p. 429.
66. Bull (1977), pp. 316–17.
67. Bull (1984), p. 18.
68. P. Keal, *Unspoken Rules and Superpower Dominance* (London, 1983), p. 210.
69. G. B. Helman and S. R. Ratner, 'Saving Failed States', *Foreign Policy*, 89 (1992–93), pp. 3–20.
70. R. Jackson, *Quasi-States: Sovereignty, International Relations and the Third World* (Cambridge, 1990).
71. Helman and Ratner (1992–93).
72. Helman and Ratner (1992–93).
73. See V. Havel's speech on Kosovo in *The New York Review of Books*, 10 June 1999, p. 6.
74. N. Chomsky, *The New Military Humanism: Lessons from Kosovo* (London, 1999).

75. A. Roberts, 'Humanitarian War: Military Intervention and Human Rights', *International Affairs*, 69 (1993), p. 449. See also Vincent and Wilson (1994).
76. See Wight (1966), p. 26; also Waltz (1979), p. 66.
77. Wight (1991), p. 159.
78. See Dunne (1998), ch. 7.
79. Bull (1984), pp. 11–12.
80. Bull (1984), p. 13.
81. Bull (1984), p. 14.
82. Bull (1984), p. 14.
83. Bull (1977), p. 267.
84. Bull (1977), pp. 254–5.
85. Bull (1977), p. 255.
86. H. Bull, 'The State's Positive Role in World Affairs', *Daedalus*, 108 (1979), pp. 111–24.
87. Bull (1977), p. 26.
88. Bull (1977), p. 26.
89. S. Hoffmann, 'International Society', in Miller and Vincent, R. J. (1990), pp. 23–4. See also I. Harris, 'Order and Justice in the Anarchical Society', *International Affairs*, 69 (1993), p. 738.
90. Wight (1991), pp. 41–2.
91. See J. MacMillan, 'A Kantian Protest Against the Peculiar Discourse of Inter-Liberal State Peace', *Millennium*, 24 (1995), pp. 549–62.
92. Wight (1991), p. 29.
93. Wight (1991), p. 73.
94. I. Kant, 'Perpetual Peace', in M. G. Forsyth, *et al.* (eds), *The Theory of International Relations: Selected Texts from Gentili to Treitschke* (London, 1970), p. 206.
95. H. Bull, 'The Theory of International Politics, 1919–1969', in B. Porter (ed.), *The Aberystwyth Papers* (London, 1969), pp. 42–3.
96. H. Bull, 'International Theory: The Case for a Classical Approach', in *World Politics*, 18 (1966), pp. 361–77.
97. Wight (1991), pp. 120 and 248.
98. H. Bull, 'Foreign Policy of Australia', *Proceedings of Australian Institute of Political Science* (Sydney, 1973), p. 137.
99. R. O. Keohane, *International Institutions and State Power: Essays in International Relations Theory*, (Boulder Colorado, 1989).
100. A. Wendt, 'Anarchy is what States Make of it', *International Organisation*, 46 (1992), pp. 391–425.
101. Wight in particular was especially interested in the different types of international society which had emerged in the context of anarchy. See his Systems of States (1977). For a parallel line of investigation from a constructivist approach, see C. Reus-Smit, *The Moral Purpose of the State: Culture, Social Identity and Institutional Rationality in International Relations* (Princeton, 1999).

102. See A. Linklater, *The Transformation of Political Community: Ethical Foundations of the Post-Westphalian Era* (Cambridge, 1998).
103. A. Watson, *Diplomacy: The Dialogue Between States* (London, 1982).
104. See R. Shapcott, 'Conversation and Co-existence: Gadamer and the Interpretation of International Society', *Millennium*, 23 (1994), pp. 57–83.
105. Linklater (1998), ch. 6.
106. See R. E. Jones, 'The English School of International Relations: A Case for Closure', *Review of International Studies*, 7 (1981), pp. 1–2. A notable exception is M. Donelan, *Elements of International Political Theory* (Oxford, 1992).
107. Bull (1977), p. 276.
108. See Jones (1981), p. 8.
109. E. H. Carr, *The Twenty Years' Crisis 1919–1939* (London, 1939) p. 12.

CHAPTER 5

Marxism

Andrew Linklater

In the mid-1840s Marx and Engels wrote that capitalist globalisation had seriously eroded the foundations of the international system of states. Conflict and competition between nation-states had not yet come to an end in their view but the main fault-lines in future looked certain to revolve around the two principal social classes: the national bourgeoisie which controlled the various systems of government and an increasingly cosmopolitan proletariat. The outline of an entirely new kind of society was already contained within the most advanced political movements of the subordinate class. Through revolutionary action, the international proletariat would embed the Enlightenment ideals of liberty, equality and fraternity in an entirely new kind of world order which would free all human beings from exploitation and domination.[1]

Many traditional theorists of international relations have pointed to the failures of Marxism as an account of world history. Marxism has been the foil for their argument that international politics have long revolved around competition and conflict between independent political communities and will do so well into the future. Realists such as Kenneth Waltz claimed that Marxism was a 'second image' account of international relations which believed that the rise of socialist as opposed to capitalist *regimes* would end conflict between states. Its utopian aspirations were bound to be dashed because the struggle for power is an inescapable outcome of international anarchy which only 'third image' analysis can explain.[2] Rationalist thinkers such as Martin Wight maintained that Lenin's *Imperialism: The Highest Stage of Capitalism* might seem to be a study of international politics but it was far too preoccupied with the economic aspects of human life to be regarded as a serious contribution to the field.[3] Marxists had underestimated the impact of nationalism, the state and war, the balance of power, international law and diplomacy on the structure of world politics.

New interpretations of Marxism have appeared over the last twenty years: the perspective has been an important weapon in the critique of realism and there have been many novel attempts to build on its ideas.[4] Its impact on the critical theory of international relations has been immense. It has been an important resource in the area of international political economy as scholars have sought to understand the interplay between states and markets, the states-system and the capitalist world economy, the spheres of power and production. For some, the collapse of the Soviet Union and the triumph of capitalism over socialism mark the death of Marxism as social theory and political practice. But it may be argued that the relevance of Marxism for the present epoch has increased with the passing of the age of bipolarity and the emergence of a new phase of globalisation.[5] Indeed a recent biography argues that with the collapse of the Soviet Union, Marx's writings which were intrigued by the ways in which capitalism broke down Chinese Walls and unified the human race, have finally come of age.[6]

One should not claim too much for Marx and Marxism despite any prescience about the way in which capitalism would become the dominant form of production across the whole world. This is not only because Marx and Marxism took the view that the triumph of capitalism would be short-lived and that its inexorable laws would bring about its destruction. Nor is it just because Marxism had a poor grasp of the importance of the nation-state and violence in the modern world,[7] a point readily conceded by Marxists in the 1970s and 1980s. It is also because modern forms of globalisation are accompanied by renewed ethnic violence and national fragmentation which Marx and Engels, prescient though they were about capitalist globalisation and increasing social inequalities, could not have foreseen. Other Marxist writers saw things differently. Lenin believed that capitalism caused national fragmentation as well as unprecedented advances in globalisation, but this is not to imply that Marxism offers the best explanation of how globalisation and fragmentation have developed in tandem in the modern era and especially since the collapse of the Soviet Union. An evaluation of the perspective cannot avoid the conclusion that Marxism was too preoccupied with systems of production and forms of class conflict to grasp the peculiarities of the modern age or to develop an adequate critical theory of modernity. But it might be found that Marxist analyses of capitalist globalisation and fragmentation invite reconsideration of Waltz and Wight's argument that Marxism cannot be regarded as a serious contribution to the study of international politics and is clearly inferior to conventional approaches in the field. It might also be argued that its project of developing a critical theory of world society is one respect in which Marxism is more sophisticated than the dominant approaches in the Anglo-American study of international politics. If so, the task is to build on its foundations and to preserve its numerous strengths without perpetuating its unmistakable errors and weaknesses.

To reconsider Marxism, Part I of this chapter describes the main features of historical materialism and explains how international relations fitted within that framework. Part II summarises key themes in the Marxist analysis of nationalism and imperialism. Part III provides a brief overview of the orthodox critique of Marxism within International Relations and explains its rehabilitation in the 1980s when political economy and critical theory came to the fore. Part IV evaluates the Marxist tradition in the light of recent developments in the theory of international relations.

I Class, Production and International Relations in Marx's Writings[8]

For Marx, human history has been a laborious struggle to satisfy basic material needs, to understand and tame the natural world, to resist class domination and exploitation, and to overcome fear and distrust of the rest of the human race. The main achievements of human history include the gradual conquest of hostile natural forces which were once beyond human control and understanding, the steady elimination of ignorance and super-stition, the growing capacity to abolish crippling material scarcity and exploitation, and the potential for remaking society so that all human beings can develop a range of creative powers not found in any other species. But modern history shaped by capitalism had unfolded tragically in Marx's view. The power of society over nature had been expanded to an unprece-dented degree but individuals had become trapped within an international social division of labour, exposed to unfettered market forces and exploited by new forms of factory production which turned workers into mere appendages to the machine.[9] Marx thought capitalism had made massive advances in reducing feelings of estrangement between societies. National-ism, he believed, had no place in the hearts and minds of the most advanced proletariat organisations which were committed to a cosmopoli-tan political project. But capitalism was a system of largely unchecked exploitation in which the bourgeoisie controlled the labour-power of the proletariat and profited from their work. It was the root cause of an alienating condition in which the human race – the bourgeoisie as well as the proletariat – was at the mercy of structures and forces which were its own creation. Marx wrote that philosophers had only interpreted the world whereas the real point was to change it.[10] An end to alienation, exploitation, and estrangement was Marx's main political aspiration and the point of his efforts to understand the laws of capitalism and the general development of human history. This was his legacy to thinkers in the Marxist tradition.

Marx believed that the historical import of the forces of production (technology) and the relations of production (specifically the division between those who own the means of production and those who must work for them in order to survive) had been neglected by members of the Hegelian movement with whom he had been closely associated in his formative intellectual years. Hegel had focused on the different forms of artistic, religious, historical, political and philosophical thinking – the diverse types of self-consciousness – which the human race had passed through in its long historical struggle to know itself. After his death, and as part of the struggle over Hegel's legacy, the Left Hegelians attacked religion, believing it was the main form of false consciousness that prevented human beings from acquiring a deep understanding of what they were and what they could become. But for Marx, religious belief was not an intellectual error which could be overcome by philosophical analysis but an expression of the frustrations and aspirations of people struggling with the material conditions of everyday life. Religion was 'the opium of the masses' and the 'sigh of an oppressed creature',[11] and revolutionaries had to understand and challenge the social conditions which gave rise to religious beliefs. 'The critique of heaven', as Marx put it, had to become 'the critique of earth'.[12]

The pivotal theme in Marx's materialist conception of history is that individuals must satisfy their material or physical needs before they can do anything else. In practice, this has meant the mass of humanity has had to surrender control of its labour-power to those that own the instruments of production simply to survive. Given the basic reality of property relations, the dominant classes have had the capacity to exploit the members of the subordinate classes, and this has been the main cause of social conflict. Marx believed that the class struggle had been the dominant form of conflict in human history, the resulting political revolutions had been the main agents of historical development while technological revolutions had been the driving-force behind social change.

Marx wrote that history was the continuous transformation of human nature.[13] Put differently, human beings do not only modify nature by working on it; they also change themselves and develop new needs. The history of the development of the human species could only be understood by tracing the development of the dominant modes of production which, in the West, included primitive communism, slave societies, feudalism and capitalism which would soon be replaced by socialism on an international scale. The fact that Marx thought socialism would be a global development deserves further comment. Although war, imperialism and commerce had destroyed the isolation of early societies, capitalism according to Marx had directed the whole human race into a single stream of world history. Few mainstream students of international relations have commented on Marx's interest in the economic and technological unification of the human race, in the widening of the boundaries of social cooperation and in the forces which block advances in human solidarity.[14] Few have commented on his fascination with the relationship between internationalisation and internationalism,[15] but these are crucial themes in his writings and they contain much that is of value for students of contemporary world politics.

In his reflections on capitalism, Marx argued that universal history came into being as the social relations of production and exchange became global and as more cosmopolitan tastes emerged in the spheres of consumption and literature. The very force which unified humanity had frustrated solidarity by pitting members of the bourgeoisie against each other as well as against the proletariat, and by forcing members of the working class to compete with each other for employment. Yet the tension between the wealth generated by capitalism and the poverty of individual life generated demands for solidarity amongst members of the exploited classes. International working class solidarity was also triggered by the fact that capitalist societies used the language of freedom and equality for all to legitimate existing social relations while systematically denying real freedom and equality to the subaltern classes.

Large normative claims are raised by the question of what it means to be really free and equal. In general, neither Marx nor Engels was interested in moral philosophy although their writings can hardly be regarded as the dispassionate analysis of nineteenth century industrial capitalism. Although they declined to ground their sociological analysis in explicitly ethical claims there is no doubt their inquiry into capitalism is normative through and through.[16] Arguably, Marx's own purpose is made clear in the introductory remarks to *The Eighteenth Brumaire of Louis Bonaparte* where he writes that human beings make their own history but not under conditions of their own choosing.[17] What this means is that humans make their own history because they possess the power of self-determination which other species do not possess or have to the same degree. That they do not make history exactly as they please is because class structures stand over human agents and constrain their freedom of action.

If this interpretation is correct then one of Hegel's most central themes survives in Marx's thought. This is the idea that in the course of their history – which for Marx is a history of the labour-process – human beings acquire a deeper appreciation of what it is to be free and a more sophisticated understanding of the social conditions which must exist if freedom is to be realised more completely. For Marx, freedom and equality in capitalist societies mean that bourgeois and proletarian enter into a labour contract as free and equal subjects, but their equal freedom is contradicted by the existence of massive social inequalities which place one at the mercy of the other. What was developing in various proletarian organisations was an understanding of how socialism could make good the claims to freedom and equality already present in capitalism. Marx's passionate condemnation of capitalism has to be seen in this light: it is a critique from within the capitalist order rather than a challenge from outside which appeals to some transcendent morality in the manner of philosophers such as Kant.

Although Marx rejected Kant's notion that human reason can uncover absolute moral truths he shared his conviction that all efforts to realise freedom within the state could be shattered by the sudden impact of external events. There is no doctrine of socialism in one country in Marx's thought: the argument is that in the context of globalisation human freedom can only be achieved through universal solidarity and cooperation. This is one reason why Marx had so little to say about international relations understood as relations between states and why he focused instead on the challenges which resulted from capitalist globalisation. Marx, and Engels in particular who was a keen student of strategy and war, were aware of the importance of geopolitics in human history and of the role of conquest in the development of larger political associations. No doubt they knew that the struggle for power involving modern European states had led to colonial expansion and the development of world trade and a global market. But the main part of their analysis was not concerned with what states had contributed to the process of globalisation but rather with how the internal dynamics of capitalism were the principal and unstoppable driving-force behind this phenomenon. States may have contributed to this process but they did so largely, and in Marx's view perhaps almost entirely, because of the internal laws of motion of the capitalist system of production.

Some of the most striking and prescient passages in Marx and Engels' writings emphasise the logic of expansionism which is peculiar to modern capitalism. The essence of capitalism is to 'strive to tear down every barrier to intercourse', to 'conquer the whole earth for its market' and to annihilate the tyranny of distance by reducing 'to a minimum the time spent in motion from one place to another'.[18] In a famous passage in *The Communist Manifesto* it was argued that:

> The bourgeoisie has through its exploitation of the world-market given a cosmopolitan character to production and consumption in every country. ... All old-fashioned national industries have been destroyed or are daily being destroyed. ... In place of the old wants, satisfied by the productions of the country, we find new wants, requiring for their satisfaction the products of different lands and climes. In place of the old local and national seclusion and self-sufficiency, we have intercourse in every direction, universal interdependence of nations. ... The bourgeoisie, by the rapid improvement of all instruments of production, by the immensely facilitated means of communication, draws all, even the most barbarian nations, into civilisation. The cheap prices of its commodities are the heavy artillery with which it batters down all Chinese walls, with which it forces the barbarians' intensely obstinate hatred of foreigners to capitulate. It compels all nations, on pain of extinction, to adopt the bourgeois mode of production ... i.e. to become bourgeois themselves. In one word, it creates a world after its own image.[19]

This remarkable statement had clear implications for revolutionary strategy. The sense of 'nationality' might already be 'dead' amongst the most enlightened members of the proletariat, but humanity was still divided into nation-states and national bourgeoisies remained in control of the state apparatus which they used to promote allegedly national interests. Each proletariat would have to settle scores with its own national bourgeoisie but the revolutionary struggle would be national only in form since the proletariat had global political objectives and aspirations.[20]

Realists such as Waltz have argued that during the First World War members of the proletariat concluded they had more in common with their own national bourgeoisie than with the proletariat in other countries. The argument was that no-one with a good understanding of nationalism, the state and war would have been surprised by this turn of events, yet many socialists were shocked by the actions of the European proletariat. For realists, the failure to anticipate this outcome demonstrates one of the central weaknesses of Marxism – its economic reductionism as manifested in its belief that understanding capitalism would reveal the mysteries of the modern world.[21] This is one of the most famous criticisms of Marxism within the field of International Relations, and there are three points to make about it.

The first is that Marx and Engels were undoubtedly aware that technological and political revolutions were transnational in character yet they displayed a strong preference for endogenous explanations of society, arguing that the great political revolutions occurred because of contradictions within separate but not autonomous societies.[22] It has been argued that the relatively peaceful nature of the international system in the middle of the nineteenth century encouraged such beliefs and that the theory of the state was eclipsed by theories of society and the economy.[23] Reflecting one of the dominant tendencies of the age, Marx argued that while relations between states were important they were 'secondary' or 'tertiary' forces in human affairs when compared with modes of production and their laws of development.[24] In a letter to Annenkov Marx asks whether 'the whole organisation of nations, and all their international relations (is) anything else than the expression of a particular division of labour. And must not these change when the division of labour changes?'[25] This is a question rather than an answer yet many have argued – Waltz is an example – that Marx and Marxism largely ignored geopolitics, nationalism and war. Even the most sympathetic reader of Marx's work has to concede that he believed that capitalism rather than nationalism and war would have the decisive impact on the future of modernity.

Second, the importance of nationalism in the 1848 revolutions and its growing appeal later in the century forced Marx and Engels to reconsider their position on national consciousness. They wrote that the Irish and the

Poles were the victims of national domination rather than class exploitation, and concluded that freedom from national dominance was essential if subordinate peoples were to become the allies of the international proletariat.[26] These remarks indicate that while Marx and Engels were primarily concerned with the class structure of capitalist societies they were well aware of the persistence of the older phenomenon of estrangement between national groups, although perhaps always inclined to the view that national differences would eventually fade away.[27] Some further adjustments to their thinking were prompted by the growing threat of inter-state violence in the last part of the nineteenth century. Engels' writings, which repeatedly emphasised the role of war throughout human history, envisaged new levels of violence and suffering in the next major European war and asserted that military competition rather than capitalist crisis might be the spark to ignite the proletarian revolution. Interestingly, Engels argued that the socialist movement had to take matters of national security and the defence of the homeland very seriously given the increased possibility of major war.[28]

Third, as Gallie has noted, these intriguing comments about nationalism, the state and war did not lead to any systematic reworking of the early statements about historical materialism.[29] An unhelpful distinction between the economic base and the legal, political and ideological superstructure of society ran through most summations of the perspective. The capitalist state was too often regarded as a passive instrument of the ruling class although it was thought capable of acquiring some degree of autonomy from ruling class forces under unusual political circumstances. Marx and Engels' political writings revealed greater subtlety but the main statements of their theoretical position continued to privilege class and production, to regard economic power as the main form of political power, and to regard the revolutionary project as fundamentally about promoting the transition from capitalism to socialism notwithstanding their sympathy for what they regarded as progressive national movements.[30]

Marx developed an analysis of capitalism which must remain the key reference point for anyone interested in the critical theory of world politics. An account of the alienating and exploitative character of industrial capitalism was linked with a political vision which looked forward to the democratisation of the labour-process as well as of the more formal political sphere which has been the main concern of democratic theory. Brilliant though the analysis was of the expansion of capitalism to all sectors of modern societies and to all parts of the globe, it is clear that the study of class domination and inequality obscured other forms of social exclusion and systematic harm which must be included in a comprehensive critical theory of world society. These include forms of domination anchored in hierarchical conceptions of race, nation and gender rather than in class-divided societies.

Marx and Engels created some of the foundations of a critical theory and it was up to later radical theorists to build on their important if flawed achievements. Something of this kind is evident in the writings of the Austro-Marxists who developed a more subtle and complex analysis of capitalist globalisation and national fragmentation in a manner that remained true to the spirit rather than the letter of the foundational texts. This is precisely what Max Horkheimer called for in the 1920s and 1930s when what came to be known as Frankfurt School critical theory was first developed.[31] Writing earlier in the century, Austro-Marxists such as Karl Renner and Otto Bauer argued that Marx and Engels had underestimated the impact of cultural differences on human history, the continuing strength of national loyalty and the need to satisfy demands for cultural autonomy in the modern world.[32] Marx and Engels had been vague on the subject of whether national differences would survive and flourish in the socialist world order. The Austro-Marxists envisaged a future in which increasing cultural diversity would be celebrated while cosmopolitanism, understood as 'friendship towards the whole human race' rather than 'the want of national attachment', would develop.[33] This was to combine a more comprehensive sociology of human affairs with a broader normative vision of the socialist project of universal emancipation.

The Austro-Marxist response to the twin forces of globalisation and fragmentation was to imagine a world in which human beings would enjoy levels of solidarity and cultural diversity which had no parallel in human history. These were controversial ideas which clashed with the socialist idea which developed in Soviet Russia under Lenin and Stalin but they indicated one way of building on the Marxian legacy. However, the emergence of Marxism-Leninism meant that what Alvin Gouldner described as the anomalies, contradictions and latent possibilities within the Marxist tradition gave way to a closed quasi-scientific system of supposed truths that destroyed the potential for further development and growth.[34] Numerous encrustations formed around Marxism in this period, as Perry Anderson noted, but the Marxist literature on nationalism and imperialism early in the twentieth century did move the discussion of capitalist globalisation and national fragmentation forward in intriguing ways.[35]

II Nationalism and Imperialism

Although Marx and Engels were mainly interested in modes of production, class conflict and the process of revolution they also analysed the movement towards the economic and technological unification of the human race and raised key questions about centrifugal and centripetal forces in capitalist societies. Their writings touched interestingly on the nature of the social bond which ties the members of one society together but also separates them from the rest of humankind, on the prospects for cooperation at the domestic and international level, and on the possibility of new forms of political community. In their account, early capitalism brought scattered and highly localised groups into single and largely homogeneous nations with clearly demarcated territories. In this initial phase the ruling classes created national bonds which united the people and inhibited the formation of subordinate class identities. As it matured, capitalism burst from its national containers. Its increasingly exploitative character in the era of globalisation led to the development of internationalist sentiments and alliances amongst members of the industrial proletariat. These early assumptions that capitalist internationalisation would be followed by socialist internationalism had to be rethought because of the revival of nationalism and the greater likelihood of systemic war.

Lenin and Bukharin developed the theory of imperialism to explain the causes of the First World War.[36] They argued that the war was the product of a desperate need for new outlets for the surplus capital accumulated by the dominant capitalist states. The theory of capitalist imperialism has been discredited on account of its economic reductionism but, despite its flaws, it was concerned with the central question of how political communities had closed in on themselves in the period in question – an inescapable preoccupation given the Marxian assumption that the main forces in world history encouraged cooperation between the proletariat of different nations.[37] Marx and Engels' primitive analysis of the relationship between nationalism and internationalism was developed in theories of imperialism which were specifically concerned with the interplay between globalisation and fragmentation.

The study of imperialism was, firstly, a critique of the liberal proposition that late capitalism was committed to free trade internationalism which would lead to peace between nations and, secondly, a restatement of Marx's position that it was the fate of capitalism to experience frequent crises. Lenin and Bukharin believed the dominant tendency of the age had created new mercantilist states which were increasingly willing to use force to achieve their economic and political objectives. National accumulations of surplus capital were regarded as the chief cause of the demise of a relatively peaceful international system although Lenin argued that the decline of British hegemony and the changing balance of power had contributed, albeit in a secondary way, to the erosion of constraints on the use of force between the major capitalist states.

Lenin and Bukharin maintained that in this context nationalist and militarist ideologies had blurred class loyalties and stymied class conflict. In *Imperialism: The Highest Stage of Capitalism* Lenin claimed that no 'Chinese wall' separates the (working class) from the other classes'. Indeed a labour aristocracy bribed by colonial profits and closely aligned with the bourgeoisie had developed in monopoly capitalist societies.[38] With the outbreak of the First World War, the working classes which had become 'chained to the chariot of ... bourgeois state power' rallied around the plea to defend the homeland.[39] But it was thought that the shift of the 'centre of gravity' from class conflict to inter-state rivalry could not last indefinitely. The horrors of war would reveal to the working classes that their 'share in the imperialist policy (was) nothing compared with the wounds inflicted by the war'.[40] Instead of 'clinging to the narrowness of the national state' and succumbing to the patriotic ideal of 'defending or extending the boundaries of the bourgeois state' the proletariat would return to the class project of 'abolishing state boundaries and merging all the peoples into one Socialist family'.[41]

As noted earlier, Marx and Engels clearly believed that capitalism created the preconditions for the extension of human loyalty from the nation to the species – and Lenin and Bukharin thought that the destruction of national community and the return to cosmopolitanism would resume after a brief detour down the disastrous path of militarism and war. The notion that the supposed superabundance of finance capital was the reason for the First World War was mistaken but that does not mean that their analysis lacks any merit. Like Marx and Engels before them they were dealing with a fundamentally important theme which has not received the attention it deserves from mainstream international relations theorists who find little or nothing of value in Marxist writings. This is the question of how political communities are shaped by the struggle between nationalism and internationalism in a world political system which is shaped by unusually high levels of global interconnectedness and national fragmentation. It is the question of how the dominant forms of solidarity – particularly the solidarity of the oppressed – are shaped by this process.

Marxist writings on nationalism dealt with these issues in greater detail. Recent claims that the contemporary world has been shaped by globalisation and fragmentation finds an interesting parallel in Lenin's thought: 'Developing capitalism knows two historical tendencies in the national question. The first is the awakening of national life and national movements, the struggle against all national oppression, and the creation of national states. The second is the development and growing frequency of international intercourse in every form, the breakdown of national barriers, the creation of the international unity of capital, of economic life in general, of politics, science etc'.[42] Globalisation and fragmentation were inter-related in Lenin's account of the uneven development of global capitalism which was taken further in what was called Third World Marxism.[43] Metropolitan core countries exploited societies in the periphery which had been brought under the dominion of capital; the latter's principal response was the struggle for national independence.

Lenin noted that particular groups such as the Jews were oppressed because of their religion and ethnicity, and that the demand for national self-determination was their immediate and unsurprising riposte. Socialists had to recognise that estrangement between religious and national groups constituted a huge barrier to universal cooperation. Although Lenin argued that socialists should support progressive national movements and try to harness them to their cause, he rejected the approach taken by the Austro-Marxists. They had advocated a federal approach to national cultures which would give them real autonomy within existing nation-states. National movements, in Lenin's view, should be forced to choose between complete secession and continued membership of the state with exactly the same rights as all other citizens. His judgement was that most national movements would decide against secession realising that small-scale societies would not enjoy the levels of economic growth achievable within more populous societies. Movements that chose to secede would gain freedom from the kind of domination which had led to national animosity and distrust and, in due course, close cooperation between the proletariats of different nations would become possible. This approach to nationalism was designed to avoid 'adapting socialism to nationalism' and to prevent the proletariat from fragmenting into 'separate national rivulets'.[44] Ethnic fragmentation was regarded as an inevitable consequence of globalisation but – the Austro-Marxists apart – the idea of proletarian internationalism trumped any notion of creating multicultural political communities.

Theories of imperialism shared Marx's belief that capitalism was progressive in that it would bring industrial development to all peoples. Western models of development would be imitated across the world. Alternative possibilities were advanced in Trotsky's law of the combined and uneven development of societies which argued that the encounter between the capitalist and pre-capitalist regions of the world would lead to entirely new types of society.[45] More recent theories of development and underdevelopment have built on this theme. Dependency theorists argued that peripheral societies failed to industrialise because of exploitative alliances between dominant class interests in the core and periphery which had no parallel in the history of Western states.[46] Peripheral societies had to secede from the world capitalist economy if they were to enjoy autonomous industrial development. World-systems theory as developed by Wallerstein also disagrees with the classical Marxist view that capitalism will bring industrial development to the world as a whole (although he argues that development does take place in what he calls the 'semi-periphery').[47] Dependency theory and the world-systems approach have been described as neo-Marxist because they do not believe that the spread of capitalism will bring industrial development to the poorer regions of the world (and because they shift the analysis from relations of production to relations of exchange). Although Marxist and neo-Marxist theories of the world economy enjoyed their greatest prominence in the 1970s and 1980s they remain important in an age of increasing global inequalities.[48]

These approaches have also been especially interested in the role of nationalism and internationalism in shaping the modern world. Third World Marxists took up the theme of uneven capitalist development and some writers argued that the proletariat in the industrial world benefits from neo-imperialism and has no interest in transnational class solidarity; these Marxists supported the national revolt of the periphery rather than the utopia of proletarian internationalism.[49] Marxists have disagreed profoundly about whether or nor to welcome nationalism in the peripheral regions of the capitalist world economy, and many have displayed considerable unease with any attempt to dilute the commitment to internationalism which runs though earlier Marxism.[50] The fact that Marxism is a Western doctrine with its roots in the European Enlightenment is the critical point. Marxist cosmopolitanism was developed when European dominance was at its height and when it was not unreasonable to assume that the non-European world would imitate not only its capitalist ways in the narrow sense but also its morality and culture. Third World Marxism was an instructive reminder that the modern world has entered the post-European age shaped by 'the cultural revolt against the West'.[51] Many non-western societies reject Western economic and political systems as well as the encroachment of alien values and beliefs which are profoundly secular and materialist, even though they cannot escape the consequences of capitalist globalisation. In this context all forms of cosmopolitanism – whether Marxist or not – are treated with suspicion.

III   The Changing Fortunes of Marxism in International Relations

To recapitulate the discussion thus far: Marxist approaches to international relations reflected on the processes which had led to the economic and social unification of the human race and they stressed the role that capitalism has played in this development. Replacing alienation, exploitation and estrangement with a form of universal cooperation which would ensure freedom for all was the main normative aspiration. The international proletariat was deemed to be the historical subject which would realise these objectives but rising nationalism and the greater risk of war in Europe led Marx and Engels to review the prospects for universal social cooperation. From the beginning through to more recent analyses of global inequality, Marxists have faced the question of whether economic internationalisation might not be followed by greater internationalism after all because strong and often deeply exclusionary national loyalties persist across the world. The main strands of critical theory have abandoned the paradigm of production, jettisoned the belief that proletariat is the privileged instrument of radical change and broken with the Marxian vision of universal emancipation. But as previously noted this does not mean that students of international relations have nothing to learn from Marxism.

The general assumption until recently was that Marxism had little if anything to offer the analyst of international relations. Realists argued that Marx and Marxism were concerned with how societies have interacted with nature rather than with how they have interacted with each other in ways which frequently lead to war. The paradigm of production was designed to analyse class structure and class conflict rather than national loyalties, state power and geopolitical competition. A failure to understand these phenomena meant that Marxists were wrong to think that capitalist globalisation would be the prelude to a more cosmopolitan world. Illustrating the point, Waltz argued that Marxists failed to appreciate that if the nation-state was to be the arena in which socialism would first be established then socialist governments would have to ensure its national survival before they could promote its global dissemination.[52] Trotsky's remark that he would issue a few revolutionary proclamations as Commissar for Foreign Affairs before closing shop has often been cited as evidence of the naivety of Marxists regarding the harsh realities of international relations.

The speed with which the Soviet regime resorted to traditional methods of diplomacy to promote national survival and security reinforced realist views. Lenin stressed in 1919 that 'we are living not merely in a state, but in a system of states'[53] – yet far from transforming the international system Marxism was transformed by it and contributed to its reproduction. The Soviet domination of Eastern Europe provoked nationalist aspirations for self-determination which realised their aspirations in many cases. Vietnam's invasion of Cambodia, and the war between China and Vietnam, were cited as evidence of the validity of the realist claim that traditional power politics would survive the transition from capitalism to state socialism.[54] The failure of Marxists to anticipate this outcome was for realists the inevitable outcome of their mistaken theory of the state.

This is a point which many Marxists conceded in the 1970s and 1980s. The essence of Marx's own position has often been thought to be contained in his remark that the state in capitalist societies is little more than the executive committee of the bourgeoisie since power in the sphere of production converts into power over society as a whole.[55] Marxists in the 1960s and 1970s moved away from this crude reductionism, arguing that the state had to have some autonomy simply to ensure the survival of capitalism or to pacify subordinate class movements – by ensuring that the labour force was provided with a basic education and health care, and that capitalism did not drive down wages to the point where the very survival of the system might be in question. A more radical path was taken by Marxists who recognised the importance of Max Weber's point that the state enjoys a monopoly control of the instruments of violence and is responsible for protecting society from internal challenges and external threats. A large literature in the 1970s and 1980s sought to reorient Marxism so that it took full account of the realm of geopolitical competition and war – a realm in which the state often has considerable autonomy from dominant class forces.[56]

At the very point when Marxism was absorbing ideas which have long been associated with classical realism, International Relations began to take account of many of the concerns of Marxists and neo-Marxists. Dependency theory was crucial here for two reasons: it forced students of international relations to analyse global inequalities which are the result of the organisation of the capitalist world economy, and it urged moral engagement with the unequal distribution of power and wealth in world society. It did so at a time when the newly independent states had forced the issue of global economic and social justice onto the diplomatic agenda.

The study of global inequality was the vehicle that brought the Marxist tradition more directly into contact with the study of international relations. Robert Cox's analysis of social forces, states and world order remains the most ambitious attempt to use historical materialism as a means of superseding statecentric international relations theory. His materialist conception of global economic and political structures focuses on the interaction between modes of production – specifically the capitalist mode – states and world order, but this is not an exercise in economic reductionism. Cox claims that production shapes other realms such as the nature of state power and strategic interaction – and to a far greater extent than traditional international relations theory has realised – but it is also shaped by them. The relative importance of each domain is an empirical question rather than a matter that can be settled a priori; however, Cox is especially interested in beginning with the sphere of production and with working out to the other constituent parts of the global order. Special emphasis is placed on the internationalisation of relations of production in the modern capitalist era and on the forms of global governance which perpetuate inequalities of power and wealth. Taking up themes which were developed by the Italian Marxist, Antonio Gramsci in the 1920s and 1930s, Cox focuses on the hegemonic character of world order, that is on how the political architecture of global capitalism maintains inequality through various permutations of coercion and consent.[57]

The neo-Gramscian school approach to international political economy has been particularly interested in understanding the origins, development and possible transformation of the modern instruments of global hegemony.[58] These instruments include close cooperation between powerful elites in core and industrialising societies and the growing network of international economic and political institutions involved in global regulation and governance.[59] The notion of 'disciplinary neo-liberalism' takes this form of investigation further by analysing the 'new constitutionalism' in which global structures force governments to bow to the dictates of neo-liberal conceptions of the state, society and economy.[60] Crucial here are the forms of surveillance and control associated with political conditionality as well as international pressures to deregulate various sectors of the domestic economy and to accede to international legal and political developments which facilitate the continuing expansion of capitalism.

These modes of explanation lend support to Fred Halliday's comment that 'the modern inter-state system emerged in the context of the spread of capitalism across the globe, and the subjugation of pre-capitalist societies. This socio-economic system has underpinned both the character of individual states and of their relations with each other: no analysis of international relations is possible without reference to capitalism, the social formations it generated and the world system they comprise'.[61] This is perfectly compatible with the realist argument that states often pursue their own agenda and act independently of dominant class forces, although it is a clear invitation not to exaggerate the autonomy of most states – especially under modern conditions of capitalist globalisation which compel all states to respect the power of global financial markets and institutions.

The continuing importance of Marxism as a resource for analysts of the global political economy reveals one aspect of its changing fortunes within the field of international relations. As we have seen, classical theorists of international relations as well as many sociologists criticised Marxism for underestimating the role of geopolitics and war in the development of human societies. This convergence of views was encouraged by the struggle between the great powers in the era of bipolarity. Marxists and their sympathisers were critical of realist arguments that strategic competition could be considered apart from the struggle between two radically different social systems and ideological perspectives, although this view had few adherents within mainstream International Relations.[62] The collapse of bipolarity and the great advances in the development of the 'global business civilisation' over the last decade have encouraged a further reassessment of Marx's writings on capitalist globalisation. The same might be said of the long tradition of Marxist literature on the relationship between capitalism and the state which still has much to contribute to the study of global governance in a period when the subordination of states to the dictates of global capitalism is – as Marxists would expect – so evident.[63] New analyses of global capitalism, international inequality, the information revolution and the changing nature of the state may rejuvenate Marxism. These are the respects in which it is best placed to contribute to the modern study of international relations.[64]

Marxism has been influential in shaping forms of international political economy which have a critical or emancipatory intent. Marx wrote about the origins and development of modern capitalism but he was especially interested in the forces that would bring about its transformation with the result that the mass of humanity would be freed from domination and exploitation. Neo-Gramscian approaches work in the same spirit by focusing on counter-hegemonic forces in world society – that is on the various groups which stand opposed to a form of world order which produces amongst other things massive global inequalities and damage to the natural environment. One of the main challenges to realism and neo-realism which draws clearly on the Marxist tradition argues that they have had a 'problem-solving' rather than a 'critical' purpose and orientation.

A distinction between problem-solving and critical theory was first made by Cox in conjunction with his much-quoted remark that 'knowledge is always for someone and for some purpose'.[65] Put another way, social inquiry is never objective and value-free but supports, however indirectly, particular conceptions of society which favour identifiable sectional interests. Cox argued that neo-realism is a version of problem-solving theory which takes the existing international order for granted and asks how it can be made to 'function more smoothly'. In the main, this meant that neo-realism concentrates on the problems resulting from strategic relations between the great powers. By contrast, critical theory asks how the existing global political and economic order came into existence and whether it might be changing. Following the example of Marx's study of capitalism, and mindful of his observation that 'all that is solid eventually melts into air',[66] critical theory focuses on opposition to the international status quo, on the forces that threaten the longer-term survival of an international order which will no doubt disappear one day and join the other dead civilisations, and on what might be the birth pangs of a different, more humane form of world political organisation. The upshot of this argument is that mainstream international theorists were too quick to dismiss Marxism on account of its economic reductionism and utopianism. What was missing from their account was any recognition of the fact that knowledge is always for someone and some purpose, and could have a critical as opposed to a problem-solving orientation. One of the main outcomes of the belated engagement with Marxism is that such considerations are now central to the theory of international relations.

Developments in international political economy have made a major contribution to what might be called the critical turn in international relations – in keeping with historical materialism the emphasis has been on the international distribution of economic and political power. Of course, this is only one strand of contemporary critical theory. Other approaches such as feminism and postmodernism have been concerned with patriarchy in international relations and with constructions of identity, otherness and difference. Admittedly these dimensions of world politics have not been central to Marxism notwithstanding past efforts to develop particular forms of cultural Marxism. Cox's version of historical materialism has taken account of the recent upsurge of identity politics associated with minority nations and indigenous peoples, in particular by focusing on the relationships between different civilisations in the post-European world order. The normative vision which runs through his writings on this subject moves beyond questions of class inequality and distributive social justice. He states that 'a post-hegemonic order would be one in which different traditions of civilisation could co-exist, each based on a different intersubjectivity defining a distinct set of values and a distinct path towards development' – similarly, 'mutual recognition and mutual understanding' is needed so that different civilisations come to enjoy their rightful place in a more just form of world political organisation.[67]

The focus on civilisation overlaps in interesting ways with the project of reconstructing historical materialism which is associated with the writings of the Frankfurt School critical theorist, Jürgen Habermas. His key point was that Marxism overestimated the importance of 'labour' for the structure of society and historical change and underestimated the role of 'interaction'. Put another way, Marxism had developed the 'paradigm of production' to understand how human beings learned how to control nature but it failed to deal with the equally important question of how human beings have learned to create orderly societies and how they have developed the capacity to rework them so that they express the will of their members. What was missing from its political economy was the 'paradigm of communication' which addresses the forms of human learning which take place within this latter sphere; and what was absent from its normative vision was the recognition that universal emancipation requires more than the conquest of nature and the destruction of class inequalities.[68] The additional ingredient in Habermas's view was progress in social communication and the radical democratisation of social, economic and political life.

The reconstruction of historical materialism has led Habermas to develop what he calls 'discourse ethics' or 'the discourse theory of morality'. The details of his argument need not concern us here, and indeed the whole argument has only the most tenuous links with the letter though not the spirit of classical Marxism which loses its identity if it surrenders the claim that class and production are the dominant forces in society and history.[69] However it is worth pausing to consider those features of the argument which have had most significance for the critical theory of international relations. Arguably the most fundamental is that modern societies no longer have secure foundations for their ethical beliefs and must surrender all hope of discovering a single moral code to which all human beings must submit. The contingency and partiality of all moral codes, and the fact of conflict between them, raises the question of whether there are any procedures which will make it possible for the exponents of different moralities to learn how to live together. The discourse theory of morality is put forward as the answer to this question. Its key requirement is that individuals must bring their different ethical positions before the tribunal of open discussion. They must be prepared to listen to all persons and to respect all standpoints, recognising that prior to dialogue itself there can be no certainty about who will learn from whom. The point of open dialogue is to establish whether or not there is any consensus regarding the best moral argument. If there is no consensus – and consensus must never be forced – they must then negotiate a just compromise between their competing positions.[70]

Two points need to be made about the outcome of Habermas's efforts to reconstruct historical materialism. First, Habermas moves beyond the paradigm of production which distinguished Marxism from other approaches to society and history. No claims are made about the primacy of the mode of production and the centrality of the class struggle in any form of life. The idea of universal emancipation as the reduction and eradication of class inequality is superseded by a vision of the good society in which there is greater human understanding and in which no-one deprives 'the other of otherness'.[71] The second point is that Habermas remains committed to the cosmopolitan project of the Enlightenment which is revised to take account of the post-European age and the circumstance of growing cultural diversity. In his writings there is no detailed account of the nature of the good society – although it is often argued that Marx provided no more than an outline of the envisaged future communist society on the grounds that revolutionaries would work this out for themselves. What is offered is a vision of global arrangements in which all human beings are equally entitled to participate in making any decision which may affect them. There is a link here with the radical democratic ethos in Marx's thought which looked forward to a world in which human beings make more of their history under conditions of their own choosing.[72] Of course, it might be argued that one does not have to be a Marxist to support this vision of cosmopolitan democracy although exponents of this ideal contend that progress towards a 'universal communication community' requires the eradication of all 'asymmetries' in society.[73] But asymmetries in this case include forms of exclusion associated with patriarchy and ethnic and racial domination as well as class inequality. Working through the logic of these claims is one of the ways in which the reconstruction of historical materialism builds on the foundations of classical Marxism.

IV   Marxism and International Relations Theory Today

Until quite recently Marxism was the dominant powerful form of critical social theory: it combined a powerful analysis of the whole development of human history with a detailed study of the evolution of capitalism and the prospects for universal emancipation. Yet the failure to break free from the paradigm of production made Marxists vulnerable to the charge of neglecting racial, ethnic, religious and gender inequality. Feminist and post-modern writers have developed new forms of critical social theory which owe very little to Marxism and many reject the idea of universal emancipation suspecting that all cosmopolitan projects contain the seeds of new forms of domination. They have the evidence of Marxism in power to support them. Efforts to reconstruct historical materialism and to import ideas from other traditions have taken place, as the development of Habermas's thought reveals. But the question that inevitably arises as a result of these challenges to, and revisions, of Marxism is whether the perspective now has a distinctive identity or a special contribution to make to the future of critical international theory.

One answer to this question argues that Marxism has been superseded by new forms of critical theory which have abandoned the idea of universal emancipation and the notion that the development of the human race can be reduced to one grand historical narrative. From this vantage-point, some may strive to reconstruct historical materialism and to transform the paradigm of production so that other dimensions of history and society are given their due, but this is to ignore deep problems in all theories anchored in the European Enlightenment. The French postmodern writer, Jean-François Lyotard argued that the belief that human history was a journey from domination and superstition to freedom and enlightenment overlooked the dark side of Western rationality and scientific progress.[74] Viewed in this light, there can be little doubt that Marx and Engels were often condescending towards, if not contemptuous of, non-western societies and were convinced that Western capitalism alone could liberate the 'historyless peoples'. Opponents of the Enlightenment have developed new forms of critical theory which challenge the ways in which individual and collective identities have been shaped by efforts to dehumanise and demean the other. Their purpose has been to celebrate human diversity and cultural difference.

Lyotard's defence of diversity led to a form of universalism in which dialogue and consent were affirmed as global principles – although this was a universalism without absolute foundations and without an explicit commitment to a philosophy of history. All human beings, he argued, have an equal right to 'establish their community by contract' using 'reason and debate'.[75] There are parallels between this position and the discourse theory of morality – and arguably with the radical democratic ethos attributed to Marx[76] – but there is also an important emphasis on the permanent danger that dialogue will end in a forced or false consensus.

It might be argued that such visions of the radical democratisation of human life need to deal with the problem of social inequality and how it prevents the establishment of community through contract and consent. In his analysis of the contemporary relevance of *The Communist Manifesto*, the leading poststructuralist writer, Jacques Derrida, makes the case for a 'new international' since 'violence, inequality, exclusion, famine, and thus economic oppression [have never] affected as many human beings in the history of the Earth and of humanity'.[77] Defending the 'spirit of Marxism', Derrida argues for revising Marx's notion of the eventual 'withering away of the state'.[78] This must now be freed from earlier claims about socialist internationalism and the dictatorship of the proletariat. The 'new International' has to protest against 'the state of international law, the concepts of state and nation' and break with inherited assumptions about exclusionary sovereign states and national conceptions of citizenship. What is envisaged are new forms of community in which the state no longer possesses 'a space which it ... dominates' and which 'it never dominated without division'.[79] The emphasis here is on new political arrangements which are more universalistic than their predecessors (because they are concerned with the right of all human beings to a decent life), more sensitive to cultural and other differences (thereby realising one of the main aspirations of the Austro-Marxists) and more committed to the reduction of global economic inequalities (so keeping faith with the central tenets of classical Marxism).[80] There is a strong invitation also to Marxists to reflect more deeply on the nature of the state, political community, international law and citizenship.

As noted earlier, mainstream international relations theorists were critical of Marxist writers who believed that globalisation would eradicate national sentiments and undermine sovereign states. Their argument was that strategic interaction far outweighs globalisation in importance, and geopolitical competition forces peoples to rely on nation-states for their security rather than support experiments in creating new forms of political community. The Marxist vision of universal solidarity had been broken on the wheel of power politics. The major wars in the first part of the twentieth century, and the bipolar struggle which dominated most of the second half of the century, made it easier for realism and neo-realism to define the study of international politics. However the key determinants of world politics do not stay constant. In some periods strategic rivalry appears to prevail; in others – in the aftermath of the Napoleonic Wars for example – economic factors assume greater importance. With the decline of bipolarity a great deal of literature has been devoted to 'the end of geopolitics' and 'the obsolescence of war'.[81] Much has been written about the new age of ethnic fragmentation and about the phenomenon which was so central to Marx's political economy – globalisation, or capitalist globalisation as Marxists would rightly prefer to call it. Strategic rivalries are less central to the world political system than they were just over a decade ago. The new agenda is concerned with increasing global inequalities and the governance of transnational capitalism, with how far the dominant states simply make the world safe for the further expansion of capital and with whether the counter-hegemonic movements in international civil society can resist the

Gramsci, Historical Materialism and International Relations (Cambridge, 1993); F. Halliday, *Rethinking International Relations* (London, 1994); V. Kubalkova and A. Cruickshank, *Marxism–Leninism and the Theory of International Relations* (London, 1980) and *Marxism and International Relations* (London, 1985); A. Linklater, *Beyond Realism and Marxism: Critical Theory and International Relations* (London, 1990); J. MacLean, 'Marxism and International Relations: A Strange Case of Mutual Neglect', *Millennium*, 17 (1988), pp. 295–31; J. Rosenberg, *The Empire of Civil Society: A Critique of the Realist Theory of International Relations* (London, 1994).

5. On these themes, see A. Gamble, 'Marxism after Communism: Beyond Realism and Historicism', *Review of International Studies*, 25 (1999), pp. 127–44.

6. F. Wheen, *Karl Marx* (London, 1999).

7. A. Giddens, *The Nation-State and Violence* (Cambridge, 1985).

8. Complex questions about the respective contributions of Marx and Engels to the development of historical materialism are beyond the scope of this essay. For further discussion, see T. Carver, *Marx and Engels: The Intellectual Relationship* (Brighton, 1983).

9. K. Marx, *Capital*, vol. 1, in McLellan (1977), p. 477.

10. K. Marx, *Theses on Feuerbach*, in McLellan (1977), p. 158.

11. K. Marx, *Towards A Critique of Hegel's Philosophy of Right: Introduction*, in McLellan (1977), p. 64.

12. Ibid., p. 64.

13. K. Marx, *Economic and Philosophical Manuscripts*, in McLellan (1977), p. 105.

14. See S. Gill, 'Gramsci and Global Politics: Towards a Post-Hegemonic Research Agenda', in Gill (1993).

15. An exception is F. Halliday, 'Three Concepts of Internationalism', *International Affairs*, 64 (1988), pp. 187–98.

16. See C. J. Brown, 'Marxism and International Ethics', in T. Nardin and D. R. Napel (eds), *Traditions of International Ethics* (Cambridge, 1992), ch. 11 and S. Lukes, *Marxism and Morality* (Oxford, 1985).

17. K. Marx, 'The Eighteenth Brumaire of Louis Bonaparte', in McLellan (1977), p. 300.

18. K. Marx, *Grundrisse* (Harmondsworth, 1973), p. 539.

19. K. Marx and F. Engels, 'Communist Manifesto', in McLellan (1977), pp. 224–5.

20. Ibid., pp. 230 and 235.

21. Waltz (1959), ch. 5

22. A. Giddens, *A Contemporary Critique of Historical Materialism* (London, 1981).

23. See W. B. Gallie, *Philosophers of Peace and War* (Cambridge, 1978).

24. Marx (1973), p. 109.

25. K. Marx, *The Poverty of Philosophy* (Moscow, 1966), p. 159.

26. K. Marx and F. Engels, *Ireland and the Irish Question* (London, 1971), p. 332; E. Benner, 'Marx and Engels on Nationalism and National Identity: A Reappraisal', *Millennium*, 17 (1988), pp. 1–23; E. Benner, *Really Existing Nationalisms: A Post-Communist View from Marx and Engels* (Oxford, 1995).

27. On this last point, see F. Halliday, *Revolution and World Politics: The Rise and Fall of the Fifth Great Power* (Basingstoke, 1999), p. 79.

28. See Gallie (1978); also E. H. Carr, 'The Marxist Attitude to War', *A History of Soviet Russia*, vol. 3, 'The Bolshevik Revolution, 1917–23', (London, 1953), pp. 549–66.

29. Gallie (1978).

30. I. Cummins, *Marx, Engels and National Movements* (London, 1980).

31. G. Friedman, *The Political Philosophy of the Frankfurt School* (New York, 1981), pp. 35–6.

32. T. B. Bottomore and P. Goode (eds), *Austro–Marxism* (Oxford, 1978).

33. See the entries under 'Cosmopolitanism' and 'Cosmophile' in *The Oxford English Dictionary*.

34. A. Gouldner, *The Two Marxisms: Contradictions and Anomalies in the Development of Theory* (New York, 1980).

35. P. Anderson, *In the Tracks of Historical Materialism* (London, 1983).

36. V. Lenin, *Imperialism: The Highest Stage of Capitalism* (Moscow, 1968); N. Bukharin, *Imperialism and World Economy* (London, 1972).

37. Linklater (1990), ch. 4.

38. Lenin (1968), p. 102.

39. Bukharin (1972), p. 166.

40. Bukharin (1972), p. 167.

41. Bukharin (1972).

42. V. Lenin, *Collected Works*, vol. 20 (Moscow, 1964), p. 27.

43. A. Emmanuel, *Unequal Exchange: A Study of the Imperialism of Trade* (New York, 1972). For a general discussion see A. Brewer, *Marxist Theories of Imperialism: A Survey* (London, 1990).

44. J. Stalin, 'Marxism and the National Question', *Collected Works* (Moscow, 1953), pp. 343 and 354.

45. B. Knei-Paz, *The Social and Political Thought of Leon Trotsky* (Oxford, 1978). Trotsky's stress on combined development is, for Halliday, of continuing value to the student of revolutions in world politics. See Halliday (1999), p. 320.

46. A. G. Frank, *Capitalism and Underdevelopment in Latin America* (New York, 1967).

47. I. Wallerstein, *The Capitalist World Economy* (Cambridge, 1979).

48. C. Thomas, 'Where is the Third World Now?', *Review of International Studies*, 25 (1999), p. 228.

49. See Emmanuel (1972).

50. T. Nairn, *The Break-up of Britain* (London, 1981); B. Warren, *Imperialism: Pioneer of Capitalism* (London, 1980).

51. C. J. Brown, 'The Modern Requirement? Reflections on Normative International Theory in a Post-Western World', *Millennium*, 17 (1988), pp. 339–48; H. N. Bull, 'Justice in International Relations', Hagey Lectures, University of Waterloo (Ontario, 1984).

52. Waltz (1959).

53. Quoted in Halliday (1999), p. 312.
54. See Giddens (1981), p. 250; Kubalkova and Cruickshank (1980).
55. K. Marx and F. Engels, 'The Communist Manifesto', in McLellan (1977), p. 223.
56. See P. Anderson, *Lineages of the Absolutist State* (London, 1974); F. Block, 'Beyond State Autonomy: State Managers as Historical Subjects', *Socialist Register* (1980), pp. 227–42; S. Brucan, *The Dialectic of World Politics* (New York, 1978); T. Skocpol, *States and Social Revolutions* (Cambridge, 1979).
57. R. W. Cox, 'Structural Issues of Global Governance: Implications for Europe', in S. Gill (ed.), *Gramsci, Historical Materialism and International Relations* (Cambridge, 1993) ch. 10.
58. Gill (1993).
59. Gill (1993). See also Cox (1983).
60. S. Gill, 'Globalisation, Market Civilisation and Disciplinary Neo-Liberalism', *Millennium*, 24 (1995), pp. 399–423.
61. F. Halliday, *Rethinking International Relations* (London, 1994) p. 61. See also Rosenberg (1994).
62. F. Halliday, *The Making of the Second Cold War* (London, 1983).
63. See S. Bromley, 'Marxism and Globalisation', ch. 14, and C. Hay, 'Marxism and the State', ch. 8, in A. Gamble *et al.* (eds) *Marxism and Social Science* (London, 1999).
64. See Gamble, 'Marxism after Communism: Beyond Realism and Historicism', (1999).
65. Cox (1981), p. 128.
66. K. Marx and F. Engels, 'The Communist Manifesto', in McLellan (1977), p. 224.
67. R. W. Cox, 'Multilateralism and World Order', *Review of International Studies*, 18 (1992), pp. 161–80, and Cox (1993), p. 265.
68. J. Habermas, *Communication and the Evolution of Society* (Boston, 1979). See also R. Roderick, *Habermas and the Foundations of Critical Theory* (London, 1986).
69. See Linklater (1990).
70. J. Habermas, *Moral Consciousness and Communicative Action* (Cambridge, 1990).
71. J. Habermas, *The Past as Future* (Cambridge, 1994), p. 119–20.
72. T. Carver, *The PostModern Marx* (Manchester, 1998).
73. K.-O. Apel, *Towards a Transformation of Philosophy* (London, 1980), p. 283 and J. Cohen, 'Discourse Ethics and Civil Society', in D. Rasmussen (ed.), *Universalism vs Communitarianism* (Cambridge, MA, 1990).
74. J.-F. Lyotard, *The PostModern Condition: A Report on Knowledge* (Manchester, 1984).
75. J.-F. Lyotard, 'The Other's Rights', in S. Shute and S. Hurley (eds), *On Human Rights: The Oxford Amnesty Lectures* (New York, 1993), p. 138.
76. Carver (1998).
77. J. Derrida, 'Spectres of Marx', *New Left Review*, 205 (May/June, 1994a), p. 32. See also J. Derrida, *Spectres of Marx: The State of the Debt, the Work of Mourning and the New International* (London, 1994b).

78. Derrida (1994a), p. 56.
79. Derrida (1994a), p. 58.
80. See also A. Linklater, *The Transformation of Political Community; Ethical Foundations of the Post-Westphalian Era* (Cambridge, 1998).
81. J. Richardson, 'The End of Geopolitics?', in J. L. Richardson and R. Leaver (eds), *Charting the Post-Cold War World* (Boulder Colorado, 1993), and J. Mueller, *Retreat from Doomsday: The Obsolescence of Major War* (New York, 1989).

CHAPTER 6

Critical Theory

Richard Devetak

Since the early 1980s international relations theory has seen the emergence of more reflective forms of theoretical inquiry as Realist, Liberal and Marxist orthodoxies in international relations have been submitted to critical scrutiny. Scholars such as Richard Ashley, Robert W. Cox, Andrew Linklater, John Maclean and Mark Hoffman began to address epistemological, ontological and normative questions, which traditionally had been marginalised, under the broad banner of critical social theory. The epistemological questions largely revolved around the relationship between knowledge and values, especially identifying latent interests guiding the main theoretical traditions of international relations. The ontological questions were concerned with identifying and analysing not just relevant agents and structures in international relations but revealing their historical transformations and complicity with various forms of domination and exclusion. The normative questions, already implicit in the epistemological and ontological aspects, were essentially driven by an interest in emancipation. Critical international theory, building especially on the lineage of emancipatory politics extending from Kant via Marx to Habermas, sought to inquire into the possibilities of transforming international relations in order to remove unnecessary constraints on achieving universal freedom and equality.

During the latter part of the 1990s a new generation of 'critical international theorists' emerged. This generation, including Karin Fierke, Stephen Gill, Kimberly Hutchings, Mark Neufeld, and Richard Shapcott among others, draws upon the lineage of emancipatory politics, but brings with it also other intellectual influences. Critical international theory has always been rather eclectic in its intellectual sources, but it is now a broader theoretical perspective incorporating elements of Aristotelean, Foucaultian, Gadamerian, Hegelian and Wittgensteinian methods and arguments. Nonetheless, if there is anything that holds this disparate group of scholars together who subscribe to 'critical theory' it is the idea that the study of international relations should be oriented by an emancipatory politics. While the removal of various forms of domination and the promotion of global freedom, justice and equality are the driving forces behind critical international theory, these are articulated on the basis of reflexive theory based on the method of immanent critique.

This chapter is divided into three main parts: firstly, a sketch of the origins of critical theory; secondly, an examination of the political nature of knowledge claims in international relations; and thirdly, a detailed account of critical international theory's attempt to place questions of community at the centre of the study of international relations.

Origins of Critical Theory

Critical theory has its roots in a strand of thought which is often traced back to the Enlightenment and connected to the writings of Kant, Hegel and Marx. Whilst this is an important lineage in the birth of critical theory it is not the only possible one that can be traced, as there is also the imprint of classical Greek thought on autonomy and democracy to be considered, as well as the thinking of Nietzsche and Weber. However, in the twentieth century critical theory became most closely associated with a distinct body of thought known as the Frankfurt school.[1] It is in the work of Max Horkheimer, Theodor Adorno, Walter Benjamin, Herbert Marcuse, Erich Fromm, Leo Lowenthal and, more recently, Jürgen Habermas that critical theory acquired a renewed potency and in which the term *critical theory* came to be used as the emblem of a philosophy which questions modern social and political life through a method of immanent critique. It was largely an attempt to recover a critical and emancipatory potential that had been overrun by recent intellectual, social, cultural, political, economic and technological trends.

Essential to the Frankfurt school's critical theory was a concern to comprehend the central features of contemporary society by understanding its historical and social development, and tracing contradictions in the present which may open up the possibility of transcending contemporary society and its built-in pathologies and forms of domination. Critical theory intended 'not simply to eliminate one or other abuse,' but to analyse the underlying social structures which result in these abuses with the intention of overcoming them.[2] It is not difficult to notice the presence here of the theme advanced by Marx in his eleventh thesis on Feuerbach: 'philosophers have only interpreted the world in various ways; the point is to change it'.[3] This normative interest in identifying immanent possibilities for social transformation is a defining characteristic of a line of thought which extends, at least, from Kant, through Marx, to contemporary critical theorists such as Habermas. This intention to analyse the possibilities of realising emancipation in the modern world entailed critical analyses of both obstructions to, and immanent tendencies towards 'the rational organization of human activity'.[4] Indeed, this concern extends the line of thought back beyond Kant to the classical Greek conviction that the rational constitution of the *polis* finds its expression in individual autonomy and the establishment of justice and democracy. Politics, on this understanding, is the realm concerned with realising the just life.

There is, however, an important difference between critical theory and the Greeks which relates to the conditions under which knowledge claims can be made regarding social and political life. There are two points worth recalling in this regard: firstly, the Kantian point that reflection on the limits of what we can know is a fundamental part of theorising, and secondly, a Hegelian and Marxian point that knowledge is always, and irreducibly, conditioned by historical and material contexts. Since critical theory takes society itself as its object of analysis, and since theories and acts of theorising are never independent of society, critical theory's scope of analysis must necessarily include reflection on theory. In short, critical theory must be self-reflective; it must include an account of its own genesis and application in society. By drawing attention to the relationship between knowledge and society, which is so frequently excluded from mainstream theoretical analysis, critical theory recognises the political nature of knowledge claims.

It was on the basis of this recognition that Horkheimer distinguished between two conceptions of theory, which he referred to as traditional and critical theories. Traditional conceptions of theory picture the theorist at a remove from the object of analysis. By analogy with the natural sciences, they claim that subject and object must be strictly separated in order to theorise properly. Traditional conceptions of theory assume there is an external world 'out there' to study, and that an inquiring subject can study this world in a balanced and objective manner by withdrawing from the world it investigates, and leaving behind any ideological beliefs, values, or opinions which would invalidate the inquiry. To qualify as theory it must at least be value-free. On this view, theory is only possible on condition that an inquiring subject can withdraw from the world it studies (and in which it exists) and rid itself of all biases. This contrasts with critical conceptions that deny the possibility of value-free social analysis.

By recognising that theories are always embedded in social and political life, critical conceptions of theory allow for an examination of the purposes and functions served by particular theories. However, while such conceptions of theory recognise the unavoidability of taking their orientation from the social matrix in which they are situated, their guiding interest is one of emancipation from, rather than legitimation and consolidation of, existing social forms. The purpose underlying critical, as opposed to traditional, conceptions of theory is to improve human existence by abolishing injustice.[5] As articulated by Horkheimer, this conception of theory does not simply present an expression of the 'concrete historical situation', it also acts as 'a force within [that situation] to stimulate change'.[6] It allows for the intervention of humans in the making of their history.

It should be noted that whilst critical theory has not directly addressed the international level, this in no way implies that international relations is beyond the limits of its concern. The writings of Kant and Marx in particular have demonstrated that what happens at the international level is of immense significance to the achievement of universal emancipation. It is the continuation of this project in which critical international theory is engaged. The Frankfurt School, however, never addressed international relations in its critiques of the modern world, and Habermas has made only scant reference to it until recently.[7] The main tendency of critical theory is to take individual society as the focus and to neglect the dimension of relations between and across societies. For critical international theory, however, the task is to extend the trajectory of Frankfurt school-critical theory beyond the domestic realm to the international, or, more accurately, global realm. It makes a case for a theory of world politics which is 'committed to the emancipation of the species'.[8] Such a theory would no longer be confined to an individual *polis*, but would examine relations between and across them, and reflect on the possibility of extending the rational, just and democratic organisation of politics across the globe.[9]

To summarise, critical theory draws upon various strands of Western social, political, and philosophical thought in order to erect a theoretical framework capable of reflecting on the nature and purposes of theory and revealing both obvious and subtle forms of injustice and domination in society. Critical theory not only challenges and dismantles traditional forms of theorising, it also problematises and seeks to dismantle entrenched forms of social life that constrain human freedom. Critical international theory is an extension of this critique to the international domain. The next part of the chapter focuses on the attempt by critical international theorists to dismantle traditional forms of theorising by promoting more self-reflective theory.

The Politics of Knowledge in International Relations Theory

It was not until the 1980s, and the onset of the so-called 'third debate', that questions relating to the politics of knowledge would be taken seriously in the study of international relations. Epistemological questions regarding the justification and verification of knowledge claims, the methodology applied, and the scope and purpose of inquiry, and ontological questions regarding the nature of the social actors and other historical formations and structures in international relations, all carry normative implications that had been inadequately addressed. One of the important contributions of critical international theory has been to widen the object domain of international relations, not just to include epistemological and ontological assumptions, but to explicate their connection to prior political commitments.

Traditional and critical conceptions of international relations theory

This section outlines the way in which critical theory brings knowledge claims in international relations under critical scrutiny. Firstly, it considers the question of epistemology by describing how Horkheimer's distinction between traditional and critical conceptions of theory has been taken up in International Relations; and secondly, it elaborates the connection between critical theory and emancipatory theory. The result of this scrutinising is to reveal the role of political interests in knowledge formation. As Robert Cox succinctly and famously said, 'theory is always for someone and for some purpose'.[10] As a consequence, critical international theorists reject the idea that theoretical knowledge is neutral or non-political. Whereas traditional theories would tend to see power and interests as a *posteriori* factors affecting outcomes in interactions between political actors in the sphere of international relations, critical international theorists insist that they are by no means absent in the formation and verification of knowledge claims. Indeed, they are *a priori* factors affecting the production of knowledge, hence Kimberly Hutchings' assertion that 'international relations theory is not only about politics, it also is itself political'.[11]

Problem-solving and critical theories

In his pioneering 1981 article, Robert Cox followed Horkheimer by distinguishing critical theory from traditional theory, or as Cox prefers to call it, problem-solving theory. Problem-solving or traditional theories are marked by two main characteristics. First by a positivist methodology; second, by a tendency to legitimise prevailing social and political structures.

Heavily influenced by the methodologies of the natural sciences, problem-solving theories suppose that positivism provides the only legitimate basis of knowledge. Positivism is seen, as Steve Smith remarks, as the 'gold standard' against which other theories are evaluated.[12] There are many different characteristics that can be identified with positivism, but two are particularly relevant to our discussion. First, positivists assume that facts and values can be separated; secondly, that it is possible to separate subject and object.[13] This results in the view not only that an objective world exists independently of human consciousness, but that objective knowledge of social reality is possible so long as values are expunged from analysis. This stems from the philosophical conviction that there is a permanent theoretical framework to which we can appeal objectively to determine legitimate knowledge claims about social reality.

Problem-solving theory, as Cox defines it, 'takes the world as it finds it, with the prevailing social and power relationships and the institutions into which they are organised, as the given framework for action'.[14] It does not question the present order, but has the effect of legitimising and reifying it. Its general aim, says Cox, is to make the existing order 'work smoothly by dealing effectively with particular sources of trouble'.[15] Neorealism, *qua* problem-solving theory, takes seriously the realist dictum to work with, rather than against, prevailing international forces. By working within the given system it has a stabilising effect, tending to preserve the existing global structure of social and political relations. Cox points out that neoliberal institutionalism also partakes of problem-solving. Its objective, as explained by its foremost exponent, is to 'facilitate the smooth operation of decentralised international political systems'.[16] Situating itself between the states-system and the liberal capitalist global economy, neoliberalism's main concern is to ensure that the two systems function smoothly in their co-existence. It seeks to render the two global systems compatible and stable by diffusing any conflicts, tensions, or crises that might arise between them.[17] Neufeld has argued that mainstream international ethics also constitutes a form of problem-solving as a result of its positivist assumptions.[18] To summarise, traditional conceptions of theory tend to work in favour of stabilising prevailing structures of world order and their accompanying inequalities of power and wealth.

The main point that Cox wishes to make about problem-solving theory is that its failure to reflect on the prior framework within which it theorises means that it tends to operate in favour of prevailing ideological priorities. Its claims to value-neutrality notwithstanding, problem-solving theory is plainly 'value-bound by virtue of the fact that it implicitly accepts the prevailing order as its own framework'.[19] As a consequence, it remains oblivious to the way power and interests precede and shape knowledge claims.

By contrast, critical international theory starts from the conviction that cognitive processes themselves are subject to political interests and so ought to be critically evaluated. Theories of international relations, like any knowledge, necessarily are conditioned by social, cultural and ideological influence, and one of the main tasks of critical theory is to reveal the effect of this conditioning. As Richard Ashley asserts, 'knowledge is always constituted in reflection of interests',[20] so critical theory must bring to consciousness latent interests, commitments, or values that give rise to, and orient, any theory. We must concede therefore that the study of international relations 'is, and always has been, unavoidably normative',[21] despite claims to the contrary. Because critical international theory sees an intimate connection between social life and cognitive processes, it rejects the positivist distinctions between fact and value, object and subject. By ruling out the possibility of objective knowledge critical international theory seeks to promote greater 'theoretical reflexivity'.[22] This includes a willingness to be open about our philosophical and political starting points, and facing the challenge of clarifying 'how our commitments and values are consistent with our (meta-)theoretical starting points'.[23] By adopting this reflexive attitude critical theory is more like a meta-theoretical attempt to examine how theories are situated in prevailing social and political orders, how this situatedness impacts on theorising, and, most importantly, the possibilities for theorising in a manner that challenges injustices and inequalities built into the prevailing world order.

Critical theory's relation to the prevailing order needs to be explained with some care. For although it refuses to take the prevailing order as it finds it, critical theory does not simply ignore it. It accepts that humans do not make history under conditions of their own choosing, as Marx observed in *The Eighteenth Brumaire of Louis Bonaparte,* and so a detailed examination of present conditions must necessarily be undertaken. Nevertheless, the order which has been 'given' to us is by no means natural, necessary or historically invariable. Critical international theory takes the global configuration of power relations as its object and asks how that configuration came about, what costs it brings with it, and what alternative possibilities remain immanent in history.

Critical theory is essentially a critique of the dogmatism it finds in traditional modes of theorising. This critique reveals the unexamined assumptions that guide traditional modes of thought, and exposes the complicity of traditional modes of thought in prevailing political and social conditions. As Seyla Benhabib pithily explains, '[t]he dogmatism of knowledge is shown to be the dogmatism of a way of life'.[24] To break with dogmatic modes of thought is to 'denaturalise' the present, as Karin Fierke puts it, to make us 'look again, in a fresh way, at that which we assume about the world because it has become overly familiar'.[25] Denaturalising '[allegedly] objective realities opens the door to alternative forms of social and political life'. Implicitly therefore critical theory *qua* denaturalising critique serves 'as an instrument for the delegitimisation of established power and privilege'.[26] The knowledge critical international theory generates is not neutral; it is politically and ethically charged by an interest in social and political transformation. It criticises and debunks theories that legitimise the prevailing order and affirms progressive alternatives that promote emancipation.

This immediately raises the question of how ethical judgments about the prevailing world order can be formed. Since there are no objective theoretical frameworks there can be no Archimedean standpoint outside history or society from which to engage in ethical criticism or judgment. It is not a matter of drafting a set of moral ideals and using them as a transcendent benchmark to judge forms of political organisation. There is no utopia to compare to facts. This means critical international theory must employ the method of immanent critique rather than abstract ethics to criticise the present order of things.[27]

The task, therefore, is to 'start from where we are', in Rorty's words,[28] and excavate the principles and values that structure our political society, exposing the contradictions or inconsistencies in the way our society is organised to pursue its espoused values. This point is endorsed by several other critical international theorists, especially Kimberly Hutchings whose version of critical international theory is heavily influenced by Hegel's phenomenological version of immanent critique. Immanent critique is undertaken 'without reference to an independently articulated method or to transcendent criteria'.[29] Following Hegel's advice, critical international theory must acknowledge that the resources for criticising and judging can only be found 'immanently', that is, in the already existing political societies from where the critique is launched. The critical resources brought to bear do not fall from the sky, they issue from the historical development of concrete legal and political institutions. The task of the political theorist therefore is to explain and criticise the present political order in terms of the principles presupposed by and embedded in its own legal, political and cultural practices and institutions.[30]

Fiona Robinson similarly argues that ethics should not be conceived as separate from the theories and practices of international relations, but should instead be seen as embedded in them.[31] In agreement with Hutchings she argues for a 'phenomenology of ethical life' rather than an 'abstract ethics about the application of rules'.[32] On her account of a 'global ethics of care', however, it is necessary also to submit the background assumptions of already existing moral and political discourses to critical scrutiny. Chris Reus-Smit makes a similar point, arguing that the pre-existing social, economic, and political contexts in which decisions about justice are made should not be immune to critique.[33] Hutchings, Robinson and Reus-Smit agree with Linklater that any critical international theory must employ a mode of immanent critique. This means that the theorist must engage critically with the background normative assumptions that structure our ethical judgments in an effort to generate a more coherent fit between modes of thought and forms of political organisation, and without relying on a set of abstract ethical principles.

Critical theory's task as an emancipatory theory

If problem-solving theories adopt a positivist methodology and end up reaffirming the prevailing system, critical theories are informed by the traditions of hermeneutics and *ideologiekritik*. Critical international theory is not only concerned with understanding and explaining the existing realities of world politics, it also intends to criticise in order to transform them. It is an attempt to comprehend essential social processes for the purpose of inaugurating change, or at least knowing whether change is possible. In Hoffman's words, it is 'not merely an expression of the concrete realities of the historical situation, but also a force for change within those conditions'.[34] Neufeld also affirms this view of critical theory. It offers, he says, a form of social criticism that supports practical political activity aimed at societal transformation.[35]

Critical theory's emancipatory interest is concerned with 'securing freedom from unacknowledged constraints, relations of domination, and conditions of distorted communication and understanding that deny humans the capacity to make their future through full will and consciousness'.[36] This plainly contrasts with problem-solving theories which tend to accept what Linklater calls the 'immutability thesis'.[37] Critical theory is committed to extending the rational, just and democratic organisation of political life beyond the level of the state to the whole of humanity.

The conception of emancipation promoted by critical international theory is largely derived from a strand of thought which finds its origin in the Enlightenment project. This project was generally concerned with breaking with past forms of injustice to foster the conditions necessary for universal freedom.[38] To begin with, emancipation as understood by Enlightenment thinkers and critical international theorists generally expresses a negative conception of freedom which consists in the removal of unnecessary, socially-created constraints. This understanding is manifest in Booth's definition of emancipation as 'freeing people from those constraints that stop them carrying out what freely they would choose to do'.[39] The emphasis in this understanding is on dislodging those impediments or impositions which unnecessarily curtail individual or collective freedom. More substantively, Ashley defines emancipation as the securing of 'freedom from unacknowledged constraints, relations of domination, and conditions of distorted communication and understanding that deny humans the capacity to make their own future through full will and consciousness'.[40] The common thrust of these understandings is that emancipation implies a quest for autonomy. 'To be free', says Linklater, is 'to be self-determining or to have the capacity to initiate action'.[41] The objective of critical international theory therefore is to extend the human capacity for self-determination.[42]

In Linklater's account of critical international theory two thinkers are integral: Immanuel Kant and Karl Marx. Kant's approach is instructive because it seeks to incorporate the themes of power, order, *and* emancipation.[43] As expressed by Linklater, Kant 'considered the possibility that state power would be tamed by principles of international order and that, in time, international order would be modified until it conformed with principles of cosmopolitan justice'.[44] Kant's theory of international relations is an early attempt to map out a critical international theory by absorbing the insights and criticising the weaknesses in Realist and Rationalist thought under an interest in universal freedom and justice. While Linklater believes Marx's approach to be too narrow in its focus on class-based exclusion, he thinks it nevertheless provides the basis of a social theory on which critical international theory must build. As Linklater observed in an early work, both Marx and Kant share 'the desire for a universal society of free individuals, a universal kingdom of ends'.[45] Both held strong attachments to the Enlightenment themes of freedom and universalism, and both launched strong critiques of particularistic lifeforms with the intention of expanding moral and political community.

To conclude this part of the chapter, critical international theory makes a strong case for paying closer attention to the relations between knowledge and interests. One of critical international theory's main contributions in this regard is to expose the political nature of knowledge-formation. Underlying all this is an explicit interest in challenging and removing socially produced constraints on human freedom, thereby contributing to the possible transformation of international relations.[46]

Rethinking Political Community

Informing critical international theory is the spirit, if not the letter, of Marx's critique of capitalism. Like Marx, critical international theorists seek to expose and analyse critically the sources of inequality and domination that shape global power relations with the intention of eliminating them. Since the mid-1990s one of the core themes that has grown out of critical international theory is the need to develop more sophisticated understandings of community as a means of identifying and eliminating global constraints on humanity's potential for freedom, equality and self-determination.[47] Linklater's approach to this task, which has set the agenda, is firstly to analyse the way in which inequality and domination flow from modes of political community tied to the sovereign state, and secondly to consider alternative forms of political community which promote human emancipation.

This section elaborates three dimensions on which critical international theory rethinks political community.[48] The first dimension is the normative and pertains to the philosophical critique of the state as an exclusionary form of political organisation. The second is the sociological dimension and relates to the need to develop an account of the origins and evolution of the modern state and states-system. Third is the praxeological dimension concerning practical possibilities for reconstructing international relations along more emancipatory and cosmopolitan lines. The overall effect of critical international theory, and its major contribution to the study of international relations, is to focus on the normative foundations of political life.

1. The normative dimension: the critique of ethical particularism and social exclusion

One of the key philosophical assumptions that has structured political and ethical thought and practice about international relations is the idea that the modern state is the natural form of political community. The sovereign state has been 'fetishised', to use Marx's term, as the normal mode of organising political life. Critical international theorists however wish to problematise this fetishisation and draw attention to the 'moral deficits' that are created by the state's interaction with the capitalist world economy. In this section I outline critical international theory's philosophical inquiry into the normative bases of political life and its critique of ethical particularism and the social exclusion it generates.

The philosophical critique of particularism was first, and most systematically, set out in Andrew Linklater's *Men and Citizens*. His main concern there was to trace how modern political thought had constantly differentiated ethical obligations due to co-citizens from those due to the rest of humanity. In practice, this tension between 'men' and 'citizens' has always been resolved in favour of citizens, or more accurately, members of a particular sovereign state. Even if it was acknowledged, as it was by most early modern thinkers, that certain universal rights were thought to extend to all members of the human community, they were always residual and secondary to particularistic ones.

Men and Citizens is, among other things, a work of recovery. It seeks to recover a political philosophy based on universal ethical reasoning which has been progressively marginalised in the twentieth century, especially with the onset of the Cold War and the hegemony of realism. That is, it seeks to recover and reformulate the Stoic-Christian ideal of human community. While elements of this ideal can be found in the natural law tradition, it is to the Enlightenment tradition that Linklater turns to find a fuller expression of this ideal. Linklater here is strongly influenced by the thought of Kant, for whom war was undeniably related to the separation of humankind into separate, self-regarding political units, Rousseau, who caustically remarked that in joining a particular community individual citizens necessarily made themselves enemies of the rest of humanity, and Marx who saw in the modern state a contradiction between general and private interests.

The point being made here is that particularistic political associations lead to inter-societal estrangement, the perpetual possibility of war, and social exclusion. This type of argument underlies the thought of several Enlightenment thinkers of the eighteenth century, including Montesquieu, Rousseau, Paine and Kant among others, for whom war was simply an expression of *ancien régime* politics and a tool of state. Marx extended the critique of the modern state by arguing that, in upholding the rule of law, private property and money, it masks capitalism's alienation and exploitation behind bourgeois ideals of freedom and equality. Modern international relations, insofar as it combines the political system of sovereign states and the economic system of market capitalism, is a form of exclusion where particular class interests parade themselves as universal.[49] The problem with the sovereign state therefore is that as a 'limited moral community' it promotes exclusion, generating estrangement, injustice, insecurity and violent conflict between self-regarding states by imposing rigid boundaries between 'us' and 'them'.[50]

Such arguments have led in recent times, and especially in a century which has seen unprecedented flows of stateless peoples and refugees, to more general and profound questions about the foundations on which humanity is politically divided and organised. In particular, as Kimberly Hutchings notes, it has led critical international theory to a 'questioning of the nation-state as a normatively desirable mode of political organisation'.[51] Consistent with other critical international theorists Hutchings problematises the 'idealised fixed ontologies' of nation and state as subjects of self-determination.[52] Hutchings goes further than Linklater however by also problematising the individual 'self' of liberalism. Her intention is to examine the status of all normative claims to self-determination, whether the 'self' is understood as the individual, nation or state.[53] But insofar as her critique is aimed at placing the 'self' in question as a self-contained entity, Hutchings' analysis complements and extends the philosophical critique of particularism undertaken by Linklater.

Richard Shapcott also continues this critique by inquiring into the way different conceptions of the 'self' shape relations to 'others' in international relations.[54] Shapcott's main concern is with the possibility of achieving justice in a culturally-diverse world. Although the main influences on his argument are Tzvetan Todorov and Hans-Georg Gadamer more than Habermas, Shapcott's critique of the self is consistent with Linklater's and Hutchings'. He rejects both liberal and communitarian conceptions of the self for foreclosing genuine communication and justice in the relationship between self and other. Liberal conceptions of the self, he says, involve a 'significant moment of assimilation' because they are incapable of properly recognising difference.[55] Communitarians, on the other hand, tend to take the limits of political community as given and, as a consequence, refuse to grant outsiders or non-citizens an equal voice in moral conversations. In other words, liberals underestimate the moral significance of national differences, while communitarians overestimate them. Both, in short, fail to do 'justice to difference'.[56]

The common project of Hutchings, Linklater and Shapcott here is to question the right to autonomy attaching to any bounded or exclusive identity. In short, a less dogmatic attitude towards national boundaries is called for by these critical international theorists; national boundaries must be recognised as 'neither morally decisive nor morally insignificant'.[57] They are perhaps unavoidable in some form. The point, however, is to ensure that national boundaries do not obstruct principles of openness, recognition and justice in relations with the 'other'.[58]

Critical international theory has highlighted the dangers of unchecked particularism which can too readily deprive 'outsiders' of certain rights. This philosophical critique of particularism has led critical international theory to criticise the sovereign state as one of the foremost modern forms of social exclusion and therefore as a considerable barrier to universal justice and emancipation. In the following section we outline critical international theory's sociological account of how the modern state came to structure political community.

2. The sociological dimension: states, social forces and changing world orders

Rejecting Realist claims that the condition of anarchy and the self-regarding actions of states are either natural or immutable, critical international theory has always been a form of small 'c' constructivism. One of its essential tasks therefore is to account for the social and historical production of both the agents and structures taken for granted by traditional theories.

Against the positivism and empiricism of various forms of realism, critical international theory adopts a more hermeneutic approach which conceives of social structures as having an intersubjective existence. 'Structures are socially constructed', that is, says Cox, 'they become a part of the objective world by virtue of their existence in the intersubjectivity of relevant groups of people'.[59] Allowing for the active role of human minds in the constitution of the social world does not lead to a denial of material reality, it simply gives it a different ontological status. Although structures, as intersubjective products, do not have a physical existence like tables or chairs, they nevertheless have real, concrete effects.[60] Structures produce concrete effects because humans act *as if* they were real.[61] It is this view of ontology which underlies Cox's and critical international theory's attempts to comprehend the present order.

In contrast to individualist ontologies which conceive of states as atomistic, rational and possessive, and as if their identities existed prior to or independently of social interaction,[62] critical international theory is more interested in explaining how both individual actors and social structures emerge in, and are conditioned by, history. For example, against the Westphalian dogma that the state is a state is a state,[63] critical international theory views the modern state as a distinctive form of political community, bringing with it particular functions, roles, and responsibilities that are socially and historically determined. Whereas the state is taken for granted by realism, critical international theory seeks to provide a social theory of the state.

Crucial to critical international theory's argument is that we must account for the development of the modern state as the dominant form of political community in modernity. What is therefore required is an account of how states construct their moral and legal duties and how these reflect certain assumptions about the structure and logic of international relations. Using the work of Michael Mann and Anthony Giddens in particular, Linklater undertakes what he calls an historical sociology of 'bounded communities'.[64]

Linklater's earlier *Beyond Realism and Marxism* had already begun to analyse the interplay of different logics or rationalisation processes in the making of modern world politics. But in *Transformation of Political Community* he carries this analysis further by providing a more detailed account of these processes and by linking them more closely to systems of inclusion and exclusion in the development of the modern state. His argument is that the boundaries of political community are shaped by the interplay of four rationalisation processes: state-building, geopolitical rivalry, capitalist industrialisation, and moral-practical learning.[65] Five monopoly powers are acquired by the modern state through these rationalisation processes. These powers, which are claimed by the sovereign state as indivisible, inalienable and exclusive rights, are: the right to monopolise the legitimate means of violence over the claimed territory, the exclusive right to tax within this territorial jurisdiction, the right to demand undivided political allegiance, the sole authority to adjudicate disputes between citizens, and the sole subject of rights and representation in international law.[66]

The combining of these monopoly powers initiated what Linklater refers to as the 'totalising project' of the modern, Westphalian state. The upshot was to produce a conception of politics governed by the assumption that the boundaries of sovereignty, territory, nationality and citizenship must be co-terminous.[67] The modern state concentrated these social, economic, legal and political functions around a single, sovereign site of governance that became the primary subject of international relations by gradually removing alternatives. Of crucial concern to Linklater is how this totalising project of the modern state modifies the social bond and consequently changes the boundaries of moral and political community. Though the state has been a central theme in the study of international relations there has been little attempt to account for the changing ways that states determine principles which, by binding citizens into a community, separate them from the rest of the world.[68]

Linklater's focus on the changing nature of social bonds has much in common with Cox's focus on the changing relationship between state and civil society.[69] The key to rethinking international relations, according to Cox, lies in examining the relationship between state and civil society, and thereby recognising that the state takes different forms, not only in different historical periods, but also within the same period.

Lest it be thought that critical international theory is simply interested in producing a theory of the state alone, it should be remembered that the state is but one force which shapes the present world order. Cox argues that a comprehensive understanding of the present order and its structural characteristics must account for the interaction between social forces, states, and world orders.[70] Within Cox's approach the state plays an 'intermediate though autonomous role' between, on the one hand, social forces shaped by production, and on the other hand, a world order which embodies a particular configuration of power determined by the states-system and the world economy.[71]

There are two fundamental and intertwined presuppositions upon which Cox founds his theory of the state. The first reflects the Marxist-Gramscian axiom that 'World orders ... are grounded in social relations'.[72] This means that observable changes in military and geopolitical balances can be traced to fundamental changes in the relationship between capital and labour. The second presupposition stems from Vico's argument that institutions such as the state are historical products. The state cannot be abstracted from history as if its essence could be defined or understood as *prior to* history.[73] The end result is that the definition of the state is enlarged to encompass 'the underpinnings of the political structure in civil society'.[74] The influence of the church, press, education system, culture, and so on, has to be incorporated into an analysis of the state, as these 'institutions' help to produce the attitudes, dispositions, and behaviours consistent with, and conducive to, the state's arrangement of power relations in society. Thus the state, which comprises the machinery of government, plus civil society, constitute and reflect the 'hegemonic social order'.[75]

This hegemonic social order must also be understood as a dominant configuration of 'material power, ideology and institutions' that shapes and bears forms of world order.[76] Each world order 'has its own specific conditions of existence and dynamics', as Stephen Gill has noted, and the task of critical international theory is to explain how the structural characteristics of world orders emerge, are consolidated, and are transformed.

The key issue for Cox therefore is how to account for the transition from one world order to another. He devotes much of his attention to explaining 'how structural transformations have come about in the past'.[77] For example, he has analysed in some detail the structural transformation that took place in the late nineteenth century from a period characterised by craft manufacture, the liberal state, and *pax britannica*, to a period characterised by mass production, the emerging welfare-nationalist state, and imperial rivalry.[78] In much of his recent writing he has been preoccupied with the restructuring of world order brought about by globalisation. In brief, Cox and his colleague Stephen Gill, have offered extensive examinations of how the growing global organisation of production and finance is transforming Westphalian conceptions of society and polity. At the heart of this current transformation is what Cox calls the 'internationalisation of the state', whereby the state becomes little more than an instrument for restructuring national economies so they are more responsive to the demands and disciplines of the capitalist global economy.[79] Drawing upon Karl Polanyi, and in a similar argument to John Ruggie, Cox sees the social purposes of the state being subordinated to the market logics of capitalism, disembedding the economy from society, and producing a complex world order of increasing tension between principles of territoriality and interdependence.[80] Some of the consequences of this economic globalisation are, as Cox notes, the polarisation of rich and poor, increasing social anomie, a stunted civil society and, as a result, the rise of exclusionary populism (extreme right, xenophobic and racist groups).[81]

The point of reflecting on changing world orders, as Cox notes, is to 'serve as a guide to action designed to change the world so as to improve the lot of humanity in social equity'.[82] After all, as both Cox and Maclean state, an understanding of change should be a central feature of any theory of international relations.[83] So it is with the express purpose of analysing the potential for structural transformations in world order that critical international theory identifies and examines 'emancipatory counterhegemonic' forces. Counterhegemonic forces could be states, such as a coalition of 'Third World' states which struggles to undo the dominance of 'core' countries,[84] or the 'counterhegemonic alliance of forces on the world scale', such as trade unions, non-governmental organisations and new social movements, which grow from the 'bottom-up' in civil society.[85] The point of critical international theory's various sociological analyses is to illuminate how already-existing social struggles might lead to decisive transformations in the normative bases of global political life.

3.   The praxeological dimension: cosmopolitanism and discourse ethics

One of the main intentions behind a sociology of the state is to assess the possibility of undoing the monopoly powers and totalising project and moving towards more open, inclusive forms of community. This reflects critical international theory's belief that while totalising projects have been tremendously successful, they have not been complete in colonising modern political life. They have not been able to 'erode the sense of moral anxiety when duties to fellow-citizens clash with duties to the rest of humankind'.[86] In this section I outline critical international theory's attempt to rethink the meaning of community in the light of this residual moral anxiety and an accumulating 'moral capital' which deepens and extends cosmopolitan citizenship. This involves not simply identifying forces working to dismantle practices of social exclusion, but also identifying those working to replace the system of sovereign states with cosmopolitan structures of global governance.

Linklater's three volumes, *Men and Citizens*, *Beyond Realism and Marxism* and *The Political Transformation of Community*, form the most sustained and extensive interrogation of political community in International Relations. In his latest offering, Linklater elaborates his argument in terms of a 'triple transformation' affecting political community. The three transformational tendencies Linklater identifies are: a progressive recognition that moral, political and legal principles ought to be universalised, an insistence that material inequality ought to be reduced, and greater demands for deeper respect for cultural, ethnic and gender differences.[87] The triple transformation identifies processes that open the possibility of dismantling the nexus between sovereignty, territory, citizenship and nationalism and moving towards more cosmopolitan forms of governance. In this respect, the praxeological dimension closes the circle with the normative dimension by furthering the critique of the modern state's particularism. However, we should note a slight revision of this critique. Modern states are not just too particularistic for Linklater's liking, they are also too universalistic.[88] He here finesses his earlier critique of particularism by acknowledging the feminist and postmodern arguments that universalism runs the risk of ignoring or repressing certain marginalised or vulnerable groups unless it respects legitimate differences. Nonetheless, it remains consistent with the Enlightenment critique of the system of sovereign states, and the project to universalise the sphere in which human beings treat each other as free and equal.

If critical international theory's overall objective is to promote the reconfiguration of political community not just by expanding political community beyond the frontiers of the sovereign state, but also by deepening it within those frontiers, then it must offer a more complex, multi-tiered structure of governance. Ultimately, it depends on reconstituting the state and its responsibilities within alternative frameworks of political action that reduce the impact of social exclusion.

The key to realising this vision is to sever the link between sovereignty and political association which is integral to the Westphalian system.[89] A post-exclusionary form of political community would be post-sovereign or post-Westphalian, according to Linklater. It would abandon the idea that power, authority, territory and loyalty must be focused around a single community or monopolised by a single site of governance. The state can no longer mediate effectively among the many loyalties, identities and interests that exist in a globalising world. Fairer and more complex mediations can only be developed, argues Linklater, by transcending the 'destructive fusion' achieved by the modern state and promoting wider communities of dialogue.[90] The overall effect would thus be to 'de-centre' the state in the context of a more cosmopolitan form of political organisation.

This requires states to establish and locate themselves in overlapping forms of international society. Linklater lists three forms. First, a pluralist society of states in which the principles of coexistence work 'to preserve respect for the freedom and equality of independent political communities'. Second, a solidarist society of states that have agreed to substantive moral purposes.[91] Third, a post-Westphalian framework where states relinquish some of their sovereign powers so as to institutionalise shared political and moral norms.[92] These alternative frameworks of international society would widen the boundaries of political community by increasing the impact which duties to 'outsiders' have on decision-making processes and contribute to what Linklater and Shapcott call 'dialogical cosmopolitanism'.[93]

Linklater and Shapcott make the case for what they refer to as 'thin cosmopolitanism'.[94] A thin cosmopolitanism would need to promote universal claims yet do justice to difference.[95] Within such a setup, loyalties to the sovereign state or any other political association cannot be absolute.[96] In recognising the diversity of social bonds and moral ties, a thin cosmopolitan ethos seeks to multiply the types and levels of political community; recognise the community of humanity at the same time as it recognises regional, national and subnational political associations. It would thus resemble the neomedieval images conjured by E. H. Carr and Hedley Bull.[97] It should be noted however that this does not mean duties to humanity override all others. There is no fixed 'moral hierarchy' within a thin cosmopolitan framework.[98] It is important to note here that this version of a thin cosmopolitanism places the ideals of dialogue and consent at the centre of its project. In this final section I outline briefly how the emphasis on dialogue is utilised in critical international theory.[99]

Linklater resorts to Habermas's notion of discourse ethics as a model for his dialogical approach. Discourse ethics is essentially a deliberative, consent-oriented approach to resolving political issues within a moral frame-work. Discourse ethics, as elaborated by Habermas, builds on the need for communicating subjects to account for their beliefs and actions in terms which are intelligible to others and which they can then accept or contest.[100] It is committed to the Kantian principle that political decisions or norms must be generalisable and consistent with the normative demands of publicity. Similarly, international norms and institutions must also be submitted to collective scrutiny and deliberation on this basis if they are to maintain legitmacy.[101] At such moments when an international principle, social norm, or institution loses legitimacy or when consensus breaks down then discourse ethics enters the fray as a means of consensually deciding upon new principles or institutional arrangements. According to discourse ethics newly arrived at political principles, norm, or institutional arrangements can only be said to be valid if they can meet with the approval of all those who would be affected by them.[102]

There are three features worthy of note for our purposes. Firstly, discourse ethics is inclusionary. It is oriented to the establishment and maintenance of the conditions necessary for open and non-exclusionary dialogue. No individual or group which will be affected by the principle, norm, or institution under deliberation should be excluded from participation in dialogue. Secondly, discourse ethics is democratic. It builds on a model of the public sphere which is bound to democratic deliberation and consent, where participants employ an 'argumentative rationality' for the purpose of 'reaching a mutual understanding based on a reasoned consensus, challenging the validity claims involved in any communication'.[103] Combining the inclusionary and democratic impulses, discourse ethics provides a method that can test which principles, norms, or institutional arrangements would be 'equally good for all'.[104] Thirdly, discourse ethics is a form of moral-practical reasoning. As such it is not simply guided by utilitarian calculations or expediency, nor is it guided by an imposed concept of the 'good life', rather, it is guided by procedural fairness. It is more concerned with the method of justifying moral principles than with the substantive content of those principles.

It is possible to identify three general implications of discourse ethics for the reconstruction of world politics which can only be briefly outlined here. Firstly, by virtue of its consent-oriented, deliberative approach, discourse ethics offers procedural guidance for democratic decision-making processes. In light of social and material changes brought about by the globalisation of production and finance, the movement of peoples, the rise of indigenous peoples and sub-national groups, environmental degradation, and so on, the 'viability and accountability of national decision-making entities' is being brought into question.[105] Held highlights the democratically-deficient nature of the sovereign state when he asks: 'Whose consent is necessary and whose participation is justified in decisions concerning, for instance, AIDS, or acid rain, or the use of non-renewable resources? What is the relevant constituency: national, regional or international?'[106] Under globalising conditions it is apt that discourse ethics raises questions not only about 'who' is to be involved in decision-making processes, but also 'how' and 'where' these decisions are to be made. For this reason critical international theory has much in common with the cosmopolitan democracy project.[107] The key here is 'to develop institutional arrangements that concretise the dialogic ideal' at all levels of social and political life.[108] This directs attention to an emerging global or international public sphere where 'social movements, non-state actors and "global citizens" join with states and international organizations in a dialogue over the exercise of power and authority across the globe'.[109] The existence of a global public sphere ensures, as Risse points out, 'that actors have to regularly and routinely explain and justify their behaviour'.[110] As Marc Lynch has shown, this network of overlapping, transnational publics not only seeks to influence the foreign policy of individual states, it seeks to change international relations by modifying the structural context of strategic interaction.[111]

Secondly, discourse ethics offers a procedure for regulating violent conflict and arriving at resolutions which are acceptable to all affected parties. Hoffman believes that the practice of third-party facilitation offers a discourse-ethical approach to the resolution of conflict. Third-party facilitation aims at achieving a non-hierarchical, non-coercive resolution of conflict by including both or all affected parties as participants in the dialogue.[112] As Fierke explains, dialogue differs from negotiation. Whereas negotiation belongs to an 'adversarial model' constructed around an 'us' versus 'them' mentality, dialogue can have a transformative affect on identities.[113] The dialogue fostered by third-party facilitation involves the conflicting parties in the reversing of perspectives and encourages them to reason from the other's point of view. As Hoffman observes, third-party facilitation seeks 'to promote a self-generated and self-sustaining resolution to the conflict'.[114] Because the outcome must be acceptable to all concerned it is more likely to promote compliance.[115] In plainly Habermasian language Hoffman says that 'third-party facilitation could be characterised as the promotion of consensual decision-making towards the resolution of conflict via a process of undistorted communication'.[116] Deiniol Jones, though more sceptical of this approach than Hoffman, also endorses third-party mediation in critical-theoretical terms, arguing that it should aim 'to enhance the strength and quality of the cosmopolitan communicative ethic'.[117]

Thirdly, discourse ethics offers a means of criticising and justifying the principles by which humanity organises itself politically. By reflecting on the principles of inclusion and exclusion, discourse ethics can reflect on the normative foundations of political life. From the moral point of view contained within discourse ethics the sovereign state as a form of community is unjust because the principles of inclusion and exclusion are not the outcome of open dialogue and deliberation where all who stand to be affected by the arrangement have been able to participate in discussion. Against the exclusionary nature of the social bond underlying the sovereign state, discourse ethics has the inclusionary aim 'to secure the social bond of all with all'.[118] In a sense it is an attempt to put into practice Kant's ideal of a community of co-legislators embracing the whole of humanity.[119] As Linklater argues, 'all humans have a *prima facie* equal right to take part in universal communities of discourse which decide the legitimacy of global arrangements'.[120] In sum, discourse ethics promotes a cosmopolitan ideal where the political organisation of humanity is decided by a process of unconstrained and unrestricted dialogue.

Conclusion

There can be little doubt that critical international theory has made a major contribution to the study of international relations. One of these contributions has been to heighten our awareness of the link between knowledge and politics. Critical international theory rejects the idea of the theorist as objective bystander. Instead, the theorist is enmeshed in social and political life, and theories of international relations, like all theories, are informed by prior interests and convictions, whether they are acknowledged or not. A second contribution critical international theory makes is to rethink accounts of the modern state and political community. Traditional theories tend to take the state for granted, but critical international theory analyses the changing ways in which the boundaries of community are formed, maintained and transformed. It not only provides a sociological account, it provides a sustained ethical analysis of the practices of inclusion and exclusion. Critical international theory's aim of achieving an alternative theory and practice of international relations rests on the possibility of overcoming the exclusionary dynamics associated with modern system of sovereign states and establishing a cosmopolitan set of arrangements that will better promote freedom, justice and equality across the globe. It is thus an attempt radically to rethink the normative foundations of global politics.

Notes

1. See M. Jay, *The Dialectical Imagination* (Boston, 1973).
2. M. Horkheimer, *Critical Theory* (New York, 1972), p. 206.
3. K. Marx, 'Theses on Feuerbach', in *Karl Marx: Selected Writings* (Oxford, 1977), p. 158.

4. Horkheimer (1972), p. 223.
5. Horkheimer (1972).
6. Horkheimer (1972), p. 215.
7. J. Habermas, *The Inclusion of the Other: Studies in Political Theory* (Cambridge, 1998), Parts III and IV.
8. A. Linklater, *Beyond Realism and Marxism: Critical Theory and International Relations* (London, 1990a), p. 8.
9. M. See Neufeld, *The Restructuring of International Relations Theory* (Cambridge, 1995), ch. 1; and R. Shapcott, *Justice, Community and Dialogue in International Relations* (Cambridge, 2001).
10. R. W. Cox, 'Social Forces, States, and World Orders: Beyond International Relations Theory', *Millennium*, vol. 10, no. 2 (1981).
11. K. Hutchings, *International Political Theory: Rethinking Ethics in a Global Era* (London, 1999), p. 69.
12. S. Smith, 'Positivism and Beyond', in S. Smith, K. Booth and M. Zalewski (eds), *International Political Theory: Positivism and Beyond* (Cambridge, 1996), p. 13.
13. On positivism see A. Linklater, 'The Achievements of Critical Theory', in Smith, Booth and Zalewski (1996), p. 281, Neufeld (1996), ch. 2, and Smith (1996).
14. Cox (1981), p. 128.
15. Cox (1981), p. 129.
16. R. O. Keohane, *After Hegemony: Cooperation and Discord in the World Political Economy* (Princeton, 1984), p. 63.
17. R. W. Cox, 'Multilateralism and World Order', *Review of International Studies*, 18 (1992a), p. 173.
18. M. Neufeld, 'Thinking Ethically – Thinking Critically: International Ethics as Critique', in M. Lensu and J.-S. Fritz (eds), *Value Pluralism, Normative Theory and International Relations* (London, 2000), p. 42.
19. Cox (1981), p. 130.
20. R. K. Ashley, 'Political Realism and Human Interests', *International Studies Quarterly*, 25 (1981), p. 207.
21. Neufeld (1995), p. 108.
22. Neufeld (1995), ch. 3.
23. Neufeld (2000), pp. 43 and 47.
24. S. Benhabib, *Critique, Norm and Utopia: A Study of the Foundations of Critical Theory* (New York, 1986), p. 30.
25. K. M. Fierke, *Changing Games, Changing Strategies: Critical Investigations in Security* (Manchester, 1998), p. 13.
26. Neufeld (1995), p. 14.
27. Linklater (1990a), pp. 22–3.
28. Quoted in Linklater (1998), p. 77.
29. Hutchings (1999), p. 99.
30. Hutchings (1999), p. 102; Fierke (1998), p. 114.

31. F. Robinson, *Globalizing Care: Ethics, Feminist Theory and International Relations* (Boulder, 1999).
32. Robinson (1999), p. 31.
33. C. Reus-Smit, 'The Normative Structure of International Society', in F. Osler Hampson and J. Reppy (eds), *Earthly Goods: Environmental Change and Social Justice* (Ithaca, 1996).
34. M. Hoffman, 'Critical Theory and the Inter-Paradigm Debate', *Millennium*, vol. 16, no. 2 (1987), p. 233.
35. Neufeld (1995), ch. 5.
36. Ashley (1981), p. 227.
37. Andrew Linklater, 'The Achievements of Critical Theory', in Booth, Smith and Zalewski (1996).
38. R. Devetak, 'The Project of Modernity and International Relations Theory', *Millennium*, vol. 24, no. 1 (1995), pp. 29–35.
39. K. Booth, 'Security in Anarchy: Utopian Realism in Theory and Practice', *International Affairs*, vol. 67, no. 3 (1991), p. 539.
40. Ashley (1981), p. 227.
41. Linklater (1990b), p. 135.
42. Linklater (1990a), p. 10.
43. Linklater (1990a), pp. 21–2.
44. A. Linklater, 'What is a Good International Citizen?' in P. Keal (ed.), *Ethics and Foreign Policy* (Canberra, 1992a), p. 36.
45. A. Linklater, *Men and Citizens in the Theory of International Relations*, 2nd edn (London, 1990b), p. 159.
46. Linklater (1990a), p. 1.
47. Linklater (1990a), p. 7.
48. A. Linklater, 'The Question of the Next Stage in International Relations Theory: A Critical-Theoretical Point of View', *Millennium*, vol. 21, no. 1 (1992), pp. 92–7.
49. Cox (1981), p. 137.
50. Linklater (1990b), p. 28.
51. Hutchings (1999), p. 125.
52. Hutchings (1999), pp. 122, 135.
53. Hutchings (1999), p. 135.
54. R. Shapcott, 'Beyond the Cosmopolitan/Communitarian Divide: Justice, Difference and Community in International Relations', in Lensu and Fritz (2000a); and Shapcott (2001), Introduction.
55. Shapcott (2000a), p. 216.
56. Shapcott (2001), ch. 1.
57. Linklater (1998), p. 61.
58. Hutchings (1999), p. 138; Linklater (1998), ch. 2; Shapcott (2000a), p. 111.
59. R. W. Cox, 'Towards a Post-Hegemonic Conceptualization of World Order: Reflections on the Relevancy of Ibn Khaldun', in E.-O. Czempiel and J. Rosenau (eds), *Governance without Government* (Cambridge, 1992b), p. 138.
60. Cox (1992b), p. 133.

61. R. W. Cox, 'Postscript 1985', in R. O. Keohane (ed.), *Neorealism and Its Critics* (New York, 1986), p. 242.
62. Reus-Smit (1996), p. 100.
63. Cox (1981), p. 127.
64. A. Linklater, *The Transformation of Political Community: Ethical Foundations of the Post-Westphalian Era* (Cambridge, 1998), chs 4–5.
65. Linklater (1998), pp. 147–57.
66. Linklater (1998), pp. 28–9.
67. Linklater (1998), pp. 29 and 44.
68. Linklater (1998), ch. 4.
69. R. Cox, 'Civil Society at the Turn of the Millennium: Prospects for an Alternative World Order', *Review of International Studies*, vol. 25, no. 1 (1999).
70. Cox (1981), pp. 137–8.
71. Cox (1981), p. 141.
72. R. W. Cox, 'Gramsci, Hegemony and International Relations: An Essay on Method', *Millennium*, vol. 12, no. 2 (1983), p. 173.
73. Cox (1981), p. 133.
74. Cox (1983), p. 164.
75. Cox (1983), p. 164.
76. Cox (1981), p. 141.
77. Cox (1986), p. 244.
78. R. W. Cox, *Production, Power and World Order: Social Forces in the Making of History* (New York, 1987).
79. R. W. Cox, 'Structural Issues of Global Governance: Implications for Europe', in S. Gill (ed.), *Gramsci, Historical Materialism, and International Relations* (Cambridge, 1993), p. 260; R. W. Cox, 'Global Restructuring: Making Sense of the Changing International Political Economy', in R. Stubbs and G. Underhill (eds), *Political Economy and the Changing Global Order* (London, 1994), p. 49.
80. Cox (1993), pp. 260–3; Cox (1994), pp. 53ff.
81. Cox (1999).
82. Cox (1999), p. 4.
83. J. Maclean, 'Marxist Epistemology, Explanations of "Change" and the Study of International Relations', in B. Buzan and R. B. Jones (eds), *Change in the Study of International Relations: The Evaded Dimension* (London, 1981b), p. 47; and R. W. Cox, 'Production, the State, and Change in World Order', in E.-O. Czempiel and J. Rosenau (eds), *Global Change and Theoretical Challenges* (Cambridge, 1989), p. 37.
84. Cox (1981).
85. Cox (1999), p. 13.
86. Linklater (1998), pp. 150–1.
87. Linklater (1998) passim.
88. Linklater (1998), p. 27.
89. Devetak (1995), p. 43.

90. Linklater (1998), pp. 60 and 74.
91. For further elaboration see R. Shapcott, 'Solidarism and After: Global Governance, International Society and the Normative "Turn" in International Relations', *Pacifica Review*, vol. 12, no. 2 (2000b).
92. Linklater (1998), pp. 166–7.
93. Linklater (1998), p. 88; Shapcott (2001).
94. Linklater (1998); Shapcott (2001).
95. Shapcott (2000a) and (2001).
96. Linklater (1998), p. 56.
97. E. H. Carr, *The Twenty Years' Crisis: 1919–1939* (London, 1946), ch. 14; Hedley Bull, *The Anarchical Society* (London, 1977), pp. 254–5; Linklater (1998), pp. 161–8 and 193–8.
98. Linklater (1998), p. 56.
99. For a critique of this application see C. Rustin, 'Habermas, Discourse Ethics, and International Justice', *Alternatives*, 24 (1999).
100. J. Habermas, *The Theory of Communicative Action, Volume 1: Reason and the Rationalization of Society* (Cambridge, 1984), p. 99.
101. Shapcott (2000b) and (2001).
102. J. Habermas, *Moral Consciousness and Communicative Action* (Cambridge, 1990) pp. 65–6.
103. T. Risse, '"Let's Argue!": Communicative Action in World Politics', *International Organization*, vol. 54, no. 1 (2000), pp. 1–2.
104. J. Habermas, *Justification and Application: Remarks on Discourse Ethics* (Cambridge, 1993), p. 151.
105. D. Held, 'Democracy: From City-States to Cosmopolitan Order', in D. Held (ed.), *Prospects for Democracy: North, South, East, West* (Cambridge, 1993), p. 26.
106. Held (1993), pp. 26–7.
107. D. Held, *Democracy and the Global Order: From the Modern State to Cosmopolitan Governance* (Cambridge, 1995); J. Bohman and M. Lutz-Bachmann (eds), *Perpetual Peace: Essays on Kant's Cosmopolitanism* (Cambridge, 1997).
108. A. Linklater, 'Transforming Political Community: A Response to the Critics', *Review of International Studies*, vol. 25, no. 1 (1999), p. 173.
109. R. Devetak and R. Higgott, 'Justice Unbound? Globalization, States and the Transformation of the Social Bond', *International Affairs*, vol. 75, no. 3 (1999), p. 491.
110. Risse (2000), p. 21.
111. M. Lynch, *State Interests and Public Spheres: The International Politics of Jordan's Identity* (New York, 1999); and Lynch, 'The Dialogue of Civilisations and International Public Spheres', *Millennium*, vol. 29, no. 2 (2000).
112. M. Hoffman, 'Third-Party Mediation and Conflict-Resolution in the Post-Cold War World', in J. Baylis and N. Rengger (eds), *Dilemmas of World Politics* (Oxford, 1992), p. 265.
113. Fierke (1998), pp. 136–7.

114. M. Hoffman, 'Agency, Identity and Intervention', in I. Forbes and M. Hoffman (eds), *Political Theory, International Relations and the Ethics of Intervention* (London, 1993), p. 206.
115. Hoffman (1992), p. 270.
116. Hoffman (1992), p. 273.
117. D. Jones, *Cosmopolitan Mediation? Conflict Resolution and the Oslo Accords* (Manchester, 1999), p. 91.
118. J. Habermas, *The Philosophical Discourse of Modernity: Twelve Lectures* (Cambridge, 1987), p. 346.
119. Linklater (1998), pp. 84–9.
120. Linklater (1998), p. 10; see also Shapcott (2000b), pp. 148–9.

CHAPTER 7

Postmodernism

Richard Devetak

Introduction

Postmodernism has been one of the most influential and controversial theoretical developments in the study of international relations. Though increasing numbers of students and scholars present their work as post-modern readings of international relations, many more see such readings as threatening the integrity and usefulness of the discipline of International Relations (IR). Postmodernism has become the latest *bête noire* of IR. As to why so much fear and loathing has been generated around postmodernism remains unclear. Part of the explanation may lie in the often impenetrable language used by some writers, but a greater part seems to lie in the narrow and dogmatic viewpoints taken by many critics. To avoid presenting post-modernism as an overly defensive theoretical perspective, this chapter will not take issue with critics directly. Instead, it will present a more positive account of postmodernism's contribution to the study of international relations.

Before going on we should point out that a great deal of disagreement exists as to what exactly postmodernism means. The meaning of post-modernism is in dispute not just between proponents and critics, but also among proponents. Indeed, many theorists associated with postmodernism never use the term, sometimes preferring the term post-structuralism, some-times deconstruction, sometimes altogether rejecting any attempt at label-ling. In lieu of a clear or agreed definition of postmodernism this chapter adopts a pragmatic and nominalistic approach. Theorists who are referred to, or who regard their own writing, as either postmodern, post-structuralist or deconstructive will be considered here as postmodern theorists.

The chapter is divided into four main parts. The first part deals with the relationship between power and knowledge in the study of international relations. The second part outlines the textual strategies employed by postmodern approaches. The third part is concerned with how post-modernism deals with the state. And the final part of the chapter outlines postmodernism's attempt to rethink the concept of the political.

Power and Knowledge in International Relations

Power and knowledge

Within orthodox social scientific accounts, knowledge ought to be immune from the influence of power. The study of international relations, or any scholarly study for that matter, is thought to require the suspension of values, interests and power relations in the pursuit of objective knowledge – knowledge uncontaminated by external influences and based on pure reason. Kant's caution that 'the possession of power inevitably corrupts the free judgment of reason', stands as a classic example of this view.[1] It is this view that Michel Foucault, and postmodernism generally, have begun to problematise.

Rather than treat the production of knowledge as simply a cognitive matter, postmodernism treats it as a normative and political matter.[2] Foucault wanted to see if there was not some common matrix which hooked together the fields of knowledge and power. According to Foucault there is a general consistency, which cannot be reduced to an identity, between modes of interpretation and operations of power. Power and knowledge are mutually supportive; they directly imply one another.[3] The task therefore is to see how operations of power fit in with the wider social and political matrices of the modern world. For example, in *Discipline and Punish* he investigates the possibility that the evolution of the penal system is intimately connected to the human sciences. His argument is that a 'single process of "epistemologico-juridical" formation' underlies the history of the prison on the one hand, and the knowledge of 'man' on the other.[4] In other words, the prison is consistent with modern society and modern modes of apprehending 'man's' world.

This type of analysis has been attempted in International Relations by various thinkers. Richard Ashley has exposed one dimension of the power-knowledge nexus by highlighting what Foucault calls the 'rule of immanence' between knowledge of the state and knowledge of 'man'. Ashley's argument, stated simply, is that, '[m]odern statecraft is modern mancraft'.[5] He seeks to demonstrate how the 'paradigm of sovereignty' simultaneously gives rise to a certain epistemological disposition and a certain account of modern political life. On the one hand, knowledge is thought to depend on the sovereignty of 'the heroic figure of reasoning man who knows that the order of the world is not God-given, that man is the origin of all knowledge, that responsibility for supplying meaning to history resides with man himself, and that, through reason, man may achieve total knowledge, total autonomy, and total power'.[6] On the other hand, modern political life finds in sovereignty its constitutive principle. The state is conceived by analogy with sovereign man as a pre-given, bounded entity which enters into relations with other sovereign presences. Sovereignty acts as the 'master signifier' as Jenny Edkins and Véronique Pin-Fat put it.[7] Both 'Man' and the state are marked by the presence of sovereignty, which contrasts with international relations which is marked, and violently so, by the absence of sovereignty (or alternatively stated, the presence of multiple sovereignties). In short, both the theory and practice of international relations are conditioned by the constitutive principle of sovereignty.

Similarly, in *Simulating Sovereignty*, Cynthia Weber provides an account of how different configurations of power and knowledge give rise to different conceptions of sovereignty, statehood and intervention. One of the questions central to her inquiry is: How are practices of power and knowledge organised to ground the notion of the sovereign state?[8] State sovereignty is not a fixed concept according to Weber. Rather, like any political concept or institution, its functions, competencies, and legitimate privileges change over time. In particular Weber is concerned with how changes in the notion of state sovereignty have been shaped by changing conceptions of intervention and modalities of punishment. She reads the historicity of state sovereignty in terms of its transgression and corrective practices. Historical configurations of power-knowledge are presented by Weber through various episodes, each of which is defined by a particular modality of punishment. The point of this is to suggest that the concept of state sovereignty as currently used wipes out the historicity of the concept by arbitrarily fixing its meaning; it loses a sense of the historical nature of sovereignty's meaning and function. Furthermore, the concept of state sovereignty depends not on the presence of a foundational political community but on practices of power-knowledge which help to constitute this apparent foundation.

Genealogy

It is important to grasp the notion of genealogy as it has become crucial to many postmodern perspectives in international relations. Genealogy is, put simply, a style of historical thought which exposes and registers the significance of power-knowledge relations. It is perhaps best known through Nietzsche's radical assault on the concept of origins. As Roland Bleiker explains, genealogies 'focus on the process by which we have constructed origins and given meaning to particular representations of the past, representations that continuously guide our daily lives and set clear limits to political and social options'.[9] It is a form of history which historicises those things which are thought to be beyond history, including those things or thoughts which have been buried, covered, or excluded from view in the writing and making of history.

In a sense genealogy is concerned with writing counter-histories which expose the processes of exclusion and covering which make possible the teleological idea of history as a unified story unfolding with a clear beginning, middle and end. History, from a genealogical perspective, does not evidence a gradual disclosure of truth and meaning. Rather, it stages 'the endlessly repeated play of dominations'.[10] History proceeds as a series of dominations and impositions in knowledge and power, and the task of the genealogist is to unravel history to reveal the multifarious trajectories that have been fostered or closed off in the constitution of subjects, objects, fields of action and domains of knowledge. Moreover, from a genealogical perspective there is not one single, grand history, but many interwoven histories varied in their rhythm, tempo, and power-knowledge effects.

Genealogy affirms a perspectivism which denies the capacity to identify origins and meanings in history objectively. A genealogical approach is anti-essentialist in orientation, affirming the idea that all knowledge is situated in a particular time and place and issues from a particular perspective. The subject of knowledge is situated in, and conditioned by, a political and historical context, and constrained to function with particular concepts and categories of knowledge. Knowledge is never unconditioned. As a consequence of the heterogeneity of possible contexts and positions, there can be no single, Archimedean perspective which trumps all others. There is no 'truth', only competing perspectives. David Campbell's analysis of the Bosnian War in *National Deconstruction* affirms this perspectivism. As he rightly reminds us, 'the same events can be represented in markedly different ways with significantly different effects'.[11] Indeed, the upshot of his analysis is that the Bosnian War can only be known through perspective.

In the absence of a universal frame of reference or overarching perspective, we are left with a plurality of perspectives. As Nietzsche put it: 'There is *only* a perspective seeing, *only* a perspective "knowing" '.[12] The modern idea, or ideal, of an objective or all-encompassing perspective is displaced in postmodernism by the Nietzschean recognition that there is always more than one perspective and that each perspective embodies a particular set of values. Moreover, these perspectives do not simply offer different views of the same 'real world'. The very *idea* of the 'real world' has been 'abolished' in Nietzsche's thought,[13] leaving *only* perspectives, *only* interpretations of interpretations, or in Derrida's terms, *only* 'textuality'.[14]

Perspectives are thus not to be thought of as simply optical devices for apprehending the 'real world', like a telescope or microscope, but also as the very fabric of that 'real world'. For postmodernism, following Nietzsche, perspectives are integral to the constitution of the 'real world', not just because they are our only access to it, but because they are basic and essential elements of it. The warp and woof of the 'real world' is woven out of perspectives and interpretations, none of which can claim to correspond to reality-in-itself, to be a 'view from nowhere', or to be exhaustive. Perspectives are thus component objects and events that go towards making up the 'real world'. In fact we should say that there is no object or event outside or prior to perspective or narrative. As Campbell explains, after Hayden White, narrative is central, not just to understanding an event, but in constituting that event. This is what Campbell means by the 'narrativizing of reality'.[15] According to such a conception events acquire the status of 'real' not because they occurred but because they are remembered and because they assume a place in a narrative.[16] Narrative is thus not simply a *re*-presentation of some prior event, it is the means by which the status of reality is conferred on events. But historical narratives also perform vital political functions in the present; they can be used as resources in contemporary political struggles.[17]

Metaphors of war and battle are central to genealogy. Genealogy is a reminder of the essential agonism in the historical constitution of identities, unities, disciplines, subjects and objects. From this perspective, 'all history, including the production of order, [is comprehended] in terms of the endless power political clash of multiple wills'.[18] Furthermore, Foucault claims as one of genealogy's express purposes the 'systematic dissociation of identity'.[19] There are two dimensions to this purpose. Firstly, it has a purpose at the ontological level: to avoid substituting causes for effects (metalepsis). It does not take unity as given but seeks to account for the forces which underwrite this apparent unity. Unity is an effect to be explained, not assumed. This means resisting the temptation to attribute essences to things or events in history, and requires a transformation of the question 'what is?' into 'how is?' For Nietzsche (and postmodernism) it is more important to determine the forces that give shape to an event or a thing than to attempt to identify its hidden, fixed essence. Ashley demonstrates an affinity with this type of question by asking, 'how, by way of what practices, are structures of history produced, differentiated, reified and transformed?'[20] Secondly, it has an ethico-political purpose to problematise prevailing identity formations which appear normal or natural. It refuses to use history for the purpose of confirming present identities, preferring to use it instead to disturb identities that have become dogmatised, conventionalised or normalised.

It is in this sense that we can understand Foucault's attempt at 'writing the history of the present'.[21] A history of the present asks: How have we made the present seem like a normal or natural point of arrival? What has been forgotten or buried in history in order to legitimise the present? How do we select and differentiate what is necessary and what can be passed over in silence when trying to make the present intelligible?

One of the important insights of postmodernism, with its focus on the power-knowledge nexus and its genealogical approach, is that many of the problems and issues studied in International Relations are not just matters of epistemology and ontology, but of power and authority; they are struggles to impose authoritative interpretations of international relations. The following section outlines a strategy which is concerned with destabilising these dominant interpretations by showing how every interpretation systematically depends on that for which it cannot account.

Textual Strategies of Postmodernism

Der Derian contends that postmodernism is concerned with exposing the 'textual interplay behind power politics'.[22] It might be better to say it is concerned with exposing the textual interplay *within* power politics, for the effects of textuality do not remain behind politics, but are intrinsic to them. The 'reality' of power politics (like any social reality) is always already constituted through textuality and inscribed modes of representation. It is in this sense that David Campbell refers to 'writing' security, Gearóid Ó Tuathail refers to 'writing' global space, and Cynthia Weber refers to 'writing' the state.[23] Two questions arise: (1) what is meant by textual interplay? and (2) how, by using what methods and strategies, does postmodernism seek to disclose this textual interplay?

Textuality is a common postmodern theme. It stems mainly from Derrida's redefinition of 'text' in *Of Grammatology*. It is important to clarify what Derrida means by text. He is not restricting its meaning to literature and the realm of ideas, as some have mistakenly thought, rather, he is implying that the world is *also* a text, or better, the 'real' world is constituted like a text, and 'one cannot refer to this "real" except in an interpretive experience'.[24] Postmodernism firmly regards interpretation as necessary and fundamental to the constitution of the social world, and it is for this reason that Derrida quotes Montaigne: 'We need to interpret interpretations more than to interpret things'.[25] Textual interplay refers to the supplementary and mutually constitutive relationship between different interpretations in the representation and constitution of the world. In order to tease out the textual interplay postmodernism deploys the strategies of deconstruction and double reading.

Deconstruction

Deconstruction is a general mode of radically unsettling what are taken to be stable concepts and conceptual oppositions. Its main point is to demonstrate the effects and costs produced by the settled concepts and oppositions, to disclose the parasitical relationship between opposed terms, and to attempt a displacement of them. According to Derrida conceptual oppositions are never simply neutral but are inevitably hierarchical. One of the two terms in the opposition is privileged over the other. This privileged term supposedly connotes a presence, propriety, fullness, purity or identity which the other lacks (for example sovereignty as opposed to anarchy). Deconstruction attempts to show that such oppositions are untenable, as each term *always already* depends on the other. Indeed, the prized term only gains its privilege by disavowing its dependence on the subordinate term.

From a postmodern perspective, the apparently clear opposition between two terms is neither clear nor oppositional. Derrida often speaks of this relationship in terms of a structural parasitism and contamination, as each term is structurally related to, and already harbours, the other. Difference *between* the two opposed concepts or terms is always accompanied by a veiled difference *within* each term. Neither term is pure, self-same, complete in itself, or completely closed off from the other, though as much is feigned. This implies that totalities, whether conceptual or social, are never fully present and properly established. Moreover, there is no pure stability, only more or less successful stabilisations as there is a certain amount of 'play', or 'give', in the structure of the opposition.

As a general mode of unsettling, deconstruction is particularly concerned with locating those elements of instability or 'give' which ineradicably threaten any totality. Nevertheless, it must still account for stabilisations (or stability-*effects*). It is this equal concern with undoing or deconstitution (or at least their ever-present possibility) which marks off deconstruction from other more familiar modes of interpretation. To summarise, deconstruction is concerned with both the constitution and deconstitution of any totality, whether a text, theory, discourse, structure, edifice, assemblage or institution.

Double reading

Derrida seeks to expose this relationship between stability-effects and destabilisations by passing through two readings in any analysis. As expressed by Derrida, double reading is essentially a duplicitous strategy which is 'simultaneously faithful and violent'.[26] The first reading is a commentary or repetition of the dominant interpretation, that is, a reading which demonstrates how a text, discourse or institution achieves the stability-effect. It faithfully recounts the dominant story by building on the same foundational assumptions, and repeating conventional steps in the argument. The point here is to demonstrate how the text, discourse or institution appears coherent and consistent with itself. It is concerned, in short, to elaborate how the identity of a text, discourse or institution is put together or constituted. Rather than yield to the monologic first reading, the second, counter-memorialising reading unsettles it by applying pressure to those points of instability within a text, discourse or institution. It exposes the internal tensions and how they are (incompletely) covered over or expelled. The text, discourse or institution is never completely at one with itself, but always carries within it elements of tension and crisis which render the whole thing less than stable.

The task of double reading as a mode of deconstruction is to understand how a discourse or social institution is assembled or put together, but at the same time show how it is always already threatened with its undoing. It is important to note that there is no attempt in deconstruction to arrive at a single, conclusive reading. The two mutually inconsistent readings, which are in a performative (rather than logical) contradiction, remain permanently in tension. The point is not to demonstrate the truthfulness or otherwise of a story, but to expose how any story depends on the repression of internal tensions in order to produce a stable effect of homogeneity and continuity.

Ashley's double reading of the anarchy problematique

Ashley's main target is the conception of anarchy and the theoretical and practical effects it produces in international relations. The anarchy problematique is Ashley's name for what he believes is the defining moment of most inquiries in International Relations. The anarchy problematique is exemplified by Oye's assertion that, 'Nations dwell in perpetual anarchy, for no central authority imposes limits on the pursuit of sovereign interests'.[27] Most importantly, the anarchy problematique deduces from the absence of central, global authority, not just an empty concept of anarchy, but a description of international relations as power politics, characterised by self-interest, *raison d'état*, the routine resort to force, and so on.

The main brunt of Ashley's analysis is to problematise this deduction of power politics from the lack of central rule. Ashley's many analyses of the anarchy problematique can be understood in terms of double reading. The first reading assembles the constitutive features, or 'hard core' of the anarchy problematique, while the second reading disassembles the constitutive elements of the anarchy problematique, showing how the anarchy problematique rests on a series of questionable theoretical suppositions or exclusions.

In the first reading Ashley outlines the anarchy problematique in conventional terms. He describes not just the absence of any overarching authority, but the presence of a multiplicity of states in the international system, none of which can lay down the law to the individual states. Further, the states which comprise this system have their own identifiable interests, capabilities, resources and territory. The second reading questions the self-evidence of international relations as an anarchical realm of power politics. The initial target in this double reading is the opposition between sovereignty and anarchy where sovereignty is valorised as a regulative ideal, and anarchy is regarded as the absence or negation of sovereignty. Anarchy takes on meaning only as the antithesis of sovereignty. Moreover, sovereignty and anarchy are taken to be mutually exclusive and mutually exhaustive. Ashley demonstrates, however, that the anarchy problematique works only by making certain assumptions regarding sovereign states. If the dichotomy between sovereignty and anarchy is to be tenable at all, then inside the sovereign state must be found a domestic realm of identity, homogeneity, order and progress guaranteed by legitimate force; and outside must lie an anarchical realm of difference, heterogeneity, disorder and threat, recurrence and repetition. But to represent sovereignty and anarchy in this way (that is, as mutually exclusive and exhaustive), depends on converting differences *within* sovereign states into differences *between* sovereign states.[28] Sovereign states must expunge any traces of anarchy that reside within them in order to make good on the distinction between sovereignty and anarchy. Internal dissent and what Ashley calls 'transversal struggles' which cast doubt over the idea of a clearly identifiable and demarcated sovereign identity must be repressed or denied to make the anarchy problematique meaningful.[29] In particular, the opposition between sovereignty and anarchy rests on the possibility of determining a 'well-bounded sovereign entity possessing its own "internal" hegemonic centre of decision-making capable of reconciling "internal" conflicts and capable, therefore, of projecting a singular presence'.[30]

The general effect of the anarchy problematique is to confirm the opposition between sovereignty and anarchy as mutually exclusive and exhaustive. This has two particular effects: (1) to represent a domestic domain of sovereignty as a stable, legitimate foundation of modern political community, and (2) to represent the domain beyond sovereignty as dangerous and anarchical. These effects depend on what Ashley calls a 'double exclusion'.[31] They are possible only if, on the one hand, a single representation of sovereign identity can be imposed, and on the other hand, if this representation can be made to appear natural and indisputable. The double reading problematises the anarchy problematique by posing two questions: firstly, what happens to the anarchy problematique if it is not so clear that fully present and completed sovereign states are ontologically primary or unitary? And secondly, what happens to the anarchy problematique if the lack of central global rule is not overwritten with assumptions about power politics?

Problematising Sovereign States

International Relations has long been concerned with states, sovereignty and violence. These are long-standing themes which draw on established traditions of international relations thinking. They are also central themes in postmodern approaches to the study of international relations. Rather than adopt them uncritically from traditional approaches, postmodernism revises them in view of insights gained from genealogy and deconstruction.

Postmodernism seeks to address a crucial issue regarding interpretations and explanations of the sovereign state that state-centric approaches have obscured, namely, its historical constitution and reconstitution as the primary mode of subjectivity in world politics. This returns us to the type of question posed by Foucault's genealogy: how, by virtue of what political practices and representations, is the sovereign state instituted as the normal mode of international subjectivity? Posing the question in this manner directs attention, in Nietzschean fashion, less to what is the essence of the sovereign state, than to how the sovereign state is made possible, how it is naturalised, and how it is made to appear as if it had an essence.

To the extent that postmodernism seeks to account for the conditions which make possible the phenomenon of the state as something which concretely affects the experience of everyday life, it is phenomenological. Yet this is no ordinary phenomenology. It might best be called a 'quasi-phenomenology', for as already noted, it is equally concerned with accounting for those conditions which destabilise the phenomenon or defer its complete actualisation. In this section postmodernism's quasi-phenomenology of the state will be explained. This comprises four main elements: (1) a genealogical analysis of the modern state's 'origins' in violence, (2) an account of boundary inscription, (3) a deconstruction of identity as it is defined in security and foreign policy discourses, and (4) a revised interpretation of statecraft. The overall result is to rethink the ontological structure of the sovereign state in order to respond properly to the question of how the sovereign state is (re)constituted as the normal mode of subjectivity in international relations.

(1) Violence

Modern political thought has attempted to transcend illegitimate forms of rule (such as tyranny and despotism) where power is unconstrained, unchecked, arbitrary and violent, by founding legitimate, democratic forms of government where authority is subject to law. In modern politics, it is reason rather than power or violence which has become the measure of legitimacy. However, as Campbell and Dillon point out, the relationship between politics and violence in modernity is deeply ambivalent, for on the one hand, violence 'constructs the refuge of the sovereign community', and on the other hand, it is 'the condition from which the citizens of that community must be protected'.[32] The paradox here is that violence is both poison and cure. It is simultaneously the thing which the modern state is designed to protect citizens against, but also that which makes possible the modern state as a shelter from violence.

The link between violence and the state is revealed in Bradley Klein's genealogy of the state as strategic subject. Klein's general purpose in *Strategic Studies and World Order* is to open up an analysis into 'the violent making and remaking of the modern world'.[33] His more particular purpose is to explain the historical emergence of war-making states. Rather than assume their existence, as many realists and neo-realists tend to do, Klein is interested in examining how political units emerge in history which are capable of relying upon force to distinguish a domestic political space from a foreign one. Consistent with other postmoderns, he argues that 'states rely upon violence to constitute themselves as states', and in the process, 'impose differentiations between the internal and external'.[34] Strategic violence does not merely 'patrol the frontiers' of the state, it 'helps constitute them as well'.[35] Violence is thus constitutive of states.

The point made by postmodernism regarding violence in modern politics needs to be clearly differentiated from traditional approaches. In general, traditional accounts take violent confrontation to be a normal and regular occurrence in international relations. The condition of anarchy is thought to incline states to war as there is nothing to stop wars from occurring. Violence is not constitutive in such accounts as these, but is 'configurative', or 'positional'.[36] The ontological structure of the states is taken to be set-up already before violence is undertaken. The violence merely modifies the territorial configuration, or is an instrument for power-political, strategic manoeuvres in the distribution or hierarchy of power. Postmodernism, however, exposes the constitutive role of violence in modern political life. As expressed by Campbell and Dillon, 'War makes the body politic (the political subject) that is invoked to sanction it'.[37] It is fundamental to the ontological structuring of states, and is not merely something to which fully formed states resort for power-political reasons. Violence is, according to postmodernism, inaugural as well as augmentative.

This argument about the intimate and paradoxical relationship between violence and political order is taken even further by Jenny Edkins who places the Nazis, concentration camps, NATO and refugee camps on the same continuum. All, she claims, are determined by a sovereign power that seeks to extend control over life. She argues that the concentration camp 'is nothing more than the coming to fruition of the horror contained in everyday existence under the sway of sovereign politics in the West'.[38] Beyond placing the West on a continuum with the concentration camps, Edkins also argues that NATO is equivalent to the Nazis insofar as its bombing campaign 'inaugurates NATO as sovereign power and at the same time legitimates its assumption of the monopoly of legitimate violence'.[39]

The controversial conclusion of Edkins' argument is that even humanitarianism can be placed on the spectrum of violence since it too is complicit with the modern state's order of sovereign power and violence, notwithstanding claims to the contrary. Famine-relief camps, she says, are like concentration camps since they are both sites of 'arbitrary decisions between life and death, where aid workers are forced to choose which of the starving they are unable to help'.[40] Famine victims appear only as 'bare life' to be 'saved'; stripped of their social and cultural being, they are depoliticised, their political voices ignored.[41] In different language, Campbell affirms this view arguing that prevailing forms of humanitarianism construct people as victims, 'incapable of acting without intervention'.[42] This insufficiently political or humane form of humanitarianism, therefore, 'is deeply implicated in the production of a sovereign political power that claims the monopoly of the legitimate use of violence'.[43] Mick Dillon and Julian Reid offer a similar reading of humanitarian responses to 'complex emergencies', but rather than assume an equivalence between humanitarianism and sovereign power, they see a susceptibility of the former to the operations of the latter. Global governance, they say, 'quite literally threatens nongovernmental and humanitarian agencies with recruitment into the very structures and practices of power against which they previously defined themselves'.[44]

(2)   Boundaries

To inquire into the state's (re)constitution, as postmodernism does, is partly to inquire into the ways in which global political space is partitioned. The world is not naturally divided into differentiated political spaces, and nor is there a single authority to carve up the world. This necessarily leads to a focus on the 'boundary question', as Dillon and Everard call it, because any political subject is constituted by the marking of physical, symbolic and ideological boundaries.[45]

Postmodernism is less concerned with *what* sovereignty is, than *how* it is spatially and temporally produced and how it is circulated. How is a certain configuration of space and power instituted? And with what consequences? The obvious implication of these questions is that the prevailing mode of political subjectivity in international relations (the sovereign state) is neither natural nor necessary. There is no necessary reason why global political space has to be divided as it is and with the same bearing. Of crucial importance in this differentiation of political space is the inscription of boundaries. Marking boundaries is not an innocent, pre-political act. It is a political act with profound political implications as it is fundamental to the production and delimitation of political space. As Gearóid Ó Tuathail affirms, '[g]eography is about power. Although often assumed to be innocent, the geography of the world is not a product of nature but a product of histories of struggle between competing authorities over the power to organize, occupy, and administer space'.[46]

There is no political space in advance of boundary inscription. Boundaries function in the modern world to divide an interior, sovereign space from an exterior, pluralistic, anarchical space. The opposition between sovereignty and anarchy rests on the possibility of clearly dividing a domesticated political space from an undomesticated outside. It is in this sense that boundary inscription is a defining moment of the sovereign state. Indeed, neither sovereignty nor anarchy would be possible without the inscription of a boundary to divide political space. This 'social inscription of global space', to use Ó Tuathail's phrase, produces the effect of completed, bounded states, usually built around what Campbell calls the 'nationalist imaginary'.[47]

However, as Connolly points out, boundaries are highly ambiguous since they 'form an indispensable protection against violation and violence; but divisions they sustain in doing so also carry cruelty and violence'.[48] At stake here is a series of questions regarding boundaries: how boundaries are constituted, what moral and political status they are accorded, how they operate simultaneously to include and exclude, and how they simultaneously produce order and violence? Clearly, these questions are not just concerned with the location of cartographic boundaries, but with how these cartographic boundaries serve to represent, limit, and legitimate a political identity. But how, through which political practices and representations, are boundaries inscribed? And what implications does this hold for the mode of subjectivity produced?

(3) Identity

There is, as Rob Walker notes, a privileging of spatiality in modern political thought and practice.[49] By differentiating political spaces, boundaries are fundamental to the modern world's preference for the 'entrapment of politics' within discrete state boundaries.[50] Postmodernism asks: how has political identity been imposed by spatial practices and representations of domestication and distancing? And how has the concept of a territorially-defined self been constructed in opposition to a threatening other?

Of utmost importance here are issues of how security is conceived in spatial terms and how threats and dangers are defined and articulated, giving rise to particular conceptions of the state as a secure political subject. Debbie Lisle has recently shown how even modern tourism participates in the reproduction of this spatialised conception of security. By continuously reaffirming the distinction between 'safety here and now' and 'danger there and then' tourist practices help sustain the geopolitical security discourse. Her reading suggests that war and tourism, rather than being two distinct and opposed social practices, are actually intimately connected by virtue of being governed by the same global security discourse.[51]

A detailed account of the relationship between the state, violence and identity is to be found in David Campbell's post-structuralist account of the Bosnian War in *National Deconstruction*. His central argument there is that a particular norm of community has governed the intense violence of the war. This norm, which he calls 'ontopology', borrowing from Derrida, refers to the assumption that political community requires the perfect alignment of territory and identity, state and nation.[52] It functions to disseminate and reinforce the supposition that political community must be understood and organised as a single identity perfectly aligned with and possessing its allocated territory. The logic of this norm, suggests Campbell, leads to a desire for a coherent, bounded, monocultural community.[53] These 'ontopological' assumptions form 'the governing codes of subjectivity in international relations'.[54] What is interesting about Campbell's argument is the implication that the outpouring of violence in Bosnia was not simply an aberration or racist distortion of the ontopological norm, but was in fact an exacerbation of this same norm.[55] The violence of 'ethnic cleansing' in pursuit of a pure, homogeneous political identity is simply a continuation, albeit extreme, of the same political project inherent in any modern nation-state. The upshot is that all forms of political community, insofar as they require boundaries, will be given to some degree of violence.[56]

Postmodernism focuses on the discourses and practices which substitute threat for difference in the constitution of political identity. Simon Dalby, for instance, explains how cold wars result from the application of a geopolitical reasoning which defines security in terms of spatial exclusion and the specification of a threatening other. 'Geopolitical discourse constructs worlds in terms of Self and Others, in terms of cartographically specifiable sections of political space, and in terms of military threats'.[57] The geopolitical creation of the external other is integral to the constitution of a political identity (self) which is to be made secure. But to constitute a coherent, singular political identity often demands the silencing of internal dissent. There can be internal others that endanger a certain conception of the self, and must be necessarily expelled, disciplined, or contained. Identity, it can be surmised, is an effect forged, on the one hand, by disciplinary practices which attempt to normalise a population, giving it a sense of unity, and on the other, by exclusionary practices which attempt to secure the domestic identity through processes of spatial differentiation, and various diplomatic, military, and defence practices. There is a supplementary relationship between containment of domestic and foreign others, which helps to constitute political identity by expelling 'from the resultant "domestic" space ... all that comes to be regarded as alien, foreign and dangerous'.[58]

If it is plain that identity is defined through difference, and that a self requires an other, it is not so plain that difference or otherness necessarily equates with threat or danger. Nevertheless, as Campbell points out the sovereign state is predicated on discourses of danger. 'The constant articulation of danger through foreign policy is thus not a threat to a state's identity or existence', says Campbell, 'it is its condition of possibility'.[59] The possibility of identifying the US as a political subject, for example, rested, during the Cold War, on the ability to impose an interpretation of the Soviet Union as an external threat, and the capacity of the US government to contain internal threats.[60] Indeed, the pivotal concept of containment takes on a Janus-faced quality as it is simultaneously turned inwards and outwards to deal with threatening others, as Campbell suggests.[61] The end result of the strategies of containment was to ground identity in a territorial state.

It is important to recognise that political identities do not exist prior to the differentiation of self and other. The main issue is how something which is different becomes conceptualised as a threat or danger to be contained, disciplined, negated or excluded. There may be an irreducible possibility that difference will slide into opposition, danger, or threat, but there is no necessity. Political identity need not be constituted against, and at the expense of, others, but the prevailing discourses and practices of security and foreign policy tend to reproduce this reasoning. Moreover, this relation to others must be recognised as a morally and politically loaded relation. The effect is to allocate the other to an inferior moral space, and to arrogate the self to a superior one. As Campbell puts it, 'the social space of inside/outside is both made possible by and helps constitute a moral space of superior/inferior'.[62] By coding the spatial exclusion in moral terms it becomes easier to legitimise certain politico-military practices and interventions which advance national security interests at the same time that they reconstitute political identities. As Shapiro puts it, 'to the extent that the Other is regarded as something not occupying the same moral space as the self, conduct toward the Other becomes more exploitive'.[63] This is especially so in an international system where political identity is so frequently defined in terms of territorial exclusion.

(4)   Statecraft

The above section has sketched how violence, boundaries and identity function to make possible the sovereign state. This only partly deals with the main genealogical issue of how the sovereign state is (re)constituted as a normal mode of subjectivity. Two questions remain if the genealogical approach is to be pursued: how is the sovereign state naturalised and disseminated? And how is it made to appear as if it had an essence?

Postmodernism is interested in how prevailing modes of subjectivity neutralise or conceal their arbitrariness by projecting an image of normalcy, naturalness, or necessity. Ashley has explored the very difficult question of how the dominant mode of subjectivity is normalised by utilising the concept of hegemony. By hegemony Ashley means not an 'overarching ideology or cultural matrix', but 'an ensemble of normalized knowledge-able practices, identified with a particular state and domestic society ... that is regarded as a practical paradigm of sovereign political subjectivity and conduct'.[64] Hegemony refers to the projection and circulation of an 'exemplary' model, which functions as a regulative ideal. Of course the distinguishing characteristics of the exemplary model are not fixed but are historically and politically conditioned. The sovereign state, as the currently dominant mode of subjectivity, is by no means natural. As Ashley remarks, sovereignty is fused to certain 'historically normalized interpretations of the state, its competencies, and the conditions and limits of its recognition and empowerment'.[65] The fusion of the state to sovereignty is, therefore, conditioned by changing historical and cultural representations and practices which serve to produce a political identity.

A primary function of the exemplary model is to negate alternative conceptions of subjectivity or to devalue them as underdeveloped, inadequate or incomplete. Anomalies are contrasted with the 'proper', 'normal', or 'exemplary' model. For instance, 'quasi-states' or 'failed states' represent empirical cases of states which deviate from the model by failing to display the recognisable signs of sovereign statehood. In this failure they help to reinforce the hegemonic mode of subjectivity as the norm, and to reconfirm the sovereignty/anarchy opposition which underwrites it.

In order for the model to have any power at all though it must be replicable; it must be seen as a universally effective mode of subjectivity which can be invoked and instituted at any site. The pressures applied on states to conform to normalised modes of subjectivity are complex and various, and emanate both internally and externally. Some pressures are quite explicit, such as military intervention, others less so, such as conditions attached to foreign aid, diplomatic recognition, and general processes of socialisation. The point is that modes of subjectivity achieve dominance in space and time through the projection and imposition of power.

How has the state been made to appear as if it had an essence? The short answer to this question is that the state is made to appear as if it had an essence by performative enactment of various domestic and foreign policies, or what might more simply be called 'statecraft', with the emphasis on 'craft'. Traditionally, statecraft refers to the various policies and practices undertaken by states to pursue their objectives in the international arena. The assumption underlying this definition is that the state is already a fully formed, or bounded, entity before it negotiates its way in this arena. The revised notion of statecraft advanced by postmodernism stresses the on-going political practices which found and maintain the state, having the effect of keeping the state in perpetual motion.

As Richard Ashley stressed in his path-breaking article, subjects have no existence prior to political practice. Sovereign states emerge on the plane of historical and political practices.[66] This suggests it is better to understand the state as performatively constituted, having no identity apart from the ceaseless enactment of the ensemble of foreign and domestic policies, security and defence strategies, protocols of treaty-making, and representational practices at the UN, among other things. The state's 'being' is thus an effect of performativity. By performativity we must understand the continued iteration of a norm or set of norms, not simply a singular act, which produces the very thing it names.[67] As Weber explains, 'the identity of the state is performatively constituted by the very expressions that are said to be its result'.[68]

It is in this sense that David Campbell, in his recent account of the war in Bosnia, focuses on what he calls 'metaBosnia', by which he means 'the array of practices through which Bosnia ... comes to be'.[69] To help come to terms with the ceaseless production of Bosnia as a state or subject Campbell recommends that we recognise that we are never dealing with a given, *a priori* state of Bosnia, but with metaBosnia, that is, the performative constitution of 'Bosnia' through a range of enframing and differentiating practices. 'Bosnia', like any other state, is always under a process of construction.

To summarise then, the sovereign state, as Weber says, is the 'ontological effect of practices which are performatively enacted'.[70] As she explains, 'sovereign nation-states are not pre-given subjects but subjects in process',[71] where the phrase 'subjects in process' should also be understood to mean 'subjects on trial' (as the French *'en procés'* implies). This leads to an interpretation of the state (as subject) as always in the process of being constituted, but never quite achieving that final moment of completion.[72] The state thus should not be understood as if it were a prior presence, but instead should be seen as the simulated presence produced by the processes of statecraft. It is never fully complete but is in a constant process of 'becoming-state'. Though 'never fully realised, [the state] is in a continual process of concretisation'.[73] The upshot is that, for postmodernism, there is statecraft, but there is no completed state.[74]

Lest it be thought that that postmodern theories of international relations mark a return to realist state-centrism, some clarification will be needed to explain its concern with the sovereign state. Postmodernism does not seek to explain world politics by focusing on the state alone, nor does it take the state as given. Instead, as Ashley's double reading of the anarchy problematique testifies, it seeks to explain the conditions which make possible such an explanation and the costs consequent on such an approach. What is lost by taking a state-centric perspective? And most importantly, to what aspects of world politics does state-centrism remain blind?

Beyond the Paradigm of Sovereignty: Rethinking the Political

One of the central implications of postmodernism is that the paradigm of sovereignty has impoverished our political imagination and restricted our comprehension of the dynamics of world politics. In this section we review postmodern attempts to develop a new conceptual language to represent world politics beyond the terms of state-centrism in order to rethink the concept of the political.

Campbell asks the question: 'can we represent world politics in a manner less indebted to the sovereignty problematic?'.[75] The challenge is to create a conceptual language that can better convey the novel processes and actors in modern (or postmodern) world politics. Campbell recommends 'thinking in terms of a *political prosaics* that understands the *transversal* nature' of world politics.[76] To conceptualise world politics in terms of 'political prosaics' is to draw attention to the multitude of flows and interactions produced by globalisation that cut across nation-state boundaries. It is to focus on the many political, economic and cultural activities that produce a 'deterritorialisation' of modern political life; activities that destabilise the paradigm of sovereignty.

The argument here draws heavily upon the philosophical work of Gilles Deleuze and Felix Guattari.[77] They have developed a novel conceptual language which has been deployed by postmodern theorists of international relations to make sense of the operation and impact of various non-state actors, flows and movements on the political institution of state sovereignty. The central terms here are reterritorialisation and deterritorialisation.[78] The former is associated with the totalising logic of the paradigm of sovereignty, or 'State-form' as Deleuze and Guattari say, whose function is defined by processes of capture and boundary-marking. The latter, deterritorialisation, is associated with the highly mobile logic of nomadism whose function is defined by its ability to transgress boundaries and avoid capture by the State-form. The one finds expression in the desire for identity, order and unity, the other in the desire for difference, flows and lines of flight.

The 'political prosaics' advocated by Campbell and others utilises this Deleuzian language to shed light on the new political dynamics and demands created by refugees, immigrants, and new social movements as they encounter and outflank the State-form. These 'transversal' groups and movements not only transgress national boundaries, they call into question the territorial organisation of modern political life. As Roland Bleiker notes, they 'question the spatial logic through which these boundaries have come to constitute and frame the conduct of international relations'.[79] In his study of popular dissent in international relations, Bleiker argues that globalisation is subjecting social life to changing political dynamics. In an age of mass media and telecommunications, images of local acts of resistance can be flashed across the world in an instant, turning them into events of global significance. Globalisation, he suggests, has transformed the nature of dissent, making possible global and transversal practices of popular dissent.[80] No longer taking place in a purely local context, acts of resistance 'have taken on increasingly transversal dimensions. They ooze into often unrecognised, but nevertheless significant grey zones between domestic and international spheres', blurring the boundaries between inside and outside, local and global.[81] By outflanking sovereign controls and crossing state boundaries, the actions of transversal dissident groups can be read as 'hidden transcripts' that occur 'off-stage', as it were, behind and alongside the 'public transcript' of the sovereign state. The 'hidden transcripts' of transversal movements are therefore deterritorialising in their function, escaping the spatial codes and practices of the dominant actors and making possible a critique of the sovereign state's modes of reterritorialisation and exclusion.[82]

This is also the case with refugees and migrants. They hold a different relationship to space than citizens. Being nomadic rather than sedentary, they are defined by movement across and between political spaces. They problematise and defy the 'territorial imperative' of the sovereign state.[83] Indeed, their wandering movement dislocates the ontopological norm which seeks to fix people's identities within the spatial boundaries of the nation-state.[84] As a consequence they disrupt our state-centric conceptualisations, problematising received understandings of the character and location of the political.

Similar arguments are advanced by Peter Nyers and Mick Dillon regarding the figure of the refugee. As Nyers argues, the figure of the refugee, as one who cannot claim to be a member of a 'proper' political community, acts as a 'limit-concept', occupying the ambiguous zone between citizen and human.[85] Dillon argues that the refugee/stranger remains outside conventional modes of political subjectivity which are tied to the sovereign state. The very existence of the refugee/stranger calls into question the settled, sovereign life of the political community by disclosing the estrangement that is shared by both citizens and refugees.[86] As Soguk and Whitehall point out, refugees and migrants, by moving across state boundaries and avoiding capture, have the effect of rupturing traditional constitutive narratives of international relations,[87] or to use Bleiker's terms, disclose a 'hidden transcript' of world politics that remains outside the reterritorialising logic of the sovereign state.

Sovereignty and the ethics of exclusion

Postmodernism's ethical critique of state sovereignty needs to be understood in relation to the deconstructive critique of totalisation and the deterritorialising effect of transversal struggles. Deconstruction has already been explained as a strategy of interpretation and criticism that targets theoretical concepts and social institutions which attempt totalisation or total stability. It is important to note that the postmodern critique of state sovereignty focuses on *sovereignty*.

The sovereign state may well be the dominant mode of subjectivity in international relations today, but it is questionable whether its claim to be the primary and exclusive political subject is justified. The most thorough-going account of state sovereignty's ethico-political costs is offered by Rob Walker in *Inside/Outside*.[88] He sets out there the context in which state sovereignty has been mobilised as an analytical category with which to understand international relations, and as the primary expression of moral and political community. Walker's critique suggests that state sovereignty is best understood as a constitutive political practice which emerged historically to resolve three ontological contradictions. The relationship between time and space was resolved by containing time within domesticated territorial space. The universal and particular was resolved through the system of sovereign states which gave expression to the plurality and particularity of states on the one hand, and the universality of one system on the other. This resolution also allowed for the pursuit of universal values to be pursued within particular states. Finally, the relationship between self and other is also resolved in terms of 'insiders' and 'outsiders', friends and enemies.[89] In deconstructive fashion, Walker's concern is to 'destabilise [these] seemingly opposed categories by showing how they are at once mutually constitutive and yet always in the process of dissolving into each other'.[90] The overall effect of Walker's inquiry into state sovereignty, consistent with the 'political prosaics' outlined above, is to question whether it is any longer a useful descriptive category and an effective response to the problems that confront humanity in modern political life.

The analysis offered by Walker suggests that it is becoming increasingly difficult to organise modern political life in terms of sovereign states and sovereign boundaries. He argues that there are 'spatiotemporal processes that are radically at odds with the resolution expressed by the principle of state sovereignty'.[91] For both material and normative reasons, Walker refuses to accept state sovereignty as the only, or best, possible means of organising modern political life. Modern political life need not be caught between mutually exclusive and exhaustive oppositions such as inside and outside. Identity need not be exclusionary, difference need not be interpreted as antithetical to identity,[92] and the trade-off between men and citizens built into the modern state need not always privilege claims of citizens above claims of humanity.[93]

To rethink questions of political identity and community without succumbing to binary oppositions is to contemplate a political life beyond the paradigm of sovereign states. It is to take seriously the possibility that new forms of political identity and community can emerge which are not predicated on absolute exclusion and spatial distinctions between here and there, self and other.[94] The practical political task is to move towards forms of state which do without the claims of territorial exclusion and supremacy as necessary constitutive features of modern politics. The practical political problems which stem from state sovereignty are brought into stark relief when considering the limited scope of democracy in modern political life.

Connolly delivers a postmodern critique which brings the question of democracy to bear on sovereignty. His argument is that the notion of state sovereignty is incompatible with democracy, especially in a globalised late modernity. The point of his critique is to challenge the sovereign state's 'monopoly over the allegiances, identifications and energies of its members'.[95] The multiple modes of belonging and interdependence, and the multiplication of global risk that exist in late modernity complicate the neat simplicity of binary divisions between inside and outside. His point is that obligations and duties constantly overrun the boundaries of sovereign states. Sovereignty, he says, 'poses too stringent a limitation to identifications and loyalties extending beyond it', and so it is necessary to promote an ethos of democracy which exceeds territorialisation by cutting across the state at all levels.[96] He calls this a 'disaggregation of democracy', or what might better be called a 'deterritorialisation of democracy'.[97] 'What is needed politically', he says, 'is a series of cross-national, nonstatist movements organized across state lines, mobilized around specific issues of global significance, pressing states from inside and outside simultaneously to reconfigure established convictions, priorities, and policies'.[98]

A similar argument is advanced by Campbell. According to Campbell, the norm of ontopology produces a 'moral cartography' that territorialises democracy and responsibility, confining it to the limits of the sovereign state.[99] But Campbell, like Connolly, is interested in fostering an ethos of democratic pluralisation that would promote tolerance and multiculturalism within and across state boundaries. By promoting an active affirmation of alterity it would resist the sovereign state's logics of territorialisation and capture.

Postmodern ethics

Postmodernism asks, what might ethics come to mean outside a paradigm of sovereign subjectivity? There are two strands of ethics which develop out of postmodernism's reflections on international relations. One strand challenges the ontological description on which traditional ethical arguments are grounded. It advances a notion of ethics which is not predicated on a rigid, fixed boundary between inside and outside. The other strand focuses on the relation between ontological grounds and ethical arguments. It questions whether ontology must precede ethics.

The first strand is put forward most fully by Ashley and Walker, and Connolly. Fundamental to their writing is a critique of the faith invested in boundaries. Again, the main target of postmodernism here is the sovereign state's defence of rigid boundaries. Territorial boundaries, which are thought to mark the limits of political identity or community, are taken by postmodernism to be historically contingent and highly ambiguous products.[100] As such, they hold no transcendental status. As a challenge to the ethical delimitations imposed by state sovereignty, postmodern ethics, or the 'diplomatic ethos' as Ashley and Walker call it, is not confined by any spatial or territorial limits. It seeks to 'enable the rigorous practice of this ethics in the widest possible compass'.[101] No demarcatory boundaries should obstruct the universalisation of this ethics which flows across boundaries (both imagined and territorial):

> Where such an ethics is rigorously practiced, no voice can effectively claim to stand heroically upon some exclusionary ground, offering this ground as a source of a necessary truth that human beings must violently project in the name of a citizenry, people, nation, class, gender, race, golden age, or historical cause of any sort. Where this ethics is rigorously practiced, no totalitarian order could ever be.[102]

In breaking with the ethics of sovereign exclusion, postmodernism offers an understanding of ethics which is detached from territorial limitations. The diplomatic ethos is a 'deterritorialised' ethics which unfolds by transgressing sovereign limits. This transgressive ethics complements the deterritorialised notion of democracy advanced by Connolly. Underlying both ideas is a critique of state sovereignty as a basis for conducting, organising and limiting political life.

The other ethical strand is advanced by Campbell. He follows Derrida and Levinas by questioning traditional approaches which deduce ethics from ontology (specifically an ontology or metaphysics of presence).[103] It does not begin with an empirical account of the world as a necessary prelude to ethical consideration. Rather, it gives primacy to ethics as, in a sense, 'first philosophy'. The key thinker in this ethical approach is Emmanuel Levinas who has been more influenced by Jewish theology than Greek philosophy. Indeed, the differences between these two styles of thought are constantly worked through in Levinas's thought as a difference between a philosophy of alterity and a philosophy of identity or totality.

Levinas overturns the hierarchy between ontology and ethics, giving primacy to ethics as the starting point. Ethics seems to function as a condition which makes possible the world of beings. Levinas offers a redescription of ontology such that it is inextricably tied up with, and indebted to, ethics, and is free of totalising impulses. His thought is antagonistic to all forms of ontological and political imperialism or totalitarianism.[104] In Levinas's schema, subjectivity is constituted through (and as) an ethical relation. The effect of the Levinasian approach is to recast notions of subjectivity and responsibility in light of an ethics of otherness or alterity. 'Ethics redefines subjectivity as ... heteronomous responsibility'.[105]

This gives rise to a notion of ethics which diverges from the Kantian principle of generalisability and symmetry. Rather than begin with the Self and then generalise the imperative universally to a community of equals, Levinas begins with the Other. The Other places certain demands on the Self, hence there is an asymmetrical relationship between Self and Other. The end result is to advance a 'different figuration of politics, one in which its purpose is the struggle *for* – or *on behalf of* – alterity, and not a struggle to efface, erase, or eradicate alterity'.[106] But as Michael Shapiro has shown, this ethos may not be so different from a Kantian ethic of hospitality that encourages universal tolerance of difference as a means of diminishing global violence.[107]

The consequence of taking postmodernism's critique of totality and sovereignty seriously is that central political concepts such as community, identity, ethics and democracy are rethought to avoid being persistently reterritorialised by the sovereign state. Indeed, de-linking these concepts from territory and sovereignty underlies the practical task of a postmodern politics. Postmodernism, as a critique of totalisation, opposes concepts of identity and community only to the extent that they are tied dogmatically to notions of territoriality, boundedness and exclusion. The thrust of postmodernism has always been to challenge both epistemological and political claims to totality and sovereignty and thereby open up questions about the location and character of the political.

Conclusion

Postmodernism makes several contributions to the study of international relations. Firstly, through its genealogical method it seeks to expose the intimate connection between claims to knowledge and claims to political power and authority. Secondly, through the textual strategy of deconstruction it seeks to problematise all claims to epistemological and political totalisation. This holds especially significant implications for the sovereign state. Most notably, it means that the sovereign state, as the primary mode of subjectivity in international relations, must be examined closely to expose its practices of capture and exclusion. Moreover, a more comprehensive account of contemporary world politics must also include an analysis of those transversal actors and movements that operate outside and across state boundaries. Thirdly, postmodernism seeks to rethink the concept of the political without invoking assumptions of sovereignty and reterritorialisation. By challenging the idea that the character and location of the political must be determined by the sovereign state, postmodernism seeks to broaden the political imagination and the range of political possibilities for transforming international relations.

Once again, however, the brunt of this ethical approach is a critique of state sovereignty. If an important political purpose is to defend alterity, then the sovereign state seems increasingly incapable of carrying out this purpose. Transversal demands for justice are being made both above and below the level of the sovereign state, and in direct challenge to its ability to accommodate them. To confine ethics to the spatial confines of the sovereign state would be to subjugate the plurality of voices to the desire for order and unity. This means rethinking notions of subjectivity, identity and the concept of the political beyond the paradigm of sovereignty. More positively, it means affirming alterity, deterritorialising responsibility, and pluralising political possibilities beyond (but including) the state.[108]

Notes

1. I. Kant, *Kant's Political Writings* (Cambridge, 1970), p. 115.
2. M. J. Shapiro, *Cinematic Political Thought: Narrating Race, Nation and Gender* (New York, 1999), p. 1.
3. M. Foucault, *Discipline and Punish* (Harmondsworth, 1977), p. 27.
4. Foucault (1977), p. 23.
5. R. K. Ashley, 'Living on Border Lines: Man, Poststructuralism and War', in J. Der Derian and M. J. Shapiro (eds), *International/Intertextual Relations: Postmodern Readings of World Politics* (Massachusetts, 1989a), p. 303.

6. Ashley (1989a), p. 264–5.
7. J. Edkins and V. Pin-Fat, 'The Subject of the Political', in J. Edkins, N. Persram and V. Pin-Fat (eds), *Sovereignty and Subjectivity* (Boulder, 1999), p. 6.
8. C. Weber, *Simulating Sovereignty: Intervention, the State and Symbolic Exchange* (Cambridge, 1995), p. 30.
9. R. Bleiker, *Popular Dissent, Human Agency and Global Politics* (Cambridge, 2000), p. 25.
10. M. Foucault, 'Nietzsche, Genealogy, History', in M. T. Gibbons (eds), *Interpreting Politics* (London, 1987), p. 228.
11. D. Campbell, *National Deconstruction: Violence, Identity, and Justice in Bosnia* (Minneapolis, 1998a), p. 33.
12. F. Nietzsche, *On the Genealogy of Morals and Ecce Homo* (New York, 1969), essay III, section 12.
13. F. Nietzsche, *Twilight of the Idols/The Anti-Christ* (Harmondsworth, 1990), p. 50–1.
14. J. Derrida, *Of Grammatology* (Baltimore, 1974), p. 158.
15. Campbell (1998a), p. 34.
16. Campbell (1998a), p. 36.
17. Campbell (1998a), p. 84; and Campbell, 'Violence, Justice and Identity in the Bosnian Conflict', in Edkins, Persram and Pin-Fat (1999), p. 31.
18. R. K. Ashley, 'The Geopolitics of Geopolitical Space: Toward a Critical Social Theory of International Politics', *Alternatives*, 12 (1987), p. 409.
19. Foucault (1987), p. 236.
20. Ashley (1987), p. 409.
21. Foucault (1977), p. 31.
22. J. Der Derian, 'The Boundaries of Knowledge and Power in International Relations', in Der Derian and Shapiro (1989), p. 6.
23. D. Campbell, *Writing Security: United States Foreign Policy and the Politics of Identity* (Minneapolis, 1992); G. Ó Tuathail, *Critical Geopolitics: The Politics of Writing Global Space* (Minneapolis, 1996); Weber (1995).
24. J. Derrida, *Limited Inc* (Evanston, 1988), p. 148.
25. J. Derrida, *Writing and Difference* (Henley, 1978), p. 278.
26. J. Derrida, *Positions* (Chicago, 1981), p. 6.
27. K. Oye, 'Explaining Cooperation Under Anarchy: Hypotheses and Strategies', *World Politics*, vol. 38, no. 1 (1985), p. 1.
28. R. K. Ashley, 'Untying the Sovereign State: A Double Reading of the Anarchy Problematique', *Millennium*, vol. 17, no. 2 (1988), p. 257.
29. Ashley (1987), p. 423; (1989), p. 299.
30. Ashley (1988), p. 245.
31. Ashley (1988), p. 256.
32. D. Campbell and M. Dillon, 'Introduction', in Campbell and Dillon (eds), *The Political Subject of Violence* (Manchester, 1993), p. 161.
33. B. Klein, *Strategic Studies and World Order: The Global Politics of Deterrence* (Cambridge, 1994), p. 139.

34. Klein (1994), p. 38.
35. Klein (1994), p. 3.
36. J. G. Ruggie, 'Territoriality and Beyond: Problematizing Modernity in International Relations', *International Organization*, vol. 47, no. 1 (1993), pp. 162–3.
37. Campbell and Dillon (1993), p. 16.
38. J. Edkins, 'Sovereign Power, Zones of Indistinction, and the Camp', *Alternatives*, vol. 25, no. 1 (2000), p. 19.
39. Edkins (2000), p. 17.
40. Edkins (2000), p. 13.
41. Edkins (2000), pp. 13–14.
42. D. Campbell, 'Why Fight? Humanitarianism, Principles, and Post-structuralism', *Millennium*, vol. 27, no. 3 (1998b), p. 506.
43. Edkins (2000), p. 18.
44. M. Dillon and J. Reid, 'Global Governance, Liberal Peace, and Complex Emergency', *Alternatives*, vol. 25, no. 1 (2000), p. 121.
45. M. Dillon and J. Everard, 'Stat(e)ing Australia: Squid Jigging and the Masque of State', *Alternatives*, vol. 17, no. 3 (1992), p. 282.
46. Ó Tuathail (1996), p. 1.
47. Ó Tuathail (1996), p. 61; Campbell (1998a), p. 13.
48. W. Connolly, 'Tocqueville, Territory and Violence', *Theory, Culture and Society*, 11 (1994), p. 19.
49. R. B. J. Walker, 'From International Relations to World Politics', in J. Camilleri, A. Jarvis and A. Paolini (eds), *The State in Transition: Reimagining Political Space* (Boulder, 1995), pp. 35–6.
50. W. Magnusson, *The Search for Political Space: Globalization, Social Movements and the Urban Political Experience* (Toronto, 1996), p. 36.
51. D. Lisle, 'Consuming Danger: Reimagining the War/Tourism Divide', *Alternatives*, vol. 25, no. 1 (2000).
52. Campbell (1998a), p. 80 and (1999), p. 27; and J. Derrida, *Spectres of Marx: The State of the Debt, the Work of Mourning, and the New International* (London, 1994), p. 82.
53. Campbell (1998a), pp. 168–9.
54. Campbell (1998a), p. 170.
55. Campbell (1999), p. 23.
56. Campbell (1998a), p. 13.
57. S. Dalby, *Creating the Second Cold War: The Discourse of Politics* (London, 1993), p. 29.
58. Campbell (1992), chs 5 and 6; and (1998a), p. 13.
59. Campbell (1992), p. 12.
60. Campbell (1992), ch. 6.
61. Campbell (1992), p. 175.
62. Campbell (1992), p. 85.
63. M. J. Shapiro, *The Politics of Representation* (Madison, 1988), p. 102.

64. R. K. Ashley, 'Imposing International Purpose: Notes on a Problematic of Governance', in E.-O. Czempiel and J. Rosenau (eds), *Global Changes and Theoretical Challenges: Approaches to World Politics for the 1990s* (Massachusetts, 1989b), p. 269.

65. Ashley (1989b), p. 267.

66. Ashley (1987), p. 410.

67. C. Weber, 'Performative States', *Millennium*, vol. 27, no. 1 (1998); Campbell (1998a).

68. Weber (1998), p. 90.

69. Campbell (1998a), pp. ix–x.

70. Weber (1998), p. 78.

71. Weber (1998), p. 78.

72. Edkins and Pin-Fat (1999), p. 1.

73. R. Lynn Doty, 'Racism, Desire, and the Politics of Immigration', *Millennium*, vol. 28, no. 3 (1999), p. 593.

74. R. Devetak, 'Incomplete States: Theories and Practices of Statecraft', in J. MacMillan and A. Linklater (eds), *Boundaries in Question: New Directions in International Relations* (London, 1995).

75. D. Campbell, 'Political Prosaics, Transversal Politics, and the Anarchical World', in M. J. Shapiro and H. Alker (eds), *Challenging Boundaries: Global Flows, Territorial Identities* (Minneapolis, 1996), p. 19.

76. Campell (1996), p. 20.

77. G. Deleuze and F. Guattari, *Anti-Oedipus: Capitalism and Schizophrenia* (New York, 1977); and *A Thousand Plateaus: Capitalism and Schizophrenia* (Minneapolis, 1987).

78. See P. Patton, *Deleuze and the Political* (London, 2000).

79. Bleiker (2000), p. 2.

80. Bleiker (2000), p. 31.

81. Bleiker (2000), p. 185.

82. Bleiker (2000), ch. 7.

83. N. Soguk and G. Whitehall, 'Wandering Grounds: Transversality, Identity, Territoriality, and Movement', *Millennium*, vol. 28, no. 3 (1999), p. 682.

84. Soguk and Whitehall (1999), p. 697. See also the essays by Jan Jindy Pettman and Nevzat Soguk in Shapiro and Alker (1996).

85. P. Nyers, 'Emergency or Emerging Identities? Refugees and Transformations in World Order', *Millennium*, vol. 28, no. 1 (1999).

86. M. Dillon, 'The Sovereign and the Stranger', in Edkins, Persram and Pin-Fat (1999).

87. Soguk and Whitehall (1999), p. 675.

88. R. B. J. Walker, *Inside/Outside: International Relations as Political Theory* (Cambridge, 1993).

89. R. Walker, 'International Relations and the Concept of the Political', in K. Booth and S. Smith (eds), *International Relations Theory Today* (Cambridge, 1995b), pp. 320–1; and Walker (1995a), p. 28.

90. Walker (1993), p. 23.
91. Walker (1993), p. 155.
92. Walker (1993), p. 123.
93. R. B. J. Walker, 'International Relations Theory and the Fate of the Political', in M. Ebata and B. Neufeld (eds), *Confronting the Political in International Relations* (London, 2000), pp. 231–2.
94. Walker (1995b), p. 307.
95. William Connolly, 'Democracy and Territoriality', *Millennium*, vol. 20, no. 3 (1991), p. 479.
96. Connolly (1991), p. 480.
97. Connolly (1991), p. 476.
98. W. Connolly, *The Ethos of Pluralization* (Minneapolis, 1995), p. 23.
99. Campbell (1998a), p. 208.
100. R. K. Ashley and R. B. J. Walker, 'Speaking the Language of Exile: Dissidence in International Studies', *International Studies Quarterly*, vol. 34, no. 3 (1990); Campbell (1998a); Connolly (1994).
101. Ashley and Walker (1990), p. 395.
102. Ashley and Walker (1990), p. 395.
103. Campbell (1998a), pp. 171–92; and see E. Levinas, *Totality and Infinity: An Essay on Exteriority* (Pittsburgh, 1969), section 1A.
104. Levinas (1969), p. 44; Campbell (1998a), p. 192.
105. Levinas quoted in Campbell (1994), p. 463 and (1998a), p. 176.
106. Campbell (1994), p. 477 and (1998a), p. 191.
107. M. J. Shapiro, 'The Events of Discourse and the Ethics of Global Hospitality', *Millennium*, vol. 27, no. 3 (1998), pp. 698–9.
108. Campbell (1998a), p. 192.

CHAPTER 8

Constructivism

Christian Reus-Smit

During the 1980s two debates structured international relations scholarship, particularly within the American mainstream. The first was between neo-realists and neoliberals, both of which sought to apply the logic of rationalist economic theory to international relations, but reached radically different conclusions about the potential for international cooperation. The second was between rationalists and critical theorists, the latter challenging the epistemological, methodological, ontological, and normative assumptions of neo-realism and neoliberalism, and the former accusing critical theorists of having little of any substance to say about 'real world' international relations. Since the end of the Cold War, these axes of debate have been displaced by two new debates: between rationalists and constructivists, and between constructivists and critical theorists. The catalyst for this shift was the rise a new constructivist approach to international theory, an approach that challenged the rationalism and positivism of neo-realism and neoliberalism while simultaneously pushing critical theorists away from metatheoretical critique to the empirical analysis of world politics.

This chapter explains the nature and rise of constructivism in international theory, situating it in relation to both rationalist and critical theories. Constructivism is characterised by an emphasis on the importance of normative as well as material structures, on the role of identity in shaping political action, and on the mutually constitutive relationship between agents and structures. When using the terms rationalism or rationalist theory, I refer not to the 'Grotian' or 'English' school of international theory, discussed by Andrew Linklater in Chapter 4, but to theories that are explicitly informed by the assumptions of rational choice theory, principally neo-realism and neoliberalism. I use the term critical theory broadly to include all post-positivist theory of the Third Debate and after, encompassing both the narrowly defined Critical Theory of the Frankfurt School and postmodern international theory, discussed by Richard Devetak in Chapters 6 and 7 respectively. After revisiting the rationalist premises of neo-realism and neoliberalism, and reviewing the broad-based critique of those premises mounted by critical theorists during the 1980s, I examine the origins of constructivism and its principal theoretical premises. I then distinguish between three different forms of constructivist scholarship in international relations: systemic, unit-level, and holistic. This is followed by some reflections on the emergent discontents that characterise constructivism as a theoretical approach, and by a discussion of the contribution of constructivism to international relations theory.

Rationalist Theory

After the Second World War realism became the dominant theory of international relations. Yet this dominance did not go unchallenged, with new theoretical perspectives emerging, forcing revisions in realist theory. In the 1970s the classical realism of Carr, Morgenthau, Claude, Niebuhr, and others was challenged by liberals, such as Robert Keohane and Joseph Nye, who emphasised interdependence between states, transnational relations, and non-state actors, particularly multinational corporations. International relations was not to be conceived as a system of colliding billiard balls, but as a cob-web of political, economic, and social relations binding sub-national, national, transnational, international, and supranational actors.[1] This view was subsequently modified to pay greater attention to the role and importance of sovereign states, with Keohane and Nye reconceiving state power in the light of 'complex interdependence'.[2] States were acknowledged to be the principal actors in world politics, but pervasive interdependence was thought to alter the nature and effectiveness of state power, with the balance of military power, so long emphasised by realists, no longer determining political outcomes, as sensitivity and vulnerability to interdependence produced new relations of power between states.

This challenge to realism did not go unanswered. As Scott Burchill explains in Chapter 3, in 1979 Kenneth Waltz published *Theory of International Politics*, in which he advanced a radically-revised realist theory, subsequently labelled neo-realism or structural realism.[3] Waltz drew on two sources of intellectual inspiration: the philosopher of science Imre Lakatos's model of theory construction, and micro-economic theory. The first led him to devise a theory with minimal assumptions, a parsimonious set of heuristically powerful propositions that could generate empirically verifiable hypotheses about international relations; the second encouraged him to emphasise the structural determinants of state behaviour. The resulting neo-realist theory built on two assumptions: that the international system is anarchical, in the sense that it lacks a central authority to impose order; and that in such a system states are primarily interested in their own survival. He went on to argue that to ensure their survival states must maximise their power, particularly their military power. Because such power is zero-sum – with an increase in the military power of one state necessarily producing a decrease in the relative power of another – Waltz argued that states are 'defensive positionalists'. They are conscious of their position within the power hierarchy of states, and at a minimum seek to maintain that position, at a maximum to increase it to the point of domination. For this reason, Waltz claimed that the struggle for power is an enduring characteristic of international relations and conflict is endemic. In such a world, he argued, cooperation between states is at best precarious, at worst non-existent.

Theory of International Politics reinvigorated realism, giving realists a new identity – as neo- or structural realists – and a new confidence to the point of arrogance. Not all were convinced, though, and criticisms mounted on several fronts. The most moderate of these came from a new school of neoliberal institutionalists, led by the repositioned Robert Keohane. Moving away from his previous concern with transnational relations and interdependence, Keohane took up the task of explaining cooperation under anarchy. Realists had long argued that if international cooperation was possible at all, it was only under conditions of hegemony, when a dominant state was able to use its power to create and enforce the institutional rules necessary to sustain cooperation between states. By the end of the 1970s, however, America's relative power was clearly on the wane, yet the framework of institutions it had sponsored after the Second World War to facilitate international economic cooperation was not collapsing. How could this be explained? In his 1984 book, *After Hegemony*, Keohane proposed a neoliberal theory of international cooperation, a theory that embraced three elements of neo-realism: the importance of international anarchy in shaping state behaviour, the state as the most important actor in world politics, and the assumption of states as essentially self-interested. He also endorsed the Lakatosian model of theory construction that informed neo-realism.[4]

Despite this common ground with neo-realism, neoliberalism draws very different conclusions about the potential for sustained international cooperation. As noted above, neoliberals accept that states have to pursue their interests under conditions of anarchy. In Axelrod and Keohane's words, anarchy 'remains a constant'.[5] Nevertheless, anarchy alone does not determine the extent or nature of international cooperation. Neorealists are closest to the mark, neoliberals argue, when there is low interdependence between states. When economic and political interactions between states are minimal, there are few common interests to spur international cooperation. When interdependence is high, however, as since the Second World War, states come to share a wide range of interests, from the management of international trade to global environmental protection. The existence of mutual interests is a prerequisite for international cooperation, but neoliberals insist that the existence of such interests does not itself explain the extent and nature of cooperative relations between states – international cooperation remains difficult to achieve. Even when states have interests in common, the lack of a central world authority often deters them from incurring the reciprocal obligations that cooperation demands. Without a central authority states fear that others will cheat on agreements; they can see cooperation as too costly, given the effort they would have to expend; and often they lack sufficient information to know that they even have common interests with other states. This not only explains why states fail to cooperate even when they have common interests, it explains how they cooperate when they do. According to neoliberals, states construct international institutions, or regimes, to overcome these obstacles to cooperation. Defined as 'sets of implicit or explicit principles, norms, rules and decision-making procedures around which actors' expectations converge in a given area of international relations', international regimes are said to raise the cost of cheating, lower transaction costs, and increase information, thus facilitating cooperation under anarchy.[6]

The debate between neo-realists and neoliberals is often characterised as a debate between those who think states are preoccupied with relative gains versus those who think states are more interested in absolute gains. Because anarchy makes states fear for their survival, and because power is the ultimate guarantor of survival, neo-realists believe that states constantly measure their power against that of other states. They constantly monitor whether their position in the international power hierarchy is stable, declining or on the rise, fearing decline above all else. This is why neo-realists are sceptical about international cooperation: if states are worried about relative gains, they will forego cooperation if they fear their gains will be less than those that accrue to others. Even if a trading agreement promises to net State A $100 million in profit, if that same agreement will net State B $200 million, State A will refuse to cooperate. In other words, the promise of absolute gains is not sufficient to encourage states to cooperate, as they are primarily interested in relative gains. Neoliberals deny that relative gains calculations pose such an obstacle to international cooperation. The world imagined by neo-realists is too simplistic, they argue. States that are confident in their survival, which amount to a significant proportion of states, are not as preoccupied with relative gains as neo-realists think; states tend to evaluate the intentions of other states as well as their relative capabilities; and when states have multiple relationships with multiple states the constant calculation of relative gains is simply impractical. Neoliberals thus characterise states, not as defensive positionalists, as neo-realists do, but as utility-maximisers, as actors that will entertain cooperation so long as it promises absolute gains in their interests.

In spite of these differences, neo-realism and neoliberalism are both rationalist theories; they are both constructed upon the choice-theoretic assumptions of micro-economic theory. Three such assumptions stand out. First, political actors, be they individuals or states, are assumed to be atomistic, self-interested and rational. Actors are treated as pre-social, in the sense that their identities and interests are autogenous. In the language of classical liberalism, individuals are the source of their own conceptions of the good. Actors are also self-interested, concerned primarily with the pursuit of their own interests. And they are rational, capable of establishing the most effective and efficient way to realise their interests within the environmental constraints they encounter. Second, and following from the above, actors interests are assumed to be exogenous to social interaction. Individuals and states are thought to enter social relations with their interests already formed. Social interaction is not considered an important determinant of interests. Third, and following yet again from the above, society is understood as a strategic realm, a realm in which individuals or states come together to pursue their pre-defined interests. Actors are not, therefore, inherently social; they are not products of their social environment, merely atomistic rational beings that form social relations to maximise their interests.

These assumptions are most starkly expressed in neo-realism. As we have seen, states are defined as 'defensive positionalists,' jealous guardians of their positions in the international power hierarchy. The formation of state interests is of complete disinterest to neo-realists. Beyond stating that international anarchy gives states a survival motive, and that over time the incentives and constraints of the international system socialise states into certain forms of behaviour, they have no theory of interest formation, nor do they think they should have.[7] Furthermore, international relations are considered so thoroughly strategic, that neo-realists deny the existence of a society of states altogether, speaking of an international system not an international society. How does neoliberalism compare? The assumption of self-interest is expressed in the neoliberal idea of states as rational egoists; actors which are concerned primarily with their own narrowly-defined interests, and which pursue those interests in the most efficacious manner possible. Like neo-realists, neoliberals treat state interests as exogenous to interstate interaction, and see no need for a theory of interest formation. In fact, explaining the origins of state interests is explicitly excluded from the province of neoliberal theory. Finally, neoliberals move beyond the stark systemic imagery of neo-realism to acknowledge the existence of an international society, but their conception of that society remains strategic. States certainly come together in the cooperative construction and maintenance of functional institutions, but their identities and interests are not shaped or constituted in any way by their social interactions.

The Challenge of Critical Theory

While neo-realists and neoliberals engaged in a rationalist family feud, critical theorists challenged the very foundations of the rationalist project. Ontologically, they criticised the image of social actors as atomistic egoists, whose interests are formed prior to social interaction, and who enter social relations solely for strategic purposes. They argued, in contrast, that actors are inherently social, that their identities and interests are socially constructed, the products of intersubjective social structures. Epistemologically and methodologically, they questioned the neo-positivism of Lakatosian forms of social science, calling for interpretive modes of understanding, attuned to the unquantifiable nature of much social phenomena and the inherent subjectivity of all observation. And normatively, they condemned the notion of value neutral theorising, arguing that all knowledge is wedded to interests, and theories should be explicitly committed to exposing and dismantling structures of domination and oppression.[8]

Beneath the umbrella of this broad critique, modern and postmodern critical theorists stood united against the dominant rationalist theories. Just as the rationalists were internally divided, though, so too were the critics. The postmodernists, drawing on the French social theorists, particularly Michel Foucault and Jacques Derrida, adopted a stance of 'radical interpretivism'. They opposed all attempts to assess empirical and ethical claims by any single criterion of validity, claiming that such moves always marginalise alternative viewpoints and moral positions, creating hierarchies of power and domination. The modernists, inspired by the writings of Frankfurt School theorists such as Jürgen Habermas, assumed a position of 'critical interpretivism'. They recognised the contingent nature of all knowledge – the inherent subjectivity of all claims and the connection between knowledge and power – but they insisted that some criteria were needed to distinguish plausible from implausible knowledge claims, and that without minimal, consensually grounded ethical principles, emancipatory political action would be impossible. Mark Hoffman has characterised this difference between modernists and postmodernists in terms of a distinction between 'anti-foundationalism' and 'minimal foundationalism'.[9]

Despite these important differences, the first wave of critical theory had a distinctive meta-theoretical or quasi-philosophical character. Critical international theorists roamed broadly over epistemological, normative, ontological, and methodological concerns, and their energies were devoted primarily to demolishing the philosophical foundations of the rationalist project. Noteworthy empirical studies of world politics were certainly published by critical theorists, but the general tenor of critical writings was more abstractly theoretical, and their principal impact lay in the critique of prevailing assumptions about legitimate knowledge, about the nature of the social world, and about the purpose of theory.[10] This general orientation was encouraged by a widely shared assumption among critical theorists about the relationship between theory and practice. This assumption was evident in the common refrain that realism constituted a 'hegemonic discourse', by which they meant two things. First, that realist assumptions, particularly dressed up in the garb of rationalism and neo-positivism, as was neo-realism, defined what counts as legitimate knowledge in the field of international relations. And, second, that the influence of these assumptions extended far beyond the academy to structure policy-making, particularly in the United States. Rationalist theories were thus doubly insidious. Not only did they dominate the discourse of international relations, to the exclusion of alternative perspectives and forms of knowledge, they informed Washington's Cold War politics, with all the excesses of power these engendered. From this standpoint, theory was seen as having a symbiotic relationship with practice, and critiquing the discourse of international relations was considered the essence of substantive analysis.[11]

Constructivism

The end of the Cold War produced a major reconfiguration of debates within the dominant American discourse of international relations theory, prompted by the rise of a new 'constructivist' school of thought. Richard Price and Chris Reus-Smit have argued that constructivism should be seen as an outgrowth of critical international theory, as its pioneers explicitly sought to employ the insights of that theory to illuminate diverse aspects of world politics.[12] Constructivism differs from first wave critical theory, however, in its emphasis on empirical analysis. Some constructivists have continued to work at the metatheoretical level, but most have sought conceptual and theoretical illumination through the systematic analysis of empirical puzzles in world politics.[13] The balance of critical scholarship has thus shifted away from the previous mode of abstract philosophical argument toward the study of human discourse and practice beyond the narrow confines of international relations theory. Where first wave critical theorists had rejected the rationalist depiction of humans as atomistic egoists and society as a strategic domain – proffering an alternative image of humans as socially embedded, communicatively constituted and culturally empowered – constructivists have used this alternative ontology to explain and interpret aspects of world politics that were anomalous to neo-realism and neoliberalism. And where earlier theorists had condemned the neo-positivist methodology of those perspectives, calling for more inter-pretive, discursive and historical modes of analysis, constructivists have employed these techniques to further their empirical explorations.

The rise of constructivism was prompted by four factors. First, motivated by an attempt to reassert the preeminence of their own conceptions of theory and world politics, leading rationalists challenged critical theorists to move beyond theoretical critique to the substantive analysis of interna-tional relations. While prominent critical theorists condemned the motives behind this challenge, constructivists saw it as an opportunity to demon-strate the heuristic power of non-rationalist perspectives.[14] Second, the end of the Cold War undermined the explanatory pretensions of neo-realists and neoliberals, neither of which had predicted, nor could adequately comprehend, the systemic transformations reshaping the global order. It also undermined the critical theorists' assumption that theory drove prac-tice in any narrow or direct fashion, as global politics increasingly demon-strated dynamics that contradicted realist expectations and prescriptions. The end of the Cold War thus opened a space for alternative explanatory perspectives and prompted critically-inclined scholars to move away from narrowly-defined metatheoretical critique. Third, by the beginning of the 1990s a new generation of young scholars had emerged who embraced many of the propositions of critical international theory, but who saw potential for innovation in conceptual elaboration and empirically-in-formed theoretical development.[15] Not only had the end of the Cold War thrown up new and interesting questions about world politics (such as the dynamics of international change, the nature of basic institutional practices, the role of non-state agency, and the problem of human rights), the ration-alist failure to explain recent systemic transformations encouraged this new generation of scholars to revisit old questions and issues so long viewed through neo-realist and neoliberal lenses (including the control of weapons of mass destruction, the role and nature of strategic culture, and the implications of anarchy). Finally, the advance of the new constructivist perspective was aided by the enthusiasm that mainstream scholars, fru-strated by the analytical failings of the dominant rationalist theories, showed in embracing the new perspective, moving it from the margins to the mainstream of theoretical debate.

Echoing the divisions within critical international theory, constructivists are divided between modernists and postmodernists. They have all, how-ever, sought to articulate and explore three core ontological propositions about social life, propositions which they claim illuminate more about world politics than rival rationalist assumptions. First, to the extent that structures can be said to shape the behaviour of social and political actors, be they individuals or states, constructivists hold that normative or idea-tional structures are just as important as material structures. Where neo-realists emphasise the material structure of the balance of military power, and Marxists stress the material structure of the capitalist world economy, constructivists argue that systems of shared ideas, beliefs and values also have structural characteristics, and that they exert a powerful influence on social and political action. There are two reasons why they attach such importance to these structures. Constructivists argue that 'material resources only acquire meaning for human action through the structure of shared knowledge in which they are embedded'.[16] For example, Canada and Cuba are both medium powers existing alongside the United States, yet the simple balance of military power cannot explain the fact that the former is a close American ally, the latter a sworn enemy. Ideas about identity, the logics of ideology, and established structures of friendship and enmity lend the material balance of power between Canada and the US and Cuba and the US radically different meanings. Constructivists also stress the importance of normative and ideational structures because these are thought to shape the social identities of political actors. Just as the institutionalised norms of the academy shape the identity of a professor, the norms of the international system condition the social identity of the sovereign state. For instance, in the age of Absolutism (1555–1848) the norms of European international society held that Christian monarchies were the only legitimate form of sovereign state, and these norms, backed by the coercive practices of the community of states, conspired to undermine Muslim, liberal or nationalist polities.

Second, constructivists argue that understanding how non-material structures condition actors' identities is important because identities inform interests and, in turn, actions. As we saw above, rationalists believe that actors' interests are exogenously determined, meaning that actors, be they individuals or states, encounter one another with a pre-existing set of preferences. Neorealists and neoliberals are not interested in where such preferences come from, only in how actors pursue them strategically. Society – both domestic and international – is thus considered a strategic domain, a place in which previously constituted actors pursue their goals, a place that does not alter the nature or interests of those actors in any deep sense. Constructivists, in contrast, argue that understanding how actors develop their interests is crucial to explaining a wide range of international political phenomenon that rationalists ignore or misunderstand. To explain interest formation, constructivists focus on the social identities of individuals or states. In Alexander Wendt's words, 'Identities are the basis of interests'.[17] To return to the previous examples, being an 'academic' gives a person certain interests, like research and publication, and being a Christian monarch in the age of Absolutism brought with it a range of interests, such as controlling religion within your territory, pursuing rights of succession beyond that territory, and crushing nationalist movements. Likewise, being a liberal democracy today encourages an intolerance of authoritarian regimes and a preference for free-market capitalism.

Third, constructivists contend that agents and structures are mutually constituted. Normative and ideational structures may well condition the identities and interests of actors, but those structures would not exist if it were not for the knowledgeable practices of those actors. Wendt's recent emphasis on the 'supervening' power of structures, and the predilection of many constructivists to study how norms shape behaviour, suggest that constructivists are structuralists, just like their neo-realist and Marxist counterparts. On closer reflection, however, one sees that constructivists are better classed as structurationists, as emphasising the impact of non-material structures on identities and interests, but just as importantly, the role of practices in maintaining and transforming those structures. Institutionalised norms and ideas 'define the meaning and identity of the individual actor and the patterns of appropriate economic, political, and cultural activity engaged in by those individuals',[18] and it 'is through reciprocal interaction that we create and instantiate the relatively enduring social structures in terms of which we define our identities and interests'.[19] The norms of the academy give certain individuals an academic identity which brings with it an interest in research and publication, but it is only through the routinised practices of academics that such norms exist and are sustained. Similarly, the international norms that uphold liberal democracy as the dominant model of legitimate statehood, and which license intervention in the name of human rights and the promotion of free trade, only exist and persist because of the continued practices of liberal democratic states (and powerful non-state actors).

Normative and ideational structures are seen as shaping actors identities and interests through three mechanisms: imagination, communication and constraint. With regard to the first of these, constructivists argue that non-material structures affect what actors see as the realm of possibility: how they think they should act, what the perceived limitations on their actions are, and what strategies they can imagine, let alone entertain, to achieve their objectives. Institutionalised norms and ideas thus condition what actors' consider necessary and possible, both in practical and ethical terms. A President or Prime Minister in an established liberal democracy will only imagine and seriously entertain certain strategies to enhance his or her power, and the norms of the liberal democratic polity will condition his or her expectations. Normative and ideational structures also work their influence through communication. When an individual or a state seeks to justify their behaviour, they will usually appeal to established norms of legitimate conduct. A President or Prime Minister may appeal to the conventions of executive government, and a state may justify its behaviour with reference to the norms of sovereignty, or in the case of intervention in the affairs of another state, according to international human rights norms. As the latter case suggests, norms may conflict with one another in their prescriptions, which makes moral argument about the relative importance of international normative precepts a particularly salient aspect of world politics.[20] Finally, even if normative and ideational structures do not affect an actor's behaviour by framing their imagination or by providing a linguistic or moral court of appeal, constructivists argue that they can place significant constraints on that actor's conduct. Realists have long argued that ideas simply function as rationalisations, as ways of masking actions really motivated by the crude desire for power. Constructivists point out, though, that institutionalised norms and ideas only work as rationalisations because they already have moral force in a given social context. Furthermore, appealing to established norms and ideas to justify behaviour is only a viable strategy if the behaviour is in some measure consistent with the proclaimed principles. The very language of justification thus provides constraints on action, though the effectiveness of such constraints will vary with the actor and the context.[21]

Given the preceding discussion, constructivism contrasts with rationalism in three important respects. First, where rationalists assume that actors are atomistic egoists, constructivists treat them as deeply social. Not in the sense that they are 'party animals', but in the sense that their identities are constituted by the institutionalised norms, values and ideas of the social environment in which they act. Second, instead of treating actors' interests as exogenously determined, as given prior to social interaction, constructivists treat interests as endogenous to such interaction, as a consequence of identity acquisition, as learnt through processes of communication, reflection on experience, and role enactment. Third, while rationalists view society as a strategic realm, a place where actors rationally pursue their interests, constructivists see it as a constitutive realm, the site that generates actors as knowledgeable social and political agents, the realm that makes them who they are. From these ontological commitments, it is clear why constructivists are called 'constructivists', for they emphasise the social determinants of social and political agency and action.

In the past decade, three different forms of constructivism have evolved: systemic, unit-level, and holistic constructivism. The first of these follows neo-realists in adopting a 'third image' perspective, focusing solely on interactions between unitary state actors. Everything that exists or occurs within the domestic political realm is ignored, and an account of world politics is derived simply by theorising how states relate to one another in the external, international domain. Wendt's influential writings provide the best example of systemic constructivism. In fact, one could reasonably argue that Wendt's writings represent the only true example of this rarified form of constructivism.[22] Like other constructivists, Wendt believes that the identity of the state informs its interests and, in turn, its actions. He draws a distinction, though, between the social and corporate identities of the state: the former referring to the status, role or personality that international society ascribes to a state; the latter referring to the internal human, material, ideological, or cultural factors that make a state what it is. Because of his commitment to systemic theorising, Wendt brackets corporate sources of state identity, concentrating on how structural contexts, systemic processes, and strategic practices produce and reproduce different sorts of state identity. Though theoretically elegant, this form of constructivism suffers from one major deficiency: it confines the processes that shape international societies within an unnecessarily and unproductively narrow realm. The social identities of states are thought to be constituted by the normative and ideational structures of international society, and those structures are seen as the product of state practices. From this perspective, it is impossible to explain how fundamental changes occur, either in the nature of international society or in the nature of state identity. By bracketing everything domestic, Wendt excludes by theoretical fiat most of the normative and ideational forces that might prompt such change.

Unit-level constructivism is the inverse of systemic constructivism. Instead of focusing on the external, international domain, unit-level constructivists concentrate on the relationship between domestic social and legal norms and the identities and interests of states, the very factors bracketed by Wendt. Here Peter Katzenstein's recent writings on the national security policies of Germany and Japan are emblematic.[23] Setting out to explain why two states, with common experiences of military defeat, foreign occupation, economic development, transition from authoritarianism to democracy, and nascent great power status, have adopted very different internal and external national security policies, Katzenstein stresses the importance of institutionalised regulatory and constitutive national social and legal norms. He concludes that:

> In Germany the strengthening of state power through changes in legal norms betrays a deep-seated fear that terrorism challenges the core of the state. In effect, eradicating terrorism and minimizing violent protest overcome the specter of a 'Hobbesian' state of nature ... In Japan, on the other hand, the close interaction of social and legal norms reveals a state living symbiotically within its society and not easily shaken to its foundation. Eliminating terrorism and containing violent protest were the tasks of a 'Grotian' community ... Conversely, Germany's active involvement in the evolution of international legal norms conveys a conception of belonging to an international 'Grotian' community. Japan's lack of concern for the consequences of pushing terrorists abroad and its generally passive international stance is based on a 'Hobbesian' view of the society of states.[24]

While not entirely disregarding the role of international norms in conditioning the identities and interests of states, Katzenstein draws attention to the internal, domestic determinants of national policies. Unit-level constructivism of this sort has the virtue of enabling the explanation of variations of identity, interest and action across states, something that systemic constructivism obscures. It follows, though, that this form of constructivism has difficulty accounting for similarities between states, for patterns of convergence in state identity and interest.

Where systemic and unit-level constructivists reproduce the traditional dichotomy between the international and the domestic, holistic constructivists seek to bridge the two domains. To accommodate the entire range of factors conditioning the identities and interests of states, they bring the corporate and the social together into a unified analytical perspective that treats the domestic and the international as two faces of a single social and political order. Concerned primarily with the dynamics of global change – particularly the rise and possible demise of the sovereign state – holistic constructivists focus on the mutually constitutive relationship between this order and the state. This general perspective has spawned two distinctive, yet complementary, analyses of international change: one focusing on grand shifts between international systems, the other on recent changes within the modern system. The former is typified by John Ruggie's path breaking work on the rise of sovereign states out of the wreck of European feudalism, work that emphasises the importance of changing social epistemes, or frameworks of knowledge.[25] The latter is exemplified by Friedrich Kratochwil's writings on the end of the Cold War, which stress the role of changing ideas of international order and security.[26] Though less parsimonious and elegant than systemic constructivism, holistic scholarship has the merit of being able to explain the development of the normative and ideational structures of the present international system, as well as the social identities they have engendered. The more concerned this form of constructivism becomes with grand tectonic transformations, however, the more structuralist it tends to become, and human agency tends to drop out of the story. Ideas change, norms evolve, and culture transforms, but these seem to move independently of human will, choice or action.

Constructivism and Its Discontents

The articulation of a constructivist theoretical framework for the study of international relations has significantly altered the axes of debate within the field. The internecine debate between neo-realists and neoliberals, which until the middle of the 1990s was still being hailed as *the* contemporary debate, has been displaced as rationalists have haphazardly joined forces to confront a common constructivist foe. The rise of constructivism has also displaced the debate between rationalists and critical international theorists. The veracity of the epistemological, methodological and normative challenges that critical theorists levelled at rationalism has not diminished, but the rise of constructivism has focused debate on ontological and empirical issues, pushing the metatheoretical debate of the 1980s off centre stage. The core debate now animating the field revolves around the nature of social agency, the relative importance of normative versus material forces, the balance between continuity and transformation in world politics, and a range other empirical-theoretical questions. This does not mean, though, that rationalism and constructivism constitute unified, unproblematic or fully coherent theoretical positions, standing pristine in opposition to one another. We have already seen the significant differences within the rationalist fold, and the remainder of this chapter considers the discontents that characterise contemporary constructivism. Four of these warrant particular attention: the disagreements among constructivists over the nature of theory, the relationship with rationalism, the appropriate methodology, and the contribution of constructivism to a critical theory of international relations.

It has long been the ambition of rationalists, especially neo-realists, to formulate a general theory of international relations, the core assumptions of which would be so robust that they could explain the fundamental characteristics of international relations, regardless of historical epoch or differences in the internal complexions of states. For most constructivists, such ambitions have little allure. The constitutive forces they emphasise, such as ideas, norms and culture, and the elements of human agency they stress, such corporate and social identity, are all inherently variable. There is simply no such thing as a universal, trans-historical, disembedded, culturally-autonomous idea or identity. Most constructivists thus find the pursuit of a general theory of international relations an absurdity, and confine their ambitions to providing compelling interpretations and explanations of discrete aspects of world politics, going no further than to offer heavily qualified 'contingent generalisations'. In fact, constructivists repeatedly insist that constructivism is not a theory, but rather an analytical framework. The one notable exception to this tendency is Wendt, who has embarked on the ambitious project of formulating a comprehensive social theory of international relations, placing himself in direct competition with Waltz. In pursuit of this goal, however, Wendt makes a number of moves that put him at odds with almost all other constructivists: namely, he focuses solely on the systemic level, he treats the state as a unitary actor, and he embraces an epistemological position called 'scientific realism'.[27] While these represent the theoretical proclivities of but one scholar, Wendt's prominence in the development of constructivism makes them important sources of division and disagreement within the new school. His recently published *Social Theory of International Relations* is the most sustained elaboration of constructivist theory yet, and for many in the field it will define the very nature of constructivism.[28] However, the vision of theory it presents is likely to be vigorously contested by other constructivists, thus forming one of the principal axes of tension within constructivism over the coming years.

The second discontent within constructivism concerns the relationship with rationalism. Some constructivists believe that productive engagement is possible between the two approaches, engagement based on a scholarly division of labour. We have seen that constructivists emphasise how institutionalised norms shape the identities and interests of actors, and that rationalists, treating interests as unexplained givens, stress how actors go about pursuing their interests strategically. The first focuses on interest formation, the second on interest satisfaction. Seeking to build bridges instead of fences between the two approaches, some constructivists see in this difference a possible division of labour, with constructivists doing the work of explaining how actors gain their preferences and rationalists exploring how they realise those preferences. Constructivism is thus not a rival theoretical perspective to rationalism at all, but rather a complimentary one. 'The result', Audie Klotz argues, 'is a reformulated, complementary research agenda that illuminates the independent role of norms in determining actors' identities and interests. Combined with theories of institutions and interest-based behavior, this approach offers us a conceptually consistent and more complete understanding of international relations'.[29] As attractive as this exercise in bridge building appears, not all constructivists are convinced. Reus-Smit has demonstrated that the institutionalised norms that shape actors' identities not only help define their interests but also their strategic rationality.[30] Attempts to confine constructivist scholarship to the realm of interest formation, and to concede rationalists the terrain of strategic interaction, have thus been criticised for propagating an unnecessarily 'thin' form of constructivism.[31]

Another discontent within constructivism involves the question of methodology. Critical theorists have long argued that the neo-positivist methodology championed by neo-realists and neoliberals is poorly suited to the study of human action, as the individuals and groups under analysis attach meanings to their actions, these meanings are shaped by a pre-existing 'field' of shared meanings embedded in language and other symbols, and the effect of such meanings on human action cannot be understood by treating them as measurable variables that cause behaviour in any direct or quantifiable manner.[32] This led early constructivists to insist that the study of ideas, norms and other meanings requires an interpretive methodology, one that seeks to grasp 'the relationship between "intersubjective meanings" which derive from self-interpretation and self-definition, and the social practices in which they are embedded and which they constitute'.[33] Curiously, these arguments have been forgotten by a number of constructivists, who defend a position of 'methodological conventionalism', claiming that their explanations 'do not depend exceptionally upon any specialized separate "interpretive methodology" '.[34] They justify this position on the grounds that the field has been bogged down for too long in methodological disputes and, at any rate, the empirical work of more doctrinaire constructivists like Kratochwil and Ruggie does not look all that different from that of conventional scholars. Neither of these grounds addresses the substance of the original constructivist argument about methodology, nor do the advocates of methodological conventionalism recognise that the similarity between mainstream empirical work and that of interpretive constructivists may have more to do with the failure of rationalists to ever meet their own neo-positivist standards. The gap between these rival methodological standpoints within constructivism is most clearly apparent in the contrast between those studies that employ quantitative methodological techniques and those that adopt genealogical approaches.[35]

The final discontent concerns the relationship between constructivism and critical international theory. It is reasonable, we have seen, to view constructivism as an outgrowth of critical theory, and Price and Reus-Smit have argued that its development has great potential to further the critical project.[36] Andrew Linklater has identified three dimensions of that project: the normative task of critically assessing and revising how political organisation, particularly the sovereign state, has been morally justified; the sociological task of understanding how moral community – locally, nationally and globally – expands and contracts; and the praxeological task of grasping the constraints and opportunities that bear on emancipatory political action.[37] Nowhere is the second of these tasks being undertaken with greater energy and rigour than within constructivism. Exploring the development and the impact of the normative and ideational foundations of international society is the constructivist stock in trade, and dialogue between constructivists and those engaged in the more philosophical project of normative critique and elaboration is the most likely path toward true praxeological knowledge. Constructivism is divided, however, between those who remain cognisant of the critical origins and potentiality of their sociological explorations, and those who have embraced constructivism simply as an explanatory or interpretive tool. Both standpoints are justifiable, and the work of scholars on both sides of this divide can be harnessed to the critical project, regardless of their individual commitments. It is imperative, though, that the former group of scholars work to bring constructivist research into dialogue with moral and philosophical argument, otherwise constructivism will lose its ethical veracity and critical international theory one of its potential pillars.

It is tempting to explain these discontents in terms of differences between modern and postmodern constructivists, differences outlined earlier. Yet disagreements over the nature of theory, the relationship to rationalism, the appropriate method, and the contribution to critical international theory do not map neatly onto the divide between minimal and anti-foundationalism. While postmodern constructivists would never advocate the development of a general theory of international relations, task-sharing with rationalists, methodological conventionalism, or pure explanation, neither would many modern constructivists. Here Ted Hopf's distinction between 'conventional' and 'critical' constructivisms may be more fruitful: 'To the degree that constructivism creates theoretical and epistemological distance between itself and its origins in critical theory, it becomes "conventional" constructivism'.[38] The discontents outlined above reflect the differences between those who have consciously or unconsciously created such distance and those who wish to stay in touch with constructivism's roots. Among the latter group, important differences remain between modernists and postmodernists. The most important of these differences concerns the questions they address, with the former focusing on *why* questions, the latter on *how* questions. For instance, Reus-Smit takes up the question of why different international societies have evolved different institutional practices to solve cooperation problems and facilitate coexistence among states, while Cynthia Weber asks 'How is the meaning of sovereignty fixed or stabilized historically via practices of international relations theorists and practices of political intervention'.[39]

The Contribution of Constructivism

In spite of these discontents, which are as much a sign of dynamism as division, the rise of constructivism has had several important impacts on the development of international relations theory and analysis. Thanks largely to the work of constructivists, the social, historical, and normative have returned to the centre stage of debate, especially within the American core of the discipline.

Until the late 1980s, two factors conspired to marginalise societal analysis in international relations scholarship. The first was the overwhelming materialism of the major theoretical perspectives. For neo-realists, the principal determinant of state behaviour is the underlying distribution of material capabilities across states in the international system, a determinant that gives states their animating survival motive, which in turn drives balance of power competition. To the extent that they discussed it, neoliberals also saw state interests as essentially material, even if they did posit the importance of international institutions as intervening variables. The second factor was the prevailing rationalist conception of human action. As we have seen, both neo-realists and neoliberals imagined humans – and by extension states – as atomistic, self-interested, strategic actors, thus positing a standard form of instrumental rationality across all political actors. When combined, the materialism and rationalism of the prevailing theories left little room for the social dimensions of international life, unless of course the social is reduced to power motivated strategic competition. Materialism denied the causal significance of shared ideas, norms and values, and rationalism reduced the social to the strategic and ignored the particularities of community, identity, and interest. By reimagining the social as a constitutive realm of values and practices, and by situating individual identities and interests within such a field, constructivists have placed sociological inquiry back at the centre of the discipline. Because of the prominence of the 'international society' school, such inquiry had never disappeared from British international relations scholarship. Constructivists, however, have brought a new level of conceptual clarity and theoretical sophistication to the analysis of both international and world society, thus complementing and augmenting the work of the English School.

By resuscitating societal analysis, the rise of constructivism has also sparked a renewed interest in international history. So long as international relations theorists were wedded to the idea that states are driven by context-transcendent survival motives or universal modes of rationality, the lessons of history were reduced to the proposition that nothing of substance ever changes. Such assumptions denied the rich diversity of human experience and the possibilities of meaningful change and difference, thus flattening out international history into a monotone tale of 'recurrence and repetition'. Historical analysis became little more than the ritualistic recitation of lines from the celebrated works of Thucydides, Machiavelli, and Hobbes, all with aim of 'proving' the unchanging nature of international relations, licensing the formulation of increasingly abstract theories. Such history had the paradoxical affect of largely suffocating the study of international history in the American core of the discipline. Aided by the momentous changes that attended the end of the Cold War, and also by the ongoing processes of globalisation, the constructivist interest in the particularities of culture, identity, interest and experience created space for a renaissance in the study of history and world politics. If ideas, norms, and practices matter, and if they differ from one social context to another, then history in turn matters. Not surprisingly, in their efforts to demonstrate the contingency of such factors and their impact on the conduct of world politics, constructivists have sought to reread the historical record, to rethink what has long been treated as given in the study of international relations. While a similar impulse came from international relations scholars inspired by the rebirth of historical sociology, constructivists have dominated the new literature on international history.[40]

Finally, constructivism may be credited with helping to reinvigorate normative theorising in international relations. Not because constructivists have been engaged in philosophical reflection about the nature of the good or the right, a project that has itself been re-energised by the multitude of ethical dilemmas thrown up by the end of the Cold War and the march of globalisation, but because they have done much to demonstrate the power of ideas, norms, and values in shaping world politics. While talk of the 'power of ideas' has at times carried considerable rhetorical force outside of academic international relations, such talk within the field has long been dismissed as naive and even dangerous idealism. Material calculations, such as military power and wealth, have been upheld as the motive forces behind international political action, and ideational factors have been dismissed as mere rationalisations or instrumental guides to strategic action. Through sustained empirical research, constructivists have exposed the explanatory poverty of such materialist scepticism. They have shown how international norms evolve, how ideas and values come to shape political action, how argument and discourse condition outcomes, and how identity constitutes agents and agency, all in ways that contradict the expectations of materialist and rationalist theories. While this 'empirical idealism' provides no answers to questions probed by international ethicists, it contributes to more philosophically-oriented normative theorising in two ways: it legitimises such theorising by demonstrating the possibility of ideas driven international change; and it assists by clarifying the dynamics and mechanisms of such change, thus furthering the development E. H. Carr's proposed 'realistic utopianism'.

Conclusion

The rise of constructivism heralds a return to a more sociological, historical and practice-oriented form of international relations scholarship. Where rationalists had reduced the social to strategic interaction, denied the historical by positing disembedded, universal forms of rationality, and reduced the practical art of politics to utility maximising calculation, constructivists have reimagined the social as a constitutive domain, reintroduced history as realm of empirical inquiry, and emphasised the variability of political practice. In many respects, constructivism embodies characteristics normally associated with the 'English School', discussed by Linklater in Chapter 4. Constructivists have taken up the idea that states form more than a system, that they form a society, and they have pushed this idea to new levels of theoretical and conceptual sophistication. Their interest in international history also represents an important point of convergence with the English School, as does their stress on the cultural distinctiveness of different societies of states. Finally, their emphasis on interpretive methods of analysis echo Hedley Bull's call for a classical approach, 'characterized above all by explicit reliance upon the exercise of judgement' rather than neo-positivist standards of 'verification and proof'.[41]

These similarities, as well as constructivism's roots in critical international theory, pose a challenge to conventional understandings of the field. An 'Atlantic divide' has long structured understandings of the sociology of international relations as a discipline, with the field seen as divided between North American 'scientists' and European (mainly British) 'classicists'. Two of the defining 'great debates' of the discipline – between realists and idealists, and positivists and traditionalists – have been mapped onto this divide, lending intellectual divisions a cultural overtone. Constructivism, however, confuses this way of ordering the discipline. Despite having taken up many of the intellectual commitments normally associated with the English School, constructivism has its origins in the United States. Its principal exponents were either educated in or currently teach in the leading American universities, and their pioneering work has been published in the premier journals and by the leading university presses. The United States also spawned much of the earlier wave of critical international theory, especially of a postmodern variety, but that work never achieved the same centrality within the American sector of the discipline. The status that constructivism has assumed within that sector, as one of the major pillars of debate, gnaws away at the foundations of the Atlantic divide, not only by diluting the 'scientism' of American scholarship, but by providing greater opportunities for dialogue across the divide between scholars who share an interest in the social dimensions of world politics.

Notes

1. R. O. Keohane and J. Nye (eds), *Transnationalism and World Politics* (Cambridge, 1972).
2. R. O. Keohane and J. Nye, *Power and Interdependence: World Politics in Transition* (Boston, 1977).
3. K. Waltz, *Theory of International Politics* (New York, 1979).
4. R. O. Keohane, *After Hegemony: Cooperation and Discord in the World Political Economy* (Princeton, 1984); R. O. Keohane, *International Institutions and State Power* (Boulder, 1989).
5. R. Axelrod and R. O. Keohane, 'Achieving Cooperation Under Anarchy: Strategies and Institutions', in D. Baldwin (ed.), *Neorealism and Neoliberalism: The Contemporary Debate* (New York, 1993), p. 86.
6. Keohane (1984), pp. 57 and 85–109.
7. Waltz (1979), pp. 91–2 and 127–8.
8. J. George and D. Campbell, 'Patterns of Dissent and the Celebration of Difference: Critical Social Theory and International Relations', *International Studies Quarterly*, vol. 34, no. 3 (1990), pp. 269–94; M. Hoffman, 'Critical Theory and the Inter-Paradigm Debate', *Millennium*, vol. 20, no. 2 (1987), pp. 169–85.
9. M. Hoffman, 'Restructuring, Reconstruction, Reinscription, Rearticulation: Four Voices in Critical International Theory', *Millennium*, vol. 20, no. 2 (1991), pp. 169–85.

10. R. Cox, *Production, Power and World Order: Social Forces in the Making of History* (New York, 1987); J. Der Derian, *On Diplomacy* (Oxford, 1987).

11. R. Price and C. Reus-Smit, 'Dangerous Liaisons? Critical International Theory and Constructivism', *European Journal of International Relations*, vol. 4, no. 3 (1998), pp. 259–94.

12. Price and Reus-Smit (1998), pp. 263–6.

13. N. Onuf, *World of Our Making: Rules and Rule in Social Theory and International Relations* (Columbia, 1989); A. Wendt, *Social Theory of International Relations* (Cambridge, 1999).

14. R. B. J. Walker, 'History and Structure in the Theory of International Relations', *Millennium*, vol. 18, no. 2 (1989), pp. 163–83.

15. For example A. Klotz, *Norms in International Relations: The Struggle Against Apartheid* (Ithaca, 1995), p. 20; R. Price, *The Chemical Weapons Taboo* (Ithaca, 1997); R. Hall, *National Collective Identity: Social Constructs and International Systems* (New York, 1999); E. Kier, *Imagining War: French and British Military Doctrine Between the Wars* (Princeton, 1997); M. Lynch, *State Interests and Public Spheres: The International Politics of Jordanian Identity* (Columbia, 1999); C. Reus-Smit, *The Moral Purpose of the State: Culture, Social Identity and Institutional Rationality in International Relations* (Princeton, 1999); N. Tannenwald, 'The Nuclear Taboo: The United States and the Normative Basis of Nuclear Non-Use', *International Organization*, vol. 53, no. 3 (1999), pp. 433–68; Heather Rae, *Pathologies of the State* (Cambridge, 2002).

16. A. Wendt, 'Constructing International Politics', *International Security* vol. 20, no. 1 (1995), p. 73.

17. A. Wendt, 'Anarchy is What States Make of It: The Social Construction of Power Politics', *International Organization*, vol. 6, no. 2 (1992), p. 398.

18. J. Boli, J. Meyer and G. Thomas, 'Ontology and Rationalization in the Western Cultural Account', in G. Thomas *et al.* (eds), *Institutional Structure: Constituting State, Society, and the Individual* (London, 1989), p. 12.

19. Wendt (1992), p. 406.

20. T. Risse, ' "Let's Argue!" : Communicative Action in World Politics', *International Organization*, vol. 54, no. 1 (2000), pp. 1–40.

21. Reus-Smit (1999), pp. 35–6.

22. Wendt (1992); Wendt (1995); Wendt (1999); and A. Wendt, 'Collective Identity Formation and the International State', *American Political Science Review*, vol. 88, no. 2 (1994), pp. 384–95.

23. P. J. Katzenstein, *Cultural Norms and National Security: Police and Military in Postwar Japan* (Ithaca, 1996); P. J. Katzenstein, *Tamed Power: Germany in Europe* (Ithaca, 1999).

24. Katzenstein (1996), pp. 153–4.

25. J. G. Ruggie, 'Continuity and Transformation in the World Polity: Toward a Neorealist Synthesis', in R. O. Keohane (ed.), *Neorealism and Its Critics* (New York, 1986) pp. 131–57; J. G. Ruggie, 'Territoriality and Beyond: Problematizing

Modernity in International Relations', *International Organization*, vol. 47, no. 1 (1993), pp. 139–74.

26. F. Kratochwil, 'The Embarrassment of Changes: Neo-realism as the Science of Realpolitik Without Politics', *Review of International Studies*, vol. 19, no. 1 (1993), pp. 63–80; R. Koslowski and F. Kratochwil, 'Understanding Change in International Politics: The Soviet Empire's Demise and the International System', in R. N. Lebow and T. Risse-Kappen (eds), *International Relations Theory after the Cold War* (New York, 1995), pp. 127–66.

27. A. Wendt and I. Shapiro, 'The Misunderstood Promise of Realist Social Theory', in K. R. Monroe (ed.), *Contemporary Empirical Theory* (Berkeley, 1997), pp. 166–90.

28. Wendt (1999).

29. Klotz (1995), p. 20.

30. Reus-Smit (1999).

31. M. Laffey and J. Weldes, 'Beyond Belief: Ideas and Symbolic Technologies in the Study of International Relations', *European Journal of International Relations*, vol. 3, no. 2 (1997), pp. 193–237.

32. C. Taylor, 'Interpretation and the Sciences of Man', in F. Dallmayr and T. McCarthy (eds), *Understanding and Social Inquiry* (Notre Dame, 1977), p. 111.

33. M. Neufeld, 'Interpretation and the "Science" of International Relations', *Review of International Studies*, 19 (1993), p. 49; F. Kratochwil and J. G. Ruggie, 'International Organization: A State of the Art on an Art of the State', *International Organization*, 40 (1986), pp. 753–75; F. Kratochwil, 'Regimes, Interpretation and the "Science" of Politics: A Reappraisal', *Millennium*, vol. 17, no. 2 (1988/89), pp. 262–84.

34. R. L. Jepperson, A. Wendt and P. J. Katzenstein, 'Norms, Identity, and Culture in National Security', in P. J. Katzenstein (ed.), *The Culture of National Security: Norms and Identity in World Politics* (New York, 1996), p. 67.

35. A. I. Johnston, *Cultural Realism: Strategic Culture and Grand Strategy in Chinese History* (Princeton, 1995); Price (1997).

36. Price and Reus-Smit (1998).

37. A. Linklater, 'The Question of the Next Stage in International Relations Theory: A Critical Theoretical Point of View', *Millennium*, vol. 21, no. 1 (1992), pp. 92–4.

38. T. Hopf, 'The Promise of Constructivism in International Relations Theory', *International Security*, vol. 23, no. 1 (1998), p. 181.

39. C. Weber, *Simulating Sovereignty: Intervention, the State, and Symbolic Exchange* (Cambridge, 1995), p. 3

40. Hall (1999); Kier (1997); Rae (2002); Reus-Smit (1999); Ruggie (1986), (1993); Thomson (1994); Weber (1995); D. Welch, *Justice and the Genesis of War* (Cambridge, 1993).

41. H. Bull, 'International Theory: The Case for a Classical Approach', in K. Knorr and J. N. Rosenau, (eds), *Contending Approaches to International Relations* (Princeton, 1969), pp. 20–38.

CHAPTER 9

Feminism

Jacqui True

Breaking with the powerful bond among men, states and war in international relations theory and practice, feminist approaches to international relations have proliferated in the post cold war era. These approaches have introduced *gender* as a relevant empirical category and theoretical tool for analysing global power relations as well as a normative standpoint from which to construct alternative world orders. Together with a range of new and previously marginalised perspectives on world politics, including postmodernism, constructivism, critical theory, and green politics, feminist theories have contested the power and knowledge of mainstream international relations over the past decade. Above all, these contemporary perspectives are shifting the study of international relations away from a singular focus on inter-state relations toward a comprehensive analysis of transnational actors and structures, and the possibilities for transformation in world order. Ironically, the collapse of communism, as the only really existing alternative to the liberal capitalist world order, has had the effect of liberating further the space for 'critical' perspectives and lessening the hold of cold war realism over the definition and discussion of international relations.

Until relatively recently, the twentieth century field of International Relations (IR) studied the causes of war and conflict, the development of diplomacy and international law, and the global expansion of trade and commerce with no particular reference to people. Indeed the use of abstract categories such as 'the state', 'the market', 'the system', predominance of strategic discourses of national interest and national security, military defence and nuclear deterrence, and research approaches such as methodological individualism and inductive reasoning have effectively removed people as agents embedded in social and historical contexts from theories of international relations. This is particularly ironic since the field itself emerged, following the harrowing end of the First World War where the loss of life was so great, in order to democratise foreign-policy making and empower people as subjects of international relations rather than mere objects of elite statecraft.[1] Nonetheless, the 'international' has come to be characterised in this discipline as the impersonal and perilous realm of 'high politics' among states. And 'the actions of states or more accurately of men acting for states' have come to dominate the substance of 'relations'.[2] So where does the study of people called 'women' and 'men' or the social construction of masculine and feminine genders fit in to this picture? How is the international system and the study of international relations gendered? To what extent do feminist perspectives help us to understand and ultimately, to transform international relations? This chapter will endeavour to explore these questions and others as they have been addressed in the rich, and diverse work of feminist international relations scholars.

The chapter is in four parts. The first part discusses the development of a feminist approach to international relations over the past decade or so. I then consider the application of the concept of gender to IR and introduce three overlapping feminist IR perspectives which variously incorporate women or gender relations as an empirical variable in global politics, render visible the hidden masculine gender of IR theories, and demonstrate the difference that feminism makes to the politics of knowing world politics. These approaches form the basis for the second, third and fourth sections of this chapter, gender as a variable in international relations, gender as constitutive of international relations, and gender as a transformative way of knowing international relations. I explore how each of these feminist perspectives has challenged the assumptions of mainstream IR and helped to construct new 'gendered' theories of global politics. I conclude the chapter by considering the future of feminist international relations scholarship at the millennium. A first generation of feminist scholars in IR provided many of the conceptual tools for revisioning IR, and a second generation of feminist scholars in IR have successfully applied gender analysis to a range of post-cold war international issues including security, foreign policy, nationalism, ethics, human rights, globalisation, and democratic transitions. However, the challenge remains to integrate a gender perspective into the mainstream study of international relations, and above all, to move feminism from the *margins* (even self-embraced ones) to the *centre* of conversation in international relations.

International relations have had great significance for patterns of gender relations just as gender dynamics have influenced global processes of militarisation and economic integration for instance. Successive world hegemons have spread modernity by globalising their own domestic norms, that included norms of private life, kinship and gender relations.[3] Indeed, the expansion of Euro-centric international society in the late nineteenth and early twentieth centuries both had emancipatory and oppressive consequences for many women in non-western countries. Great Britain imposed metropolitan gender relations on her colonial territories. This had the effect of modernising (and sometimes outlawing) traditional patriarchal practices, such as sati, purdah, footbinding, and genital mutilation that often oppress women, as well as codifying 'native' laws and traditions in patriarchal forms, thus causing women to lose previous rights to land and resources. The United States has also promoted 'civilised' norms of gender around the globe and extended ideas and movements for gender equality abroad as an integral part of its world leadership. During the Allied occupation following World War Two, for example, America reconstructed and liberalised the economies of Europe and Japan, and played a central role in the democratisation of their political systems. American reform of the Japanese constitution was successful in enfranchising women, although its democratic propaganda was only partially able to break down traditional patriarchal authority. The idea that the spread of American influence would improve the lives of foreign women, Emily Rosenberg argues, 'comprises a consistent trope of American exceptionalism.'[4] In today's context of intensified globalisation, where American hegemony is contentious, gender relations are being re-shaped by marketisation, democratisation and liberalisation. Many scholars argue that these new forms of economic and cultural globalisation are opening spaces for women's empowerment.

The emergence over the past decade or so of feminist approaches to international relations has been hastened by the rise of a global women's movement. The United Nations Decade for Women, 1975–85, and the related four world women's conferences encouraged this flourishing of transnational feminist activism and placed the issue of gender inequality on the global agenda, and that of many states.[5] Increasingly, advocates for women's rights have gone around, below and above the state in order to rectify gender injustices.[6] Nation-states traditionally have provided few spaces for women's organising or for the articulation of women's interests. Thus, the transnational advocacy of feminist networks has increased the pressure on individual states to address persistent gender inequities and recognise women's human rights.[7] Indeed, the diffusion of 'gender mainstreaming' policies and institutional mechanisms to promote gender equality within international organisations and across states has been quite spectacular.[8]

In the world of international security and foreign policy-making, gender injustice is increasingly being acknowledged as a key concern. As just one indication of this, in October 1999, foreign ministers from 14 nations wrote a letter to Kofi Annan, the Secretary General of the United Nations, calling for measures that would end the widespread transnational trafficking of human beings – predominantly women and children – in the service of prostitution, domestic servitude, and other forms of profiteering.[9] These actions were prompted by the networking efforts of international women's non-governmental organisations to place sex trafficking on the agenda of individual governments and international organisations, and the new presence of feminist-oriented women in foreign-policy decision-making roles. For her part, Madeleine K. Albright has made special efforts to promote global gender issues in her role as US Secretary of State. As she said, in a speech given at the Department of State, 'working with a variety of agencies and forward-looking NGOs ... we have made tremendous gains ... from curbing violence against women to fostering participation in the global economy. Meanwhile, we have brought international women's issues into the mainstream of our foreign policy, which is right where they belong'.[10] Thus, while the International Relations discipline is yet to converse seriously with feminist perspectives and face up to the reality of gendered power relations, it is clear that many nation-states are.[11]

For more than a decade now, feminist international relations scholars have offered fresh and intriguing insights on global politics. Following on the wave of the worldwide feminist revolution, Cynthia Enloe dared to suggest that 'the personal which is political' is also, quite likely, 'international.' In *Bananas, Beaches and Bases* (1989), she exposed how international politics frequently involves intimate relationships, personal identities and private lives. These informal politics are altogether less transparent than the stuff of official politics and they are typically ignored by IR scholars. Taking the view from below, feminists have sought to demonstrate that gender relations are integral to international relations. Diplomatic wives smooth over the workings of power among states and statesmen, opaque but trustworthy marital contracts facilitate transnational money laundering and sex trafficking, global icons like *Carmen Miranda* and *Cosmopolitan* conquer foreign cultures and prepare them for the onslaught of western capitalism, women and men organize in kitchens, churches and kin-communities to overthrow authoritarian regimes and make peace in the face of brutal conflict.

Focusing on politics at the margins dispels the assumption that power is what comes out of the barrel of a gun or ensues from the declarations of world leaders. Indeed, feminist efforts to reinterpret power suggest that international relations scholars have underestimated the pervasiveness of power, and precisely what it takes, at every level and every day, to reproduce a grossly uneven and hierarchical world order.[12] Mainstream IR scholars are infamous for their poor observation of contemporary changes in states and in world politics. To see this, we need not look far, nor think solely in terms of feminist perspectives as valid counterpoints to the mainstream. The failure to anticipate the collapse of the Soviet Bloc is the most salient of many instances that show how rigid adherence to particular state-centric understandings of politics and power can seriously impede our ability to recognise and comprehend new political phenomena.

Feminist contributions to international relations are not just about adding women to the study of world politics; they are more fundamental. A variety of feminist scholars have shown that the structures, history, and knowledge about international relations are all gendered. Recognising the gendered construction of IR and building on the insights of feminist scholars in other fields of study, a first generation of feminist international relations in the late 1980s sought to challenge the conventional ontological and epistemological focus of the field by engaging in what was called the 'third-debate' among positivist and post-positivist international relations scholars discussed in the previous chapters. In this debate, feminist scholars contested the exclusionary, state-centric and positivist nature of the discipline primarily at a metatheoretical level.[13] Many of these feminist contributions sought to deconstruct and subvert *realism*, the dominant 'power politics' explanation for post-war international relations. Often implicit in their concern with gender relations was the assumption of a feminist standpoint epistemology. Such as standpoint maintained that women's lives 'by no means spectacular, banal in fact' afford us a more critical and comprehensive understanding of international relations than the objectivist view of the realist theorist or foreign policy lens of the statesman.[14]

The first generation preoccupation with metatheory obviously had its limits given feminism's normative claim to provide a radical alternative to realism.[15] As Richard Price and Christian Reus-Smit have argued 'the third debate was inward looking, concerned primarily with undermining the foundations of dominant discourses in International Relations.'[16] While feminist theoretical and epistemological challenges to IR opened the space for critical scholarship, they begged the question of what a feminist perspective on world politics would look like substantively, and how distinctive it would be.[17] Enloe proposed a decade ago that feminist theorising about international relations be linked to transnational feminist organising and 'rooted in clear explanations of how women from different, often unequal societies, are used to sustain the world patterns that feminists seek to change.'[18]

A number of developments have occurred in the International Relations field in the 1990s. *Constructivism*, combining the insights of critical international theory and rationalist calls for a research programme, has emerged as a 'middle ground' in international relations,[19] and normative, philosophical and historical approaches are increasingly welcome in the mainstream.[20] Ten years after the first journal in the field devoted a special issue to 'women and international relations' much has also been accomplished by feminist IR scholars, short of transforming the gender-blind study of international relations. Most thorough introductory and advanced courses on international relations theory worldwide now consider gender issues or feminist perspectives as a result of the publication of several exemplary texts and monographs by feminist IR scholars.[21] A number of the key disciplinary journals have published whole issues on the subjects of women, gender and feminism in international relations. Further, in 1999 the *International Feminist Journal of Politics* was established to promote dialogue among scholars of women's studies, politics and international relations due, in large part, to the efforts of feminist IR scholars. But as Ann Tickner has articulated, mainstream international relations scholars 'just do not understand' feminist approaches.[22] They have failed to integrate feminist theories of international politics on account of methodological differences and because feminist perspectives are often concerned with issues and problems outside of those raised by conventional IR analysts. At the same time, feminist scholars have not always spoken in dialects discernible to traditionally-trained IR specialists or indeed, seen dialogue with mainstream perspectives as likely to advance, rather than co-opt, feminist contributions. Thus, a need has arisen for studies that can empirically and theoretically refine 'first generation' theories of international relations and engage mainstream IR.

A 'second-generation' of feminist research promises a new phase in the development of feminist international relations. An emerging body of scholarship seeks to make gender a central analytic category in studies of foreign policy, security, global political economy through an exploration of particular historical and geographic contexts. More cautious and precise in its analytic use of the concept of gender, and more closely tied to developments in critical international theory, constructivism, post-Marxist political economy, feminist historical and anthropological methods, the next generation of feminist scholarship should be able to provide empirical support for first generation challenges, while also generating new theoretical insight on the gendering of global politics.

The Concept of Gender in International Relations

Gender refers to the asymmetrical social constructs of masculinity and femininity as opposed to ostensibly 'biological' male-female differences (although postmodern feminists contend that both sex and gender are socially constructed categories).[23] The hegemonic western brand of masculinity is associated with autonomy, sovereignty, the capacity for reason and objectivity, universalism and men, whereas the dominant notion of femininity is associated with the absence or lack of these characteristics. In this construction of gender, to be masculine is expressly 'not' to be feminine. A common assumption is that gender identities are natural or 'human nature' and not subject to human constitution or agency. When this assumption about gender is applied to other social and political phenomena it has political effects in terms of reproducing the status quo or existing power relations. As Joan Scott has stated, 'the binary opposition and the social process of gender relationships [have] both become part of the meaning of power itself' and, 'to question or alter any aspect of it, threatens the entire system.'[24]

In the realm of international relations, the routine practices of militaries replicate these hegemonic gender identities by training soldiers both to protect 'womenchildren' through killing and at the same time to deride their presence along with gays and lesbians, and to suppress emotions associated with bodily pain and caring.[25] Military training, in Barbara Roberts words is 'socialization into masculinity carried to the extremes'.[26] But feminist IR is not limited to the observation that masculinities and femininities, play a role in international relations, as 'just warriors' and 'beautiful souls', on the war and home fronts respectively. Rather, feminist IR scholars seek to illuminate how the entire enterprise of international relations is a gendered construction, including the processes of militarisation and capitalist globalisation, and the practices of state sovereignty.

Historically, the boundaries of gender and the state have excluded women from domestic and international political life, and engendered international relations as the virtual preserve of men and as a primary site for the construction of masculinities through the control and domination of women. Patriarchal structures and gendered symbolism within and across states have rationalised changing power relationships while maintaining a semblance of material and ideological continuity in world order. This points holds true whether the change has been from absolutist to modern states, feudalism to capitalism or from nation-state to global governance.

Gender troubles

In recent years there has been much controversy over the application of gender in IR and in feminist studies generally. In IR two main criticisms of gender as a concept have arisen. The first criticism is that the analytic use of gender masks other forms of oppression prevalent in global politics. Speaking to a western women's studies audience in the 1980s from a third world feminist standpoint, Chandra Mohanty criticised western feminist scholarship for constructing the victimised 'third world woman' based on universal, western assumptions of gender, emptied of all historical, cultural and geographical-specificity, including realities of race and class oppression.[27] As in the adage, 'the master tools won't bring down the master's house', Mohanty made the point that western categories cannot be used to challenge the imposition of western categories and imperialist structures in non-western societies.

The implications of this third world feminist challenge for feminist IR is that gender is a biased concept which cannot be easily applied across states or globally. Indeed, if, as feminist scholars argue, gender relations are culturally and historically constructed, then it also follows that they cannot be the same everywhere. Nonetheless, there is a tendency in feminist IR to focus on gender constructions at the global level.[28] Such analyses often lead to the 'overgeneralisation of women's experiences, neglecting diversity as well as sources of resistance and change. They underestimate the interplay of the global and the local in the construction of gender relations'.[29] To be sure, the social and cultural practices which construct gender are now increasingly global, but they are nonetheless altered at local levels and in specific historical and discursive contexts. Thus, even while feminist IR scholars are concerned foremostly with global politics, their applications of gender must be grounded in local analysis and understanding as well. Gender identities and relations are constantly being renegotiated and transformed, especially in light of local and national responses to globalisation. It is well-recognised in feminist political economy for instance, that there are diverse national gender regimes that shape the global integration of national political economies and culture.

A second criticism concerns the confusion over the apparent conflation of *sex* and *gender*. Sally Baden and Anne-Marie Goertz in their article, 'Who needs [sex] when you have [gender]?' discuss the contestation over the concept of gender at the fourth world women's conference in Beijing.[30] In that global forum many women's rights advocates from developing countries argued that attempts to make women visible in development had been in many ways undermined by the shift to gender analysis. At the same time, fundamentalist Christian women from the United States and other countries decried the use of gender in international discourse for its feminist connotations and misrecognition of the biological differences between men and women. At the same time, in the IR field critics have contended that the introduction of *gender* is just another synonym for *women*.[31] In the article, 'Does "gender" make the world go round?', Adam Jones charged that feminist scholars have focused on women to the exclusion of men in world politics because of their implicit feminist standpoint.[32] In his view, the assumption that women are always victims and men oppressors has impoverished feminist analysis of important dimensions of the gendering process at the global level.

Contrary to these criticisms, contemporary feminist IR scholars have underscored the point that gender is a *relational* concept based on the analysis of masculinity and femininity, men as well as women, by foregrounding the study of men and masculinities in international relations.[33] The authors of *The 'Man' Question* contend that international politics and institutions are themselves vital sites for the construction of masculinities and masculine identity.[34] In her book, *Manly States*, Charlotte Hooper reveals how *multiple* masculinities are produced in and through the competing discourses of international relations.[35] While critical of previously monolithic analyses of masculinity and power in the study of IR, she nonetheless argues that 'such a strategy may have been necessary for feminists to get an initial grip on IR, but perhaps now we need to pay more attention to relatively unexamined differences.'[36] Building on Ann Tickner's earlier application of the concept of 'hegemonic masculinity' to international relations,[37] Hooper differentiates hegemonic and subordinate masculinities in the context of global power relations.

Recognising the western imperialism behind universal categories of 'woman' or 'man', a second generation of feminist scholars is increasingly moving beyond the explanation of international and global processes through generic concepts of *patriarchy* or *gender* hierarchy. Rather, they are exploring the dynamic relationship between the global political economy, the state, and culturally, geographically-specific gender relations. There is also a realisation that gender as a concept cannot be used to explain everything.[38] It is not always the most salient aspect of the international or global phenomena we are seeking to comprehend. Moreover, for the purposes of advancing feminist perspectives in the study of international relations, it is important to consider how, why, and when gender is a salient or the most salient factor in 'making the world go round.'

Gender as a Variable in Global Politics

The first feminist challenge to IR contends that women's lives and experiences have been excluded from the study of international relations and female scholars from the brotherhood of the IR field. This 'sexist' exclusion has resulted in research which presents only a partial malestream view of international reality, in a field in which the dominant theories claim to explain 'the reality' of world politics.[39] It is not that women have not been present or their experiences relevant to IR. Rather, as Cynthia Enloe's work demonstrates, women are and have always been part of international relations – if we choose to see them there. Moreover, it is in part because women's lives and experiences have not been empirically researched in the context of world politics, as Grant and Newland argue, that IR has been 'excessively focused on conflict and anarchy and a way of practising statecraft and formulating strategy that is excessively focused on competition and fear'.[40] Studies of the norms and ideas that make the reproduction of the state-system possible and analysis of the structural violence (poverty, environmental injustice, socio-political inequality) that underpins direct violence are seen as secondary to the manly study of war and conflict in IR due to their association with domestic 'soft' politics. As a result, IR scholars continue to theorise politics and the international realm 'in a way that guarantees that women will be absent from their inquiry, and that their research agendas remain unaltered'.[41]

Taking gender seriously involves recognising over fifty per cent of the world's population, correcting the denial or misrepresentation of women in world politics due to false assumptions that male experiences can count for both men and women, and that women are either absent from international political activities or not relevant to global processes.[42] On a world scale women are a disadvantaged group: they own one per cent of the world's property and resources, perform sixty per cent of the labour, are the majority of refugees, illiterate and poor persons. Yet women are central to the survival of families and communities and also at the forefront of environmental, peace, indigenous, nationalist and other global social movements. International processes and interactions often have causes and consequences that affect men and women differently.[43] Moreover, the failure to resolve global dilemmas of poverty, pollution, nuclear proliferation and so on, is in part, a result of the neglect of women's contributions to political–economic development and the lack of support of these contributions by international aid agencies and governments.[44]

In recent years, gender-sensitive research has taken a variety of forms in IR. Feminist scholarship on global restructuring has analysed how the processes of global economic integration create gender identities and inequalities. Research in the 1970s and 1980s on the role of women in international economic development first identified the gender dynamics of capitalist expansion in the South. This scholarship revealed how western gender divisions of labour were created in modernising societies when men's labour was extracted for capitalist, cash-cropping production and women were left in charge of subsistence production. The field of 'women in international development' (commonly referred to as *WID*) documented how male bias in the development process has led to poor implementation of projects and unsatisfactory policy outcomes.[45] It made visible the central role of women as subsistence producers and providers of basic needs in developing countries. WID was motivated less by a concern to integrate women into processes of development than by the need to recognise and support women's already integral role in development.[46]

WID policy studies have shown that the most efficient allocation of development assistance is to provide women with appropriate agricultural technology, credit financing, education and health resources. The gains from targeting women are greater for the overall community. The United Nations estimates, for example, that while women's farming accounts for one half of the food production in the developing world, it provides three-quarters of domestic food supply for family-households.[47] However, in the late 1980s there was shift from studying women in development (WID) to analysing gender and development (GAD).[48] GAD Studies sought to reform gender-blind multilateral agencies, such as the World Bank, and government aid policies, that have taken men as the normative agents and distributors of development, and have at the same time, failed to effectively address the basic needs of developing countries, sometimes even exacerbating their problems of malnutrition-hunger, pauperisation, disease, and 'overpopulation'.[49] Indeed, many GAD specialists and local women themselves believe that development projects for women and by women while in themselves important, contain lessons that need to be extended to a country's whole model of social and economic development.

Economic globalisation has intensified social and economic polarisation, both within and across states. In particular, it has increased inequality between men and women – as manifest, for example, in the feminisation of poverty and the gendered international division of labour.[50] In the late 1980s and 1990s, feminist scholars revealed the expanding gender gap in work hours, income, resources and power, intensified by third world debt crises, structural adjustment policies (SAPs) in the South and state restructuring in the North.[51] As national and international economic policies have become increasingly governed by the global imperatives of export earnings, financial markets and comparative labour costs, states have failed to deliver social welfare services and to maintain their previous commitments to near full employment and the well being of national populations. This shift from largely (domestic) state to (global) market provision of public services has imposed a disproportionate burden on women to pick up the slack of the state.[52]

Feminist scholarship has also highlighted the importance of flexible female labour in state and corporate strategies for global competitiveness.[53] Economic globalisation has been accompanied by a worldwide expansion in the use of female labour. Guy Standing argues that a process of 'global feminisation' is occurring as many occupations and tasks formerly dominated by men have become low wage, insecure, often part-time or contract-based temporary female employment with few social benefits.[54] 'Free-trade' export processing zones in developing countries, for example, are heavily reliant on young women's labour. Global cities, the nodal points for global financial markets and economic transactions, are also dependent on a class of women workers.[55] As Lily Ling and Kimberly Chang point out, domestic workers, typically immigrant women of colour who service the masculinised corporate elite, are the 'intimate others' of economic globalisation.[56] An ever darker 'underside' of globalisation can be seen in the phenomenal growth of sex-tourism, *male*-order brides, and most gravely, the international trafficking of women and girls for prostitution.[57] For subordinate states in the world system, these economic activities are key sources of foreign exchange and thus national income.

But women are not only victimised by the global process of structural change, in many cases they are empowered by it. Feminist researchers have considered how global capitalism shapes women's subjectivities and transforms local gender relations. In contrast to feminist scholars who analyse globalisation one-dimensionally as a structurally determining process that reinforces patriarchal relationships, these researchers highlight subtle forms of empowerment and cultural change in the lives of differently located women. Naila Kabeer, for example, has investigated how changing material incentives provided by the re-siting of transnational corporations' garment production, opened up possibilities for Bangladeshi poor women to make a better living and at the same time to challenge patriarchal gender arrangements.[58] A similar case of global restructuring disrupting local gender arrangements has been observed along the US–Mexico border. There, in the Macquiladora factories, women are often the favoured employees (maquiladora) while men, now the majority of the unemployed, are supported by their wives and daughters' wages.[59]

Gender relations are integral to the changing structures of global production, but feminist research on global media and consumer marketing suggests that representations of difference conveyed through gender are also a strategic aspect of the quest for global competitiveness among corporations and states.[60] For their part, multinational corporations play up gender identities and symbols in order to expand consumer markets and profit margins. At the same time, the spread of consumption, cultural production, and information in the global economy has enabled women and men to create new identities as individuals and citizens. Women's empowerment by global media in particular, may allow them to challenge gender divisions of labour and power in the labour market and family.[61] In sum, feminist research on globalisation foregrounds the interplay between gender identities and the cultural as well as the material dimensions of integration.

Feminist studies of global governance reveal the gendered construction of international organisations (IOs).[62] IOs more so even than national decision-making institutions are dominated by elite men. They privilege priorities such as global economic growth, competition and enterprise over domestic societal wellbeing and human development.[63] Feminist scholars have observed the effects of recent efforts to 'mainstream gender' in global governance institutions.[64] These initiatives have allowed more women to join their policy-making ranks. Women now head many of the United Nations' agencies, including the World Health Organisation, the United Nations Childrens Fund, the Office of the High Commissioner for Refugees, the World Food Programme and the World Population Fund. The Deputy Secretary General and the High Commissioner for Human Rights are also both women. Nonetheless, as feminists point out, in institutions such as the United Nations, women continue to be ghettoised in agencies specifically concerned with women's and children's issues or as secretarial helpmates, and are only gradually coming to have influence over the larger United Nations global security and development agenda.[65] Sandra Whitworth and Catherine Hoskyns look at how changing assumptions about gender relations and gender equality have been institutionalised in the International Labour Organisation (ILO), and the organisations of the European Union, respectively.[66] Whitworth shows how assumptions about gender relations in the ILO shaped policies that have had gender-discriminatory effects in national and international labour markets.[67] She also notes that the ILO has begun to reflect upon the implications of its past practices for women's inequality. Hoskyns discusses the EU's European Court of Justice's bold precedent laws that have forced state jurisdictions to harmonise their national laws to uphold equal opportunities and gender equity.[68] She also considers how women's movements in member states have successfully used the EU's supranational body of law and policy to address gender disparities at the national level. Here, gender-sensitive analysis shows how the pooling of state sovereignty in the process of regional integration has been used to extend women's social citizenship rights within states.

Interconnected with gender-sensitive research on international political economy and global governance, feminists have examined the gendered context of global environmental politics, a growing concentration in the IR discipline.[69] Various studies expose women's unequal responsibility for sustaining the ecological resource (water, soil, fuel) balance necessary for daily subsistence and sustainable development. They point out that women are the first to suffer the effects of resource depletion and environmental degradation and are the chief caretakers in times of scarcity, hunger and natural disaster. Maria Mies contends that women, colonies and natural resources share systematic exploitation as expendable resources by men and developed world capitalists.[70] Feminists argue that gender ideologies of 'nature as woman and woman as nature' underlie today's masculine quests to control and subjugate 'her' to grander projects of development and globalisation.[71] In her book, *Earth Follies*, Joni Seager asserts that it is masculinist national and global institutions dominated by instrumental rationality, including science, the state, and the eco-conservationist establishment, that structure our relationship (of domination) to the environment and which are most responsible for environmental calamities. Eco-feminist critiques deconstruct the masculine gender bias of these institutions and suggest environmentally sustainable alternatives which stress women's autonomy and local self-reliance within and in relation to eco-systems.[72]

In the realm of foreign policy, feminist analyses reveal gender as a variable by exposing the dominant male gender of policymakers and the gendered assumption that these policymakers are strategically rational actors who make life and death decisions in the name of an abstract conception of the 'national interest.' As Nancy McGlen and Meredith Sarkees have assessed in their study of the foreign-policy and defence establishment, women are rarely 'insiders' of the actual institutions that make and implement foreign policy and conduct war.[73] In 1999, the fact that 14 women are currently foreign ministers suggests that this male dominance is undergoing some change. At the same time, feminist foreign policy analyses have opened up new substantive areas of policy-making and research in the relations between states, such as 'sex trafficking' now one of the most lucrative global criminal rackets and a critical security issue on the global agenda.[74] In addition, feminist empiricists analyse the persistent 'gender-gap' in the foreign policy beliefs of men and women foreign policy-making elites and citizens; women leaders and citizens in western states are consistently more likely to oppose the use of force in international actions and are typically more supportive of humanitarian interventions.[75] Attitudes toward gender equality are good predictors of more pacific attitudes to international conflict.[76] However, our preoccupation with statesmen and women prevents us from seeing the multiple non-state actors who also play significant roles in foreign-policy making.

Women are more likely to be among the group of non-state actors in world politics. Indeed, as Deborah Stienstra states, 'women have been organising [autonomously] at the global level for at least 150 years'.[77] In recent years, women have played key roles in transnational social movements, such as the global movement to ban landmines, the campaign for nuclear disarmament, and the feminist network protesting violence against women globally has been particularly significant.[78] At the local level, women activists have theorised the relationship between global processes, such as militarisation, and economic globalisation and community self-determination and quality of life. In the Pacific Islands, French Polynesian and Micronesian women have protested against French and American nuclear colonisation, the displacement of their traditional homelands, and the health deformities and diseases suffered by their children. In the troubled conflict zones of the world, Israel/Palestine and the former Yugoslavia, groups known as Women in Black have protested against the escalation of militarism, weaponry and war, and men's violence against women and children.[79]

In Cynthia Enloe's telling women are providers of a whole range of support services for militarisation (domestic, psychological, medical, and sexual); they are reserve armies in home industries, transnational peace activists, soldiers as well as the mothers of soldiers, and revolutionary actors in national liberation struggles and civil wars.[80] If we see militarisation as a social process consisting of many gendered assignments that make possible those ultimate acts of state violence, then, she argues, the official provision of sexual services on military bases for example can be seen as a central factor in military policy and foreign intervention. In her book, *Sex Among Allies*, Katherine Moon argues that the exploitative sexual alliances between Korean prostitutes (kijich'on women) and US soldiers defined and supported the unequal military alliance between the US and South Korea in the post-war era.[81] Moreover, she states, the South Korean government's weakness in foreign policy abetted its authority and sexist control in their domestic policymaking.[82]

Feminist scholarship exposes the gendered foundations of militaristic foreign policies: men sacrifice their lives in war to protect the motherland as home and the home as a mothering space. Indeed, the gender dichotomies of 'just warrior-beautiful soul' and militarised masculinity-domesticated femininity continue to reflect the imagery of war and violence around the world,[83] even now as women are increasingly in combat roles and peacekeeping has in many places replaced war-mongering.[84] As soldiers trained for combat, women simultaneously subvert the association of masculine citizenship with military service and are co-opted as women into perhaps the most male dominated and masculinist social institution.[85] As civilians, women and children are victims of rape, abuse and murder during war. They bear the social opportunity costs of military build-up and the escalation of domestic violence that is usually associated with the external use of military force. The establishment of domestic violence hotlines across the former states of the Federal Republic of Yugoslavia, for example, allowed the phenomenal increase in violence against women during the war to be documented. As a result of militarisation around the world, and the gender persecution that is one of its most stark expressions, women and children today make up more than two-thirds of the world's official refugee population.[86]

Alongside the growing importance of international law in the post-cold war era, feminist scholars have documented the recognition of gender justice as a norm in international society. Human rights instruments and declarations at the global level, for example, the women's convention (CEDAW), increasingly acknowledge the gender-specificity of human rights.[87] In 1990, Amnesty International, the global human rights NGO recognised women's human rights by adding gender-persecution to its list of forms of political persecution.[88] Governments and international institutions have followed suit. Canada, for example, was the first state to give asylum to women refugees who fear persecution for not conforming to their society's 'traditions,' such as forced marriage, bride-burning, dowry deaths, sexual abuse, domestic violence, genital-mutilation, rape, forced sterilisation and abortion, practices of purdah and veiling.[89] The United States has in addition to developing a sort of 'state feminism' for abroad under the leadership of Secretary Albright and First Lady, Hillary Clinton, been under citizen pressure to place economic and political sanctions on Afghanistan for its abrogation of women's fundamental human rights.[90] As a result of the lobbying of transnational feminist networks and the widespread media coverage of rape as a specific war strategy in Yugoslavia, rape is now considered a war crime under the 'Geneva Convention Against War Crimes'.[91] Until the recent Yugoslav conflict, states and international agencies interpreted the persecution of women as a matter of personal privacy and cultural tradition.[92]

Recent exploration in feminist international relations research include theoretical and regional studies of gender, nationalism, and citizenship. In general, these studies argue that gender is a constitutive dimension of political identity, because politics has been associated exclusively with the masculine public sphere and the activities of men, separated from the private sphere identified with femininity and women's activities. Nationalisms and national identities are gendered insofar as they privilege masculine representations of the nation in war/sacrifice/heroism, and legitimate men's control over women's bodies on the basis that they are the mothers of the nation and the embodiment of male national honour.[93] Women are biological, and social reproducers, as well as cultural signifiers of group identity. They are thus central to the construction of national boundaries and vulnerable to masculine control over their sexuality and reproductive labour.[94] The naturalisation of gender hierarchies inside nations, commonly prefigures the legitimate domination of 'others'/foreigners outside national boundaries. In the Yugoslav civil war and conflict over Kosovo, for example, gender was a marker of ethnicity and the rape of women of the 'other' ethnic group was used as a weapon of war.[95]

A number of post cold war feminist studies focus on the transformations in gender relations before and after communism in Eastern Europe and the former Soviet Union, and in the post-authoritarian democracies of Latin America.[96] For feminist scholars of international relations, the region of Eastern Europe, where the main alternative to the liberal capitalist world system previously existed, has been of most interest. To varying degrees across this region, women have been instrumentalised as reproducers of the nation, sex objects, and encouraged to return to the private household due to the new capitalist democracies' rescinding former social(ist) full employment, reproductive rights and social welfare.[97] Feminist studies document how western market forces and civil society have advanced eastwards through commodification processes that tend to operate with a gender bias. Compelling evidence shows that opening borders to foreign investment and rapidly privatising formerly nationalised economies have intensified employment discrimination against women and other kinds of gender-based injustice. These processes have also produced a thriving sex market, including many well-documented instances of the forced prostitution of women and girls. Furthermore, the new civil societies in Eastern Europe are not necessarily public spaces where women gather or are even welcome. Indeed, as a number of feminist scholars have observed, the processes of political change in post-communist societies seem to demonstrate the *masculine* constitution of liberal democracy. Nonetheless, the spread of markets and democracy has been mediated by domestic institutions and local agents in Eastern Europe and has not been wholly negative from a gender perspective. Liberalisation and democratisation have produced some positive opportunities and unintended consequences for women in particular, contrary to many initial feminist analyses of post-communism.[98] A gender perspective allows us to better discern both the *limits* and the *possibilities* of liberal internationalism by considering how far and in what ways the global processes of diffusing capitalism and democracy are meaningful for different groups of citizens, including women. Such normative concerns and criteria are grossly absent from neoliberal institutionalist approaches to IR.

Bringing women's lives into view through gender-sensitive research has policy-relevant and material effects. Indeed, feminists argue that only when women are recognised as fundamental players in economic and political processes will they share an equal role in societal decision making. By redressing the empirical neglect of women and gender relations, feminist IR scholars both improve our understanding of global politics and help to put women's voices and concerns on the global agenda. But in order to integrate gender into the mainstream of the IR discipline, it is necessary to challenge its conceptual framework which has excluded women from the study of international relations in the first place. The next section discusses the shift from including women's lives in accounts of IR to illuminating gender as a category of analysis and critical lens for theorising world politics. Feminist empiricism is complemented by a feminist standpoint that unmasks the gender bias of IR's core concerns and key concepts and reconstructs them as if women mattered.

Gender as Constitutive of International Relations

The second feminist challenge to the IR canon contends that women have not been studied in IR because the conceptual framework of the entire field is gendered. IR's key concepts are neither generic nor neutral but derived from a social and political context where 'the problem of patriarchy is repressed'.[99] Feminists argue, for instance, that notions of power, sovereignty, autonomy, anarchy, security, and the levels of analysis, man, the state and the international system are inseparable from the patriarchal division of public and private. They are identified with men's rather than women's experiences and forms of knowledge. Thus, in this view, IR is not just gender-biased, premised on the very exclusion of women and feminine attributes, but gender is world-constitutive.[100] Dominant malestream theories of IR such as realism and neo-realism which claim to describe or explain the world *as it is* 'shape our behaviours with concrete consequences for the real world of actors and events'.[101] They are partly responsible for making the world *as it is*, for the reproduction of global hierarchies of gender and other social identities such as race, class, and ethnicity. Theorising, as Burchill articulates in the introduction to this edition, is 'the process by which we give meaning to an allegedly objectified world "out there" '. IR's conceptual framework is but one, essentially-contested attempt to make sense of world politics.

From a feminist perspective, the mainstream field's failure to see the socially constructed boundaries of gender, the state and international relations has limited its ability to explain historical change and continuity in world politics.[102] Feminist scholars of IR have shown how state formation and the expansion of an 'international society' of states are implicated in the construction of gender differences through the establishment of divisions between public/private, state/society and domestic/international. The creation of a patriarchal division between public and private spheres within states, relegated women to subordinate family-households where they have often been invisible to social and political analysts. At the same time, the territorial borders of the sovereign state, which separate 'inside' from 'outside', the domestic polity from the international realm, and citizens from foreigners, have been symbolically defined and enforced by women's bodies, as seen most graphically in the male violation of territorial integrity and nation-state identity through rape.

Taken together, these boundaries of gender and the state have excluded women from domestic and international political life, and engendered international relations as the virtual preserve of men and as a primary site for the construction of masculinities through the control and domination of women. In particular, the discursive separation of domestic politics from international politics and concomitant neo-realist aversion to the 'domestic analogy',[103] obscures the prior gendered public–private division within states and masculine aversion to the latter's association with emotion, subjectivity, reproduction, the body, femininity and women. Both mainstream and critical theories of world politics overlook this private sphere because it is submerged within the domestic analogy itself.[104]

For feminists, the independence of domestic politics from international politics cannot be the basis for a disciplinary boundary, since anarchy outside often supports [gender] hierarchy at home and 'the international' has been very much about the management of change in domestic political orders.[105] Throughout modern history, for example, women have been told that they will receive equal human rights, equality with men, after the war, after liberation, after the national economy has been rebuilt, and so on: but after all of these 'outside' forces have been conquered, the commonplace demand is for things to go back to normal, and women to a subordinate place. In the contemporary context of global restructuring, states summon the deterministic discourse of 'there is no alternative' but to conform to external market forces in order to legitimise their repressive internal social and economic policies. This neoliberal discourse has implications for gender relations, since women in their family and community roles are shock-absorbers of market forces and the privatisation of state sectors. As Cynthia Enloe has observed 'states depend upon particular constructions of the domestic and private spheres in order to foster smooth(er) relationships at the public/international level'.[106]

In spite of feminist efforts to theorise the relationships between gender, domestic and international politics, IR's conventional levels of analysis mystifies them by treating the individual, the state, and the international system as distinct analytic units. This theoretical schema has become 'the most influential way of classifying explanations of war, and indeed of organising our understanding of inter-state relations in general'.[107] However, Ann Tickner has sought to deconstruct each level of analysis as a starting point for re-constructing a relational, gender-sensitive theory of world politics.[108] Through a feminist lens, the traditional generic actors and units of analysis in IR, statesmen and nation-states in the context of an international system, are revealed as social constructions based on a gender-specific, masculine mode of being and knowing. Moreover, they assume men's autonomy from women, and the denigration of characteristics and actors associated with femininity.[109] Taking gender seriously renders the divisions between the individual, state, and international system not only less potent – insofar women are excluded from all levels and each level is preconditioned by an image of rational man – but simply one way to represent the world.

'Man'

Sovereign man constitutes the dominant model of agency in conventional IR theories and is typically used by analogy to explain inter-state behaviour. The concepts of anarchy and sovereignty are also derived from this understanding of rational, autonomous agency. Richard Ashley writes that the ontology of sovereign man 'betokens a "rational identity" a homogeneous and continuous presence that is hierarchically ordered, that has a unique centre of decision presiding over a coherent self, and that is demarcated from, and in opposition to, an external domain of difference and change that resists assimilation to its identical being'.[110] The external domain of difference against which this self is defined, is as much the feminine concrete other inside the domestic sphere, as it is an abstract conception of international anarchy outside. Feminists such as Ann Tickner and Christine Sylvester claim that this is not a generic, generalisable ontology of human nature and behaviour, but rather an exclusionary masculine model of agency derived from a context of unequal gender relations, where primarily women's childrearing and caregiving work supports the development of autonomous male selves. The vast majority of people and social relationships that cannot be interpreted as coherent rational selves are thus denied agency in international politics. IR theory, Newland and Grant argue is 'constructed overwhelmingly by men working with mental models of human activity seen through a[n elite] male eye and apprehended through a[n elite] male sensibility'.[111]

In realist and liberal IR theory, rational, self-interested and autonomous man stands as a metaphor for all of human nature. He is abstracted from situatedness in the concrete world, from a place in time and space (that is, from family, community and history), from particular prejudices, interests and needs. By reference to the egoistic behaviour of this Hobbesian and/or Waltzian man in the competitive 'state of nature,' IR theorists explain the workings of the inter-state system. Rousseau's stag hunt allegory, for instance, the prisoners dilemma, chicken and other gaming theory allow the fiction of these presocial abstract individuals to persist for the purposes of logical postulation on the nature of the international system. Such a stripped-down understanding of human agency, however, can only be arrived at when one assumes a male standpoint.[112] Feminist theorists are suspicious of such theoretical models which deny the centrality of human relatedness, and repress the way affective relations constitute distinctive human subjectivities. Some feminists posit an alternative *female* model of the individual as connected, interdependent and interrelated. Carole Gilligan has suggested that women can approximate either human nature model, in the present socially-constructed order, as both connected and autonomous individuals, whereas men can only fulfil the model of the autonomous and separate individual.[113] Moreover, Joan Tronto has argued that there is a fundamentally different conception of the self, and the relation between the self and other in feminine and masculine images.[114] However, most feminist IR scholars are sceptical of positing a nurturing account of feminine nature to correct the gender-bias of Waltzian man. He is in any case, 'an anthropologically inaccurate representation of the earliest people or human nature that does not consider that [some] women nurtured, no matter what [some] men did'.[115]

Feminists seek to move beyond fixed, gendered conceptions of human agency. Some scholars look for emancipatory models of human agency at the margins, among third world women and human rights activists for instance.[116] According to Ann Tickner, a feminist perspective could transform IR by posing richer, alternative models, that take account of both production and reproduction, redefine rationality to be less exclusive and instrumental, and respect human relationships (across all levels) as well as our interdependent relation with nature.[117] Such models, Tickner stresses, would better conceptualise individuals and states as both autonomous and connected, and as having multiple identities, sovereignties and relations. In other words, feminist alternatives to IR's levels of analysis do not resort to more universal abstractions, but demand greater historical and cultural contextualisation in order to more adequately map the complexity and indeterminacy of human agency.

Reductionist arguments that explain international conflict over time through conceptions of 'evil' human nature are typical in classical and neo-realist IR. Hans Morgenthau argued that the objective 'national interest' is rooted deeply in human nature and thus, in the actions of statesmen.[118] Despite his advocacy of a systemic theory of IR, Kenneth Waltz frequently applies the analogy between man and the state as proof of the hostile reality that he observes in the anarchical system as a whole: '[a]mong men as among states there is no automatic adjustment of interests. In the absence of a supreme authority there is then the constant possibility that conflicts will be solved by force'.[119] Similarly, while Waltz prefers international anarchy as the most potent explanation for war he embraces Alexander Hamilton's polemic set forth in the Federalist papers: 'to presume a lack of hostile motives among states is to forget that men are ambitious, vindictive and rapacious'.[120] The upshot of this man/state analogy for feminist analysis, Sylvester argues, is that if man is rational–or rather, rationality is equated with men's behaviour–and the social institutions he creates are also rational, then the state itself bears a male-masculine identity.[121]

'The state'

According to the constitutive principle of territoriality the modern state is simultaneously differentiated along two axes, inside-outside and public-private.[122] Sovereignty is the formal principle which institutionalises *public* authority in mutually exclusive domains:[123] it assumes boundaries between us and them, order and anarchy, domestic and international, public and private. Andrew Linklater theorises the problem of political obligation with the rise of the modern state and the formation of territorial boundaries that divide men from citizens, insiders from outsiders and differentiate men's private morality as members of humanity from public morality among citizens.[124] While critical of IR theories that assume the centralised state as an ontological given, these historicised accounts of state-formation nonetheless ignore the gendered differentiation of public-private spaces and moralities and their implications for international relations.

The boundaries of the IR discipline are marked by the boundaries of the state and the stigma of the domestic analogy. They are also marked by IR analysts' efforts to evade all reflection on state of gender relations and gendered states. Both in its structural origins and its contemporary manifestations the state is the centralised, main organiser of gendered power, working in part through the manipulation of public and private spaces. It is not a 'coherent identity subordinate to the gaze of a single interpretative centre'. This notion reflects, rather, an the idealised model of western manhood that mystifies the state's patriarchal foundations.[125] Feminists argue that the state manipulates gender identities for its own project of unity in hierarchy. Men are socialised to identify with constructions of masculinity which emphasise autonomy, male superiority, fraternity, strength, protector roles, and ultimately the bearing of arms. Women on the other hand are taught to defer, as wives and daughters, to the protection and stronger will of men, while providing the emotional, economic and social support systems for men's activities. The state legitimises and regulates this naturalised gender order for its own authority purposes: sovereign relations with other states, outside, and man's relation to woman, inside, define the internal constitution of sovereign man and sovereign state.

Masculinist domination is integral to and institutionalised within the state-system. Spike Peterson argues that there was an intersection of domination practices with modern state-formation, involving capitalist accumulation, the rise of western science and objectivist dualistic metaphysics.[126] Together, she says, these historical processes, marginalised women in a private, exclusively reproductive realm of necessity and supported men's citizenship in a public realm defined by the political apparatuses of the state. Earlier state transition from kinship to citizen-based societies, Peterson contends, established a gender hierarchy inextricable from the metaphysics of identity over difference, mind over body, culture over nature, and order over chaos. Gendered divisions of identity (masculine over feminine) and labour (production over reproduction) in public and private spheres were formative of and constituted by these other dualisms in the territorial and ideological shift to nation-states. Modern state formation, thus, has its origins in early Athenian state formation, with the institutionalised separation between the *oikos* (household) and the *polis* (public sphere), and privileging of Greek elite male citizen-warriors as the source and strength of the democratic polity over all those who labour and therefore do not have the time to participate.

Consistent with this genealogy of gendered state-formation, the boundaries of the state are strengthened by their association with naturalised gender boundaries and masculine agency. Sovereign states require 'others' to establish their very existence: men and states stand against anarchy 'outside', and are distinguished from women and feminised others 'inside'. While it is true that the propriety of moral responsibility distinguishes the private sphere and the domestic state from the international realm in realist thought, the private and international realms are similarly subordinate to the domestic state, and its sovereign order of justice and rationality. The ontology of conventional IR thus conceives the private sphere, like the international sphere where order is seen as the primary consideration, as a natural realm of disorder; where women are represented as reproductive beings akin to nature, who like nature must be controlled. The lower being represented by women, the body, and the anarchical system must be subordinated to the higher being present in the mind, rational man, and the order of states. Jean Elshtain insists that the realist narrative of IR in particular, pivots on this public-private division and its essentialist construction of femininity and masculinity as the cause of disorder and the bringer of order respectively.[127] She recounts St. Augustine's scornful interpretation of the *Pax Romana* in which he equates sovereign absolutism and the terrible sway of Rome with masculinity, and femininity with alien forces, 'aliena', the unruly She who can disorder. The male, like Machiavelli's virtuous Prince, is the bearer of order, who must tame capricious female forces, domestically and externally. Otherness within (women, femininity) and others outside (barbarians, foreigners, other states) threaten the coherent identities of men and states, whose security rests on the establishment of fixed, gendered boundaries.

This symbolic codification of boundaries has real political implications for gender relations and the lives of women. State coercive apparatuses celebrate the agency of soldiers and statesmen and devalue the agency of women, who defend homes, families and communities, but are rendered increasingly 'insecure' by war and male violence. The assumption in IR that states are orderly and domesticated, moreover, masks the masculinist social control that women are subjected to: through direct violence (murder, rape, battering, incest), but also ideological constructs, such as 'women's work' and the cult of motherhood that justify structural violence – inadequate health care, sexual harassment, and sex segregated wages, rights and resources.[128]

Further, Peterson argues that states are directly implicated in violence against women in their non-intervention in domestic violence, their definition of rape from a male standpoint, and indirectly complicit in the masculinist, heterosexist ideology they promote in education, media images, military indoctrination, welfare policies, and patriarchal law.[129] Similarly, dominant IR theories are complicit with masculinist violence against women when they deny or exclude analysis of the gender struggles that go on inside-outside states – that suggest the state itself is a site of struggle. Feminists, however, challenge the constructed boundaries of domestic-international and public-private, that distinguish legitimate from illegitimate force, and en-gender the coercive meaning(s) of order, anarchy and 'security'.

Non-feminist critical IR theories enrich our knowledge by incorporating an historical understanding of the state and state-making in the study of IR. But these theories do not similarly incorporate an historical understanding of the construction of gender, and the institutionalisation of gender hierarchies within and across states. However, by neglecting to analyse the historically-constituted gender boundaries of states critical IR theories overlook one of the most potent ways of constructing and legitimating boundaries of political authority.

Key concepts

Power, rationality, security and sovereignty are the constitutive concepts which underpin the levels of analysis in IR, and the hegemonic realist theories which claim to explain 'the reality' of world politics in a more limited sense as 'inter-national relations'. As already argued, these concepts are gender-biased, derived from the above androcentric accounts of men (human nature), the state, and the system of states as ahistorical fixities made self-evident by reference to a gendered state of nature (the natural state of egoistic, rational men). Feminist scholars of IR have analysed the 'gender-specificity' of each of these key terms and suggested how mystification of their gendered rather than generic foundations limits our ability to explain and understand the multiple realities of world politics.

Because of the dominance of realist accounts, power in IR theory is almost exclusively conceived of as 'power-over': the power to force or influence someone to do something that they otherwise would not.[130] An individual's power rests on his or her autonomy from the power of others. In this view, power cannot be shared nor can power be readily increased by relationships with others in the context of interdependent or common interests. The accumulation of power capabilities and resources, according to Morganthau, is both an end and a means to security. In the context of an anarchical state system which is interpreted as necessarily hostile and self-helping, states that act 'rationally' instinctively deduce their national interests as their maximisation of power-over other states. The Waltzian notion of power is only mildly different. Waltz conceptualises power as a means for the survival of a state but not as an end-goal in itself, to the extent that a stable, bipolar, balance of power configuration exists between states. Consequently, in the Waltzian world view, the only power that really matters is the power-capability of 'Great Powers', whose bipolar or multipolar arrangement brings limited order to an anarchic international realm.

How is the concept of power gendered? In her critique of Morganthau's six principles of power politics, Ann Tickner argues that the realist understanding of power is androcentric.[131] It is unique to male self-development and objectivist knowing in patriarchal societies where men's citizenship and personal authority rests on their head-of-household power-over women's sexuality and labour. This concept of power also rests on a particularly gender-specific notion of autonomous agency – man and the state – that makes human relationships and affective connections invisible. If the human world is exhaustively defined by such gendered constructions of 'power-over', how then do children get reared, collective movements mobilise and everyday life get reproduced? It is incoherent to posit self-help as the essential feature of world politics, Christine Sylvester argues when many 'relations international' go on within households and other institutions, such as diplomatic negotiations, trade regimes, and the socialisation of future citizens, that are not based on self-help alone, but which take interdependent relations between self and other as the norm.[132] The realist and liberal assumption that men and states are mutually-exclusive and self-sufficient atoms presents power politics as a self-fulfilling prophecy. Power politics, however, is a gendered and, therefore, partial account of world politics because its conceptualisation of power depends upon the exclusive agency of rational man.

When Cynthia Enloe writes that paying attention to women can expose how much power it takes to maintain the international political system in its present form she is not referring to the sheer coercive power of men and states.[133] Rather, she is intimating that power is a complex phenomenon of social forces that interpellates and reproduces our personal and sexual identities as men, women and national citizens. In order to understand the nature of power at the international level, feminist and other critical theorists urge that we study the domestic and transnational social relations that not only support the foreign policies of states but actually constitute and reproduce the state as the institution with a monopoly over the use of legitimate force.

Rationality in the realist paradigm is the instrumental reason which determines the world-view of states and statesmen. It conditions their perception of the international sphere as an anarchical – without formal structure or order – and hostile space where states are rendered mutually insecure in their attempts to achieve security by offensive–defensive military means. Exclusive national interests and the unitary action of states are deduced from the rationality postulate. To the extent that states share common interests, the theory of rational action tells us that these cannot be realised outside of a juridico-legal order with coercive power, and where there is no world government to regulate and enforce agreements.

Feminists argue that this realist form of rationality is gendered. It cannot see relationships, other than self-help relationships, between people and states. State identities and interests moreover, are interpreted as exogenous not endogenous to state interaction.[134] This is because rationality is a particular disembodied and detached masculine way of seeing the world. This model of knowledge takes the world as 'given' and as inherently conflictual because it portends to know from a position 'outside', removed from the reality of social relations embedded in interdependencies. Further, this rational knowledge is made possible by the gendered division of labour which holds women responsible for human relationships and the reproduction of everyday life, making co-operation for them a daily reality, and relieving men of these necessities. Rational thinkers such as men and states do not figure in their cost-benefit analyses of foreign policies (military build-up, war mobilisation, economic liberalisation or protection), the social costs that are borne by 'private' family-households and communities. This is because the context for neo-realist and neo-liberal conceptions of rationality is the gender-specific, male-dominated preserve of public institutions, including the market economy. The dominance of the objective, 'rational' knowledge-interest in IR theory and practice leaves women and feminist theorists to make visible such relationships between the local and the global, the personal and the political.

Security, as theorised by neo-realists and neoliberals, is not what it sounds like from feminist points of view. Rather, security is conventionally defined in IR as the stability provided by militaristic states whose nuclear proliferation, ironically, is seen to prevent total war, if not many limited wars fought on proxy territory. Typically, security is examined only in the context of the presence and absence of war, because the threat of war is considered endemic to the sovereign state-system where security is zero-sum and by definition 'national'. This conception of security presupposes what Peterson terms a 'sovereignty contract' established between states.[135] According to this imaginary contract the use of military force is a necessary evil to prevent the outside – difference, irrationality, anarchy and potential conflict – from conquering the inside of homogeneous, rational and orderly states. States, on this view, are a kind of 'protection racket' that by their very existence as bully 'protectors' create threats outside and then charge for the insecurity that these bring to their 'protected' population 'inside'. In the name of protection, states demand the sacrifice of gendered citizens: soldiers through military conscription and mothers who devote their lives to socialising these dutiful citizens for the sovereign state.[136]

Like the state which has a monopoly on legitimate force, the institution of marriage has a monopoly on legitimate reproduction and property inheritance and acts as a protection racket, specifically for women. Women seek security in marriage and the protection of a husband from the violence of other men or males in general, and from the economic insecurity of a international division of labour which devalues work associated with women and locates females in the poorest paid and least secure sectors of the labour force. As such, men and states, domestic and international violence, are inextricably related. The limited security provided by protection rackets allows them to consolidate their centralised authority over other men and states, but more importantly over women and nature, on who they depend for a source of exploitable resources, for the socio-cultural and biological reproduction of power relations.

But how has the national state come to be the ultimate arbiter of power, security and freedom? How is it that we have come to believe in the state's protection from threats of death or conquest? Or rather, from feminist perspectives, ' "[t]hrough" what identities do we seek "security" '?[137] Jean Elshtain genealogically traces gendered identities of just warriors and beautiful souls, as the constitutive leading roles in narratives of war and peace, from Hegel's philosophical state to the contemporary state of realist IR.[138] Internalising an identity, a name, is one of the most potent expressions of a power relationship. Indeed, the power of the 'protector' depends upon structural demands for protection and their embodiment in the 'protected'.

In sum, as a result of taking women's experiences of protection rackets seriously, feminists urge that 'security' must be redefined. In particular, what is called 'national security' is profoundly endangering to human survival and sustainable communities.[139] State security apparatuses create their own security dilemmas by purporting androcentric control and power-over to be the name of the game; a game we are persuaded to stay in order to achieve the absolute and relative gains of state security. Tickner argues, however, that ideas and key concepts such as 'rationality', 'security', and 'power' might be building blocks of explanation for a feminist theory of international politics.[140] There is nothing inherent in the terms which suggests that they must be discarded, rather it is their narrow and exclusionary meanings in IR theory and practice, which is problematic for feminists. Peterson and Runyan claim that it is dichotomous thinking (inside–outside, sovereignty–anarchy, domestic–international) that prevents IR theory from being able to 'conceptualise, explain, or deliver the very things it says it is all about – security, power and sovereignty'.[141] For feminists it can only *re*-present the same dualisms, and reproduce the self-fulfilling security dilemma and the perpetuity of masculine power politics.

Gender as Transformative of International Relations

In the prior sections of this chapter the ontological contributions of feminism to IR were surveyed. However, as Scott Burchill clarifies in his introduction, ontological questions about 'what is a knowable reality' depend upon an epistemological stance. Feminist post-positivists argue that epistemological stances depend upon ontological positions 'from which to know': the positive pursuit of objectivity, for instance, is dependent upon particular masculine subjectivities. In contrast, positivist methods in IR subordinate questions of ontology – the specificity of the knowing-subject and subjects of knowledge – to questions of epistemology – universalising levels of abstraction and the quest for universal knowledge. Feminist perspectives subvert this patriarchal-ordering by exposing the male-masculine ontologies behind positivist epistemologies.

In this section the epistemological significance of feminist IR is discussed in relation to the ontological claims of the category of 'woman', women as an identity group, and gender as a unit of analysis, presented above. By arguing that gender-difference is constitutive of world politics, feminists have deconstructed the defining abstractions of sovereign man and state and opened spaces for theorising women's experience in world politics. But this is only a starting point for feminist goals of transforming social hierarchies because feminist projects of reconstruction entail the concurrent deconstruction of 'sovereign woman'.[142] In other words, gender is a *transformative* macro-political category, not because once we understand it at work, we can do away with it, but because once we understand it we can transform how it works at all levels of social and political life.

Feminist postmodern theorists challenge the hierarchical dichotomies order-anarchy, dependency-sovereignty, domestic-international, subject-object which have traditionally defined the theory and methods of IR. Jean Elshtain and Christine Sylvester refuse to include women in IR on the basis of their dichotomous conflation with peace, co-operation, concrete subjectivity, and domestic(ated) politics, that mirrors men's conflation with war, competition, abstract objectivity and international anarchical politics.[143] Instead, they have problematised the defining dichotomies of the field that are reinforced through their association with the masculine-feminine gender dichotomy. They question how gender hierarchies are constructed, legitimated and resisted and how they serve to naturalise other forms of superordination in world politics. From this perspective, gender or sexual difference is not just about the relations between male-masculine and female-feminine but about the politics of knowledge, how and from what position we can know, and signifying human relationships of power more generally.

The stance of objectivity is exposed as androcentric for claiming universal validity, when it is actually only congruent with elite male perspectives and masculine attributes.[144] In the same way, the abstractions, sovereign man and woman, are criticised for masking their white, western identity and rendering differences among women and men according to race, class, ethnicity, nationality, and so on, invisible. But what do the global differences and similarities among women, in addition to those between men and women, say about the politics of knowing and doing IR?

If asking questions about women's location in world politics, addressed in the first feminist challenge to IR, is dependent upon the second challenge, 'bringing gender in' as a theoretical construct in order to account for women's marginalisation in IR, feminist postmodernists rethink binary gender 'not as the essence from which social organization can be explained but as a variable ... *which must be explained'*.[145] While modern feminist theories created the category of gender, to explain the social construction of women's oppression, postmodern feminist theories historicise gender as an analytical device, complicit with patriarchal orderings and harbouring its own exclusions, that must be deconstructed also. It is a tragic irony that 'women became a [homogeneous] identity ... to fight the way that women have been relegated to the [homogeneous] category woman'.[146] As an essentially-contested political-theoretical movement, however, feminism expresses the paradoxical tension between 'needing to speak and act as women *qua* woman [and] needing an identity not overdetermined by our gender'.[147] This makes feminist identity and solidarity problematic insofar as achieving its goal of deconstructing the bonds of binary gender, depends on organising 'as women'. Contrary to the tenets of 1970s radical feminisms, there is no easily realised, readily mobilised, global sisterhood.[148] Rather, 'feminist internationality', as Christina Gabriel and Laura Macdonald establish in their analysis of North American women's transnational organising in the context of the North American free trade agreement (NAFTA), must be created by acknowledging and confronting, not ignoring, the differences among women.[149] The very tension between modern and postmodern epistemologies which has divided malestream social and political theorists, including IR theorists, is the source of contemporary feminism's theoretical dynamism and political relevancy. Postmodern feminism acknowledges the lack of a foundational collective subject 'woman', and a relatively bounded realm of the political, as well as the need to make a difference to women's daily lives, with the realisation that it is the superordinate category 'woman/women' that has historically served to marginalise females.

In his discussion of Marxism in this edition, Andrew Linklater argues that the status of universalism is the key to the current debate between different modes of critical theory. This debate surrounding the nature of the universal and particular-universal relations of power takes on special and heightened meaning in the context of feminist IR theorising which seeks to conceptualise global-local relations and feminist politics on an international scale. Thus, the threefold feminist epistemologies most commonly identified in IR writings as *feminist empiricism, feminist standpoint*, and *feminist postmodernism* are not autonomous or necessarily contradictory approaches to gender-sensitive and gender-transformative knowledge in IR.[150] On the contrary, these epistemologies are distinctive and interrelated feminist challenges to the authority and masculine dominance of science itself.[151] They share a normative struggle to sustain connections to practical feminist politics and the concrete workings of gendered power. The act of feminist theorising is itself a conscious political practice inescapably implicated with power. Symbolically, 'woman' has been constructed as antithetical to the grand project of abstract theory, and this has had profound implications for women's practice of theorising, be it feminist or not. In some senses, however, feminists have always been doing theory postpositively by starting from the everyday lives of women and striving to create contingent intellectual spaces in meaningful relation to concrete practices. A number of scholars have brought the insights of feminist *praxis*, in particular, the feminine ethic of care and women's social activism in developing countries, to bear on debates about the ethics of international aid, humanitarian intervention, and human rights instruments.[152] Academic feminism is about cultivating connections between theory and practice, knowledge and politics, deconstruction and reconstruction. Feminists argue that 'we can't separate our lives from the accounts given of them', that the articulation of our experience is part of our experience.[153] In the IR field, it is especially apparent that feminist theory-is-practice, given that women are the absences on which the identity of the field itself has been established.

Feminist IR epistemologies

Cynthia Enloe's work has greatly inspired feminist international relations, perhaps because her research most radically subverts conventional ways of knowing and doing IR. To make sense of international politics, Enloe analyses the (extra)ordinary lives of women from below – which the history of the discipline would tell us is the least likely place for 'high politics'. But it is in these 'lesser known' places that we see 'gender makes the world go round', that the personal is the political *and* the international (Enloe 1989). Enloe reveals constructions of masculinity and femininity at the heart of state legitimation, social processes of militarisation, nationalist struggles, successful capitalist accumulation and post-cold war reconstruction. For example in *The Morning After: Sexual Politics at the End of the Cold War*, she considers the withdrawal of Russian mothers' support for the Soviet army, due to the gross and unaccountable sacrifice of their sons in the USSR–Afghanistan war, as one of many personal expressions of gendered power that led to the delegitimisation of the Soviet regime and the end of the cold war.[154] Further, analysing the Gulf war from a feminist perspective, Enloe challenges the 'us-versus-them' construction of the conflict between Iraq and the Rest (symbolised by the veiled Arab woman and the liberated US woman soldier) by focusing on women's war stories and experiences, not featured in the multinational media coverage: the sexual abuse and harassment of US soldiers, the rape of Filipino servants by, and in the homes of, their Kuwaiti employers, Iraqi soldiers' rape of Kuwaiti women, and Kuwaiti women's struggle to be included in the suffrage of their so-called democratic country. Enloe's method encourages us to broaden conventional ways of knowing 'the truth' of international politics, and to question from whose perspective state 'legitimate' force is the most significant expression of violence and potent explanation for war.

In *Feminist Theory and International Relations for a Postmodern Era*, Christine Sylvester suggests an alternative postmodern feminist epistemology, variously referred to as 'homesteading', 'empathetic co-operation', or postmodern feminism.[155] Women as actors and gender as an analytic variable, she argues, are homeless in IR, where the exclusionary homesteads of nation-states dominate without reference to or recognition of the historical centrality of (gendered) households and multiple, shifting political identities. IR theory is also attached to the fixed homesteads of 'man' and 'the state'. However, Sylvester contends that the epistemological practice of 'homesteading' 'reconfigures "known" subject statuses [such as binary gender] in ways that open up rather than fence in terrains of meaning, identity and place in IR'.[156] From Sylvester's postmodern feminist perspective 'all places to speak and act as women are problematic', because they are socially and historically constructed and exclude other contestatory identities.[157] But she argues that women can be agents through creative and mobile acts of homesteading, that admit a sense of homelessness in fixed positions – our identity slippage as women – and thus refuse our inherited statuses and places in IR. Effectively, Sylvester relinquishes the pure feminist standpoint position that women's experience can constitute the ground(s) for a more critical and universal theory of IR, in favour of multiple feminist standpoints that question the discipline's exclusionary constitution.

Cross-cultural understanding and feminist strategies, in the context of these multiple standpoints and differences among women, however, demand 'empathetic co-operation'.[158] This method advocates intersubjective conversations between selves and others (for example, realists and neo-liberals, postmodern feminists and non-feminists in IR) that are not fixed to any one identity but can 'root and shift' from narrowly construed positions and engage in learning processes of mutual transformation. Feminist theory for a postmodern era has the potential, Sylvester claims, to heighten the modern-postmodern epistemological crisis that the field of IR would like to ignore: Postmodern feminism demonstrates that it is possible to do research and make knowledge claims, despite there being no given ontological starting points for theories of international relations.[159]

In her article 'The Women/Woman Question in International Relations', Marysia Zalewski favourably compares the ostensibly opposed feminist standpoint and postmodern epistemologies of Enloe and Sylvester.[160] By making women in world politics visible, she says, Cynthia Enloe adds new voices, from new places, not traditionally discussed in terms of IR, that contribute alternative ways of conceptualising relations internationally. Enloe's seemingly ontological approach actually challenges given ways of thinking about IR, including the dominant objectivist approach: for instance, asking why we have typically only seen statesmen and soldiers in IR, leads us to question the identity of the knowers and the particular ways of knowing institutionalised in IR. Moreover, by introducing vastly different worldviews of women who are differently situated in the present world order, Enloe practically exemplifies the postmodern feminist perspective that there are multiple standpoints from which to view IR, and that each reveals diverse realities and relationships.

In sum, feminist IR epistemologies emphasise the falsity of knowing international relations from fixed ontological positions and objective epistemological perspectives. Sovereign woman/women, unlike sovereign man in mainstream IR theories, cannot be a foundational epistemic category for alternative feminist IR theories. Rather, a feminist perspective seeks to contextualise theoretical claims, theorise relationships, situate political struggles and homestead subjectivities on personal, local, national, transnational, regional, and global levels, with the knowledge that these are interconnected.

Mainstreaming Feminism in International Relations?

As I noted in the introduction to this chapter, in recent years feminist scholars have sought to challenge the conventional focus of International Relations from a range of perspectives. Initial efforts of this kind were undertaken as critiques of realist International Relations. But because this critique was developed primarily at the metatheoretical level, the question remained open as to just what a feminist perspective on world politics would look like substantively, and how distinctive it would be from the perspectives that feminist scholars were opposing. Undoubtedly, previous efforts to establish a feminist approach to international relations have cleared the way for new thinking. But too often that thinking has gone on at the margins of the discipline and, rather than engage the mainstream, feminist scholars have occasionally appeared to take misguided pride in being perpetually misunderstood or ignored. A 'second wave' of feminist international relations scholarship seeks to address a myriad of key questions and issues in contemporary International Relations and International Political Economy doing so in a manner that empirically and theoretically integrates gender. The distinguishing feature of these second generation studies is a more contextualised and empirically-grounded exploration of gender relations and their interactions with processes of global transformation. This second generation also engages with other perspectives in mainstream IR, such as constructivist, critical theory and liberal institutionalist perspectives. The point of this is to make gender analysis and feminist perspectives central to the study of global politics.

I want to reflect now upon the future directions of feminist IR scholarship. In the coming years, I believe that feminist scholars will, above all else, have to engage in more self-conscious dialogue with a variety of other perspectives on global politics. This means being open to the interventions of non-feminist scholars and policy-oriented analysts who have a common interest in gender and international relations issues. Such conversation across identities need not take away from the distinctiveness of feminist contributions, but it will more likely result in these contributions being taken to heart.

In the past, some feminists have sought to converse with postmodernists who share their concern with the exclusionary discourses of international relations, and their awareness of the inextricable relation between the production of IR knowledge and the reproduction of global power relations.[161] But, as Rebecca Grant writes 'the newest IR theory is radical but comes without the guarantee of being feminist'.[162] Postmodern IR is mancraft without statecraft. Rather than postmodernism, Sandra Whitworth has observed that critical theory is the perspective most amenable to a dialogue with feminism in International Relations.[163] As well, she and other feminist scholars have noted that 'feminist questions [concerning International Relations] can be raised most successfully in the subfield of international political economy'. Although IPE has typically neglected gender dynamics, the neo-Gramscian stress placed on culture and ideology as an integral part of the global political economy provides an opening for feminist studies of international political economy.[164]

Critical theory approaches to international political economy pay special attention to ideas and identities, exploring and illuminating how they matter in the process of global structural change. A focus on gender relations extends this approach to international political economy by showing how the structures of the global political economy are articulated in concrete terms, not merely in *class* but in *gender* relations.[165] Both feminist and critical theory approaches to IPE consider how social hegemony is constructed in civil society through elements of popular culture, identification and 'common sense'. Together these perspectives underscore the key insight that change in world order begins at home, through changes in identities and ideas at the domestic level (although always in relation to global forces).

Feminist approaches also advance constructivist approaches to international relations by uncovering the processes through which identities and interests, not only those of states but of *key social constituencies*, are shaped at the global level.[166] In particular, Elisabeth's Prugl exemplifies this feminist constructivist approach in her study of home-workers in the global political economy.[167] Prugl shows how transnational discourses of gender in international organisations such as the ILO and global solidarity networks have been powerful forces in determining the plight of these workers around the world.

Integrating gender perspectives into critical theory and constructivist approaches to the study of world order, represents an important strategy for engaging with other scholars of international relations. Once we recognise the tight connections between ideas and cultural norms and aspects of international politics and economics, integrating a gender perspective becomes a relatively straight-forward exercise. Nonetheless, it is an exercise that can have important payoffs in terms of generating new insights into the processes associated with local and global transformations. Yet an even more stretching task involves finding ways to alert proponents of 'mainstream' international relations to the illuminating effects that can come from viewing social and political processes from a gender perspective. To do this successfully, feminist scholars must be prepared to bring their theoretical and empirical strengths to bear on the study of a full range of issues, and definitely not cede key areas of study to scholars working in the realist and neoliberal institutionalist paradigms. This need not entail capitulation to positivist social science, but rather in line with feminism's fundamentally reconstructive purposes, it calls for theoretically-informed empirical and normative studies that reflexively explore and defend feminist approaches to international relations.

Where feminist attempts to engage mainstream IR result in dialogue with those working out of other perspectives, then opportunities for the sharing of theoretical insights and research strategies are more likely to arise. In any event, feminist scholars should recognise their relative proximity to the mainstream and the extent to which their work implicitly or explicitly engages it. Moreover, to avoid charges of hypocrisy when we are doing research in different parts of the world, especially in non-western or less-privileged places, we should remember that we are rarely seen as 'on the margins' to those who we are studying. In fact, far from being marginalised, feminists face immense and exciting opportunities to surprise mainstream IR scholars through developing and articulating alternatives to the intellectual status-quo.

Conclusion

The three feminist challenges discussed in this chapter, arguing that gender is a variable, a constitutive theoretical, and transformative epistemic category in IR scholarship, suggest further that the actual practice of world politics has suffered from its neglect of feminist perspectives. Feminists argue that malestream visions of international relations distort our knowledge of both 'relations' and the ongoing transformations of the 'international'. Their adoption and embodiment of positivist forms of knowing has produced only very simplistic co-relational knowledge claims that reproduce the dichotomies which have come to demarcate IR. These dichotomies are gendered: they define power as power over 'others', autonomy as reactive and not relational, international politics as the absence of women and the negation of domestic politics, and objectivity as the lack of (feminised) subjectivity. They render women and gender invisible because they fail to see the political significance of fundamentally gendered divisions of public and private institutionalised within and by the state and state-system. They also ignore the political activities and activism of women: whether they are mobilising for war, protesting state abrogation of their rights or organising for the international recognition of women's human rights. In sum, approaches to international relations that fail to take gender seriously overlook critical aspects of world order.

International Relations as a discipline is currently in a state where the mainstream has been shown to have major blindspots with respect to social and political change. This conceptual blindness frequently leads to empirical blindness. It is not surprising then that IR analysts are often caught offguard by events in world politics, such as the so-called 'Battle of Seattle' in November 1999 where a transnational social movement in *formation* blocked the meeting of the World Trade Organisation, to name just one. Clearly, a rethinking of the basic assumptions of this discipline remains urgent if scholars want to understand global politics in the twenty-first century. Feminist scholarship of the sort I have reviewed here offers a way out of the darkness. If one wants to gain fresh insights into the processes of transformation in world order, averting one's gaze from the processes of state formation and cozying up to elites has its limits as a research strategy. In contrast, feminist perspectives reveal that in many instances, the sites of global power and transformation are not just the domain of political and economic elites; such sites also exist in the nooks and crannies of societies. Realist and liberal expectations about the nature of states and international relations are both disrupted when a feminist perspective is brought to bear. Feminist perspectives help us to recognise power shifts within nation-states that have ramifications for world order. Surely, observing and interpreting such power shifts as they arise in a variety of global and local venues constitute core functions of International Relations scholarship.

Notes

1. C. Hill, 'Where are we going? International Relations, the voice from below', *Review of International Studies*, vol. 25, no. 1 (1999), pp. 107–22.
2. K. Waltz, *Man, the State, and War: A Theoretical Analysis* (New York, 1959), pp. 122–3 and 230.
3. P. Taylor, 'What's Modern about the Modern World System?' *Review of International Political Economy*, vol. 4, no. 39 (1997), pp. 270–86.

4. E. Rosenberg, 'Consuming Women: Images of Americanization in the 'American Century', *Diplomatic History*, vol. 23, no. 2 (1999), p. 481.
5. M. A. Chen, 'Engendering World Conferences: The International Women's Movement and the UN', in T. G. Weiss and L. Gordenker (eds), *NGOs, The UN, and Global Governance* (Boulder, 1996), pp. 139–58. E. Dorsey, 'The Global Women's Movement: Articulating a New Vision of Global Governance', in P. Diehl (ed.), *The Politics of Global Governance: International Organizations in an Interdependent World* (Boulder, 1997), pp. 335–60.
6. See C. Bunch, 'On Globalizing Gender Justice: Women of the World Unite', *The Nation*, 11 September 1995, pp. 230–6; also J. Scott, C. Kaplan and D. Keates, *Transitions, Environments and Translations: Feminisms in International Politics* (New York, 1997); A. Heitlinger (ed.), *Émigré Feminisms: Transnational Perspectives* (Toronto, 1999).
7. K. Sikkink and M. Keck, *Activists Beyond Borders: Advocacy Networks in International Politics* (Ithaca ,1998).
8. J. True and M. Mintrom, 'Transnational Networks and Policy Diffusion: The Case of Gender Mainstreaming', *International Studies Quarterly*, vol. 45, no. 1, (2001).
9. United Nations News Agency, '14 Women Ministers Seek to End to Human Trafficking', 15 October 1999.
10. See J. Mattras and M. Lightman, 'Clinton's second term: making women's rights a foreign policy issue', *Presidential Studies Quarterly*, 27 (1997), pp. 121–5.
11. See J. A. Tickner, 'You Just Don't Understand: Troubled Engagements Between Feminist and IR Theorists', *International Studies Quarterly*, 41 (1997), pp. 611–32. For a further elaboration of the tensions and possibilities of conversations between feminist and non-feminist IR scholars see J. A. Tickner, *Gendering World Politics: Issues and Approaches in the Post-Cold War Era* (New York, 2001).
12. C. Enloe, 'Margins, silences, and bottom-rungs: how to overcome the underestimation of power in the study of international relations', in S. Smith, K. Booth and M. Zalewski (eds), *International Theory: Positivism and Beyond* (Cambridge, 1997), pp. 186–202.
13. See J. Steans, *Gender and International Relations: An Introduction* (New Brunswick, 1998), p. 36.
14. S. Drakulic, *How We Survived Communism and Even Laughed* (New York, 1993), p. xv. Feminist IR standpoint perspectives argue that knowledge which emerges from women's experiences 'on the margins' of world politics is more 'objective' since it is not as complicit with, or blinded by existing institutions and power relations; C. Sylvester, *Feminist Theory and International Relations in a Postmodern Era* (Cambridge, 1994), p. 13; R. O. Keohane, 'International Relations Theory: Contributions of a Feminist Standpoint', *Millennium*, vol. 18, no. 2 (1989), p. 245. For further explication of feminist standpoint epistemology as applied to international relations, see J. A. Tickner, *Gender in International Relations* (New York, 1992); M. Zalewski, 'Feminist Standpoint

Theory Meets International Relations Theory', *The Fletcher Forum for World Affairs*, vol. 75, no. 1, (1993), pp. 13–32. See also Sandra Harding, *The Science Question in Feminism* (Ithaca, 1986); N. Hartsock, 'The Feminist Standpoint: Developing the Ground for a Specifically Feminist Historical Materialism', in S. Harding and M. B. Hintikka (eds), *Discovering Reality* (Dordrecht, 1983), pp. 283–310.

15. A. S. Runyan and V. S. Peterson, 'The Radical Future of Realism: Feminist Subversions of IR Theory', *Alternatives*, 16 (1991), pp. 67–106.

16. R. Price and C. Reus-Smit, 'Dangerous Liasions: The Constructivist-Critical Theory Debate in International Relations', *European Journal of International Relations*, vol. 4, no. 3 (1998), p. 263.

17. Marysia Zalewski addresses these questions in 'Well, what is the feminist perspective on Bosnia?', *International Affairs*, vol. 71, no. 2 (1995), pp. 339–51.

18. C. Enloe, *Bananas, Beaches, and Bases: Making Feminist Sense of International Politics* (London, 1989), p. 18.

19. E. Adler, 'Seizing the middle ground: Constructivism in world politics', *European Journal of International Relations*, vol. 3, no. 3 (1997), pp. 319–63.

20. O. Waever, 'The rise and fall of the interparadigm debate.' in K. Booth, S. Smith and M. Zalewski (eds), *International Relations Theory: Post-Positivism and Beyond* (Cambridge, 1997), p. 168.

21. See Enloe (1989); C. Enloe, *The Morning After: Sexual Politics at the End of the Cold War* (Berkeley, 1994); also C. Enloe, *Maneuers: The International Politics of Militarizing Women's Lives* (Berkeley, 2000); V. S. Peterson and A. S. Runyan, *Global Gender Issues*, 2nd edn (Boulder, 1999); Sylvester (1994); J. J. Pettman, *Worlding Women: A Feminist International Politics* (New York, 1996); Steans (1998).

22. Tickner (1997).

23. J. Butler, *Gender Trouble: Feminism and the Subversion of Identity* (New York, 1990); M. Gatens, *Feminism and Philosophy* (Bloomington, 1991).

24. J. W. Scott, *Gender and the Politics of History* (New York, 1988), p. 48.

25. C. Cohn, 'Gays in the Military: Texts and Subtexts', in M. Zalewski and J. Parpart (eds), *The Man Question in International Relations* (Boulder, 1998).

26. B. Roberts, 'The Death of Machothink: Feminist Research and the Transformation of Peace Studies', *Women's Studies International Forum*, 7 (1984), p. 197.

27. C. Mohanty, 'Under Western Eyes: Feminist Scholarship and Colonial Discourses', in C. Mohanty, T. A. Russo and L. Torres (eds), *Third World Women and the Politics of Feminism* (Bloomington, 1991).

28. S. Whitworth, *Feminism and International Relations: Towards a Political Economy of Gender in Interstate and Non-Governmental Institutions* (London, 1994); E. Prugl, *The Global Construction of Gender: Home-Based Work in the Political Economy of the Twentieth Century* (New York, 1999).

29. E. K. Baines, 'Gender Construction and the Protection Mandate of the UNHCR: Responses from Guatemalan Women', in E. Prugl and M. K. Meyer, (eds), *Gender Politics and Global Governance* (Lanham, 1999), p. 251; also F.

Miller, 'Feminisms and Transnationalism', *Gender and History*, vol. 10, no. 3 (1998), pp. 569–80.

30. S. Baden and A.-M. Goetz, 'Who needs [sex] when you can have [gender]? Conflicting discourses on gender at Beijing', *Feminist Review*, 56 (1997), pp. 2–25.

31. See T. Carver, *Gender is Not a Synonym for Women* (Boulder, 1996).

32. A. Jones, 'Does "gender" make the world go round? Feminist critiques of International Relations', *Review of International Studies*, vol. 22, no. 4 (1996), pp. 245–53.

33. Zalewski and Parpart (1998).

34. Zalewski and Parpart (1998); C. Hooper, 'Masculinist Practices and Gender Politics: The Operation of Multiple Masculinities in International Relations', in Zalewski and Parpart (1998), p. 38.

35. C. Hooper, *Manly States: Masculinities, International Relations, and Gender Politics* (New York, 2000).

36. Hooper (1998), p. 32.

37. Tickner (1992).

38. J. Large, 'Disintegration Conflicts and the Restructuring of Masculinity', *Gender and Development*, (1997), pp. 23–30.

39. F. Halliday, 'Hidden from International Relations: Women and the International Arena', *Millennium*, vol. 17, no. 3 (1988), pp. 419–28.

40. R. Grant and K. Newland (eds), *Gender and International Relations* (London, 1991), p. 5.

41. G. A. Steuernagel, 'Men do not do Housework! The Image of Women in Political Science', in M. Paludi and G. A. Steuernagel (eds), *Foundations for a Feminist Restructuring of the Academic Disciplines* (New York, 1990), pp. 79–80.

42. L. Alexandre, 'Genderizing International Studies: Revisioning Concepts and Curriculum', *International Studies Notes*, vol. 14, no. 1 (1989), p. 6.

43. Halliday (1988), pp. 419–28.

44. Peterson and Runyan (1999).

45. See K. Newland, 'From Transnational Relationships to International Relations: Women in Development and the International Decade for Women', *Millennium*, vol. 17, no. 3 (1988).

46. M. Mies, *Patriarchy and Accumulation on a World Scale* (London, 1986); M. Mies, V. Bennholdt-Thomsen and C. von Werlhof (eds), *Women: The Last Colony* (London, 1988); L. Beneria (ed.), *Women and Development: The Sexual Division of Labor in Rural Societies* (New York, 1982); S. E. Charlton, J. Everett and K. Staudt (eds), *Women, the State, and Development* (Albany, 1989).

47. United Nations, *The World's Women's Progress* (New York, 2000).

48. A.-M. Goetz, 'Feminism and the claim to know: contradictions in feminist approaches to women in development', in Grant and Newland (1991); D. Elson (ed.), *Male Bias in the Development Process* (New York, 1991); N. Kabeer, *Reversed Realities: Gender Hierarchies in Development Thought* (London, 1994); G. Sen and C. Grown, *Development Crises and Alternative Visions: Third World*

Women's Perspectives (New York, 1986); E. M. Rathergeber, 'Gender and Development in Action', in M. H. Marchand and J. L. Parpart (eds), *Feminism/Postmodernism/Development* (London, 1995).

49. See R. O'Brien, A.-M. Goetz, J. A. Scholte and M. Williams, 'The World Bank and Women's Movements', in *Contesting Global Governance: Multilateral Economic Institutions and Global Social Movements* (Cambridge, 2000); also C. Miller and S. Razavi (eds), *Missionaries and Mandarins: Feminist Engagement with Development Institution* (London, 1998); K. Staudt (ed.), *Women, International Development, and Politics: The Bureaucratic Quagmire*, 2nd edn (Philidelphia, 1997); N. Kardam, *Bringing Women in: Women's Issues in International Development Programs* (Boulder, 1991).

50. I. Bakker (ed.), *The Strategic Silence: Gender and Economic Policy* (London, 1994); M. Marchand and A. S. Runyan (eds), *Gender and Global Restructuring: Sites, Sightings and Resistances* (New York, 2000); S. Sassen, *Globalization and its Discontents* (New York, 1998); UNDP, *Human Development Report 1999. Globalization with a Human Face* (Oxford, 1999).

51. H. Afshar and C. Dennis, *Women and Adjustment in the Third World* (London, 1992); Vickers (1991); Moghadam (1993); P. Sparr (ed.), *Mortgaging Women's Lives: Feminist Critiques of Structural Adjustment* (London, 1994); M. Porter and E. Judd (eds), *Feminists Doing Development: A Practical Critique* (London, 2000).

52. See 'The invisible heart' in UNDP, *Human Development Report 1999. Globalization with a Human Face* (Oxford, 1999).

53. A. Ong, 'The gender and labor politics of postmodernity.' in L. Lowe (ed.), *The Politics of Culture Under the Shadow of Capital* (Durham, 1997); S. Sassen, 'Notes on the Incorporation of Third World Women into Wage Labor through Immigration and Offshore Production', in *Globalization and its Discontents* (New York, 1998); S. Mitter, *Common Fate, Common Bond: Women in the Global Economy* (London, 1986).

54. G. Standing, 'Global Feminization Through Flexible Labor', in C. K. Wilber and K. P. Jameson (eds), *The Political Economy of Development and Underdevelopment*, 5th edn (New York, 1992), pp. 346–75.

55. S. Sassen, *The Global City: New York, London, Tokyo* (Princeton, 1991).

56. K. Chang and L. H. M. Ling, 'Globalization and its Intimate Other: Fillipina Domestic Workers in Hong Kong', in Marchand and Runyan (2000); D. Stasiulis and A. B. Bakan, 'Negotiating Citizenship: The case of foreign domestic workers in Canada', *Feminist Review*, 57 (1997), pp. 112–39; C B. Chin, *In Service and Servitude: Foreign Female Domestic Workers and the Malaysian Modernity Project* (New York, 1998); E. Boris and E. Prugl (eds), *Homeworkers in Global Perspective* (New York, 1996).

57. J. Pettman, 'An international political economy of sex', in *Worlding Women: Towards a Feminist International Politics* (New York, 1996); M. Specter, ' "Traffickers" New Cargo: Naïve Slavic Women', *The New York Times*, 11 January 1998; 'New Cargo: The Global Business of Trafficking in Women', *Refuge*, special issue, vol. 12, no. 1 (1999).

58. Kabeer (1994).

59. J. Nash and M. Fernandez-Kelly (eds), *Women, Men, and the International Division of Labor* (Albany, 1983).

60. S. Sassen, 'Toward a Feminist Analytics of the Global Economy', in *Globalization and its Discontents* (New York, 1998).

61. See, for example, Kabeer (1994); A. Ong, *The Spirits of Resistance and Capitalist Discipline* (Albany, 1987); J. True, 'Expanding Markets and Marketing Gender: The Integration of the Post-Socialist Czech Republic', *Review of International Political Economy*, vol. 6, no. 3 (1999), pp. 360–89.

62. See E. Prugl and M. K. Meyer, *Gender Politics and Global Governance* (Lanham, 1998).

63. K. Ferguson, *The Feminist Case Against Bureaucracy* (Philidelphia, 1984).

64. See, for example, L. Reanda, 'Engendering the United Nations: The Changing International Agenda.' *European Journal of Women's Studies*, 6 (1999), pp. 49–68.

65. H. Pietila and J. Vickers, *Making Women Matter: The Role of the United Nations*, 3rd edn (London, 1996).

66. S. Whitworth, *Feminism and International Relations: Towards a Political Economy of Gender in Interstate and Non-Governmental Institutions* (London, 1994); C. Hoskyns, *Integrating Gender: Women, Law and Politics in the European Union* (London, 1996).

67. S. Whitworth, 'Gender, International Relations and the Case of the ILO', *Review of International Studies*, vol. 20, no. 9 (1994), pp. 388–405.

68. See C. Hoskyns, 'Gender Issues in IR: the Case of the European Community', *Review of International Studies*, 20 (1994), pp. 225–39; also J. A. Caporaso and J. Jupille, 'The Europeanization of Gender Equality Policy and Domestic Structural Change', in M. G. Cowles, J. A. Caporaso and T. Risse (eds), *Europeanization and Domestic Structural Change* (Ithaca, 2001).

69. J. Seager, *Earth Follies: Coming to Feminist Terms with the Global Environmental Crisis* (New York, 1993); K. Litfin, 'The gendered eye in the sky: A Feminist Perspective on earth observation satellites', *Frontiers*, vol. 18, no. 2 (1997), pp. 26–47; D. Rocheleau, B. Thomas-Slayter and E. Wangari (eds), *Feminist Political Ecology: Global Issues and Local Experiences* (New York, 1996); M. Waring, *If Women Counted: A New Feminist Economics* (San Francisco, 1988); S. Dalby, 'Security, Modernity and Ecology: The Dilemmas of Post-Cold War Security Discourse', *Alternatives*, 17 (1992), pp. 95–134.

70. Mies (1986).

71. V. Shiva and M. Mies, *Ecofeminism* (London, 1993); C. Merchant, *The Death of Nature: Women, Ecology, and the Scientific Revolution* (New York, 1980).

72. V. Shiva, *Staying Alive: Women, Ecology, and Development* (London, 1988).

73. N. E. McGlen and M. R. Sarkees (eds), *Women in Foreign Policy: The Insiders* (New York, 1993).

74. A recent US–CIA report titled 'International Trafficking in Women to the United States: A Contemporary Manifestation of Slavery' documents the rise

of this global underground criminal industry. J. Brinkley, 'C.I.A. Depicts a Vast Trade in Forced Labour, A New Slavery is Growing in the US, CIA Report finds', *The New York Times*, 2 April 2000, pp. A1, 18.

75. J. Rosenau and O. Holsti, 'Women Leaders and Foreign Policy Opinions' in E. Boneparth and E. Stoper (eds), *Women, Power, and Politics* (New York, 1982). Contrary to gender gaps in the West, Mark Tessler, J. Nachtwey, and Audra Grant have found there to be no significant gender differences in attitudes toward international conflict and use of force in the Middle East region. (M. Tessler, J. Nachtwey and A. Grant, 'Further Tests of the Women and Peace Hypothesis: Evidence from Cross-national Survey Research in the Middle East', *International Studies Quarterly*, vol. 43, no. 3 (1999), pp. 519-31).

76. M. Tessler and I. Warriner, 'Gender, Feminism and Attitudes toward International Conflict: Exploring Relationships with Survey Data from the Middle East', *World Politics*, 49 (1997), pp. 250–81.

77. D. Stienstra, *Women's Movements and International Organizations* (Toronto, 1994), p. xii. See also L. Rupp, *Worlds of Women: The Making of an International Women's Movement* (Princeton, 1997).

78. E. Friedman, 'Women's Human Rights: The Emergence of a Movement'. in J. Peters and A. Wolper (eds) *Women's Rights/Human Rights: International Feminist Perspectives* (New York, 1995); A. M. Clark, E. J. Friedman and K. Hochstetler, 'The Sovereign Limits of Global Civil Society: A Comparison of NGO Participation in UN World Conferences on the Environment, Human Rights, and Women', *World Politics*, 51 (1998), pp. 1–35; J. Williams and S. Goose, in A. Maxwell, R. Cameron, J. Lawson and B. W. Tomlin (eds), *To Walk Without Fear: The Global Movement to Ban Landmines* (Toronto, 1998); A. S. Runyan, *Feminism, Peace, and International Politics: An Examination of Women Organizing Internationally for Peace and Security*, PhD dissertation, American University, 1988.

79. S. Sharoni, 'Middle-East Politics Through Feminist Lenses: Toward Theorize International Relations from Women's Struggles,' *Alternatives*, 18 (1993), pp. 5–28; T. Jacoby, 'Feminism, Nationalism and Difference: Reflections on the Palestinian Women's Movement', *Women's Studies International Forum*, vol. 22, no. 5, (1999), pp. 511–23; M. Korac, 'Ethnic nationalism, war and the patterns of social, political and sexual violence against women: the case of post-Yugoslav countries', *Identities*, vol. 5, no. 2 (1998), pp. 153–81. Also, C. Cockburn, *The Space Between Us: Negotiating Gender and National Identity in Conflict Zones* (London, 1998).

80. Enloe (1989), (2000); A. Rao (ed.), *Women's Studies International: Nairobi and Beyond* (New York, 1991).

81. K. Moon, *Sex Among Allies: Military Prostitution in US–Korea Relations* (New York, 1997).

82. Moon (1997), p. 151.

83. J. B. Elshtain, *Women and War* (New York, 1987); J. Stiehm, 'The Protected, the Protector, the Defender', in J. Stiehm (ed.), *Women and Men's Wars* (Oxford, 1983); B. Reardon, *Sexism and the War System* (New York, 1985).

84. S. Whitworth, *Warrior Princes and the Politics of Peacekeeping: A Feminist Analysis* (Boulder, forthcoming); J. H. Stiehm, 'United Nations Peacekeeping: Men and Women's Work', in E. Prugl and M. K. Meyer (eds), *Gender Politics and Global Governance* (Lanham, 1998).

85. See, for example, the American film *GI Jane* and discussion of it in the *International Journal of Feminist Politics*, vol. 1, no. 1, (1999); F. D'Amico and L. Weinstein (eds), *Gender Camouflage: Women in the US Military* (New York, 1999); C. Enloe, *Khaki is You: The Militarization of Women's Lives* (London, 1983); C. Becraft, *Women in the Military, 1980–1990* (Washington, 1991).

86. Baines (1999).

87. See S. Cartwright, 'Bridging national policies and international commitments: the question of the status of women', *UN Chronicle*, vol. 35, no. 1, (1998), pp. 24–5; A. Ackerly and S. M. Okin, 'Feminist Social Criticism and the International Movement for Women's Rights as Human Rights', in I. Shapiro and C. Hacker-Cordon (eds), *Democracy's Edges* (Cambridge, 1999); Peters and Wolper (1995); J. Kerr (ed.), *Women's Rights as Human Rights* (London, 1993); N. La Violette and S. Whitworth, 'No Safe Haven: Sexuality as a Universal Human Right and Gay and Lesbian Activism in International Politics', *Millennium*, vol. 23, no. 3 (1994), pp. 563–88.

88. Amnesty International, *Women in the Front Lines: Human Rights Violations Against Women* (New York, 1990).

89. 'Where in the World is there Safety for Me?: Women Feeling Gender-Based Persecution', in Peters and Wolper (1995).

90. See the US Vital Voices Initiative, <http://www.secretary.state/gov/www/picw/index.html>; R. Schuktheis, 'Afghanistan's Forgotten Women,' *Genders*, 27 (1998).

91. See E. Philapose, 'The Laws of War and Women's Human Rights,' *Hypatia*, vol. 11, no. 4 (1996); C. N. Niarchos, 'Women, war, and rape: challenges facing the international tribunal for the former Yugoslavia', *Human Rights Quarterly*, 17 (1995), pp. 649–90.

92. A. Rao, 'The Politics of Gender and Culture in International Human Rights Discourse', in Peters and Wolper (1995).

93. See N. Yuval-Davis, *Gender and Nation* (New York, 1997).

94. Moghadam (1993); Pettman (1996).

95. S. Meznaric, 'Gender as an Ethno-Marker: Rape, War and Identity Politics in the Former Yugoslavia' in V. Moghadam (ed.), *Identity Politics and Women* (Boulder, 1996).

96. J. Jaquette and S. Wolchik, *Women and Democracy* (Baltimore, 1998); B. Einhorn, *Cindarella Goes to Market: Women's Movements in East-Central Europe* (London, 1993); G. Waylen, 'Women and Democratisation: Conceptualising Gender Relations in Transition Politics', *World Politics*, 46 (1994), pp. 327–54; J. True, 'Gendering Post-Socialist Transitions,' in Marchand and Runyan (2000); UNDP, 'A Worsening Record on Gender Equality', in *Transition 99* (Oxford, 1999), ch. 6; see also L. Racioppi and K. O'Sullivan, 'Organizing Women

Before and After the Fall: Women's Politics in the Soviet Union and Post-Soviet Russia', *Signs*, vol. 20, no. 4, (1995); I. Miethe, 'From Mothers of the Revolution to Fathers of Unification', *Social Politics*, 6 (1999).

97. M. Molyneux, 'Women's Rights and the International Context: Some Reflections on the Post-Communist States' *Millennium*, vol. 23, no. 2 (1994), pp. 287–313.

98. See True (1999); J. True, *Engendering Transformations: Re-Constructing States and Civil Societies in Post-Socialist Europe*, PhD dissertation, York University, 2000.

99. C. Pateman, 'Introduction', in C. Pateman and E. Gross, 'Feminist Challenges: Social and Political Thought' (Sydney, 1986), p. 5.

100. Grant (1991), p. 21.

101. Peterson and Runyan (1999), p. 3.

102. V. S. Peterson, 'Transgressing Boundaries: Theories of Gender, Knowledge and International Relations', *Millennium*, vol. 21, no. 2 (1992), pp. 183–206.

103. The 'domestic analogy' refers to explanations of inter-state relations based on comparable or causal dynamics inside domestic(ated) states. See Suganami (1989).

104. Sylvester (1994); R. B. J. Walker, 'Gender and Critique in the Theory of International Relations', in V. S. Peterson (ed.), *Gendered States: Feminist (Re)visions of International Relations Theory* (Boulder, 1992).

105. Sylvester (1994), p. 104.

106. Enloe (1989), p. 131.

107. R. B. J. Walker, 'Realism, Change and International Political Theory', *International Studies Quarterly*, vol. 31, no. 1 (1987), p. 67.

108. Tickner (1992); see also V. S. Peterson and J. True, 'New Times and New Conversations', in Zalewski and Parpart (1998).

109. Sylvester (1994).

110. R. Ashley, 'Untying the Sovereign State: A Double Reading of the Anarchy Problematique', *Millennium*, vol. 17, no. 2 (1988), p. 230.

111. Newland and Grant (1991), p. 1.

112. See C. di Stefano, 'Masculinity as Ideology in Political Thought: Hobbesian Man Considered', *Women's Studies International Forum*, 6 (1983).

113. See C. Gilligan, *In a Different Voice: Psychological Theory and Women's Development* (Cambridge, 1982).

114. J. Tronto, 'Woman, the State and War: What Difference Does Gender Make?' in V. S. Peterson (ed.), *Clarification and Contestation: A Conference Report* (Los Angeles, 1989).

115. J. B. Elshtain, 'Reflections on War and Political Discourse: Realism, Just War, and Feminism in a Nuclear Age', *Political Theory*, 13 (1985), p. 41.

116. See B. A. Ackerly, *Political Theory and Feminist Social Criticism* (Cambridge, 2000).

117. J. A. Tickner, 'On the Fringes of the World Economy: A Feminist Perspective', in C. Murphy and R. Tooze (eds), *The New International Political Economy* (Boulder, 1991), pp. 204–6.

118. J. A. Tickner, 'Hans Morganthau's Political Principles of Political Realism: A Feminist Reformulation', *Millennium*, vol. 17, no. 3 (1988).

119. Waltz (1959), p. 188.

120. Waltz (1959), p. 238.

121. C. Sylvester, 'The Emperors' Theories and Transformations: Looking at the Field through Feminist Lens', in D. Pirages and C. Sylvester (eds), *Transformations in the Global Political Economy* (London, 1990).

122. J. Ruggie, 'Territoriality and Beyond: Problematizing Modernity in International Relations', *International Organization*, vol. 47, no. 1 (1993), pp. 149–74.

123. J. Ruggie, 'Continuity and Transformation in the World Polity: Towards a Neo-Realist Synthesis', in R. O. Keohane (ed.), *Neorealism and its Critics* (New York, 1986).

124. A. Linklater, *Men and Citizens in the Theory of International Relations* (London, 1990).

125. Harding (1989), p. 86.

126. Peterson (1992).

127. Elshtain (1992).

128. V. S. Peterson, 'Security and Sovereign States: What is at Stake in Taking Feminism Seriously?' in Peterson (1992), p. 46.

129. Peterson (1992), pp. 46–7.

130. See J. Jaquette, 'Power as Ideology: A Feminist Analysis'. in J. H. Stiehm (ed.), *Women's Views of the Political World of Men* (Dobbs Ferry, 1984).

131. Tickner (1988).

132. C. Sylvester, 'Feminist Theory and Gender Studies in International Relations', *International Studies Notes*, vol. 16, no. 1 (1992), pp. 32–8.

133. Enloe (1997).

134. See A. Wendt, *The Social Theory of International Politics* (Cambridge, 2000).

135. Peterson (1992), pp. 47–8.

136. J. B. Elshtain, 'Sovereignty, Identity, Sacrifice.' in Peterson (1992).

137. Peterson (1992), p. 53.

138. Elshtain (1985).

139. Tickner (1992).

140. Tickner (1991).

141. Runyan and Peterson (1991), p. 70

142. Sylvester (1994); N. Persram, 'Politicizing the Feminine, Globalizing the Feminist', *Alternatives*, 19 (1994), pp. 275–313; S. J. Ship, 'And What About Gender? Feminism and International Relations Theory's Third Debate', in W. S. Cox and C. T. Sjolander (eds), *Beyond Positivism: Critical International Relations Theory* (Boulder, 1994); Mohanty, Russo and Torres (1991).

143. Elshtain (1987); C. Sylvester, 'The Dangers of Merging Feminist and Peace Projects', *Alternatives*, vol. 8, no. 4 (1987), pp. 493–510.

144. E. A. Grosz, 'The Intervention of Feminist Knowledges' in B. Cane, E. A. Grosz and M. de Lepervanche (eds), *Crossing Boundaries: Feminisms and the Critique of Knowledges* (Sydney, 1988).

145. Scott (1988), p. 2.

146. A. Snitow, 'A Gender Diary', in A. Harris and Y. King (eds), *Rocking the Ship of the State: Towards a Feminist Peace Politics* (Boulder, 1989), p. 38.

147. Snitow (1989), p. 38.

148. Laura Busheikin discusses the difficulties of forging solidarity between East and West feminists since the fall of Soviet communism in 'Is Sisterhood really Global? Western Feminism in Eastern Europe', in T. Renne (ed.), *Ana's Land: Sisterhood in Eastern Europe* (Boulder, 1997).

149. C. Gabriel and L. Macdonald, 'Women's Transnational Organizing in the Context of NAFTA: Forging Feminist Internationality', *Millennium*, vol. 23, no. 3 (1994), p. 535.

150. C. Weber, 'Good Girls, Little Girls, and Bad Girls: Male Paranoia in Robert Keohane's Critique of Feminist International Relations', *Millennium*, vol. 23, no. 2 (1994), pp. 337–49.

151. K. McClure, 'The Issue of Foundations: Scientized Politics, Politicized Science and Feminist Critical Practice', in J. W. Scott and J. Butler (eds), *Feminists Theorize the Political* (New York, 1992), p. 359.

152. F. Robinson, *Globalizing Care: Ethics, Feminist Theory, and International Relations* (Boulder, 1999); Ackerly (2000). Also O. O'Neill, 'Justice, Gender and International Boundaries', *British Journal of Political Science*, 20 (1989), pp. 439–59; M. Cochran, *Normative Theory in International Relations: A Pragmatic Approach* (Cambridge, 1999).

153. M. Lugones and E. Spelman, 'Have We Got a Theory for You! Feminist Theory, Cultural Imperialism, and the Demand for "The Woman's Voice" ', *Women's Studies International Forum*, 6 (1983), p. 573.

154. C. Enloe, *The Morning After: Sexual Politics at the End of the Cold War* (Berkeley, 1994).

155. Sylvester (1994).

156. Sylvester (1994), p. 2

157. Sylvester (1994), p. 12.

158. Sylvester, (1994); also, C. Sylvester, 'Empathetic Co-operation: A Feminist Method for IR', *Millennium,* vol. 23, no. 2 (1994b).

159. Sylvester (1994b), p. 317.

160. M. Zalewski, 'The Women/Woman Question in International Relations', *Millennium*, vol. 23, no. 2 (1994), pp. 407–23.

161. For example, C. Weber, *Faking It: US Hegemony in a Post-Phallic Era* (Minneapolis, 1999); Sylvester (1994).

162. Grant (1991), p. 21.

163. S. Whitworth, 'Gender and International Relations: Beyond the Interparadigm Debate', *Millennium,* vol. 18, no. 2 (1989), pp. 265–72.

164. S. Whitworth, 'Theory as Exclusion: Gender and International Political Economy', in R. Stubbs and G. R. D. Underhill (eds), *Political Economy and the Changing Global Order* (London, 1995), pp. 116 and 125.

165. For an overview of historical materialist approaches to international relations see S. Gill (ed.), *Gramsci, Historical Materialism, and International Relations* (Cambridge, 1993). For feminist studies that draw on critical IPE analysis see also Chin (1998); L. H. Ling, *Post-colonial IR: Conquest and Desire between Asia and the West* (London, 2001).
166. For an example of a social constructivist approach to international relations see Wendt (2000).
167. Prugl (1999).

CHAPTER 10

Green Politics[1]

Matthew Paterson

Introduction

Of all the perspectives discussed in this book, Green Politics is perhaps the newest. While there has been a significant amount of writing within IR on this topic in the last few years, it has as yet at best an underdeveloped position in International Relations (IR).[2] However, Green Politics has emerged as a significant political force in many countries from the mid-1970s onwards, and it has a position which is explicitly global in character, and which addresses global politics in a distinctive fashion. Many of the writings of Green thinkers, and practices of Green movements, contain both analyses of the dynamics of global politics, and normative visions concerning the restructuring of world politics. This chapter aims to outline strands of Green Political thought which could be used to develop a Green theoretical position on IR, and arguments made in the emerging literature in the field. This Green position of course has features in common with others presented in this volume, and I will aim to highlight these in the conclusion. The chapter will focus, however, on what is distinctive about a Green position.

The Chapter is organised through a discussion of two main sets of literature which can be used to develop a Green position on IR/global politics. These are the literature on Green Political Theory and that on 'Global Ecology'.[3] I will outline what general arguments are made by these writers in this introductory section. The chapter will then draw out the themes from both which help us construct a Green position in IR. I will do this through what I argue are the key strands of Green politics – ecocentric ethics, limits to growth, and decentralisation of power. Together, these two literatures provide an *explanation* of the destruction of the rest of nature by human societies, and a *normative* foundation for resisting this destruction and creating sustainable societies.

First it is necessary to make an important distinction, between Green Politics and *environmentalism*.[4] This will become clearer later in the chapter, but here it is important to note that environmentalists, broadly speaking, accept the framework of the existing political, social, economic and normative structures of world politics, and seek to ameliorate environmental problems within those structures, while Greens regard those structures as the main origin of the environmental crisis and therefore contend that they are structures which need to be challenged and transcended. Although obviously a crude simplification of the variety of positions adopted by those in the Green, and broader environmental movement, it serves a useful function here as a representation of ideal types. This is the case because it becomes clear that there is no distinctive *environmentalist* position on IR. As is obvious from even the most cursory literature survey of the mainstream IR literature on environmental problems, the environmentalist position is easily compatible with the liberal institutionalist position outlined most clearly by Keohane.[5] In fact most writers within IR who write on environmental problems, and who are clearly motivated by the normative concerns adopted by environmentalists, adopt liberal institutionalist positions (as discussed in Chapter 2).[6] The analytic concern is with the response of the states-system to environmental problems, focusing on the emergence of 'international environmental regimes', while the underlying assumption is that the states-system can respond effectively to those problems. By contrast, Green Politics rejects the idea that the states-system, and other structures of world politics, can provide such a response. The contrast between Green Politics and environmentalism neatly mirrors one between critical and problem-solving theory, with Greens focusing on the need for global-scale political transformation rather than institutional tinkering. This chapter will not therefore discuss the mainstream IR literature on environmental problems.

Green Political Theory

There is now a well-developed literature on Green Political Theory (GPT), which gives a useful base for Green ideas about IR. Three major works suggest slightly different ideas about the defining characteristics of Green Politics. Eckersley suggests that the defining characteristic is ecocentrism – the rejection of an anthropocentric world-view which places moral value only on humans in favour of one which places independent value also on ecosystems and all living beings.[7] Goodin also places ethics at the centre of the Green position, suggesting that a 'Green theory of value' is at the core of Green political theory. His formulation is that for a Green theory of value, the source of value in things is the fact that they have a history of having been created by natural processes rather than by artificial human ones.[8]

Dobson is the one of these three to have two defining characteristics of Green Politics.[9] One is the rejection of anthropocentrism, as outlined by Eckersley. The other however is the 'limits to growth' argument about the nature of the environmental crisis. Greens suggest that it is the exponential economic growth experienced during the last two centuries which is at the root cause of the current environmental crisis. Thus it is not the belief in an environmental crisis which is defining, but the particular (and unique) understanding which Greens have of the nature of that crisis which makes them distinctive.

Dobson's position is the most convincing, in my view. A reduction of the Green position to an ethical stance towards non-human nature, without a set of arguments about why the environment is being destroyed by humans, seems to me to lose much of what is central to Greens' beliefs. It is also highly indeterminate politically, as I will show below. Goodin's formulation is also highly problematic, as he posits a notoriously dubious distinction between things which are 'natural' and those which are 'artificial' which cannot be even loosely sustained.

However, I would argue that a third key plank of Green politics can also be identified, that of decentralisation. There is an ongoing debate both about whether this is a key and necessary part of Green politics at all, but also whether it is something which is derived from the arguments about ecocentric ethics and limits to growth, or is something which can be regarded as a Green principle in its own right.[10] I do not propose to answer the second of these debates directly, but against writers like Goodin and Eckersley, I will try to show below that decentralisation is a key plank of Green Politics. I devote most space in the chapter to this debate, both because of the contested nature of this claim, and also because it is where the implications for IR are most tangible.

Global ecology

In the early 1990s a literature emerged which builds on the basic Green principles outlined above and provides an analysis of the present situation which is consistent with them. In other words, while GPT provides a normative foundation for a Green view of global politics, 'global ecology' provides an explanatory foundation.[11] This literature can be associated most centrally with the writings of Wolfgang Sachs, Pratap Chatterjee and Matthias Finger, *The Ecologist* magazine, *Third World Resurgence*, and Vandana Shiva. This literature has two central themes: development as the root cause of environmental problems; and the protection and reclamation of 'commons' as central to the Green vision.

A background concern for Sachs and others is that the practices of the environmental movement worldwide have been diluted and coopted in the 1980s. He writes that:

> Once, environmentalists called for new public virtues, now they call for better managerial strategies. Once, they advocated more democracy and local self-reliance, now they tend to support the global empowerment of governments, corporations and science. Once, they stove for cultural diversity, now they see little choice but to push for a worldwide rationalisation of life-styles.[12]

Reflecting the historical specificity of these works, but also helping illustrate their ideas, a prevalent theme is a critique of UNCED, or the 'Earth Summit'.[13] While mainstream environmentalist accounts of UNCED usually regard the conference as having been a tremendous success for environmentalists and for the environment, marking the culmination of years of effort in getting politicians to take environmental problems seriously, Chatterjee and Finger see it rather differently.[14]

They suggest that UNCED was a failure for the environmental movement, since it marked the final cooptation of environmentalism by ruling elites. 'In fact, the UN Conference in Rio inaugurated environmentalism as the highest state of developmentalism'.[15] Governments managed to shore up their own power by using environmental groups to legitimise them. Mainstream environmental groups made UNCED look like a genuine attempt by governments and other actors to deal with global environmental problems. Also, Multinational Corporations, organised in such groups as the Business Council for Sustainable Development, were able to use the Conference to present themselves as legitimate actors on the world stage, and as the people with the expertise to deal with environmental problems. They highlight the irony of this by noting that one PR company which offered to promote UNCED free of charge, Burson-Marstellar, had previously worked for Exxon during the Valdez oil spill, Union Carbide during Bhopal, and the US nuclear industry after Three Mile Island.[16] Multinationals were given privileged access by the UNCED Secretariat to the proceedings, relative to environmental groups. Those groups were used by the Conference's organisers mainly as legitimising tools. Thus the environmental movement left the UNCED process more divided than before, partly because of the tactics of many of its members of cooperation with governments and multinationals, but partly also because of the inherent set up of the Conference which favoured well-organised, large groups over the diverse, wide variety of groups which make up the environmental movement. Mainstream groups such as WWF (and even Greenpeace) had been coopted by governments, while those who maintained an oppositional posture were even further marginalised.

The concern of these writers therefore is to reclaim a set of beliefs about the nature of the ecological crisis which emphasise that radical social and political changes are necessary in order to respond to those problems. The analysis is again that it is not possible to simply adapt existing social institutions to deal with environmental problems – entirely new ones will have to be developed. There is a lineage back to Green writers of the early 1970s, such as Schumacher, which is clearly intended.

Ecocentrism[17]

A central tenet of Green thought is the rejection of anthropocentric ethics in favour of an ecocentric approach. For Eckersley ecocentrism has a number of central features. Firstly, it involves some empirical claims. These involve a view of the world as ontologically composed of interrelations rather than individual entities.[18] All beings are fundamentally 'embedded in ecological relationships'.[19] Consequently, there is no convincing criteria which can be used to make a hard and fast distinction between humans and non-humans.[20]

Secondly, it has an ethical base. Eckersley rejects anthropocentrism on consequentialist grounds, suggesting that it leads to environmentally de-vastating results, but also argues for ecocentrism on deontological grounds.[21] Since there is no convincing reason to make rigid distinctions between humans and the rest of nature, a broad emancipatory project, to which she allies herself, ought to be extended to non-human nature. Ecocentrism is about 'emancipation writ large'.[22] All entities are endowed with a relative autonomy, within the ecological relationships in which they are embedded, and therefore humans are not free to dominate the rest of nature.

Ecocentrism therefore has four central ethical features which collectively distinguish it from other possible ethical positions towards the environment.[23] Firstly, it recognises the full range of human interests in the nonhuman world. Secondly, it recognises the interests of the nonhuman community. Thirdly, it recognises the interests of future generations of humans and nonhumans. Finally it adopts a holistic rather than an atomistic perspective – that is, it values populations, species, ecosystems and the ecosphere as a whole as well as individual organisms.[24]

Many challenge both whether ecocentrism is descriptively a necessary component of Green ideology, or whether it is an adequate or desirable basis for a political theory. Normatively, for example, both Barry and Hayward question both the intellectual coherence and strategic viability of ecocentrism, and argue for a 'soft' anthropocentrism as the basis for Green politics.[25] Hayward, for example, argues that the rejection of anthropocentrism in much Green thought is misplaced – what Greens seek typically to criticise should more accurately be thought of as either specie-sism (arbitrary and unjustifiable discrimination against or oppression of organisms by species) or human chauvinism (attempts to specify the relevant criteria of ethical judgment which invariably benefit humans at the expense of other species). Anthropocentrism is not necessarily the problem in either of these cases, and in fact a proper respect for humanity may in fact itself lead to respect for other species as well.[26] Nevertheless, despite the details of their arguments, Hayward and Barry both agree that a radical thinking of the ethical relationship between humans and the rest of 'nature' is a fundamental part of Green politics.

Limits To Growth, Post-Development

A second plank of a Green position is the belief in limits to the growth of human societies. Although the idea clearly has a long lineage, the immediate impetus for arguments concerning limits to growth came from an influential, controversial and very well-known book published in 1972, *The Limits to Growth.*[27] The argument there was that exponential economic and population growth of human societies was producing an interrelated series of crises. This exponential growth was producing a situation where the world was rapidly running out of resources to feed people or to provide raw material for continued industrial growth (exceeding *carrying capacity* and *productive capacity*), and simultaneously exceeding the *absorptive capacity* of the environment to assimilate the waste products of industrial production.[28] The team of researchers led by Donella Meadows produced their arguments based on computer simulations of the trajectory of industrial societies. They predicted that at current rates of growth, many raw materials would rapidly run out, pollution would quickly exceed the absorptive capacity of the environment, and human societies would experience 'overshoot and collapse' some time before 2100.

The details of their predictions have been fairly easily refuted.[29] However, Greens have taken their central conclusion–that exponential growth is impossible in a finite system – to be a central plank of their position.[30] Dobson suggests there are three arguments which are important here.[31] Firstly, technological solutions will not work – they may postpone the crisis but cannot prevent it occurring at some point. Secondly, the exponential nature of growth means that 'dangers stored up over a relatively long period of time can very suddenly have a catastrophic effect'.[32] Finally, the problems associated with growth are all interrelated. Simply dealing with them issue by issue will mean that there are important knock-on effects from issue to issue–solving one pollution problem alone may simply change the medium through which pollution is carried, not reduce pollution.

From this Greens get their notions of sustainability. While environment-alism concentrates on 'sustainable development',[33] which presumes the compatibility of growth with responding to environmental problems, Greens reject this. Sustainability explicitly requires stabilising, and in the industrialised countries almost certainly reducing, throughputs of materials and energy.[34] This requires the wholesale reorganisation of economic systems.

As the notion of sustainable development became fashionable in the 1980s, and as the specific predictions of the MIT team concerning resource exhaustion proved inaccurate, belief in limits subsided. But in the 1990s, a politics rejecting economic growth as the primary purpose of governments and societies reemerged. It came, however, less out of the computer-mod-elling scientistic methods of Meadows *et al.* (although her team did produce a 20-year-on book *Beyond the Limits*[35]), than out of emerging critiques of development in the South from the late 1980s onwards. Such 'post-devel-opment' perspectives draw heavily on postmodernism and feminism, and have been used greatly by Greens in the North to develop the 'global ecology' perspective.[36] Through the critique of 'development', economic growth became again the subject of critique, although in this vein its ecological consequences were much more closely connected by its critics to its social consequences.[37]

Writers such as Sachs do not believe the term development can be retrieved.[38] They are highly critical of the term 'sustainable development', in widespread use in environmentalist circles, suggesting that this merely serves to make it easier for ruling elites to coopt environmentalism. Sachs writes, illustrating this argument well:

> The walls of the Tokyo subway used to be plastered with advertising posters. The authorities, aware of Japan's shortage of wood pulp, searched for ways to reduce this wastage of paper. They quickly found an 'environmental solution'; they mounted video screens on the walls and these now continuously bombard passengers with commercials – paper problem solved.[39]

In other words, elites manage to deal with environmental problems dis-cretely, while in practice ongoing development undermines any ameliora-tive effect which a particular response, such as changing the medium of advertising on the underground, may have.

One of the reasons why the 'global ecology' writers object to develop-ment is the limits to growth arguments, abandoned by much of the envir-onmental movement during the 1980s. Implicit throughout their work is a need to accept the limits imposed by a finite planet, an acceptance which is ignored by the planet's managers and mainstream environmentalists.

'In the eyes of the developmentalists, the "limits to growth" did not call for abandoning the race, but for changing the running technique', writes Sachs.[40] They are also sceptical of the idea that it is possible to decouple the concept of development from that of growth. While many environmentalists try to distinguish the two by stating, in Daly's words, that 'growth is quantitative increase in physical scale while development is qualitative improvement or unfolding of potentialities', others would suggest that in practice it is impossible to make such neat distinctions.[41] For the practitioners of sustainable development, 'sustainable growth' and 'sustainable development' have usually been conflated, and certainly the Brundtland Commission regarded a new era of economic growth as essential or sustainable development (WCED, 1987).

However, there are a number of more nuanced arguments which they make. While accepting limits in principle, they would be critical of the scientistic fashion in which Meadows *et al.* demonstrated limits – that computer modelling approach would itself lead easily to a 'global environmental management' form of response which entrenched the power of elites. This was of course one critique of the Limits to Growth in the 1970s, that it was too technocratic. They would also agree with another significant criticism of the Limits to Growth, for example by Cole *et al.*, that their models had no social content.[42] The social effects of growth, and the social context of developing sustainable societies, is crucial for these writers.

The Ecologist suggests that one of the central features of development is enclosure, or the turning of common spaces into private property.[43] This was central to modernising agriculture in England before the industrial revolution, and they suggest it is a central part of development practice throughout the world at the present. It is important to development because it is an act of appropriation which makes commodity production possible. Commons were organised largely (but not exclusively) outside the market, making efficient accumulation difficult. Enclosure makes this possible. However, the effects of enclosure are to take decision-making away from those who depend on local resources, which in turn makes environmental degradation more likely, as well as being socially divisive. This argument is closely tied to the argument in favour of the commons, explored below.

As a consequence of enclosure, access to resources is denied, which concentrates resources and power in the hands of fewer people. Development is thus necessarily inegalitarian, since it depends on continuous appropriation. Inequality has been one of the central ideological arguments governments have often made for economic growth; that within inequality, growth enables the worst off to get better off.[44] An anti-ecological dynamic is therefore built into development. This also illustrates how the global ecology writers make close links between the damaging human effects of development and the damaging ecological effects of development.

Development therefore entrenches the power of the already powerful. This can be seen on the global level – in the global economy in which the North dominates, and can insulate itself from (many) socio-ecological effects of development, such as through exporting dirty industries to developing countries. It can also be seen at the micro-level, for example in the 'Green revolution' in the 1970s, which concentrated power and land in the hands of the rich farmers, at the expense of the poor who could not afford the fertilisers and pesticides to support the new strains of crops.[45]

A central part of this concentration of power is to do with knowledge. The appropriation of spaces previously held in common empowers 'experts' and denies indigenous knowledges as it transforms those spaces into objects for commodity production. This means that the techniques involved in attempts to manage those spaces are turned over to scientists, and other development experts.[46]

This involves privileging western technology and knowledge over non-Western knowledges. Thus 'technology transfer' becomes central to solving environmental problems – the idea that 'advanced' Western technology is needed to help developing countries develop in an 'environmentally friendly' way. McCully provides a compelling critique of technology transfer regarding climate change, showing how past attempt at technology transfer, through development aid, have reproduced the problems associated with development outlined above.[47]

As mentioned above, development necessarily is about creating commodity production where previously it had not prevailed. This is of course closely linked to the emergence of instrumental rationality and individualism, which, as mentioned above while discussing Carolyn Merchant, has turned 'nature' into 'natural resources', to be plundered by humans. Development is therefore about an ideological shift of world-view, a major part of which is towards seeing the environment purely in human-instrumental terms.

Closely allied to this is the idea that development progressively 'rationalises' the natural world. It turns it into a set of countable species, some of which are useful (to be preserved) some of which are not (to be destroyed if in the way of progress). This way of seeing nature has historically reduced biological diversity, and arguably necessarily does so.

The global ecology writers therefore present a powerful set of arguments as to how development is inherently anti-ecological. This is not only because of abstract limits to growth type arguments, but because they show in a more subtle fashion how development in practice undermines sustainable practices. It takes control over resources away from those living sustainably in order to organise commodity production, it empowers experts with knowledges based on instrumental reason, it increases inequality which produces social conflicts, and so on.

Green Restructurings of Global Politics

A central question for us here is the position which Green Politics has concerning questions of world order, and particular world order reform. Although some arguments made by environmentalists concerning such institutional reform have clear connections to other traditions, what I argue is the most plausible and representative account of what Greens believe provides a distinctive account of what forms of global political restructuring are required. This is therefore the third plank of a Green Politics – decentralism. However, whether this is a key principle of Green Politics or not is certainly contested, as will be obvious below.

On the basis of her account of ecocentric ethics, Eckersley develops a political argument from this which is statist in orientation. Although she does not adopt the position of the 'eco-authoritarians' such as Ophuls, Hardin or Heilbroner, she suggests, in direct contradiction to ecoanarchism which is widespread in Green political thought, that the modern state is a necessary political institution from a Green point of view.[48] She suggests that ecocentrism requires that we both decentralise power down within the state, but also centralise power up to the regional and global levels.

For Eckersley, then, new forms of global political structures are required from an ecocentric point of view. This is necessary in order to protect nature. Arguing against the anarchist interpretation of Green politics (see below) she says that a 'multitiered' political system, with dispersal of power both down to local communities and up to the regional and global levels is the approach which is most consistent with ecocentrism.[49] If all power is decentralised, she suggests, there will be no mechanisms to coordinate responses to regional or global environmental problems, or to redistribute resources from rich to poor regions of the world.[50] Her argument is premised on ecocentric ethics and the priority to protect the rest of nature, the social justice consequences of ecocentrism, and the urgency of the ecological crisis. Arguing against ecoanarchists, she suggests that:

> in view of the urgency and ubiquity of the ecological crisis, ultimately only a supraregional perspective and multilateral action by nation States can bring about the kind of dramatic changes necessary to save the 'global commons' . . . .[51]

Her arguments elsewhere are also premised on the urgency of the ecological crisis. 'Indeed, the urgency of the ecological crisis is such that we cannot afford *not* to "march through" and reform the institutions of liberal parliamentary democracy . . . and employ the resources . . . of the State to promote national and international action.'[52]

This position could be developed within a conventional perspective on IR (such as liberal institutionalism) to look at the character of a wide variety of interstate treaties and practices. The most obvious would be those regarding Biodiversity, acid rain or climate change. But it could also be developed for global economic institutions such as the World Bank, or the military practices of states. A broad critique of the major global institutions from an ecocentric position could be fairly easily established, especially considering the very different ethical basis underlying this position in contrast to that which informs international treaties and other international practices. This critique would show how the main international practices are based on an anthropocentric ethic which puts human material interests first, and disregards that of ecosystems or other species. This is even the case for environmental treaties. For example, while ostensibly about protecting biodiversity, the substance of the Biodiversity Convention signed in 1992 is primarily couched in terms of protecting the gene pool for the biotechnology industry.[53] And the objective of the Climate Change Convention, also signed in 1992, while stating that the aim is to 'prevent dangerous anthropogenic interference with the climate system', which could have an ecocentric interpretation, quickly goes on to say that this is 'to ensure that food production is not threatened and to enable economic development to proceed in a sustainable manner'.[54] As a consequence the implications of ecocentric ethics could be limited to a critique of the content of international practices, rather than the structure of international relations.

But her account could also be developed in the context of the literature on 'global environmental governance', which implies forms of governance emerging which do not rely solely on sovereign states.[55] One view of this is that we are currently witnessing a simultaneous shift of authority up to international/transnational institutions, and down to local organisations.[56] Rosenau makes this claim concerning patterns of authority in global politics in general, but also specifically in relation to global environmental politics.[57] For Hempel, such forms global environmental governance are emerging because the spatial scale of the state is inadequate to dealing with the scales of environmental change. The state is simultaneously too small and too big to deal effectively with such change, and thus practices of governance move towards regional and global levels and at the same time towards local levels, in response. Eckersley's position is a normative claim justifying such shifts in authority.

But this interpretation of ecocentrism advanced by Eckersley is challengeable. Ecocentrism is in itself politically indeterminate. It can have many variants, ranging from anarchist to authoritarian, with Eckersley's version in the middle of the continuum.

The predominant alternative interpretation within Green thought suggests that it is the emergence of modern modes of thought which is the problem from an ecocentric point of view. The rationality inherent in modern Western science is an instrumental one, where the domination of the rest of nature (and of women by men) and its use for human instrumental purposes have historically at least been integral to the scientific project on which industrial capitalism is built. Carolyn Merchant's *The Death of Nature: Women, Ecology and the Scientific Revolution* is the classic account of the emergence of this rationality in the Scientific Revolution of the sixteenth and seventeenth centuries.[58] In other words, environmental ethics are given a historical specificity and material base – the emergence of modern forms of anthropocentrism are located in the emergence of modernity in all its aspects.

This interpretation argues therefore that since modern science is inextricably bound up with other modern institutions such as capitalism, the nation-state and modern forms of patriarchy, it is inappropriate to respond by developing those institutions further, centralising power through the development of global and regional institutions. Such as response will further entrench instrumental rationality which will undermine the possibility for developing an ecocentric ethic. An ecocentric position therefore leads to arguments for scaling down human communities, and in particular for challenging trends towards globalisation and homogenisation, since it is only by celebrating diversity that it will be possible to create spaces for ecocentric ethics to emerge. This argument is developed by the 'global ecology' writers outlined below.

Adding in questions of limits to growth reinforce this reading of the implications of ecocentrism for politics. The implications for global political structures then clearly become considerable. O'Riordan presents a useful typology of positions which emerge from the limits to growth version of sustainability which Greens adopt.[59] The first is very similar to that outlined by Eckersley – that the nation-state is both too big and too small to deal effectively with sustainability, and new regional and global structures (alongside decentralisation within the state) are needed to coordinate effective responses.

A second interpretation, prevalent in the 1970s but virtually absent from discussions in the 1980s, is what O'Riordan calls 'centralised authoritarianism'. This generally follows the logic of Garrett Hardin's 'tragedy of the commons' which suggested that resources held in common would be overused.[60] This metaphor led to the argument that centralised global political structures would be needed to force changes in behaviour to reach sustainability.[61] In some versions, this involved the adoption of what were called 'lifeboat ethics'.[62] The idea was that the scarcity outlined by Meadows *et al.* meant that rich countries would have to practise triage on a global scale – to 'pull up the ladder behind them'. This argument, largely an ecological version of the world government proposals of some versions of liberal internationalism (see Chapter 2) has however been rejected by Greens, with a few exceptions.

The third position is similar to the above in that it suggests authoritarianism may be required, but rejects the idea that this can be on a global scale. The vision here is for small scale, tightly knit communities run on

hierarchical, conservative lines with self-sufficiency in their use of resources.[63] It shares with the above position the idea that it is freedom
and egoism which has caused the environmental crisis, and these tendencies need to be curbed to produce sustainable societies. In some versions,
these communes would be inward looking and explicitly xenophobic.[64]

The final position which O'Riordan outlines is termed by him the 'anarchist solution'. This has become the position adopted by Greens as the best
interpretation of the implications of limits to growth. For many, it is also
regarded as a principle of Green politics in its own right (for example,
decentralisation is a one of the four principles of Green Politics in the
widely cited *Programme of the German Green Party*[65]). The term 'anarchist'
is used in this typology loosely. It means that Greens envisage global
networks of small-scale self-reliant communities.[66] This position would
for example be associated with people like E. F. Schumacher, as well as
bioregionalists such as Kirkpatrick Sale.[67] It shares the focus on small-scale
communities with the previous position, but has two crucial differences.
Firstly, relations within communities would be libertarian, egalitarian, and
participatory. This reflects a very different set of assumptions about the
origins of the environmental crisis; rather than being about the 'tragedy of
the commons' (which naturalises human greed), it is seen to be about the
emergence of hierarchical social relations, and the channelling of human
energies into productivism and consumerism.[68] Participatory societies
should provide means for human fulfilment which do not depend on high
levels of material consumption. Secondly, these communities, while self-
reliant, are seen to be internationalist in orientation. They are not cut off
from other communities, but in many ways conceived of as embedded in
networks of relations of obligations, cultural exchanges, and so on.[69]

Greens also often object to the State for anarchist reasons. For example,
Spretnak and Capra suggest that it is the features identified by Weber as
central to statehood which are often the problem from a Green point of
view.[70] Bookchin gives similar arguments, suggesting that the State is the
ultimate hierarchical institution which consolidates all other hierarchical
institutions.[71] Carter suggests that the State is part of the dynamic of
modern society which has caused the present environmental crisis. He
outlines a 'environmentally hazardous dynamic', where '[a] centralized,
pseudo-representative, quasi-democratic state stabilizes competitive, inegalitarian economic relations that develop "non-convivial", environmentally
damaging "hard" technologies whose productivity supports the (nationa-
listic and militaristic) coercive forces that empower the state'.[72] Thus the
State is not only unnecessary from a Green point of view, it is positively
undesirable.

This is perhaps the most important theme coming out of Green Politics
for IR. One of the best known Green Political slogans is 'think globally, act
locally'. While obviously also fulfilling rhetorical purposes, it is often seen

to follow from the two above principles. It stems from a sense that while that global environmental and social/economic problems operate on a global scale, they can only be successfully responded to by breaking down the global power structures which generate them through local action and the construction of smaller scale political communities and self-reliant economies.

One of the best developed arguments for decentralisation within Green Political Theory is given in John Dryzek's *Rational Ecology*. Dryzek summarises the advantages of decentralisation thus; small-scale communities are more reliant on the environmental support services in their immediate locality and therefore more responsive to disruptions in that environment.[73] Self-reliance and smallness shortens feedback channels, so it is easier to respond quickly before disruptions become severe. He also suggests that they are more likely to develop a social ontology which undermines pure instrumental ways of dealing with the rest of nature, commonly identified by Greens (and others) as a cause of environmental problems.[74]

The 'global ecology' writers also reinforce this Green Political theory argument for decentralisation of power. At the same time, they give this argument a political economy, by which I mean they make it so that it is not only a question of the scale of political organisation, but also a reorganisation of the structural form of political institutions, and in particular a reconceptualisation of how economic production, distribution and exchange – the direct way in which human societies transform 'nature' – is integrated into political life. Their positive argument is that the most plausibly Green form of political economy is the 'commons'.[75] This argument is most fully developed by the editors of *The Ecologist* magazine in their book *Whose Common Future? Reclaiming the Commons*.[76]

The argument is essentially that common spaces are sites of the most sustainable practices currently operating. They are under threat from development which continuously tries to enclose them in order to turn them into commodities. Therefore a central part of Green Politics is resistance to this enclosure. But it is also a (re)constructive project – creating commons where they do not exist.

Commons regimes are difficult to define, as *The Ecologist* suggest. In fact they suggest that precise definitions are impossible, as the variety of commons around the world defy clear description in language. The first point of definition is a negative one however. The commons is not the commons as referred to by Garrett Hardin.[77] His 'tragedy of the commons', where the archetypal English medieval common gets overgrazed as each herder tries to maximise the number of sheep they graze on it, is in practice not a commons, but an 'open access' resource.[78]

Commons, therefore, are not anarchic in the sense of having no rules governing them. They are spaces whose use is closely governed, often by informally defined rules, by the communities which depend on them. They depend for their successful operation on a rough equality between the members of the community, as imbalances in power would make some able to ignore the rules of the community. They also depend on particular social and cultural norms prevailing, for example, the priority of common safety over accumulation, or distinctions between members and non-members (although not necessarily in a hostile sense, or one which is rigid and unchanging over time).[79]

Commons are therefore clearly different from private property systems. However, commons are also not 'public' spaces in the modern sense. Public connotes open access under control by the State, while commons are often not open to all, and the rules governing them do not depend on the hierarchy and formality of state institutions. A further difference from 'modern' institutions is that they are typically organised for the production of use values rather than exchange values, that is, they are not geared to commodity production. This makes them not susceptible to the pressures for accumulation or growth inherent in capitalist market systems.

Commons are therefore held to produce sustainable practises for a number of reasons. First, the rough equality in income and power means that none can usurp or dominate the system. 'Woods and streams feeding local rivers remained intact because anyone degrading them had to brave the wrath of neighbours deprived of their livelihood, and no one was powerful enough to do so'.[80] Second, the local scale at which they work means that the patterns of mutual dependence make cooperation easier to achieve.[81] Third, this also means that the culture of recognising one's dependence on others and therefore having obligations, is easily entrenched. Finally, commons make practices based on accumulation difficult to adopt, usufruct being more likely.

One of the great strengths of *The Ecologist's* work is the way in which the argument is richly illustrated. I will give just a few examples here. At a general level, they highlight how many people throughout the world are dependent on commons, despite the globalisation of capitalism. For example, 90 per cent of the world's fishers depend on small inshore marine commons, catching over half of all the fish eaten.[82]

In the Philippines, Java and Laos, irrigations systems are run by villages communally, with water rights decided at the village level. Even in the North, they suggest, communities still exist which manage resources communally – for example lobster harvesters in Maine.[83] In parts of India, villages based on Gandhian principles known as *gramdam* villages enable sustainable practices to flourish. In these villages, all land within the village boundary is controlled by the *gram sabha*, composed of all the adults in the village.[84] They quote Agarwal & Narain on how one such village, Seed near Udaipur, operates:

The common land has been divided into two categories – one category consists of lands on which both grazing and leaf collection is banned and the second category consists of lands on which grazing is permitted but leaf collection or harming trees is banned. The first category of land is lush green and full of grass which villagers can cut only once a year ... Even during the unprecedented drought of 1987, Seed was able to harvest 80 bullock cartloads of grass from this parch. The grass was distributed equitably amongst all households.[85]

The idea of the commons is clearly very consistent with the arguments from GPT about the necessity of decentralisation of power, and grassroots democracy. However it supplements it by showing how small scale democratic communities are the most likely to produce sustainable practices within the limits set by a finite planet.

Objections to Green arguments for decentralisation

Much of the academic literature on Green Politics in the 1990s questioned the Green commitment to decentralisation.[86] In addition, Doherty and de Geus suggest that Green parties have scaled back their commitments during the 1990s in response to electoral success and the corresponding need for 'realism'.[87] Objections to decentralisation tend to come in three forms.

First is a claim that small-scale anarchistic communities would be too parochial and potentially self-interested to provide atmospheres conducive to cross-community cooperation. 'One of the major fears of observers outside the Green movement is that its picture of localized politics smacks of a petty parochialism, which would be both undesirable and unpleasant to live with', writes Dobson.[88] Part of this argument is therefore that it would be stultifying or oppressive for those within the community, but it also suggests that they would be unconcerned with effects across their borders.

This argument is generally empirical in character; that in human societies (historical and present) organised on such a small scale such a parochial character is pervasive, and that a universalistic ethics which Greens also espouse only emerged in modernity, with its nation-states, cities, and so on.[89] However, it is also heightened by the writings of some Greens. One Green anarchist writes that 'If there is much social mixing between the groups, if people work outside the group, it will weaken the community bond ... xenophobia is the key to the community's success'.[90] Many other Greens are of course aware of the argument. Goldsmith *et al.* wrote as early as 1972 that 'we would stress that we are not proposing that they (small-scale communities) be inward-looking, self-obsessed or in any way closed to the rest of the world'.[91]

Whether or not Greens have an adequate answer to this problem, this objection to the anti-statist position is a very odd argument. The objection that small-scale communities may be too parochial could just as easily be a charge levelled against sovereign states. It is the practice of sovereignty which enables states to be primarily self-regarding, and avoid any sense that they have fundamental obligations to the rest of the world.[92] And the sorts of communities Greens envisage are precisely post-sovereign communities. Confederations of small-scale communities could be organised in such a way that effects on other communities would have to be taken into account in decisions. But even if this is rejected as naive, the point that is missed in this objection is that no particular political form (arguably excepting world government, but that has its own problems) could *guarantee* that communities would be concerned with effects on other communities. Solving that problem is a question of political culture, not political structure.

A second objection is that while Greens' advocacy of decentralisation clearly involves an explicit rejection of the contemporary sovereign states-system, this undermines Greens' claims to global relevance. Decentralised small-scale communities, it is claimed, will have little chance of developing effective mechanisms for resolving global environmental problems. The most developed argument of this sort is put by Bob Goodin.

Goodin's argument (and that of others) is that since many environmental problems are transnational or even global in scope, global cooperation to respond to these problems is necessary. This is a reasonable enough argument. But he then goes on to argue that the State, with sovereign rights intact, is a necessary political form to procure this cooperation. This turn in the argument is perhaps less convincing.

Goodin's focus is on the logic of collective action, using game-theoretic arguments.[93] He reviews a number of models of cross-community cooperation on transboundary issues under a Green scenario of decentralisation towards small-scale self-reliant communities, and concludes that even under the most favourable scenario, solutions to this problem 'must necessarily involve revesting at least some of those powers in centralized coordinating agencies at the global level'.[94]

Goodin outlines four well-known games which could be said to model cooperation between small-scale anarchistic communities: Prisoner's Dilemma, Chicken, Assurance, and Altruism.[95] His concern is to try to show that for each of these, substantial powers may have to be transferred to institutions well beyond the local level, right up to the global level. The problem gets less acute as we move through his four models towards Altruism (which he reasonably suggests approximates the Green utopia), but he argues it applies there also. This model assumes that all the communities have a fully 'green' culture, in that they follow Green ethical norms as he outlines them, and base their decisions on norms which are global in orientation – they are not purely interested in the quality of their own environment.

As he notes, this does not produce an Altruist's Dilemma mirroring a Prisoner's Dilemma, since each community would be concerned with the total payoffs for all communities, rather that simply the payoffs of the other players (which would produce such a Dilemma).[96] However, he suggests that there will still be a significant need for coordinating mechanisms. In particular, even if Green communities abided by Green norms, they will still need information about what other communities are doing on a particular problem in order to find out what precisely they need to do about that problem. Thus 'there will still be a need for a central coordinating mechanism to collate everyone's action plans'.[97]

Goodin then argues that 'the role [of centralised agencies] will be greater, the need for sanctioning powers more urgent, the more the situation resembles the Polluter's-cum-Prisoner's Dilemma'.[98] There seem to me to be two major flaws in his argument here. Firstly, there is a great difference between 'organized information-pooling' and 'sanctioning powers' which, although Goodin is obviously aware of it, glosses over its importance for Green conceptions of where political authority would lie.[99] If the State is the focus of the discussion, then only where sanctioning powers are concerned would we be fully talking about something resembling a State. It doesn't seem to me that Greens who reject the idea of global political authorities should have any problem with institutions concerned with information-pooling across communities.

Secondly, Goodin makes much too much of the need for *sanctioning* powers in the Prisoner's Dilemma situation. Much contemporary theorising about international cooperation has highlighted how extensive cooperation can be produced despite the lack of enforcement powers in international agencies, relying on the sort of information-pooling which Goodin highlights would be necessary 'even' in the altruist case.[100] This undermines his case that institutions with effective authority beyond the local level would be required.

This problem of coordination is not one to which Green positions are uniquely vulnerable. All social arrangements, including the present one, require some form of coordination of action between social units to respond to transboundary environmental problems. Of course, Greens are arguing for a system where power is decentralised as much as possible, so they may be seen to be especially vulnerable to this problem. However, if Goodin has failed to show that Greens need envisage anything more than information-pooling institutions, then Green proposals are left with the advantage that radical decentralisation makes environmental management on the ground more practicable, using many of the arguments given by Dryzek earlier.

Two further arguments could be mentioned from a game-theoretic point of view which Goodin and other critics of the decentralist version of Green politics do not discuss. Firstly, collective action is commonly argued to be easier to achieve in situations where the number of players in a game is small.[101] This is primarily because it is easier for members of a system to monitor the actions of others, so 'defection' (in the game theoretic language) is less likely, and easier to punish.[102] If Green proposals for decentralisation were to take place the number of players in a global game would go up, and therefore cooperation would be more difficult to achieve. Dryzek considers this question. However, as he points out, this works two ways:

> Coordination among social actors ... is clearly facilitated by smallness of size in the social unit. This small scale leads, *ceteris paribus*, to the existence of large numbers of such units. And the larger the number of social units, the more problematical is coordination above the local level.[103]

In other words this is an inevitable dilemma; we either make coordination between units more difficult by decentralising, or make coordination within units more difficult by maintaining centralised forms of social organisation.

Secondly, cooperation is usually held to be only possible in situations where player A knows that player B will in fact implement an agreement signed. The confidence needed to make an Assurance game produce co-operation (or make strategies of reciprocity work in a Prisoners' Dilemma) would not be forthcoming, and players would 'defect' to avoid the costs of cooperation without the public good being provided. State sovereignty could be interpreted, and seems to be implicitly by Goodin *et al.*, as fulfilling this condition. If sovereign practices were abandoned, and we were in a situation of loose collections of anarchistic communities confederating at various levels up to the global in forms such as Bookchin's 'Community of communities' , then at the global level, no player would be able to guarantee that agreements they sign will in fact be implemented.[104]

However, in practice it is currently the case that despite the institution of State sovereignty, there remains a significant implementation deficit on many environmental problems by nation-states. It is highly plausible to argue that most agreements signed are done so while negotiators know that implementation will only be patchy. Yet cooperation persists between sovereign states on environmental (and other) issues. There thus seems no reason to believe that removing sovereignty would make cooperation between communities significantly more difficult to achieve. While the degree of coercion which a Green 'Community of communities' would have over communities in matters of meeting basic ecological responsibilities and guaranteeing human rights would be significantly less than those which presently existing sovereign, Weberian, states, the arguments that this would make cooperation between such 'Communities of communities' is unconvincing.

A third objection to the Green argument I have outlined is rather different. Rather than arguing that Greens' attempts to abandon sovereignty and decentralise power means there is insufficient coordinating capacity, much of the recent literature on Green Politics in IR has argued that Green Politics remains overly committed to a sovereign model of politics.[105] Kuehls, Dalby and Stewart, and from a different theoretical background, Wapner, all advance such an argument.[106] Dalby suggests, while agreeing with Green critiques of 'global environmental management', that:

> The political dilemma and the irony here is that the alternative to global management efforts – that of political decentralization and local control, which is often posited as the political alternative by green theory – remains largely in thrall to the same limited political imaginary of the domestic analogy, and avoids dealing with the hard questions of coordination by wishing them away.[107]

The second part of this critique, concerning questions of coordination, is the second objection dealt with above. But the earlier part of Dalby's critique is that Greens remain committed to a sovereign model of politics, the 'domestic analogy'. In a different theoretical context, the same form of critique is made by Wapner in his account of 'world civic politics'.[108] Decentralisation of power, as Wapner or Dalby read the Green decentralist position, is simply a matter of recreating existing political institutions, sovereign states, at much more local, 'human scale' levels. But this is a misreading. Green decentralists do base much of their arguments on questions of scale. But they are also clear that such decentralisation for ecological purposes involves creating fundamentally different political institutions. That is clear by the way that many such writers are explicitly opposed to institutions and practices of sovereignty; as Helleiner points out, this has always been an intended implication of the slogan 'Think Globally, Act Locally' (see more below).[109] It is also clear that such decentralisation also arises from Green concerns with hierarchy and domination. So the state is not simply about the scale of political institutions, but also their form.

Kuehls does recognise that Bookchin, who he discusses as an exemplar of this Green localist position, is anti-state (it would be difficult to avoid this conclusion). But somehow Kuehls implies that Bookchin remains committed to the state as a model of political organisation, as the site of politics:

> Ophuls's and Bookchin's theories are easily placed onto O'Riordan's and Dobson's matrix of ecopolitical thought due to their similar orientation to state and sovereignty. Although one [Ophuls] endorses the state as an appropriate place for ecopolitics and the other holds the state to be the absolute negation of an appropriately ecological politics, both reify the state as the locus of political activity – for good or bad.[110]

This conclusion seems perverse to me. Bookchin is held to negate the state but be committed to it as the locus of political activity. His anti-state position must therefore be an anti-political position, suggesting that in his 'utopia' (for want of a better term) there would be no politics. This seems a bizarre reading of Bookchin, who would be entirely happy with the notion that politics occurs outside the realms of the state, as Kuehls (and others discussed in this chapter) assert. A model of politics, like Bookchin's 'municipal confederalism', which rejects the state, necessarily rejects sovereignty, and is therefore open to possibilities for global coordination which Dalby and many others imply is necessary.

Both sets of writers – Dalby, Stewart and Kuehls from poststructuralist frameworks, and Wapner and Lipschutz from liberal-pluralist ones – suggest that a more appropriate way to understand forms of governance in relation to environmental politics is to abandon spatial-territorial conceptions of politics totally.[111] In an age of globalisation, they both suggest, that transnational network forms of governance are emerging, not least to deal with ecological problems, which make possible an alternative form of politics. But much of the problem with this formulation is it takes as given the political-economically driven processes of globalisation which undermine traditional forms of politics, and fails to imagine the possibility of resisting globalisation, not in order (as social democrats such as Hirst and Thompson or Weiss want) to revitalise the national state, but to make possible a more thoroughgoing decentralisation of political life.[112] The 'networks' of global civil society as envisaged by Wapner and Lipschutz may be appropriate modes of facilitating inter-community cooperation to get round the coordination problems discussed above, but it is not necessary to make them the site of politics itself.

There are therefore good reasons to be sceptical of critics of Green politics who focus on the inadequacies of Greens' proposed restructuring of global politics. This is strengthened by some of the arguments made by the 'global ecology' writers, who focus on how the 'commons' are a form of political and social space which are the most conducive to sustainable practices (contrary to the suggestions of Garrett Hardin and others), a position which strengthens arguments for decentralisation. Despite some challenges in the 1990s, it certainly still remains the case that for most writers on the subject from diverse perspectives, the political implications of Green politics are in the direction of radical decentralisation of power.[113]

Conclusions

These two literatures support each other. GPT outlines basic principles of ecocentrism, limits to growth, and decentralisation of power. For other IR traditions the central point here is the particular way in which Greens reject the states-system, arguing primarily for decentralising political communities below the nation-state, rather than for new forms of global political authority. This involves decentralisation not only of political organisation, but economic and social organisation as well. They also argue for abandoning traditional sovereign systems and practices in favour of more mixed locations of authority. Global ecology complements this by suggesting in rich detail how contemporary political-economic practices undermine the sustainability of human societies, and how those power structures need to be challenged to create sustainable societies. Their focus on 're-claiming the commons' supports the decentralisation argument in GPT.

The introduction to the book outlined some of the central questions and distinctions concerning theoretical traditions in IR. Green Politics should clearly be regarded as a critical rather than problem-solving theory. It is one however which aims to be both explanatory and normative – it tries both to explain a certain range of phenomena and problems in global politics, and provide a set of normative claims about the sorts of global political changes necessary to respond to such problems.[114] Writers within this tradition have to date spent less time engaging in constitutive-theoretical activity – reflecting on the nature of their theorising *per se*, although there is attention, in particular among the writers in what I have called the 'global ecology' school to power/knowledge questions.[115]

For Greens, the central object of analysis and scope of enquiry is the way in which human societies destroy other species and ecosystems. Such destruction is deplored both because of the independent ethical value held to reside in such organisms and ecosystems, and because human society ultimately depends on the successful function of the biosphere as a whole for its own survival. Regarding IR specifically, Greens focus on the way in which prevailing political structures and processes contribute to this destruction. The purpose of enquiry is thus explicitly normative – to understand how global political structures can be reformed to prevent such destruction and provide for a sustainable human relationship to the planet and the rest of its inhabitants. Like idealism (see Chapter 2), the normative imperative is the original impulse in Green Politics – the explanation of environmental destruction comes later. Methodologically, while Greens are hostile to positivism, not least because of its historical connection to the treating of 'nature' (including humans) as objects, purely instrumentally, there is no clearly identifiable 'Green' methodology. Finally, Greens share with many other perspectives a rejection of any claimed separation of IR from other disciplines. As the introductory chapter suggests, the possibility of the emergence of a distinct Green perspective in IR has seen the breaking down of disciplinary boundaries.

Regarding other IR traditions, Green Politics has a number of features in common with many other critical approaches. Firstly, it shares the rejection of a hard and fast fact/value distinction with feminism, critical theory, and poststructuralism, by making clear attempts to integrate normative and explanatory concerns. Its conception of theory is clearly incompatible with positivist conceptions which have such a clear distinction. Secondly, it shares an interest in resisting the concentration of power, the homogenising forces in contemporary world politics, and the preservation of difference and diversity with poststructuralism and feminism. Thirdly, it shares a critique of the states-system with critical theory and others, although it adopts a position which rejects the idea of global power structures to emerge in correspondence with some idea of a 'global community' in favour of decentralising power away from nation-states to more local levels. While for critical theorists such as Linklater, the idea of community at the global level is about balancing unity and diversity rather than one which wishes to create a homogenous global identity, there is a much stronger sense in Green politics that community only makes sense at the very local level – the idea of a 'global community' is for Greens nonsensical, if not potentially totalitarian.[116] Nevertheless, there is a shared sense that the purpose of theory is to promote emancipation.[117] Allied to this normative rejection of the states-system is a rejection of a clear empirical split between domestic and international politics shared in particular with pluralists such as John Burton, but also with Marxists, critical theorists, and feminists. Greens would not think it useful therefore to think for example in terms of 'levels of analysis', a form of thinking still prevalent in realism, as it arbitrarily divides up arenas of political action which should be seen as fundamentally interconnected. Finally, there is a clear focus on political economy, and the structural inequality inherent in modern capitalist economies also focused on by Marxists and dependency theorists.

However, in contrast in particular to poststructuralism, it shares to an extent an element of modernist theorising, in the sense that Greens are clearly trying to understand the world in order to make it possible to improve it. For Hovden, this makes it more compatible with Frankfurt school type critical theory and feminism than with poststructuralism, as these both have a clear emancipatory normative goal, and in particular a clearer sense that their explanations or interpretations of the world are connected to a clear political project.[118] This is linked to poststructuralism's rejection of foundationalism, which marks a clear difference from Green Politics, which necessarily relies on fairly strong foundational claims, of both the epistemological and ethical variety. However, this argument should not be pushed too far, as there are also tensions with the way in which critical theory tries to reconstruct Enlightenment rationality. Eckersley, for example, makes much of attempts by Habermas in particular (she contrasts Habermas to Marcuse) to reclaim science for radical political purposes, suggesting that it necessarily ends up justifying human domination of nature.[119] I would ultimately concur with Mantle , who argues that the closest connections which Green theory has to other approaches in IR are to feminism.[120]

Green theory therefore clearly has its own distinctive perspective. The focus on humanity-nature relations and the adoption of an ecocentric ethic with regard to those relations, the focus on limits to growth, the particular perspective on the destructive side of development, and the focus on decentralisation away from the nation-state are all unique to Green Politics. This chapter has illustrated how the purpose of Green theory within IR is to provide an explanation of the ecological crises facing humanity, to focus on that crisis as possibly the most important issue for human societies to deal with, and to provide a normative basis for dealing with it.

Notes

1. I am grateful to John Barry, Scott Burchill, Richard Devetak, Andrew Linklater, Peter Newell, Ben Seel, and Richard Shapcott for helpful comments on an earlier version of this piece, and to Eric Helleiner for comments on the chapter in the first edition.

2. See for example E. Laferriere and Peter Stoett, *International Relations Theory and Ecological Thought* (London, 1999); E. Laferriere, 'Emancipating International Relations Theory: An Ecological Perspective', *Millennium*, vol. 25, no. 1 (1996), pp. 53–76; E. Hovden, 'As if nature doesn't matter: ecology, regime theory and international relations', *Environmental Politics*, vol. 8, no. 2 (1999), pp. 50–74; D. Mantle, 'Critical Green Political Theory and International Relations Theory–Compatibility or Conflict', PhD thesis, Keele University, 1999; E. Helleiner, 'International Political Economy and the Greens', *New Political Economy*, vol. 1, no. 1 (1996), pp. 59–78. See also E. Helleiner, 'New Voices in the Globalization Debate: Green Perspectives on the World Economy', in R. Stubbs and G. Underhill (eds), *Political Economy and the Changing Global Order*, 2nd edn (Oxford, 2000), pp. 60–9.

3. On Green Political Theory see A. Dobson, *Green Political Thought* (London, 1990); R. Eckersley, *Environmentalism and Political Theory: Towards an Ecocentric Approach* (London, 1992); R. Goodin, *Green Political Theory* (Cambridge, 1992); T. Hayward, *Ecological Thought: An Introduction* (Cambridge, 1995); J. Barry, *Rethinking Green Politics: Nature, Virtue and Progress* (London, 1999). On Global Ecology see W. Sachs (ed.), *The Development Dictionary: a Guide to Knowledge as Power* (London, 1992); W. Sachs (ed.), *Global Ecology: A New Arena of Political Conflict* (London, 1993); P. Chatterjee and M. Finger, *The Earth Brokers: Power, Politics and World Development* (London, 1994); The Ecologist, *Whose Common Future? Reclaiming the Commons* (London, 1993).

4. For example Dobson (1990).

5. R. O. Keohane, *International Institutions and State Power: Essays in International Relations Theory* (Boulder, 1989).

6. This can be seen in major works such as P. M. Haas, R. O. Keohane and M. A. Levy, *Institutions for the Earth: Sources of Effective Environmental Protection*

(Cambridge, 1993); P. M. Haas, *Saving the Mediterranean: The Politics of International Environmental Cooperation* (New York, 1990); O. R. Young, *International Cooperation: Building Regimes for Natural Resources and the Environment* (New York, 1989); O. R. Young, *International Governance: Protecting the Environment in a Stateless Society* (New York, 1994); A. Hurrell and B. Kingsbury, *The International Politics of the Environment* (Oxford, 1992); G. Porter and J. W. Brown, *Global Environmental Politics* (Boulder, 1991); or J. Vogler, *The Global Commons: A Regime Analysis* (London, 1995).

7. Eckersley (1992).
8. Goodin (1992), p. 27.
9. Dobson (1990).
10. See Dobson (1990); Helleiner (2000).
11. I use the term in inverted commas here because at times the writers mentioned use it ironically, at other times descriptively. For example, M. Finger, 'Politics of the UNCED Process', in Sachs (1993), pp. 36–48, uses it to denote the environmentalist discourse which emerged in the 1980s which globalised environmental problems for the first time (closely tied to the discourse of sustainable development). On the other hand, W. Sachs, 'Global Ecology and the Shadow of 'Development', (1993a), pp. 3–21, refers to it simply to describe the conflicts occurring over the set of issues often organised around the global themes of environment and development. I am also using a convenient heading to tie together a range of writers, not all of whom would use this tag to define themselves. My point however is that there has been a resurgence of radical environmentalist writing in the early 1990s centred around these writers, whose work adds to GPT and some loose heading is required to tie them together.
12. Sachs (1993), p. xv.
13. This was held in Rio de Janeiro in June 1992. It was the UN's response to the wave of interest in environmental issues in the late 1980s and early 1990s. It was the biggest diplomatic gathering on any topic ever held. Among other things, treaties on Climate Change and Biodiversity were signed, and an 800-page document called Agenda 21 was agreed, which is a wishlist of possible actions governments could take to achieve sustainable development. For a straightforward overview, see M. Grubb, M. Koch, A. Munson, F. Sullivan and K. Thomson, *The Earth Summit Agreements: A Guide and Assessment* (London, 1993). The fullest treatment of this is in Chatterjee and Finger (1994).
14. As do others in this school. See for example N. Hildyard, 'Foxes in Charge of the Chickens', in Sachs (1993), pp. 22–35; *The Ecologist* (1993), pp. 1-2; P. Doran, 'The Earth Summit (UNCED): Ecology as Spectacle', *Paradigms*, vol. 7, no. 1 (1993), pp. 55–65; or many contributors to the journal *Third World Resurgence*.
15. Sachs (1993a), p. 3.
16. Chatterjee and Finger (1994), p. 119.
17. This section will follow Eckersley's *Environmentalism and Political Theory*, largely for reasons of simplicity, but also because her book still represents the

most developed application of ecocentric ideas to politics. For other ecocentric works, see for example C. Birch and J. B. Cobb, *The Liberation of Life: From the Cell to the Community* (Cambridge, 1981); or W. Fox, Toward a Transpersonal Ecology: *Developing New Foundations for Environmentalism* (Boston, 1990).

18. Eckersley (1992), p. 49.
19. Eckersley (1992), p. 53.
20. Eckersley (1992), pp. 49–51.
21. Eckersley (1992), p. 52.
22. Eckersley (1992), p. 53.
23. The other positions which Eckersley identifies are resource conservation, human welfare ecology, preservationism and animal liberation (1992), ch. 2.
24. Eckersley (1992), p. 46.
25. Barry (1999): Hayward (1995), (1998).
26. Hayward (1998), pp. 46–9.
27. D. Meadows *et al.*, *The Limits To Growth*, (London, 1972).
28. Dobson (1990), p. 15; Meadows *et al.* (1972).
29. The classic early critique was provided by researchers at the University of Sussex: H. S. D. Cole, C. Freeman, M. Jahoda and K. L. R. Pavitt, *Thinking About the Future: A Critique of the Limits to Growth* (London, 1973). For many of the raw materials they predicted would run out by 2000 there are in fact now greater reserves than there were in 1972 (reserves being related to price – the higher the price, the greater amounts are recoverable).
30. To see this at work in Green writings, see for example P. Bunyard and F. Morgan-Grenville (eds), *The Green Alternative* (London, 1987); J. Porritt, *Seeing Green* (Oxford, 1986); C. Spretnak and F. Capra, *Green Politics: The Global Promise* (London, 1984); F. E. Trainer, *Abandon Affluence!* (London, 1985).
31. Dobson (1990), pp. 74–80.
32. Dobson (1990), p. 74.
33. This concept was originally used in the *World Conservation Strategy* developed by the International Union for the Conservation of Nature; IUCN, *World Conservation Strategy* (Gland, 1980), and popularised by the Brundtland Commission, or World Commission on Environment and Development; WCED, *Our Common Future – Report of the World Commission on Environment and Development* (Oxford, 1987).
34. K. Lee, 'To De-Industrialize – is it so irrational?', in A. Dobson and P. Lucardie (eds), *The Politics of Nature: Explorations in Green Political Theory* (London, 1993), pp. 105–17.
35. See D. Meadows and J. Randers, *Beyond the Limits* (London, 1992).
36. For example A. Escobar, *Encountering Development: The Making and Unmaking of the Third World* (Princeton, 1995); V. Shiva, *Staying Alive: Women, Ecology and Development* (London, 1988).
37. Of course some of the critics of growth in the 1970s also focused on its social consequences (for example, F. Hirsch, *The Social Limits to Growth* (London 1976); I. Illich, *Energy and Equity* (London, 1974); I. Illich, *Tools for Conviviality*

(London, 1975); A. Gorz, *Ecology as Politics* (London, 1980). The 'global ecology' writers in the 1990s talk much more of development than growth, although part of their critique presumes that it is for all practical purposes impossible to separate the two. For others focusing specifically on growth, see R. Douthwaite, *The Growth Illusion* (Dublin 1992); M. Wackernagel and W. Rees, *Our Ecological Footprint: Reducing Human Impact on the Earth* (Gabriola Island, 1996); D. Booth, *The Environmental Consequences of Growth: Steady-State Economics as an Alternative to Ecological Decline* (London, 1998).

38. I present here what seems to me the strongest version of the argument. Some Greens do believe it is more fruitful to try to reconstruct the term development, rather than to reject it. However, they would be equally critical of the forms of development criticised by writers mentioned in this section. A debate about whether to reject or reconstruct notions such as development can easily collapse into a simple terminological dispute which is not particularly important. The important point here is that if development is understood as necessarily involving quantitative growth of the system, greater complexity of technological systems, increasing economic interconnections across the globe, then Greens are clearly opposed to it.

39. Sachs (1993a), p. 3.

40. Sachs (1993a), p. 10.

41. H. Daly, 'Toward Some Operational Principles of Sustainable Development', *Ecological Economics*, vol. 2, no. 1 (1990), pp. 1–6, in P. Ekins, 'Making Development Sustainable', in Sachs (1993), pp. 91–103.

42. Cole *et al.* (1973).

43. *The Ecologist* (1993).

44. This is of course not necessarily inconsistent with an argument, that economic growth (at least under capitalism) necessarily increases inequality. Inequality increases while the poor are bought off through quantitative increases in their own consumption, produced by growth in the system as a whole.

45. For example Trainer (1985), pp. 139–41; S. George, *How the Other Half Dies* (Harmondsworth, 1977).

46. *The Ecologist* (1993), pp. 67–70; see also A. Gorz, 'Political Ecology: Expertocracy versus Self-Limitation', *New Left Review*, 202 (1994), pp. 55–67.

47. P. McCully, 'The case against climate aid', *The Ecologist*, vol. 21, no. 6 (1991), pp. 244–51.

48. W. Ophuls, *Ecology and the Politics of Scarcity* (San Francisco, 1977); G. Hardin, 'The ethics of a lifeboat', *BioScience*, 24 (1974); R. Heilbroner, *An Inquiry into the Human Prospect* (New York, 1974). See also Barry (1999), ch. 4.

49. Eckersley (1992), pp. 144, 175 and 178.

50. Like many other Greens, she suggests that social justice, in the form of at least a considerably more egalitarian world than that which currently exists, is an integral part of ecocentric ethics.

51. Eckersley (1992), p. 174.

52. Eckersley (1992), p. 154.

53. Chatterjee and Finger (1994), pp. 41-3; A. Kothari, 'The Politics of the Biodiversity Convention', *Economic and Political Weekly*, 27 (1992), pp. 749-55.

54. United Nations, *Framework Convention on Climate Change* (New York, 1992), Article 2.

55. For an overview of debates concerning global environmental governance, see M. Paterson, 'Overview: Interpreting trends in global environmental governance', *International Affairs*, vol. 75, no. 4 (1999), pp. 801-17.

56. For example in J. Rosenau, 'Governance, Order, and Change in World Politics', in J. N. Rosenau and E.-O. Czempiel (eds), *Governance Without Government: Order and Change in World Politics* (Cambridge, 1992); L. Hempel, *Environmental Governance: the Global Challenge* (Washington, 1996).

57. J. N. Rosenau, *Turbulence in World Politics: a Theory of Change and Continuity* (Princeton, 1990); J. Rosenau, 'Governance, Order, and Change in World Politics', in J. N. Rosenau and E.-O. Czempiel (eds), *Governance Without Government: Order and Change in World Politics* (Cambridge, 1992).

58. C. Merchant, *The Death of Nature: Women, Ecology and the Scientific Revolution* (San Francisco, 1980).

59. T. O'Riordan, *Environmentalism*, 2nd edn (London, 1981), pp. 303-7; also Dobson (1990), pp. 82-3.

60. G. Hardin, 'The Tragedy of the Commons', *Science*, 162 (1968), pp. 1243-8.

61. Examples of this would be Ophuls (1977); Hardin (1974).

62. Hardin (1974).

63. For example Heilbroner (1974); The Ecologist, *Blueprint for Survival* (Harmondsworth, 1972).

64. R. Hunt, *The Natural Society: a basis for Green Anarchism* (Oxford, no date).

65. *Programme of the German Green Party* (London, 1983).

66. There is an important, although never clearly defined, difference between self-sufficient and self-reliant. The former implies that there should be no trade or other exchange of material resources between communities, while self-reliant is a less strong injunction, merely that communities should be primarily only dependent on their own resources, using exchange with other communities where they cannot produce particular items themselves.

67. Bioregionalists argue that ecological societies should be organised with natural environmental features such as watersheds forming the boundaries between communities. E. F. Schumacher, *Small is Beautiful* (London, 1976); K. Sale, *Human Scale* (San Francisco, 1980).

68. M. Bookchin, *The Ecology of Freedom: The Emergence and Dissolution of Hierarchy* (Palo Alto, 1982).

69. The notion of subsidiarity is often used in Green discourse. It is not however used in the way that many governments use it – to protect their rights against those of supranational organisations (the classic case being the UK government in relation to the EU). In the green version, it has radical implications for decentralisation of power to the local level, with power only

transferred up to higher levels if deemed necessary – local levels deciding what constitutes necessary.

70. Spretnak and Capra (1984), p. 177.
71. M. Bookchin, *Toward an Ecological Society* (Montreal, 1980).
72. A. Carter, 'Towards a Green Political Theory', in A. Dobson and P. Lucardie (eds), *The Politics of Nature: Explorations in Green Political Theory* (London, 1993), pp. 39–62; see also D. Wall, 'Towards a Green Political Theory – In Defence of the Commons?' in P. Dunleavy and J. Stanyer (eds), *Contemporary Political Studies: Proceedings of the Annual Conference*, Political Studies Association (Belfast, 1994), pp. 13–28.
73. J. Dryzek, *Rational Ecology: Environment and Political Economy* (Oxford, 1987), ch. 16.
74. Dryzek (1987), p. 219; see also H. Ward, 'Green arguments for local democracy', in D. King and G. Stoker (eds), *Rethinking Local Democracy* (London, 1996), pp. 130–57; or *The Ecologist* (1993), for extended discussions of similar arguments.
75. It will be clear from what follows that this is a usage of commons which regards the term 'global commons', in widespread use in mainstream environmental discussions to refer to problems such as global warming or ozone depletion, for example, Vogler (1995); S. J. Buck, *The Global Commons: An Introduction* (London, 1998), as nonsensical.
76. *The Ecologist* (1993).
77. Hardin (1968).
78. *The Ecologist* (1993), p. 13.
79. *The Ecologist* (1993), p. 9.
80. *The Ecologist* (1993), p. 5.
81. This has a lot in common with the game-theoretic arguments discussed below which often emphasise how in small scale systems it is easier to generate cooperation than in large scale systems.
82. *The Ecologist* (1993), p. 7; E. Ostrom, *Governing the Commons: The Evolution of Institutions for Collective Action* (Cambridge, 1990), p. 27.
83. *The Ecologist* (1993), p. 7.
84. *The Ecologist* (1993), p. 190.
85. *The Ecologist* (1993), pp. 190–1; A. Agarwal and S. Narain, *Towards Green Villages: A Strategy for Environmentally-sound and Participatory Rural Development* (New Delhi, 1989), p. 23.
86. For example Goodin (1992); M. de Geus, 'The Ecological Restructuring of the State', in B. Doherty and M. de Geus (eds), *Democracy and Green Political Thought* (London, 1995).
87. B. Doherty and M. Geus, 'Introduction', in Doherty and de Geus (1995) p. 4.
88. Dobson (1990), p. 101; see also p. 124.
89. I have not however seen an argument which demonstrates why this would necessarily happen when modern societies with modern universalistic

sensibilities try to reorganise themselves along ecoanarchist lines, which would seem to me to be important for this case to be convincing.

90. Hunt (no date), p. 3, quoted in Wall (1994), p. 19.

91. *The Ecologist* (1972), p. 53; Goodin (1992), p. 153; see also Ward (1996).

92. States may have emerged as part of the phenomenon of modernity, and therefore be affected by the rise of universalistic ethics, but they remain accountable only to those within the territory they control (if to anyone at all), and are therefore unlikely to be particularly concerned about the effects of their actions on those living outside their borders.

93. Goodin (1992), pp. 156–68; He also has an argument against decentralisation on the grounds of democracy. He suggests that decentralisation simply gives people 'more and more power over less and less' (1992), p. 150.

94. Goodin (1992), p. 168; Goodin is in fact arguing here for some proto-world government. However, his argument is also that something which we approximate to the State, in this context some ultimate focus of authority, is necessary.

95. For an introduction to the basics of game-theoretic models and analysis, see for example J. Elster (ed.), *Rational Choice* (Oxford, 1986). For applications to IR, see K. A. Oye (ed.), *Cooperation under Anarchy* (Princeton, 1986).

96. Goodin (1992), p. 165.

97. Goodin (1992), p. 166.

98. Goodin (1992), p. 167.

99. Goodin (1992), p. 167.

100. See for example A. Chayes and A. H. Chayes, 'On compliance', *International Organization*, vol. 47, no. 2 (1993), pp. 175–205.

101. R. Axelrod, *The Evolution of Cooperation* (New York, 1984); R. Axelrod and R. O. Keohane, 'Achieving Cooperation under Anarchy: Strategies and Institutions', in Oye (1986). However, powerful arguments are made by M. Taylor, *The Possibility of Cooperation* (Cambridge, 1987), ch. 1, that these claims about the importance of the size of the group are false. I am grateful to Hugh Ward for pointing this out.

102. Axelrod and Keohane (1986), pp. 234–8.

103. Dryzek (1987), p. 231.

104. M. Bookchin, 'Libertarian Municipalism: An Overview', *Society and Nature*, vol. 1, no. 1 (1992); J. Barry, 'Towards a Theory of the Green State', in S. Elworthy, *et al.* (eds), *Perspectives on the Environment 2* (Aldershot, 1995), p. 194.

105. This passage is a summary of a longer account of these arguments which I give elsewhere – see 'Globalisation, governance and resistance' in M. Paterson, *Understanding Global Environmental Politics: Domination, Accumulation, Resistance* (Basingstoke, 2000), ch. 7.

106. T. Kuehls, *Beyond Sovereign Territory: The Space of Ecopolitics* (Minneapolis, 1996); S. Dalby, 'Ecological Metaphors of Security: World Politics in the Biosphere', *Alternatives*, vol. 23, no. 3 (1998); C. Stewart, 'Old Wine in Recycled Bottles: The Limitations of Green International Relations Theory', paper

presented to the BISA Annual Conference, Leeds (December, 1997); P. Wapner, *Environmental Activism and World Civic Politics* (New York, 1996).

107. Dalby (1998), p. 13.

108. Wapner (1996).

109. Helleiner (1996).

110. Kuehls (1996), p. 106.

111. R. D. Lipschutz, 'From place to planet: Local knowledge and global environmental governance', *Global Governance*, vol. 3, no. 1 (1997), pp. 83–102.

112. P. Hirst and G. Thompson, *Globalization in Question: The International Economy and the Possibilities of Governance* (Cambridge, 1996); L. Weiss, *The Myth of the Powerless State* (Cambridge, 1988).

113. For example Helleiner (2000); T. Luke, *Ecocritique: Contesting the Politics of Nature, Economy, and Culture* (Minneapolis, 1997); R. Bryant and S. Bailey, *Third World Political Ecology* (London, 1997), p. 4.

114. Although I have not had space here to consider this question, they could also be argued to have a distinctive account of political agency and transformation, focusing on resistance to the encroachment on commons by global capital and the state and network forms of organisation. See for example M. Paterson, 'Globalisation, ecology, and resistance', *New Political Economy*, vol. 4, no. 1 (1999a), pp. 129–46; Paterson (2000), ch. 7; B. Taylor (ed.), *Ecological Resistance Movements: The Global Emergence of Radical and Popular Environmentalism* (Albany, 1995).

115. For an exception, see P. Doran, 'Earth, power, knowledge: towards a critical global environmental politics', in J. MacMillan and A. Linklater (eds), *New Directions in International Relations* (London, 1995), pp. 193–211; or Laferriere and Stoett (1999).

116. A. Linklater, *The Transformation of Political Community* (Cambridge 1998). For an account with many similarities to that of Linklater in relation to environmental politics, see N. Low and B. Gleeson, *Justice, Society and Nature* (London, 1998), ch. 7. Further on 'global community' see examples from G. Esteva and M. S. Prakash, 'From Global Thinking to Local Thinking', in M. Rahnema (ed.) with V. Bawtree, *The Post-Development Reader* (London, 1997), originally in *Interculture*, vol. 29, no. 2 (1996).

117. Laferriere (1996); Laferriere and Stoett (1999).

118. Hovden (1999).

119. Eckersley (1992), ch. 5.

120. Mantle (1999).

Index